MW00484356

Computer Accounting
with
Peachtree Complete® 2004
for
Microsoft Windows®

Release 11.0

Eighth Edition

Carol Yacht, M.A.

McGraw-Hill
Irwin

Boston   Burr Ridge, IL   Dubuque, IA   Madison, WI   New York   San Francisco   St. Louis
Bangkok   Bogotá   Caracas   Kuala Lumpur   Lisbon   London   Madrid   Mexico City
Milan   Montreal   New Delhi   Santiago   Seoul   Singapore   Sydney   Taipei   Toronto

About the Author:

Carol Yacht is a textbook author and educator with a teaching career of more than 30 years. She has taught at Yavapai College; West Los Angeles Community College; California State University, Los Angeles; Beverly Hills High School and Adult School. Carol started teaching computer accounting in 1978. She is the editor of Communicator, the American Accounting Association's two-year college section publication. Carol has worked for IBM Corporation as an education instruction specialist, and served on the Computer Education Task Force and Hospitality Committee for the National Business Education conferences. Carol earned her AS degree from Temple University, BS degree from the University of New Mexico, and MA degree from California State University, Los Angeles.

Publisher: *Stewart Mattson*
Sponsoring editor: *Steve Schuetz*
Developmental editor: *Jennifer Jelinski*
Senior supplement producer: *Susan Lombardi*
Senior digital content specialist: *Brian Nacik*
Production supervisor: *Debra Sylvester*
Cover designer: *Kami Carter*
Marketing manager: *Katherine Mattison*
Media technology producer: *Gregory Bates*

COMPUTER ACCOUNTING WITH PEACHTREE COMPLETE® 2004 FOR MICROSOFT® WINDOWS® RELEASE 11.0
Carol Yacht, M. A.

Published by McGraw-Hill/Irwin, an imprint of The McGraw-Hill Companies, Inc., 1221 Avenue of the Americas, New York, NY 10020. Copyright © 2005, 2004, 2003, 2002, 2000, 1999, 1998 by The McGraw-Hill Companies, Inc. All rights reserved.

No part of this publication may be reproduced or distributed in any form or by any means, or stored in a database or retrieval system, without the prior written consent of The McGraw-Hill Companies, Inc., including, but not limited to, in any network or other electronic storage or transmission, or broadcast for distance learning.

Some of the material with permission of Peachtree Software.
©1992-2003 Peachtree Software. All rights reserved.

1 2 3 4 5 6 7 8 9 0 QPD/QPD 0 9 8 7 6 5 4

ISBN 0-07-283594-X

www.mhhe.com

The McGraw·Hill Companies

Preface

Computer Accounting with Peachtree Complete 2004, Release 11, Eighth Edition, teaches you how to use Peachtree Complete Accounting 2004 software. Peachtree Complete Accounting 2004 is widely used by individuals, businesses, and accountants. For more than 25 years, Peachtree Software has produced award-winning accounting software.

System Requirements

- IBM PC compatible 233 MHz Pentium computer minimum; 350 MHz Pentium II or higher recommended.
- Windows XP/2000/ME/98 or Windows NT 4.0 with Service Pack 6. Multi-user optimized for Windows XP/2000/98/Windows NT 4.0 (peer-to-peer network), Windows NT server or Novell Netware Network 4.x - 5.x.
- Microsoft Internet Explorer 6.0 provided on CD requires 70 MB. Online features require Internet access.
- 64 MB of RAM (minimum); 128 MB of RAM recommended.
- Display settings of at least High Color (16 bit). SVGA video. 800 X 600 resolution with small fonts.
- 80-140 MB of free hard disk space.
- At least 256-color, 64K colors (or higher); SVGA video; 800 x 600 resolution with small fonts.
- CD-ROM drive.
- Windows supported printer.
- Mouse or compatible pointing device.
- One Zip™ drive disk. One CD for a CD-RW drive. Ten blank, formatted disks. The author suggests that you reformat floppy disks.
- *Optional requirement:* Microsoft Excel and Word 97 and higher.

NEW *The software, Peachtree Complete Accounting 2004, Educational Version, Release 11, is included with the textbook.* See Appendix A, pages 675–680 for software installation instructions.

 Read Me

Install the educational version of Peachtree Complete Accounting 2004 in the school's computer lab. This ensures software compatibility between the school and students' off-site installation.

NEW *Textbook website at www.mhhe.com/yacht2004.*

PEACHTREE COMPLETE ACCOUNTING 2004, RELEASE 11

Each textbook includes a copy of the software, Peachtree Complete Accounting 2004, Release 11, Educational Version. A software site license is included for installation on individual or networked computers. Install the software packaged with the textbook in the school's computer lab to ensure compatibility with the software that your students install on their home or office computers.

NEW *PowerPoint slides for Chapters 1 - 18 on the textbook's website at* http://www.mhhe.com/yacht2004.

NEW *Read Me reminders and troubleshooting tips in the textbook and on the website.*

Computer Accounting with Peachtree Complete 2004, Eighth Edition, shows you how to set up service, merchandising, nonprofit, and manufacturing businesses. When you complete this book you will have a working familiarity with Peachtree Complete Accounting 2004 software. The Part 1, 2, 3, and 4 introductions include a chart showing you how many disks are needed to make backups in each chapter.

NEW PEACHTREE COMPLETE ACCOUNTING 2004 FEATURES

* The sample companies are set up for March 2007 transactions.
* The Open Company screen shows the directory where Peachtree is stored.
* Open the previous company from the File menu.
* Restore Wizard lets you restore an existing company *or* a new company.
* *Enhanced* Account Reconciliation.
* The task bar is redesigned; for example, click on the T-account icon to add/change/or delete accounts in the chart of accounts on the fly.
* Globally change chart of accounts IDs.
* Quick entry in an easy-to-use **checkbook register**.
* Use drill down to go to the original entry window.
* Spell-check as you type.
* Use the Next/Back button on maintenance and task screens.
* Email forms.
* Vendor payment terms are tracked in the cost of sales account Purchase Discounts.

PART 1: EXPLORING PEACHTREE COMPLETE ACCOUNTING 2004

There are two sample companies included with the software: Bellwether Garden Supply and Pavilion Design Group. Bellwether Garden Supply is a retail business and service company that demonstrates inventory and job tracking capabilities. Pavilion Design Group is a service company that demonstrates time and billing.

In Part 1 of the book, you will complete eight chapters that demonstrate how Peachtree is used. This introduces you to the procedures that will be used with all the chapters of the textbook.

NEW *Chapter 1, Exploring PCA 2004, includes steps for using Peachtree's Restore Wizard.*

NEW *Chapter 7, Financial Statements, shows you how to drill down from reports to the original transaction entry.*

Chapter 8, Pavilion Design Group, shows you how to use Peachtree's time and billing features.

PART 2: PEACHTREE COMPLETE ACCOUNTING 2004 FOR SERVICE BUSINESSES

Chapters 9, 10, Project 1, and Project 1A are included in this section of the book. The work completed in Chapter 9 is continued in Chapter 10. The accounting cycle is completed for the fourth quarter of the year.

NEW *In Chapter 9, Maintaining Accounting Records for Service Businesses, you set up two service companies with Peachtree's simplified chart of accounts. You use Peachtree's Account Register to drill down to the Cash Account Register. You also use Peachtree's enhanced account reconciliation.*

Chapter 10, Completing Quarterly Activities and Closing the Fiscal Year, shows you how to complete adjusting entries, print financial statements, and close the fiscal year.

NEW *Project 1, Lena Becker, Consultant, is a comprehensive project that reviews what you have learned in Chapters 9 and 10.*

Project 1A, Student-Designed Service Business, shows you how to design a service business from scratch. You set up the business, choose a chart of accounts, create a Balance Sheet, write business transactions, complete the computer accounting cycle, and close the fiscal year.

PART 3: PEACHTREE COMPLETE ACCOUNTING 2004 FOR MERCHANDISING BUSINESSES

Chapters 11, 12, 13, 14, Project 2, and Project 2A are included in this section of the book. Students set up two merchandising businesses in Chapter 11. The work started in Chapter 11 is continued in chapters 12, 13 and 14.

Chapter 11, Accounts Payable, shows you how to use Peachtree's accounts payable system.

NEW *In Chapter 11, Accounts Payable, Vendor defaults/payment terms are set up to automatically track purchase discounts as cost of sales. For purchase returns, use vendor credit memos.*

NEW *In Chapter 12, Accounts Receivable, use Credit Memos for sales returns.*

Chapter 12, Accounts Receivable, shows you how to use Peachtree's accounts receivable system. Chapter 13, Merchandise Inventory, shows you how to use Peachtree's perpetual inventory system. Chapter 14, Payroll, shows you how to use Peachtree's payroll system.

NEW *Chapter 14, Payroll, includes automatic payroll tax calculations. Example payroll tax withholding tables are included with the educational version software.*

NEW *Project 2, Copper Bicycles, is a comprehensive project that incorporates what you have learned in Chapters 11 through 14.*

Project 2A, Student-Designed Merchandising Business, asks you to create a merchandising business from scratch.

PART 4: ADVANCED PEACHTREE COMPLETE ACCOUNTING 2004 APPLICATIONS

Chapters 15, 16, 17, 18, Project 3, Project 4, and Project 4A are included in this section of the book. Chapter 15, Customizing Forms, shows you how to use Peachtree's forms designer. Chapter 16, Import/Export, shows you how to export data from Peachtree Complete Accounting 2004 to a word processing program. Chapter 17, Using Peachtree Complete Accounting 2004 with Microsoft Excel and Word, shows you how to use Peachtree with two Microsoft Office 97 or later applications. Chapter 18, Dynamic Data Exchange (with Excel), shows you how to share data with Microsoft Excel for Windows.

NEW *Chapter 17, Using Peachtree Complete Accounting 2004 with Microsoft Excel and Word, shows you how to combine two financial statements on one Excel spreadsheet.*

NEW *Chapter 18, Dynamic Data Exchange (with Excel), includes steps for downloading files from Peachtree's website.*

NEW *Project 3, Valley Computers, is a nonprofit business.*

NEW *Project 4, Woods Manufacturing, Inc., is the culminating project in your study of Peachtree Complete Accounting 2004.*

Project 4A, Student-Designed Project, allows you to write another month's transactions for one of the four projects that you have completed.

The textbook ends with three appendixes: Appendix A, Software Installation & Using the Website; Appendix B, Review of Accounting Principles; and Appendix C, Glossary. The glossary is also included on the textbook website at www.mhhe.com/yacht2004.

Index: Each chapter in the book ends with an index. The index at the end of the book is an alphabetic listing of the chapter indexes.

Carol Yacht

Carol Yacht, Author
Computer Accounting with Peachtree Complete 2004, 8e
www.mhhe.com/yacht2004
carol@carolyacht.com

Acknowledgments

I would like to thank the following colleagues for their help in the preparation of this book: Brent Gordon; Steve Schuetz; Jennifer Jelinski; Susan Lombardi, Ed Przyzycki; Beth Woods, CPA; Sharon Clarke, Accountant; Matt Lowenkron; and Brice Wood. A special thank you to the following accounting professors who made many valuable suggestions.

Diane Ardans, American River College
Robert S. Beattie, Hudson Valley CC
Linda Bolduc, Mt. Wachusett College
Judye Cadle, Tarleton State University
Paul Cameron, Texas A & M University
Brenda Catchings, Augusta Tech. Institute
Robert Dansby, Columbus Tech. Institute
Alan Davis, Comm. Coll. of Philadelphia
Dave Davis, Vincennes University
Jeff Decker, University of Hawaii
Kevin Dooley, Kapi`olani Comm. College
David R. Fordham, James Madison Univ.
Stephen Fogg, Temple University
Michael Fujita, Leeward Community College
Bill Gaither, Dawson Community College
Diane Glowacki, Tarrant County Jr. College
Bill Guidera, Texas State Technical College
Jean Guttman, University of So. Maine
Norma Hall, Manor Junior College
Jim Hale, Vance-Granville Community Coll.
Mark Henry, Victoria College
Geoffrey Heriot, Greenville Tech. College
Jeff Jackson, San Jacinto College
Robert Jackson, Ivy State Tech College
Margie Johnson, Pima Community College
Bob Johnson, Jefferson College
William Lambert, University of Houston
Bev Kibbey, International Business College
Judy Kidder, Mohave Community College
Alex Kogan, Rutgers University
Linda Kropp, Modesto Junior College
Bruce Lindsey, Genesee Community Coll.
Susan Looney, Mohave Community Coll.
Susan Lynn, University of Baltimore
Charles McCord, Portland Comm. College
Jack Neymark, Oakton Community College

Nancy O'Connor, Whittier Adult School
Pat Olson, Moraine Park Technical College
Sandra O'Meara, Santa Barbara Comm. Coll.
Vincent Osaghae, Chicago State University
Gary A. Parker, DeKalb Technical Institute
Timothy Pearson, West Virginia University
Simon Petravick, Bradley University
Joel Peralto, Hawaii Community College
Gerald Peterka, Mt. San Jacinto College
Tom Pinckney, Trident Technical College
Mildred Polisky, Milwaukee Area Tech. College
Robert Porter, Cape Fear Community College
Susan Pope, University of Akron
Charlotte Pryor, University of Southern Maine
Iris Lugo Renta, Interamerican University
Betty J. Reynolds, Arizona Western College
Monique Ring, So. New Hampshire University
Lou Rosamilla, Hudson Valley Community Coll.
Diane Sandefur, Elliott Bookkeeping School
Art Schroeder, Louisiana State University
Deborah Seehorn, NC Dept of Education
Marilyn St. Clair, Weatherford College
Donald Schwartz, National University
Warren Smock, Ivy Tech State College
Tom Sentman, Skadron College
Marie Stewart, Newport Business Institute
Mel Sweet, University of Connecticut
Laurie Swinney, University of Nebraska
Greg Thom, Parkland Community College
Gene Trenary, San Juan College
Tom Turner, Des Moines Area Community Coll.
Jamie Vaught, Southeast Community College
Steve Walsh, Clark College
Mazdolyn Winston, Calhoun Community Coll.
W. Brian Voss, Austin Community College
Dan Zhu, University of Iowa

I would also like to extend a special thank you to my students and appreciation to the many professors who stay in touch.

Table of Contents

Comment: The timetable for completion shown on the next page is meant as a guideline for in-class lecture/discussion/ demonstration and hands-on work. Work not accomplished in class is homework. In most Accounting classes, students can expect to spend approximately 2 hours outside of class for every hour in class.

TIMETABLE FOR COMPLETION		Hours
Part 1: Exploring Peachtree Complete Accounting 2004		
Chapter 1	Introduction to Bellwether Garden Supply	2.0
Chapter 2	Vendor Transactions	1.0
Chapter 3	Customer Transactions	1.0
Chapter 4	Employees	1.0
Chapter 5	General Ledger and Inventory	1.0
Chapter 6	Job Cost	2.0
Chapter 7	Financial Statements	1.0
Chapter 8	Pavilion Design Group: Time & Billing	1.0
	Subtotal Part 1	10.0
Part 2: Peachtree Complete Accounting 2004 for Service Businesses		
Chapter 9	Maintaining Accounting Records for Service Businesses	2.5
Chapter 10	Completing Quarterly Activities and Closing the Fiscal Year	2.0
Project 1	Lena Becker, Consultant	2.5
Project 1A	Student-Designed Service Business	2.0
	Subtotal Part 2	*9.0*
Part 3: Peachtree Complete Accounting 2004 for Merchandising Businesses		
Chapter 11	Accounts Payable	3.0
Chapter 12	Accounts Receivable	2.5
Chapter 13	Merchandise Inventory	2.0
Chapter 14	Payroll	2.0
Project 2	Copper Bicycles	3.5
Project 2A	Student-Designed Merchandising Business	3.0
	Subtotal Part 3	*16.0*
Part 4: Advanced Peachtree Complete Accounting 2004 Applications		
Chapter 15	Customizing Forms	1.0
Chapter 16	Import/Export	1.0
Chapter 17	Using Peachtree Complete Accounting 2004 with Microsoft Excel and Word	1.0
Chapter 18	Dynamic Data Exchange (with Microsoft Excel)	1.0
Project 3	Valley Computers	1.0
Project 4	Woods Manufacturing, Inc.	3.0
Project 4A	Student-Designed Project	2.0
	Subtotal Part 4	*10.0*
	TOTAL HOURS: PARTS 1, 2, 3, 4	**45.0**

Exploring Peachtree Complete Accounting 2004

Part 1 shows you how to use Peachtree Complete Accounting 2004. You learn about the basic features of PCA. The purpose of Part 1 is to help you become familiar with the software rather than to test accounting knowledge. Beginning with Chapter 9, computer accounting skills are reviewed in more depth. In Chapters 9 through 18, you set up 11 businesses from scratch. Part 1 introduces you to Peachtree and the two sample companies that are included with the software.

Part 1 includes eight chapters:

Chapter 1: Introduction to Bellwether Garden Supply
Chapter 2: Vendor Transactions
Chapter 3: Customer Transactions
Chapter 4: Employees
Chapter 5: General Ledger and Inventory
Chapter 6: Job Cost
Chapter 7: Financial Statements
Chapter 8: Pavilion Design Group: Time & Billing

The instructions in this book were written for Peachtree Complete Accounting 2004 (abbreviated PCA). PCA requires that you use the Windows XP/2000/Me/98 or Windows NT 4.0 with Service Pack 6 operating system.

Windows[1] uses pictures or **icons** to identify tasks. This is known as a **graphical user interface (GUI)**. For example, PCA uses common icons or symbols to represent tasks: a file folder, a trash can for deleting, an hourglass to show that the program is waiting for a task to be performed, a printer, etc. You can also use a **mouse**, **trackball** or other pointing device in addition to the keyboard to perform various tasks.

The way personal computer software looks and works can be described by the acronym **WIMP** -- Windows, Icons, Menus, and Pull-downs.

---

[1] Words that are boldfaced and italicized are defined in the Glossary. The Glossary is on the textbook's website at http://www.mhhe.com/yacht2004.

The chart below shows that you need 14 blank, formatted disks to back up data in Part 1, Chapters 1 - 8. This assumes a 3½" floppy 1.44 MB disk. Since Peachtree backs up to the current point in the data, the author suggests that you reformat disks used in earlier chapters. You can also back up to the hard drive, network or other media.

Chapter	Disk Label	Backup Name	Kilobytes	Page Nos.
1	Disk 1 of 14	a:\bgs[2]	1,227 KB	15-19
	Disk 2 of 14	a:\Chapter 1	1,228 KB	41-42
	Disk 3 of 14	a:\Exercise 1-2	1,228 KB	49-50
2	Disk 4 of 14	a:\Chapter 2	1,230 KB	80
	Disk 5 of 14	a:\Exercise 2-2	1,228 KB	86-87
3	Disk 6 of 14	a:\Chapter 3	1,238 KB	123
	Disk 7 of 14	a:\Exercise 3-2	1,239 KB	128
4	Disk 8 of 14	a:\Chapter 4	1,257 KB	151
	Disk 9 of 14	a:\Exercise 4-2	1,256 KB	156
5	Disk 10 of 14	a:\Chapter 5	1,249 KB	181
	Disk 11 of 14	a:\Exercise 5-2	1,252 KB	187
6	Disk 12 of 14	a:\Chapter 6	1,247 KB	199
	Disk 13 of 14	a:\Exercise 6-2[3]	1,251 KB	203
7	--	No backups in Chapter 7	--	--
8	Disk 14 of 14	a:\Chapter 8	566 KB	237-238

The Disk Label column numbers the floppy disks. The size of your backup files may differ from the amounts shown.

The author suggests that you reformat floppy disks for use with later chapters. For example, you may reformat the disk used to back up Chapter 1 (disk 2 of 14) when you are ready to back up Chapter 3 (disk 6 of 14). Since the *work in Chapters 1–7 is cumulative*, you should have data backed up through Exercise 2-2 *before* you reformat the Chapter 1 disk (disk 2 of 14).

You may back up to a floppy disk, network location, hard drive location, CD-RW drive, or other media (Zip or Jazz drive). One Zip disk or CD-R will hold all the back up data in Chapters 1–18.

---

[2]This is the first backup (disk 1 of 14) and includes beginning data for Bellwether Garden Supply. Keep this disk in a safe place and do *not* reformat it.

[3]This back up file will be used in Part 4, Chapters 15, 16, 17, and 18. You should *not* reformat the Exercise 6-2.ptb back up.

Chapter 1

Introduction to Bellwether Garden Supply

SOFTWARE OBJECTIVES: In Chapter 1, you will use the software to:

1. Start Peachtree Complete Accounting 2004 (PCA).[1]
2. Explore the sample company, Bellwether Garden Supply.
3. Back up Bellwether Garden Supply data.
4. Restore data with Peachtree's restore Wizard.
5. Operate Peachtree's drop-down lists, lookup fields, toolbar, and navigation aid.
6. Navigate Windows Explorer.
7. Explore Peachtree Today to link to the Internet and learn about software features.
8. Make three backups: 1) one blank, formatted disk to back up starting data for Bellwether Garden Supply; 2) one blank, formatted disk for the Chapter 1 backup; 3) one blank formatted disk for the Exercise 1-2 backup.[2]

WEB OBJECTIVES: In Chapter 1, you will do these Internet activities:

1. Use PCA to link to Peachtree's website at http://www.peachtree.com.
2. Link to Peachtree Software's newsroom page.
3. Select two product news articles and write an essay about each press release.
4. Use your Internet browser to go to the book's website at http://www.mhhe.com/yacht2004.
5. Complete the first web exercise in Part 1.

Peachtree Complete Accounting 2004 (PCA) is similar to other programs that use Windows. If you have used other Windows programs, you will see the similarities in the menus and windows, entering and saving data, and selecting icons. If you are not familiar with Windows, using PCA will

---

[1] If Peachtree Complete Accounting 2004 is not installed see Appendix A, Installing the Software, pages 675-680. The sample companies must be installed to complete Chapters 1–8.

[2] Refer to the chart on page 2, for information about backing up data.

---

help you become familiar with the Windows operating system.

MOUSE AND KEYBOARD BASICS

One of the first decisions you need to make is whether you want to use your mouse or keyboard. The instructions in this book assume that you are using a mouse. When the word click is used in the instructions, it means to use your mouse, but you can also use the keyboard. The instructions below explain how to use your mouse or keyboard.

Using the Mouse

➢ To single click: position the mouse cursor over what you want to select and click the left mouse button once.

➢ To double-click: position the mouse cursor over your selection and click the left mouse button twice, quickly.

➢ Use the right mouse button the same way you use the left mouse button.

Using the Keyboard

➢ If there is an underlined letter in the menu or option you want to select, hold down the **<Alt>**[3] key and the underlined letter to make the selection.

➢ If you have already held down the **<Alt>** key and the underlined letter and more selections appear with underlined letters, just type the underlined letter to select the item.

Using Shortcut Keys

Shortcut keys enable you to perform common operations by using two or more keys together. The tables on the next page show the shortcut keys.

---

[3]The greater and lesser signs are used around words to indicate individual keys on your keyboard; for example, **<Alt>** is for the Alternate key, **<Enter>** for the Enter/Return key, **<Ctrl>** is for the Control key, **<Esc>** is for the Escape key.

<Ctrl> + <Letter> Shortcuts	
<Ctrl> + <X>	Cut
<Ctrl> + <C>	Copy
<Ctrl> + <V>	Paste
<Ctrl> + <E>	Erase
<Ctrl> + <N>	New Company
<Ctrl> + <O>	Open Company
<Ctrl> + <B>	Back Up Company
<Ctrl> + <R>	Restore Company
<Ctrl> + <P>	Print purchase orders, quotes, invoices, payments or reports
<Ctrl> + <F>	Find
<Ctrl> + <D>	Find Next
Function Key Shortcuts	
<F1>	Displays the online Help
<Ctrl> + <F4>	Closes the current window
<Alt> + <F4>	Closes the application window
<Ctrl> + <F6>	Moves to the next window
<Shift> + <Ctrl> + <F6>	Moves to the previous window
<F10>	Toggles the menu bar
<F5>	Saves the current record in maintenance windows

PCA'S STARTUP SCREEN

Peachtree's startup screen gives you a number of options.

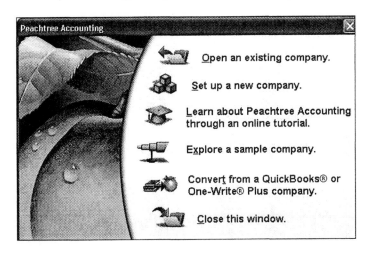

From the startup screen, you can Open an existing company, Set up a new company, Learn about Peachtree Accounting through an online tutorial, Explore a sample company, Convert a QuickBooks® or One-Write® Plus company, or Close this window.

Notice that there is an X in a box () on the upper right-hand side of the smaller Peachtree Accounting window.

If you click on the ☒ on the Peachtree Accounting title bar with your left mouse button, the window closes and your screen displays the File, Options, Help menu bar

Peachtree Accounting
File   Options   Help

Comment
The screen illustrations in this text were done with Windows XP and Peachtree Complete Accounting 2004, Educational Version.

THE WINDOWS ENVIRONMENT

One of the benefits of Windows is that it standardizes terms and operations used in software programs. Once you learn how to move around in PCA's menus, you will also know how to use other Windows applications.

To learn more about the Windows environment, let's look at a PCA screen. The screen illustration on the next page shows the parts of a PCA window as well as the menu bar for Bellwether Garden Supply. In Windows 98, notice that each word on the menu bar has an underlined letter. (If you are using Windows XP, menu bar selections do *not* show underlined letters.) If your menu bar selections have underlined letters that means you can make a selection by typing **<Alt>** and the underlined letter or by clicking on your selection with the mouse. Each time you make a menu bar selection, a pull-down menu appears.

For now, let's study the parts of the window shown below. Some features are common to all software programs that are written for Windows. For example, in the upper right corner is the Minimize �button, Double Window ▣ button, and the Close ☒ button. The title bar, window border, and mouse pointer are also common to Windows programs. Other features are specific to PCA: menu bar, toolbar, and navigation aid.

Windows programs all use menus in the form of horizontal menu bars and pull-down menus. The contents of these menus will differ depending on the application you are using. PCA's menu bar and pull-down menus are specific to the features needed for general ledger accounting.

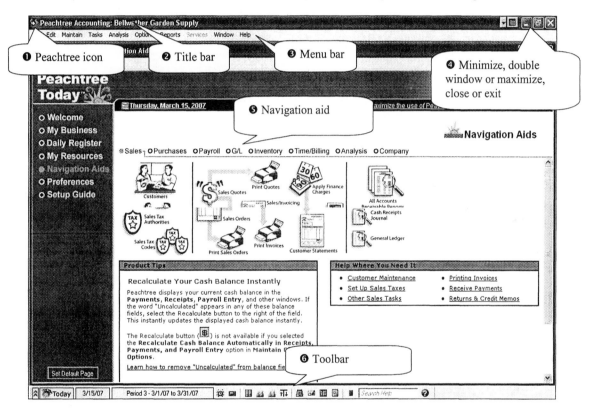

❶ Peach icon: Click on the Peach icon and a pull-down menu appears with options such as: Move, Size, Minimize, Maximize, Close, Next.

❷ *Title Bar* The bar at the top of your screen. When a company is open in PCA, the name of the company is displayed on the Title Bar. If your window is minimized, you can put your mouse on the Title Bar, click and hold the left mouse button and drag the window around the *desktop*. The title bar shows Peachtree Accounting: Bellwether Garden Supply.

❸ Menu Bar: In PCA 2004, Educational Version, there are nine menu bar selections. If your menu bar selections have underlined letters, that means you can make a selection by typing **<Alt>** and the underlined letter. For example, in Windows XP if you press the <Alt> key then press the <F> key, the menu bar shows underlined letters as well as the pull-down menu. You can also click with your left-mouse button on the menu bar headings to see a submenu of options.

❹ Minimize ▬, Double Window ▣, or Maximize ▣, and Close or Exit ✖ buttons: Clicking once on Minimize ▬ reduces the window to a button on the *taskbar*. In Windows, the [start] button and taskbar are located at the bottom of your screen. Clicking once on Double Window ▣ returns the window to its previous size. This button appears when you maximize the window. After clicking on the Double Window ▣ button, the symbol changes to the Maximize ▣ button. Click once on the Maximize ▣ button to enlarge the window. Click once on the Exit or Close ✖ button to close the window, or exit the program.

❺ Navigation Aid[4]: Peachtree offers a graphical alternative to the menu bar. The major functions of the program are represented as icons or pictures that show you how tasks flow through the system. You can click on an icon and perform that function.

❻ Toolbar: The gray bar[5] at the bottom of the window shows help information about the current field, today's date or system date, and the current accounting period. The toolbar also includes icons viewing action items; a calculator; and other icons for quick access to Peachtree's features. Move your mouse over the icons to see what

---

[4]If the Navigation Aid is not displayed on our screen, from the menu bar, select Options, click on View Navigation Aid to place a check mark next to it.

[5]Screen colors may differ. Check with your instructor if you have a question.

they do. You can hide the toolbar by unchecking the View Custom Toolbar option on the Options pull-down menu.

TYPICAL WINDOWS USED IN PCA

When you make a menu bar selection, a window displays. You can enter information into that window by using your mouse to click on icons or by typing on your keyboard.

The screen illustration below is the Maintain Customers/Prospects window, one that is typical of PCA. There are four sections on this window: ❶ the icon bar, ❷ the lookup field (magnifying-glass icon), ❸ Previous record or Next record, ❹ tabs, and ❺ the drop-down lists (down arrow).

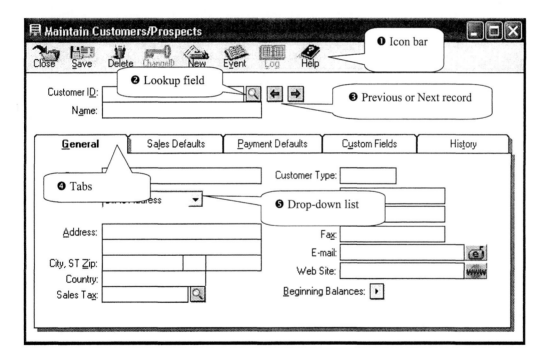

❶ *Icon bar*[6]: The icon bar shows pictures of commands or additional information that pertains to the window. Some icons are common to all windows while other icons are specific to a particular window. The icons included in the Maintain Customers/Prospects window are:

 Close: This closes the window without saving any work that has been typed since the last time you saved.

 Save: This saves record information you have entered such as addresses, telephone numbers, contacts for vendors, customers, employees, etc.

 Delete: If you select this while using a selection from the Maintain menu, the record (customer, vendor, etc.) you're working with will be deleted. When you're finished deleting, select Close, in order to delete the records.

 Change ID: When a customer record is displayed on the screen, you may change the information for that customer.

 New: If you select this while using a selection from the Maintain menu, this will clear the record that is displayed and allow you to enter a new one. This can be used with the following Maintain pull-down menu items: Customers/Prospects, Vendors, Employees/Sales Reps, Chart of Accounts, Inventory Items, and Jobs.

Event: This allows you to schedule an event for a Customer/Prospect. You can choose to have events display or not display in Action Items. Events that you schedule will appear on the Events Tab of Action Items for the date scheduled. You can use this to log notes about telephone calls, meetings, letters, or any other type of activity. Use Action Items to show a list of the day's priorities or to create a list of future activities.

Log: This shows you events recorded for an individual over a range of time that you specify. You can *filter* this list to see only certain types of activities and whether they're completed or not.

---

[6]Notice that familiar business items are used for icons: file folder (Close), floppy disk and Rolodex card (Save), and a trash can (Delete).

You can mark activities as completed by placing a mark in the far left column. Double-clicking on any of the *line items* will take you to the Create an Event window. Line items appear on many of Peachtree's windows. On color monitors, a magenta line is placed around the row (line item) you select.

Help: This icon is displayed on most windows. Selecting this icon gives you information specific to the current window. The fields of the window are often listed at the bottom of the help message. When you have a question about how to use Peachtree, clicking on the Help icon often answers it.

❷ *Lookup Field*: The most common field you will type in is called the text field. Sometimes the program will tell you if you type incorrect information, but often you can type whatever you want. A magnifying-glass icon indicates lookup fields. When you are in the text field portion of the lookup field, the cursor changes to an I-bar with a plus sign and question mark **<I +?>**. (For example, when you move the cursor to the Vendor ID field on the Tasks/Payments window, the **<I +?>** appears.) In a lookup field, you can either select from a list of records, such as vendors, customers, accounts, etc. or you can type a new record. You use one of the methods shown below to display a list or type a new record:

To display a list	To enter a new record
In the text field, click on the magnifying-glass icon.	In the text field, type a **<+>**.
In the text field, type a **<?>**.	Double-click in the text field.
In the text field, click the right mouse button.	Click on the magnifying-glass icon, and then select New.

❸ Previous or Next Record. Click on either the left arrow for the previous record; or the right arrow for the next record.

❹ *Tabs*: The tabs that are shown in the Maintain Customers/Prospects window are General, Sales Defaults, Payment Defaults, Custom Fields, and History. Once a customer is selected, you can select one of these folders to display information about a customer.

❺ *Drop-Down List*: The down arrow means that this field contains a list of information from which you can make a selection. Many of PCA's windows have drop-down lists that appear when you click on a down arrow next to a field. You can press **<Enter>** or click on an item to select it from the list.

THE SAMPLE COMPANY: BELLWETHER GARDEN SUPPLY

Bellwether Garden Supply is one of the sample companies included with PCA. You get a sampling of features that are developed in greater detail as you complete this book. The purpose of using the sample company is to help you become familiar with the software.

GETTING STARTED

Follow these steps to start Peachtree Complete Accounting 2004 (PCA):

1. Start Windows. If Peachtree Complete Accounting 2004 is not installed on your computer, refer to Appendix A for installing the Peachtree Complete Accounting CD that is included with this textbook.

2. When Peachtree Complete Accounting 2004 (PCA) was installed, an icon was created for Peachtree. Place the mouse pointer on the Peachtree icon and double-click with the left mouse button to start PCA. (Or, click on Start, All Programs, Peachtree Complete Accounting Educational Version 2004. Then, select Peachtree Complete Accounting Educational Version 2004.) The startup screen is shown on the next page.

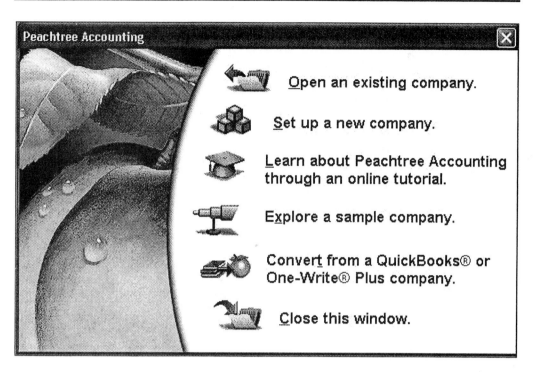

3. The Peachtree Accounting screen appears. From the startup screen, you can Open an existing company; Set up a new company; Learn about Peachtree Accounting through an online tutorial; Explore a sample company; Convert a QuickBooks® company or One-Write® Plus Company; or Close this window.

4. Click on Explore a sample company (or hold down the **<Alt>** key and press **<X>**).

Troubleshooting: What if the startup screen does not appear? That means someone has turned off this option. Follow these steps to open the sample company if the startup screen did not display.

1. At the Peachtree Accounting menu bar, click on File. The file menu drops down.
2. Click on Open Company. The Open Company window displays.
3. In the Companies list, highlight Bellwether Garden Supply. Then click

   | OK |

---

5. The Explore a Sample Company screen appears.

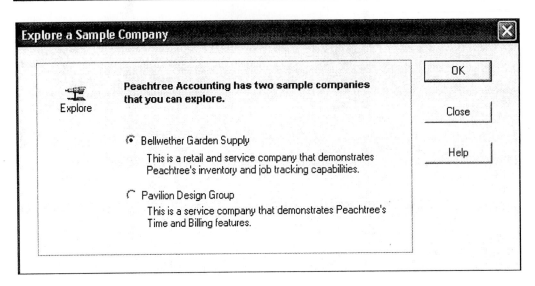

6.   PCA 2004, has two sample companies: Bellwether Garden Supply and Pavilion Design Group. In Chapters 1 – 7, you will use Bellwether Garden Supply to explore Peachtree. Then, in Chapter 8, you will use Pavilion Design Group to see how Peachtree's time and billing feature works. Make sure that Bellwether Garden Supply is selected. Click [OK].

7.   The Peachtree Today - Welcome screen appears. Read the information on this screen, then click ☒ on the Peachtree Today title bar to close this window.

DISPLAYING PRODUCT INFORMATION

1. After closing the Peachtree Today window, the menu bar for Bellwether Garden Supply appears. From the menu bar, click on Help, then About Peachtree Accounting.

This screen shows the copyright information and the Release, Build, Serial Number, Installed Tax Service, and Registered Tax Service. The Release of the educational version is Peachtree Complete® Accounting 2004; the Build No. is 11.0.00.029E, and the Serial Number is Educational Version. If you are using the commercial version of Peachtree, your Release, Build, and Serial Number will differ. The Installed Tax Service and Registered Tax Service could also differ.

To see if software or text updates have been made, periodically check the Textbook Updates link on the book's website at www.mhhe.com/yacht2004.

2. Click [OK] to close the Product Information window. You are returned to the menu bar.

BACKING UP BELLWETHER GARDEN SUPPLY

Before you begin to make changes to Bellwether Garden Supply, you should back up the sample company data. When using PCA, information is automatically saved to the hard drive of the computer. In a classroom setting, a number of students may be using the same computer. This means that when you return to the computer lab or classroom, your data will be gone. *Backing up* your data simply means saving it to a floppy disk (or other media), so that it will be available when you want to work again.

Comment

The author suggests using a blank, formatted disk to make the first back up of Bellwether Garden Supply data. PCA compresses the backup file, which makes the data smaller.

You should have at least two chapters of data backed up before reformatting a disk used in an earlier chapter. For example, you may reformat the disk used to back up Chapter 1 (disk 2 of 18) when you are ready to back up Chapter 3. Refer to the chart on page 2 for backup information.

When you back up, you are saving to the current point in Peachtree. Each time you make a backup, you should type a different backup name (file name) to distinguish between them. In this way, if you need to *restore* an earlier backup, you have the data for that purpose.

In the business world, backups are unique to each business: daily, weekly, monthly. Think of your backups this way and you will see why individual backups for different points in the data are necessary. *You should never leave the computer lab without first backing up your data.*

Follow these steps to back up Bellwether Garden Supply:

1. Put a blank, formatted disk in drive A. The text directions assume you are using a blank, formatted disk in drive A for backing up Bellwether Garden Supply. *If you have a CD-RW disk drive or Zip disk drive, you can use one CD-R or Zip disk for all the backups in the textbook (Chapters 1 through 18).*

2. From the menu bar, click on File, then select Back Up. The Back Up Company window appears. If necessary, uncheck the box next to Include company name in the backup file name.

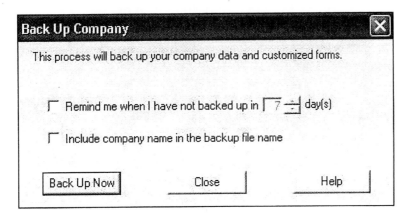

3. Click 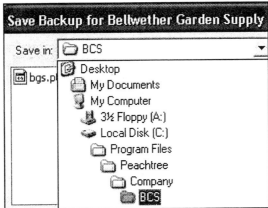.

4. The Save in field shows the default location for your backup. If you do *not* change the Save in location, you will be saving to the hard drive. Click on the down-arrow in the Save in field. The list that displays shows you the location on your hard drive for the sample company files.

5. Since you are going to back up to drive A, if necessary, scroll up the list, then click 3½ Floppy (A:) to select drive A.[7] Observe that the File name field shows the default name. In the File name field, highlight the default file name and then type **bgs** as the file name.

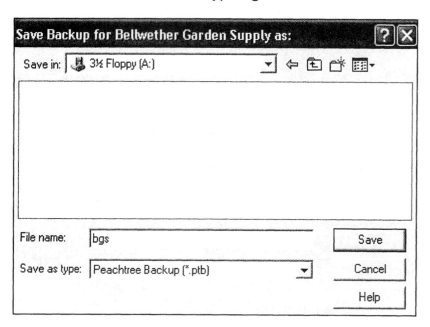

Observe that the Save as type field shows that you are making a Peachtree Backup (*.ptb), which is abbreviated ptb. This is the standard default for Peachtree backups.

Comment

If your Save as type field does *not* show Peachtree Backup (*.ptb), follow these steps:

1. Click on the 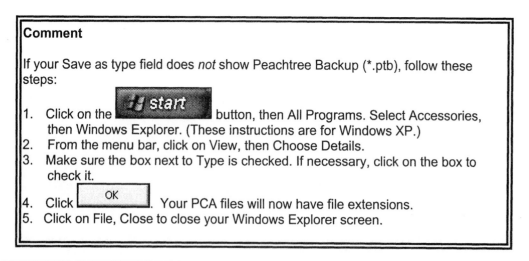 button, then All Programs. Select Accessories, then Windows Explorer. (These instructions are for Windows XP.)
2. From the menu bar, click on View, then Choose Details.
3. Make sure the box next to Type is checked. If necessary, click on the box to check it.
4. Click [OK]. Your PCA files will now have file extensions.
5. Click on File, Close to close your Windows Explorer screen.

---

[7]If you are backing up to a CD-RW or Zip drive, substitute the appropriate drive letter.

6. Click .

7. A screen pops up that says This company backup will require approximately 1 diskette.

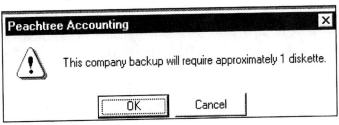

8. Click [OK]. Another screen pops up that says Please insert the first disk. . . .

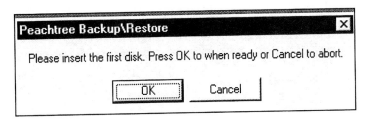

9. Click [OK]. When the Back Up Company scale is 100% completed, you have successfully backed up the sample company. This takes a few moments. Your screen is returned to Bellwether's menu bar.

Follow these steps to see the size of the backup file.

1. Click on the [start] button. Then select All Programs. From the drop-down list, select Accessories, then Windows Explorer. (*Hint: These instructions are for Windows XP; they may differ for other Windows versions.*)

2. In the Address field, click on the down-arrow, then select drive A (3½ Floppy (A:). If necessary, select View, Details to see the screen illustration below.

The Name of the file is bgs.ptb; the Size of the file is 1,227 KB;[8] and file Type is PTB File. Compare this information to the bcs folder on your hard drive (C:\Progam Files\Peachtree\Company\Bcs), which is 7.63 MB (megabytes). Since the Peachtree backup file is 1,227 KB, and a disk holds 1.44 MB of data, you will be able to save one Bellwether backup file on one blank, formatted disk.

Refer to the chart on page 2 for disk, back up, and kilobyte information. Since Peachtree backs up to the current point, you should periodically reformat disks. (*Hint: Remember to have at least two chapters backed up before you reformat.*)

If you do not want to reformat disks, you will need 14 blank, formatted disks to back up Chapters 1–8. Remember to refer to the chart on page 2 to see how many disks you will need for backing up Part 1 of the book. You can also reformat disks used in earlier chapters.

Follow these steps to exit Peachtree:

1. Close any opened windows. From the menu bar, click on File, Exit.

2. You are returned to your Windows desktop.

USING WINDOWS EXPLORER

The instructions on pages 16–19 show you how to use Peachtree's Back Up feature. You learned that when you back up the company file to drive A (or other location), the information is compressed or made smaller. Peachtree's Back Up feature works with their Restore feature, which is shown on pages 23–26. *What if your instructor prefers that all of the company files be copied or saved?*

1. Your Windows desktop should be displayed on your screen.

2. If your desktop has a Windows Explorer icon double-click on it. Or, click on the **start** button; select All Programs, then Accessories; then Windows Explorer.

---

[8]You may notice that the size of your backup file differs from the amount of kilobytes shown on page 19. This is okay.

3. In the Address field, select drive C. Then, open the folder for Bellwether Garden Supply: C:\Program Files\Peachtree\Company\BCS (this is the default location for Peachtree; your location may differ).

4. Right-click on the BCS folder. A drop-down menu appears. Left-click on Properties.

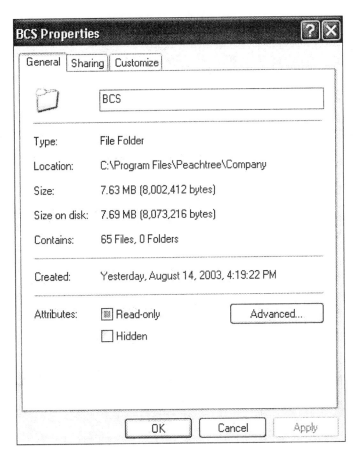

5. Observe that the size of the BCS folder is 8,002,412 bytes (or 7.63 MB). That means this file is too large for one blank formatted disk, which holds 1,440,000 bytes. If you want to copy the entire folder to a disk, you will need to have a Zip drive or CD-RW drive. The steps in the Copying the Bcs folder to a Zip Drive or CD-RW Drive show you how to do that. Peachtree folders need read and write access in order to be used. Floppy disk drives, Zip disk drives and CD-RW disk drives are read/write.

6. Click [OK] to close the BCS Properties window. Click ✖ on the C:\Program Files\Peachtree\Company title bar to close Windows Explorer.

Copying the Bcs Folder to a Zip Drive or CD-RW Drive

The steps that follow show you how to copy the BCS folder to a Zip disk or to a CD-RW drive. If your Zip drive or CD-RW drive is located in a different location, substitute that drive letter. Depending on what software you are using to copy CDs, your instructions may differ.

1. If necessary, click on File, Exit to exit Peachtree and return to your desktop. Put a Zip disk into your computer or a CD-R disk in your CD-RW drive. In this example, drive E is used for the Zip drive and drive F to identify the CD-RW drive. (Substitute the correct drive letter for your computer.)

   If you are copying files to a CD, a window may pop-up that asks What do you want Windows to do? In this example, the Open writable CD folder using Windows Explorer was selected.

2. Locate the BCS folder on your hard drive. The default location is C:\Program Files\Peachtree\Company\BCS. Click on BCS to select it. On the left side of your screen, there is a File and Folder Tasks list. Click on <u>Copy this folder</u>.

3. When the Copy Items window pops up, select the appropriate Zip drive or CD-RW drive to copy to. In this example CD Drive (F:) is shown. You should select the correct drive on your computer for either your Zip drive or CD-RW drive.

4. Click on [Copy]. A screen pops up showing the files are being copied. If you are copying the files to a CD, make the selections to write the files to your CD.

---

5. To check that the file was copied, make sure your CD disk or Zip disk is in the drive, then go to the appropriate drive right-click on the BCS folder and select Properties. The BCS Properties window should look similar to the one shown on page 21, under step 4.

6. Click ☒ on the title bar to close the windows.

When you copy the BCS folder from drive C to a Zip disk or CD-RW drive, you are copying all the files contained in the folder. Remember, backing up files compresses the data (or makes the file smaller). Copying the entire folder allows you to have all the BCS files on external media. When you want to return to where you left off, you can use Windows Explorer to copy and paste these files from your Zip disk or CD to Peachtree's program path and Bellwether's folder (subdirectory) on drive C– C:\Program Files\Peachtree\Company\BCS.

Remember, the instructions in the textbook teach you how to use Peachtree's Back Up and Restore features. Check with your instructor for his or her preference.

USING PEACHTREE'S RESTORE WIZARD

In order to start where you left off the last time you backed up, you use Restore. Your school may prefer that you use Windows Explorer to copy/paste instead of Peachtree's Restore feature. You may need to check with your instructor on the preferred method. This book uses Peachtree's Restore feature.

Follow these steps to use Peachtree's Restore feature.

1. Start Peachtree in the usual way.

2. On the startup screen, click on E̲xplore a sample company. Make sure Bellwether Garden Supply is selected. Click | OK |.

3. To restore Bellwether's files, do the following:

    a. Put your backup disk in drive A.

    b. From the menu bar, click on File, then Restore. The Restore Wizard – Select Backup File window appears.

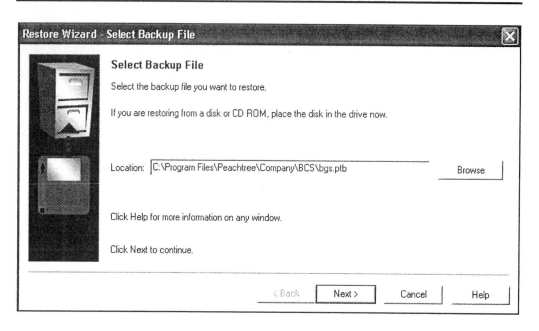

c. In the Location field, click _____. In the Look in field, select drive A. Highlight the bgs.ptb file.

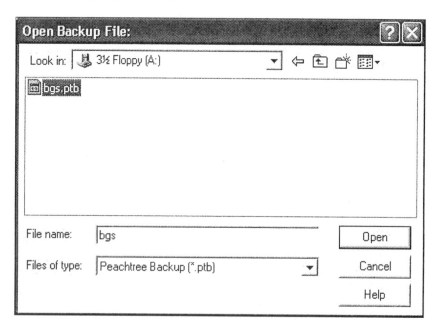

d.   Click [Open]. The Select Backup File screen appears. Observe that the Location field shows A:\bgs.ptb. (If your backup file is in a different location, it will appear in the Location field. If necessary, you can also click [Browse].)

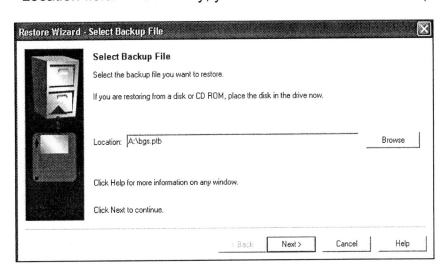

e.   Click [Next >]. The Select Company screen appears. Observe that An Existing Company is the default. The Company Name field shows Bellwether Garden Supply and the Location shows Bellwether's location.

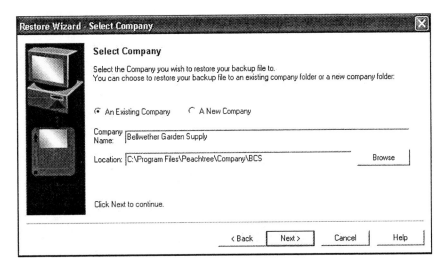

Read Me

Observe that there are two options on the Select Company screen: An Existing Company (which is the default) *and* A New Company. If you select A New Company, then the company will be named exactly as the backup file you selected. Here is how that works.

1. Click on the radio button next to A New Company.
2. Look at the Location field. The subdirectory for Bellwether has changed to \belgarsu. (When you accepted the default for An Existing Company the subdirectory showed \bcs.)

This is an important distinction. You can restore to an existing company—one that is previously set up—*or* you can restore to a new company, bypassing the process of setting up a new company. (Setting up a new company is shown in Chapter 9.) Let's say you wanted to restore a backup file for a company that was *not* set up in Peachtree. Some schools delete subdirectories from the hard drive; for example, you have a back up file but the company, in this case Bellwether Garden Supply, is *not* listed as a Peachtree company. If you start Peachtree and you *cannot* select Bellwether, use the Restore Wizard to select A New Company. Using your backup file, and the selection for A New Company, you are able to get started where you left off the last time you used Peachtree.

Remember to select An Existing Company before continuing with step f.

f.   Read the information on the screen, then click [Next >].

The Restore Options screen appears. Make sure that the check mark is next to Company Data.

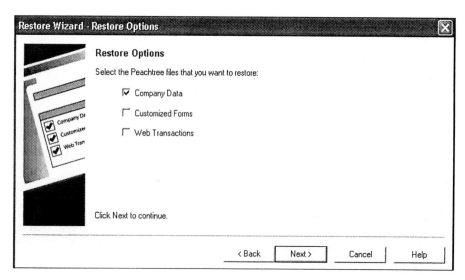

g. Click . The Confirmation screen appears.

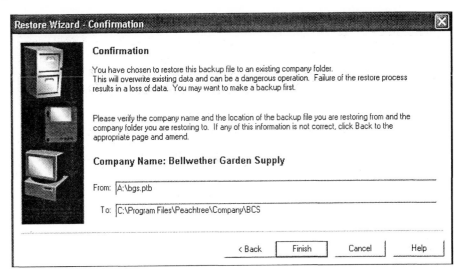

Restore Wizard - Confirmation

Confirmation

You have chosen to restore this backup file to an existing company folder. This will overwrite existing data and can be a dangerous operation. Failure of the restore process results in a loss of data. You may want to make a backup first.

Please verify the company name and the location of the backup file you are restoring from and the company folder you are restoring to. If any of this information is not correct, click Back to the appropriate page and amend.

Company Name: Bellwether Garden Supply

From: A:\bgs.ptb

To: C:\Program Files\Peachtree\Company\BCS

< Back   Finish   Cancel   Help

h.   Read the information on the Confirmation screen, then click
Finish . Your backup data starts to restore. When the scale is
100% completed, the Bellwether Garden Supply data is restored.
On Peachtree Today's title bar, click ☒ to close the Peachtree
Today window.

Now that you have restored Bellwether's files, you are ready to continue using the sample company. *Remember before you exit PCA, make a backup of your work.*

USING PEACHTREE TODAY

The instructions that follow assume PCA was just installed and is being used for the first time. If PCA has been used before, your Peachtree Today window may look different.

At the bottom of your screen on the toolbar, there is a 🔥Today icon. If necessary, click on the 🔥Today icon and the Peachtree Today window pops up. If your Peachtree Today window is already displayed on your screen, continue with the next section.

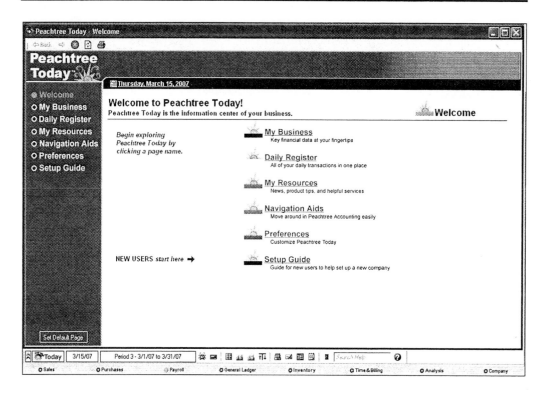

Your screen may differ. This is okay. Read the information on this screen to become familiar with what it says. You may want to explore some of the links. The underlined words are links to other information.

Follow these steps to try one of the links.

1. Move your cursor over My Business. Observe that your cursor changes to a hand. (If you do *not* have a My Business link, go to step 2.)

2. Click once on the My Business link. (If PCA has been used before, click on the My Business radio button on the left side of Peachtree Today's window).

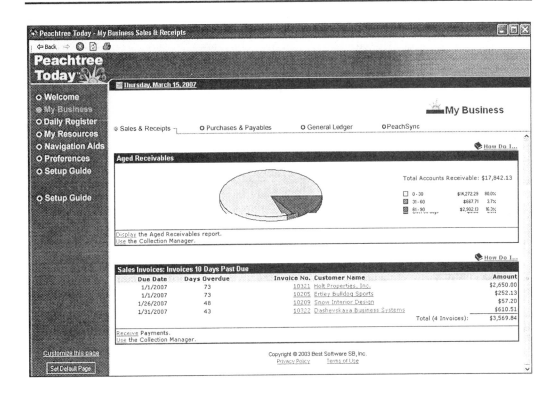

3. If necessary, scroll down the screen to see more. You can also explore additional links by clicking on another tab.

4. When you are through, click ⊠ on the Peachtree Today - My Business Sales & Receipts title bar.

Peachtree Today - My Business Sales & Receipts

5. You are returned to Bellwether Garden Supply's menu bar.

To hide the Peachtree Today window at startup, follow these steps.

1. On the toolbar, click on the ⬚Today icon. The Peachtree Today – Welcome window appears.

2. Click on the ⬚Preferences Customize Peachtree Today link.

3. If necessary, scroll down the screen to go to the Start Up area. Observe that there is a check mark next to Display Peachtree Today each time this company is opened. Click on the box to uncheck it.

Start Up

☐ Display Peachtree Today each time this company is opened.

4. Click on the ☒ on the Peachtree Today – Preferences General title bar.

To check that Peachtree Today no longer displays at startup, follow these steps.

1. From Bellwether's menu bar, click on File, Exit. You are returned to your Windows desktop.

2. Restart Peachtree. At the startup menu, select Explore a sample company. Make sure that the radio button for Bellwether Garden Supply is selected, then click on ⟨ OK ⟩.

3. When Bellwether starts, the Peachtree Today window is *not* displayed on your screen. If Peachtree Today is displayed, complete the steps that follow.

   a. Link to Preferences.

   b. Scroll down the screen to the Start Up section.

   c. Make sure the box is unchecked next to Display Peachtree Today each time this company is opened. Close the Peachtree Today window.

MENU BAR

PCA's menu bar has ten pull-down menus: File, Edit, Maintain, Tasks, Analysis, Options, Reports, Services (this selection is active on the commercial version and inactive on the educational version), Window, and Help.

Follow these steps to explore the menu bar.

1. From the menu bar, click on File to see its pull-down menu, or if you prefer, press <Alt> + F to display the File pull-down menu. If you use <Alt> + F instead of your mouse, notice that the individual letters on the menu bar are underlined. In this example, the mouse was used.

In order to show these File pull-down menu selections, the General Ledger Trial Balance was displayed from the Reports pull-down menu.

The File pull-down menu allows you to open an existing company, open the previous company, create a new company, print, print preview, setup the page, back up and restore data, make an online backup (if you subscribe to this service), import files into PCA from other programs, export files from PCA to other programs, verify data, load and edit payroll tax tables, and exit.

Pull-down menu choices that are followed by an *ellipsis* are associated with *dialog boxes* or screens that supply information about the window you are using. An arrow (▶) next to a menu item (Payroll Tax Tables) indicates that there is another pull-down menu or submenu with additional selections.

To cancel the pull-down menu, click on File or **<Esc>**.

2. Click on Edit to see its pull-down menu.

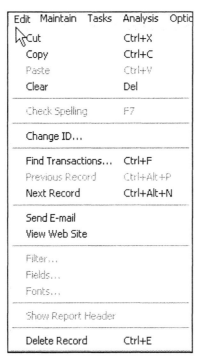

In order to show these Edit selections, the Maintain Customers/ Prospects window was opened. Then, one of the customer records was selected. The grayed-out selections are inactive.

The Edit pull-down menu allows you to cut, copy, paste, and clear objects from one place to another via the Windows feature called the clipboard. Change ID allows you to change information in maintenance windows. You can also spell check and find transactions. You can Send E-mail and view web pages. You can also filter records, locate fields, change fonts, and show headers. Delete Record allows you to delete maintenance records.

3. Click on Maintain to see its pull-down menu.

The Maintain pull-down menu allows you to enter, view, or edit required information for your company's customers or prospects, vendors, employees or sales reps, chart of accounts, inventory items, item prices, and job costs. You can also edit company information; enter memorized transactions; or go to *default* information, sales tax codes, and passwords. Defaults are commands that PCA automatically selects. Default information automatically displays in windows. You can change the default by choosing another command.

4. Click on Tasks to see its pull-down menu.

The Tasks pull-down menu allows you to enter quotes and sales orders, sales invoices, receipts, finance charges, select for deposit, issue credit memos, purchase orders, purchases for inventory, select bills to pay, make payments, write checks, issue vendor credit memos, display account registers, record time and expenses, record payroll information, and make general journal entries. You can also make inventory adjustments, assemblies, reconcile bank statements, void checks, and enter action items. With the System selection, another pull-down menu displays with choices such as post and unpost (available with batch posting), change the accounting period, use the year-end wizard, and purge old or inactive transactions.

5. Click on Analysis to see its pull-down menu.

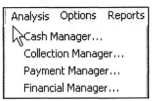

The Analysis pull-down menu allows you to view customized graphics developed for specific companies. You can use the cash manager, collection manager, payment manager and financial manager.

6. Click on Options to see its pull-down menu.

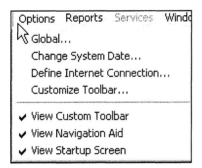

The Options pull-down menu allows you to set *global options* for a company, change the system date, define your Internet connection, and customize the toolbar. Global options are settings that affect the entire program. When you set global options for one company, you set them for all companies.

The check marks next to View Custom Toolbar, View Navigation Aid, and View Startup Screen sets these options on your Peachtree screen. If they are unchecked these options will not display.

7. Click on Reports to see its pull-down menu.

The Reports pull-down menu allows you to *queue* reports for printing or display reports on your screen. You can also create and edit the format for reports, forms, and financial statements. The My Business selection takes you to Peachtree Today – My Business Sales & Receipts window. This screen was shown on page 28. You can also print or display daily registers. The Crystal Report Designer allows you to access, analyze, report and share data.

8. The Services pull-down menu is inactive in the educational version of PCA. On the commercial version of Peachtree Complete 2004, the Services pull-down menu has selections for Peachtree Today, Check for Updates, Credit Card Authorization, Internet Postage, My Web Site, Peachtree Web Services, and the Peachtree Web Transaction Center.

9.   Click on Window to see its pull-down menu. (*Hint:* To see these choices, click on 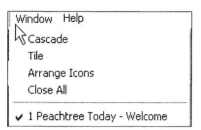 on the toolbar. The Maintain/Customers Prospects and general ledger report windows were closed.)

The Window pull-down menu allows you to arrange how the windows and icons are displayed and close all open windows. Cascade allows you to display document windows in overlapping format on the screen. Tile allows you to display windows side by side, with no window overlapping any other window. You can also select Arrange Icons to change the look of your desktop. Close All allows you to close all the windows at once. According to the list shown on the Window pull-down menu, there is one window open: 1 Peachtree Today - Welcome.

10.   Click on Help to see its pull-down menu.

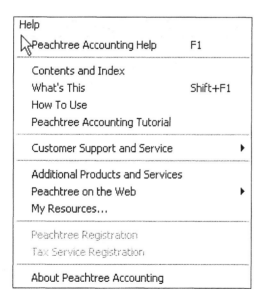

The Help pull-down menu allows you to open a window of context-sensitive help, run tutorials for PCA and Windows, and display file statistics. Additional Products and Services includes information about Peachtree Software. Select About Peachtree Complete Accounting to display product information. How to display product information was shown on page 15.

BECOMING AN EMPLOYEE OF BELLWETHER GARDEN SUPPLY

Before you add yourself as an employee of Bellwether Garden Supply, let's learn how to use the Navigation Aid to open the Maintain Employees window. The Navigation Aids are listed across the bottom of your screen. They are: Sales, Purchases, Payroll, General Ledger, Inventory, Time & Billing, Analysis, and Company. (*Hint: If the Navigation Aids are* not *shown on the bottom of your screen, click Options from the menu bar. Click on View Navigation Aid to place a check mark next to it.*)

Follow these steps to use the Navigation Aid to add yourself as an employee. Close the Peachtree Today window before you begin.

1. At the bottom of your screen, click on the Payroll Navigation Aid
    Payroll . The Peachtree Today - Navigation Aids Payroll window pops up.

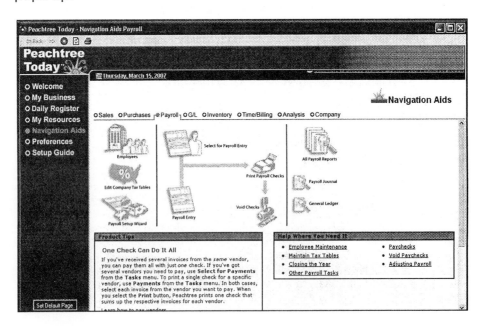

The Payroll Navigation Aid flow chart shows what happens when a Payroll Entry is made. Observe the links on the flow chart. These selections can also be made from the Maintain, Tasks, and Reports pull-down menus. The Payroll Navigation Aid organizes information into three sections.

a. Maintenance selections include links to Employees, Edit Company Tax Tables, and the Payroll Setup Wizard.

b. Task selections include links to Select for Payroll Entry, Payroll Entry, Print Payroll Checks, and Void Checks.

c. Report selections include links to All Payroll Reports, Payroll Journal, and General Ledger.

2. Click [Employees]. The Maintain Employees/Sales Reps window appears.

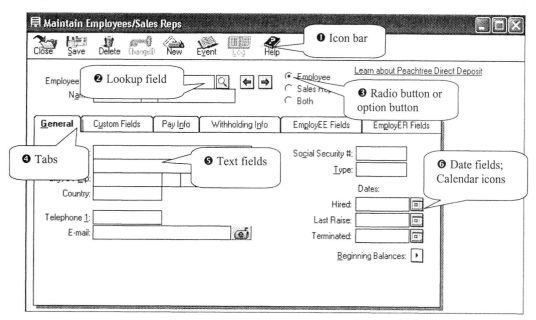

❶ The icon bar at the top of most windows shows graphical representations of commands or functions that are accessible from the window.

❷ Lookup fields have a text field and a magnifying-glass icon. When you are in the text field portion of the lookup field, the cursor changes to an I-bar and a question mark **< I ? >**. Click the left mouse button on the magnifying-glass icon, or type a question mark **<?>** in the text field, or click the right mouse button to display lists.

❸ *Radio Button or Option Button:* These buttons allow you to select one by clicking with the mouse or using the space bar. The default is Employee shown by the radio button next to Employee.

❹ Tabs are common to most PCA windows. They provide a subtitle to the various screens that store and organize information. Here, for example, the information you can choose to track is subdivided into six categories: General, Custom Fields, Pay Info, Withholding Info, EmployEE Fields, and EmployER Fields.

❺ Text fields are rectangles or fields where information is typed.

❻ Date fields; Calendar icons: You can type dates in the text field or click on the calendar icons. The date is selected by clicking within the calendar icon.

Adding Yourself as an Employee

Follow these steps to add yourself as an employee.

1. Type an Employee ID code for yourself in the Employee ID field. For example, type **CYACHT-01** (type *the first initial of your first name, your full last name, a hyphen, zero, then one); use all capital letters* and press **<Enter>**.[9]

---

[9]All ID codes are case-sensitive which means that cyacht-01 and CYACHT-01 are considered different codes. Capital letters sort before lowercase letters.

2. In the Name field, type your first name, press **<Enter>**; type your middle initial, if any, press **<Enter>**, then type your last name. Press **<Enter>** two times.[10]

3. In the Address field, type your street address. There are two lines so you can enter an ATTENTION line or P.O. Box, if necessary. If you are using just one line for your address, press **<Enter>** two times to go to the City, ST Zip fields.

4. In the City, ST Zip field, type your city, state (two-digits), and zip code, pressing **<Enter>** after each.

5. None of the other information is required. You will work with the other fields in the Payroll chapter. Click on the ⬛Save icon or press the function key **<F5>** to save your entries.

   To check that your Employee ID has been added, click on the magnifying glass next to the Employee ID text field.

6. Select Close or **<Esc>** to return to the menu bar. Close the Payroll Navigation window.

BACKING UP CHAPTER 1 DATA

Follow these steps to back up Chapter 1 data:

1. Put a blank, formatted disk in drive A.

2. From the menu bar, select File, then Back up. Make sure that the box next to Include company name in the backup file name is *unchecked*.

3. Click on the ⬛Back Up Now button.

4. Click on the down-arrow in the Save in field. If necessary, scroll up the list, then click on 3½ Floppy (A:) to select drive A.

5. Type **Chapter 1** in the File name field.

---

[10]You can use **<Enter>** or **<Tab>** to move from field to field. Use **<Shift>+<Enter>** or **<Shift>+<Tab>** to move back a field. You can also hold the **<Alt>** key and press the underlined letter of a text box to move between fields.

6. Click on the [Save] button.

7. When the screen prompts that This company backup will require approximately 1 diskette, click on [OK].

8. When the screen prompts you to insert the first disk, click on [OK]. When the Back Up Company scale is 100% completed, you have successfully backed up to the current point in Chapter 1. You are returned to the menu bar.

9. Click on File, Exit to exit Peachtree.

MANUAL VS. COMPUTERIZED ACCOUNTING

Because there are differences between manual and computerized accounting systems, you will notice in several instances that the procedures used in PCA are slightly different than those outlined in the steps of the manual accounting cycle.

The differences between the Manual and Computer Accounting Cycle are shown on the next page. The first step of the Computer Accounting Cycle is New Company Set Up, which includes the option for selecting a Chart of Accounts. The Manual Accounting Cycle does not include a New Company Set Up. In manual accounting, the chart of accounts is the same as the accounts in the general ledger.

Step five of the manual cycle shows a worksheet. There is no worksheet in the computerized cycle.

In PCA you can complete account reconciliation. Account reconciliation automates bank reconciliation.

Another important difference is that in the Computer Accounting Cycle, the adjusting entries are journalized and posted before printing the financial statements.

In the computerized cycle, Step 10, change accounting periods, is similar to closing the month manually except that the temporary accounts maintain balances so a post-closing trial balance is not available. PCA tracks income and expense data for an entire year. At the end of the year, all revenue and expense accounts are closed to equity.

MANUAL ACCOUNTING CYCLE	PCA's COMPUTER ACCOUNTING CYCLE
1. Analyze transactions	1. New Company Set up. (You have the option of selecting a chart of accounts.)
2. Journalize entries.	2. Analyze transactions.
3. Post to the ledger.	3. Journalize entries.
4. Prepare unadjusted trial balance.	4. Post to the ledger.
5. Prepare worksheet.	5. Print general ledger trial balance (unadjusted).
6. Prepare financial statements: income statement, statement of changes in owner's equity, and balance sheet.	6. Account reconciliation: reconciling the bank statement.
7. Adjust the ledger accounts: journalize and post adjusting entries.	7. Journalize and post adjusting entries.
8. Close the temporary accounts: journalize and post the closing entries.	8. Print the general ledger trial balance (adjusted).
9. Prepare post-closing trial balance.	9. Print financial statements: balance sheet, income statement, statement of cash flow, and statement of changes in financial position.
10. Reverse entries (optional).	10. Change accounting periods.
Interpret accounting information	

	INTERNET ACTIVITY
	The *Internet* is a worldwide electronic communication network that allows for the sharing of information. The *World Wide Web* (WWW) or Web is a way of accessing information over the Internet. To read about the differences between the Internet and the Web, go to www.webopedia.com/DidYouKnow/Internet/2002/Web_vs_Internet.asp. To make an Internet connection, your computer must be equipped with a *modem*. The word modem is an abbreviation of **Mo**dulator/**Dem**odulator. A modem is a device that translates the digital signals from your computer into analog signals that can travel over telephone lines. There are also wireless radio modems, cable modems, and T-1 lines for faster connections.
1.	Start Windows, then PCA. Open Bellwether Garden Supply. Minimize Peachtree, and then connect to your Internet browser.
2.	Maximize Peachtree. Start Peachtree Today. (*Hint: If necessary, click on the Today icon on the toolbar.*) Select My Resources 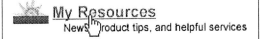. (*Hint: You must be connected to the Internet. If a window pops up that asks if you want to make an Internet connection, follow the screen prompts to make a connection. A window may pop up that says You are about to enter a server-provided Internet Resource. Click on OK to continue.*)
3.	If necessary, scroll down the screen to the Stay in Touch with Peachtree section. Click on Peachtree.com.
4.	Websites are time and date sensitive. When using the Internet, be aware that changes will likely take place. For purposes of this assignment, you will link to Peachtree's press releases. When you place your cursor over News a drop-down list appears. Select Press Releases. Then, link to ▷ Product News . The Peachtree Newsroom page appears.
5.	Select two links from the list of press releases. Using a word processing program, write an essay about each site you selected. Remember to include the website address of each link. Your summary for each site selected should be no more than 100 words or less than 75 words.
6.	From your Internet browser, go to the textbook's website at http://www.mhhe.com/yacht2004. Link to the Student Edition.
7.	Link to Internet Activities, then Part 1 Internet Activities for Chps 1-8. You may open or save these web exercises. Complete the Web Exercises for Chap. 1.
8.	Complete the first activity, ACCOUNTING MONOPOLY – Chapter 1. This is a group activity. Check with your instructor regarding this assignment.

SUMMARY AND REVIEW

SOFTWARE OBJECTIVES: In Chapter 1, you used the software to:

1. Start Peachtree Complete Accounting 2004 (PCA).
2. Explore the sample company, Bellwether Garden Supply.
3. Back up Bellwether Garden Supply data.
4. Restore data with Peachtree's restore Wizard.
5. Operate Peachtree's drop-down lists, lookup fields, toolbar, and navigation aid.
6. Navigate Windows Explorer.
7. Explore Peachtree Today to link to the Internet and learn about software features.
8. Make three backups: 1) one blank, formatted disk to back up starting data for Bellwether Garden Supply; 2) one blank, formatted disk for the Chapter 1 backup; 3) one blank formatted disk for the Exercise 1-2 backup.

WEB OBJECTIVES: In Chapter 1, you did these Internet activities:

1. Used PCA to link to Peachtree's website at http://www.peachtree.com.
2. Linked to Peachtree Software's newsroom page.
3. Selected two product news articles, and wrote an essay about each press release.
4. Used your Internet browser to go to the book's website at http://www.mhhe.com/yacht2004.
5. Completed the first web exercise in Part 1.

GOING TO THE NET

> **Comment**
>
> The textbook website at http://www.mhhe.comyacht2004 has a link to Textbook Updates. Check this link for updated Going to the Net exercises.

Access the Career Development website at
http://www.net-temps.com/careerdev/index.htm?type=careertalk&channel=fin&topic=careers
Read the article Careers in Accounting & Finance.

1. What three skills are essential for those seeking careers in accounting and finance?
2. What is the preferred educational background for an accountant?

3. List five career opportunities in accounting and finance.

True/Make True: Write the word True in the space provided if the statement is true. If the statement is not true, write the correct answer.

1. If there is an underlined letter in the menu or option you want to select, hold down the **<Alt>** key and the underlined letter to make the selection.

_____

_____

2. The menu items that have an arrow next to them indicate that there is another pull-down menu with additional selections.

_____

_____

3. Shortcut keys enable you to use Peachtree's mouse.

_____

_____

4. In this book, the greater and lesser signs are used to indicate individual keys on the keyboard; for example <Tab>.

_____

_____

5. You can close the application you are working with if you single click with your mouse on the close button (☒).

_____

_____

6. You can hide the toolbar on your screen by unchecking that option on the Options menu.

_____

_____

7. In PCA, some icons are common to all windows while other icons are specific to a particular window.

_____

_____

8. The Navigation Aid is shown at the top of your window.

_____

_____

9. The most common field you will type in is called the drop-down list.

_____

_____

---

10. The extension used for Peachtree backups is .XLS.

Exercise 1-1: Follow the instructions below to complete Exercise 1-1:

1. Start Windows, then PCA. Start the sample company, Bellwether Garden Supply.

2. Follow these steps to restore your data from the end of Chapter 1:

   a. Put your Chapter 1 backup disk in drive A. You made this backup on pages 41-42.

   b. From the menu bar, click on File, Restore.

   c. From the Select Backup File screen, click `Browse`. The Open Backup File screen pops up.

   d. Click on the down-arrow in the Look in field. Then click on 3½ Floppy (A:) to select drive A (or the appropriate place for your backup file).

   e. Click on the Chapter 1.ptb file to highlight it. The File name field displays Chapter 1.

   f. Click on the `Open` button.

   g. Make sure that the Location field shows A:\Chapter 1.ptb (or the appropriate location for your backup file). Click `Next >`.

   h. From the Select Company screen make sure that the radio button next to An Existing Company is selected. The Company name field shows Bellwether Garden Supply; the Location field shows C:\ProgramFiles\Peachtree\Company\BCS (or the appropriate location on your computer). Click `Next >`.

---

i.   The Restore Options screen appears. Make sure that the box next to Company Data is *checked*. Click | Next > |.

j.   The Confirmation screen appears. Check the From and To fields to make sure they are correct. Click | Finish |. When the Restore Company scale is 100% completed, your data is restored and you are returned to the menu bar.

k.   Remove the backup disk.

3. Continue using PCA and complete Exercise 1-2.

Exercise 1-2: Follow the instructions below to complete Exercise 1-2:

1. Add Leif Fowler as the new employee.

Employee ID:	LFOWLER-01 [use all caps; use a zero]
Name:	Leif Fowler
Address:	12 North Oak Street
City, ST Zip:	Decatur, GA 30030

2. Follow these steps to back up Exercise 1-2:

a. Put a blank, formatted disk in drive A.

b. From the menu bar, select File, then Back up.

c. Click on the | Back Up Now | button.

d. Click on the down-arrow in the Save in field. If necessary, scroll up the list, then click on 3½ Floppy (A:) to select drive A.

e. Type **Exercise 1-2** in the File name field.

f. Click on the | Save | button.

g. When the screen prompts that This company backup will require approximately 1 diskette, click on | OK |.

h. When the screen prompts you to insert the first disk, click on
   | OK |. When the Back Up Company scale is 100%
   completed, you have successfully backed up to the current point in
   Chapter 1. You are returned to the menu bar.

3. Click on File, Exit to exit Peachtree.

CHAPTER 1 INDEX

Chapter 2 | Vendor Transactions

SOFTWARE OBJECTIVES: In Chapter 2, you will use the software to:

1. Restore data from Exercise 1-2.
2. Enter a purchase order.
3. Enter and post a vendor invoice in the Purchases/Receive Inventory window.
4. Go to the Payments window to pay a vendor.
5. Print a check in payment of the vendor invoice.
6. Analyze payments and vendor credit memos.
7. Make two backups: one blank, formatted disk for Chapter 2; one blank, formatted disk for Exercise 2-2.[1]

WEB OBJECTIVES: In Chapter 2, you will do these Internet activities:

1. Use your Internet browser to go to the book's website at http://www.mhhe.com/yacht2004.
2. Complete the Internet activity for Accounting Students.
3. Use a word processing program to write a summary about the website(s) that you visited.

In Chapter 2 you will learn about how Peachtree works with vendors. The first thing you will do is select Purchase Orders from the Tasks menu.

When Bellwether Garden Supply orders inventory from vendors, Account No. 12000, Inventory, is debited. Accounts Payable and the vendor account is credited. Vendors offer Bellwether a **purchase discount** for purchase invoices paid within a discount period. Purchase discounts are cash discounts from vendors in return for early payment of an invoice; for example, 2% 10, net 30 days. If Bellwether pays an invoice within 10 days, they can deduct two percent from the invoice amount. Otherwise, the net amount is paid within 30 days. In this chapter, you learn how PCA handles accounts payable transactions with vendors.

---

[1]Refer to the chart on page 2 for backing up data.

GETTING STARTED

Follow these steps to start PCA:

1. Start Windows and Peachtree in the usual way.

2. Start the sample company, Bellwether Garden Supply.

RESTORING DATA FROM CHAPTER 1

On pages 48 and 49, you backed up (saved) Exercise 1-2. In order to begin where you left off, you must restore your data from Exercise 1-2. Restoring will allow you to start where you left off at the end of Chapter 1.

Follow these steps to restore your Exercise 1-2 data:

1. Put your Exercise 1-2 backup disk in drive A. This backup was made on pages 48 and 49.

2. From the menu bar, click File, Restore.

3. From the Select Backup File screen, click [Browse]. The Open Backup File screen pops up.

4. Click on the down-arrow in the Look in field. Then click on 3½ Floppy (A:) to select drive A (or the appropriate place for your backup file).

5. Click on the Exercise 1-2.ptb file to highlight it. The File name field displays Exercise 1-2. Click [Open].

6. Make sure that the Location field shows A:\Exercise 1-2.ptb (or the appropriate location for your backup file). Click [Next >].

7. From the Select Company screen make sure that the radio button next to An Existing Company is selected. The Company name field shows Bellwether Garden Supply; the Location field shows C:\ProgramFiles\Peachtree\Company\BCS (or the appropriate location on your computer). Click [Next >].

8. The Restore Options screen appears. Make sure that the box next to Company Data is *checked*. Click [Next >].

9. The Confirmation screen appears. Check the From and To fields to make sure they are correct. Click [Finish]. When the Restore Company scale is 100% completed, your data is restored and you are returned to the menu bar.

10. Remove the backup disk.

ACCOUNTS PAYABLE TASKS

Vendor transactions are a five-step process:

1. Maintain Vendors: Set up a new vendor.

2. Purchase Orders: Order items from one of Bellwether's vendors.

3. Purchase Invoices: Receive inventory or services from one of Bellwether's vendors. Apply a purchase order to a purchase invoice.

4. Payments: Pay a vendor or record a cash purchase. (PCA also includes vendor credit memos.)

5. Print Checks: Print a check for payment to a vendor or expenses.

The Purchase Order Window

Purchase orders are used to place an order from a vendor. When you post a purchase order, you do not update any accounting information. In an accrual-based accounting system, the accounting information is updated when you receive the items from the purchase order.

Changing Global Settings for Accounting Behind the Screens

Peachtree is a double-entry accounting system. There is a selection in Options/Global that allows you to hide general ledger accounts. This is called Accounting Behind the Screens. The PCA screens in this book show the general ledger accounts. To check the Accounting Behind the Screens settings, follow the steps shown below.

1. From the menu bar, click Options, then Global. The Accounting tab should is already selected. The boxes in the section Hide General Ledger Accounts *must* be unchecked. (If necessary, click on the boxes to uncheck them.)

Hide General Ledger Accounts

☐ Accounts Receivable (Quotes, Sales Orders, Invoicing, Credit Memos, Receipts)
☐ Accounts Payable (Purchase Orders, Purchases, Credit Memos, Payments)
☐ Payroll Entry

3. Observe that two boxes are checked in the Other Options section: Warn if a record was changed but not saved and Recalculate

Other Options

☑ Warn if a record was changed but not saved
☐ Hide inactive records
☑ Recalculate cash balance automatically in Receipts, Payments, and Payroll Entry
☐ Use Timeslips Accounting Link

cash balance automatically in Receipts, Payments, and Payroll Entry. Make sure *both* of these Other Options boxes are checked.

4. Click on the General tab. Make sure your Line Item Entry Display has 2 Line selected; and that the Smart Data Entry area has both boxes checked.

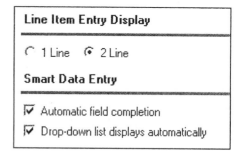

Line Item Entry Display

○ 1 Line   ⊙ 2 Line

Smart Data Entry

☑ Automatic field completion
☑ Drop-down list displays automatically

5. Click [OK].

6. From the menu bar, click Tasks, then select Purchase Orders. The Purchase Orders window displays.

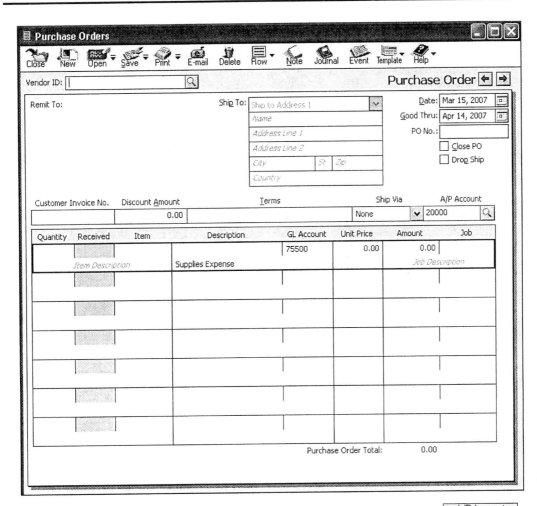

If your screen does not show an A/P Account lookup field
or a GL Account column, the option to hide general ledger
accounts is selected.

Uncheck the Hide General Ledger Accounts boxes in
Options/Global. (*Hint: See the instructions at the top of page 56 for
changing the global setting.*)

6.   Your cursor is in the Vendor ID lookup field. Type **A** (use capital A).
     AARON-01 displays in the lookup field.

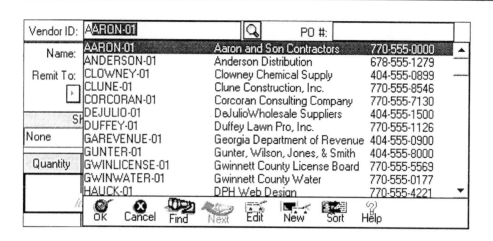

Comment

If the Vendor ID field is not completed, the Automatic Field Completion option is *not* selected. Click on Options, then Global. Click on the General tab. In the Smart Data Entry section, make sure that a check mark is placed next to Automatic field completion. Click ___OK___ when you are finished.

---

7.   Click on the Date field. Highlight the date, then type **28** and press **<Enter>**. Your cursor moves to the Good Thru field. To accept the 30-day expiration, press **<Enter>**. Your cursor moves to the PO No. field.

8.   Click on the Quantity column. Type **20** as the Quantity.

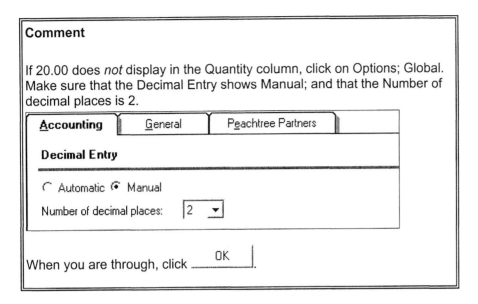

Comment

If 20.00 does *not* display in the Quantity column, click on Options; Global. Make sure that the Decimal Entry shows Manual; and that the Number of decimal places is 2.

| <u>A</u>ccounting | <u>G</u>eneral | P<u>e</u>achtree Partners |

Decimal Entry

   ◦ Automatic ⊙ Manual

Number of decimal places: | 2 ▾ |

When you are through, click ___OK___.

9. Press **<Enter>**. Your cursor is in the Item column.

10. Click once on the magnifying-glass icon in the Item column. Double-click on AVRY-10150 Bird Bath - Stone Gothic 2pc. The Description column is automatically completed.

11. Press the **<Enter>** key and your cursor moves to the GL Account column. Notice that Account No. 12000 is automatically selected. Account No. 12000 is the Inventory account. The word Inventory is also displayed in the line below the Description.

12. Press the **<Enter>** key to go to the Unit Price column. The 51.95 unit automatically displays.

13. Press the **<Enter>** key to go to the Amount column. Peachtree calculates the quantity times the unit price and enters the result in the Amount column (20 X $51.95 = $1,039.00).

14. Press the **<Enter>** key to go to the Job column. The Job column is also a lookup field. It contains a list of the jobs and their descriptions. Since Bellwether does not apply this purchase to a job, press the **<Enter>** key to skip this field.

Your cursor is ready to enter a new transaction. Complete the following information:

> Quantity: **50**
> Item: **AVRY-10100** - Bird House Kit

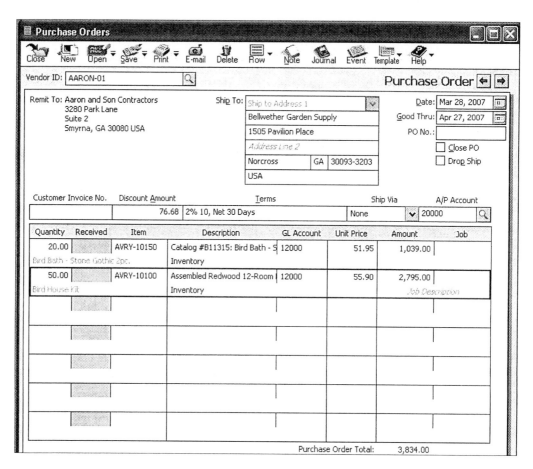

15. Click . The Accounting Behind the Screens, Purchase Order Journal window displays. Compare your screen to the one shown on the next page.

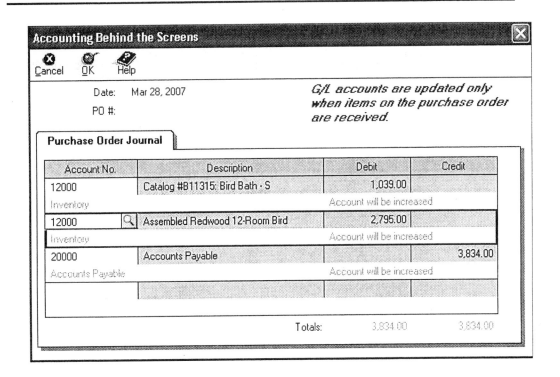

16.   Click **OK**. You are returned to the Purchase Orders window.

Printing Purchase Orders

When you select the **Print** icon, PCA will print the purchase order and post the purchase order journal. Follow these steps to print the purchase order:

1.   Click **Print**.

2.   The Print Forms: Purchase Orders window pops up. Accept the default for First PO Number temp1 by clicking **Print**. The purchase order starts to print. Purchase Order No. temp1 is shown on the next page.

	Ship To:
Aaron and Son Contractors 3280 Park Lane Suite 2 Smyrna, GA 30080 USA	Bellwether Garden Supply 1505 Pavilion Place Norcross, GA 30093-3203 USA

3/28/07	4/27/07	BEL005
2% 10, Net 30 Days		None

AVRY-10150	Catalog #B11315: Bird Bath – Stone Gothic 2pc.	20.00	51.95	1,039.00
AVRY-10100	Assembled Redwood 12-Room Bird House on 14 ft. pole. Attracts Purple Martins, Bluebirds and Wrens	50.00	55.90	2,795.00

Comment

The purchase order form that printed is called PO Preprinted. To type a different form, click Change Form . Then, select PO Plain as the form to print. When you select a different form, the information is the same but the look of the form changes.

---

3.   Click Close to return to the menu bar.

The Purchases/Receive Inventory Window

The first step is to select Purchases/Receive Inventory from the Tasks pull-down menu. In PCA, the Purchases/Receive Inventory window is the Purchase Journal. The Apply to Purchases tab is the default. The lower half of the screen shows columns for Quantity, Item (inventory items), Description, GL Account, Unit Price, Amount, and Job. Observe that the default for the A/P Account is 20000, Accounts Payable. The Purchases/Receive Inventory window looks like a purchase order. Similar to other PCA windows, the icon bar appears at the top of the window.

Follow these steps to learn how to process vendor transactions:

1. From the menu bar, select Tasks, then Purchases/Receive Inventory. Your cursor is in the Vendor ID field.

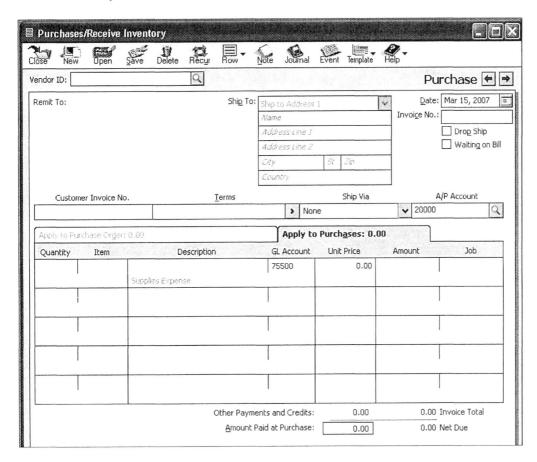

2. With the cursor in the Vendor ID text field, press the plus key: **<+>** and the Maintain Vendors window displays.

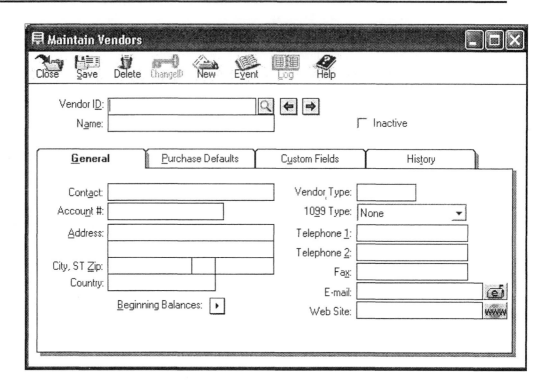

Observe that there are four tabs on the Maintain Vendors window: General, Purchase Defaults, Custom Fields, and History.

Adding a New Vendor

You are going to enter a new vendor: AA Landscaping. Since a *coding system* has already been set up for vendors in Bellwether, you will continue to use the same one. The coding system used has uppercase letters and numbers. To be consistent, AA Landscaping will use AA-01. Notice that the name of the company is typed in all capital letters followed by a hyphen, then a zero, and the number one: AA-01.

What if two companies have the same name, such as, AA Landscaping and AA Suppliers? They could be coded as AALAND-01 and AASUP-01.

You should be consistent so that others working in your company can guess what a customer or vendor code is from the company's name. This is accomplished when you set up a logical, consistent coding system. Remember codes are **case sensitive** which means that you must type either upper or lowercase letters: AA-01 is not the same as AA-01.

You have choices for coding in PCA. Here are some other suggestions for coding AA Landscaping:

AA: the first three letters of the company's name.

AAL-01:   the first three letters of a company's name, the first letter of the second name, a hyphen, and a two-digit number.

AALAND: an alphabetic code for a company name, using the first and second names for a total of eight characters.

Follow these steps to continue in the Maintain Vendors window:

1. Make sure the Maintain Vendors window is displayed. Type **AA-01** in the Vendor I<u>D</u> field and press **<Enter>**. A vendor list drops down. AA Landscaping is *no*t one of Bellwether's vendors.

2. Press the **<Enter>** key. Your cursor is in the N<u>a</u>me field.

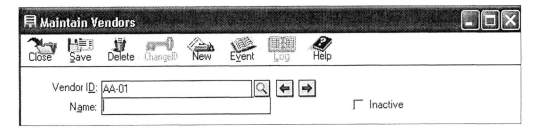

3. Type **AA Landscaping** and press **<Enter>**.

4. Your cursor is in the Cont<u>a</u>ct field. The person who handles sales for AA is Cindy Barber. Type **Cindy Barber** and press **<Enter>** two times.

5. Your cursor is in the <u>A</u>ddress field. Skip the <u>A</u>ddress, City, ST <u>Z</u>ip, and Country fields. For now, you are going to use only one more field in the Maintain Vendors window: Vendor Type. You use the Vendor Type field to classify vendors. You could classify vendors as Service or Supply to indicate what type of goods you purchase from them.

6. With your mouse, click in the Vendor Type text field and type **SUPPLY** (use all capital letters) to classify AA.

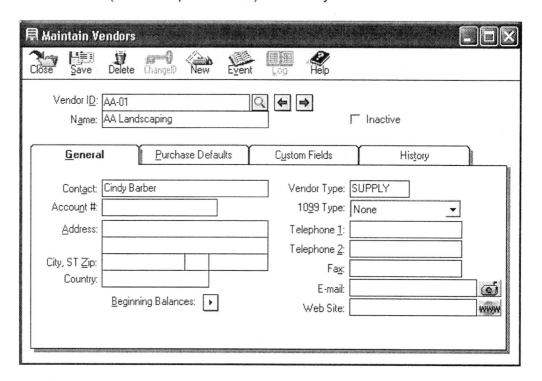

If you need to move between fields to make corrections, use the **<Tab>** key to move forward and the **<Shift> + <Tab>** to move backwards.

7. Click on the <u>P</u>urchase Defaults tab. Notice that the Vendor I<u>D</u> and N<u>a</u>me fields stay the same: AA-01 and AA Landscaping.

8. Click on the magnifying-glass icon in the Pur<u>c</u>hase Acct field. A pop-up list of accounts displays.

9. Scroll up the list. Double-click on Account No. 57200, Materials Cost.

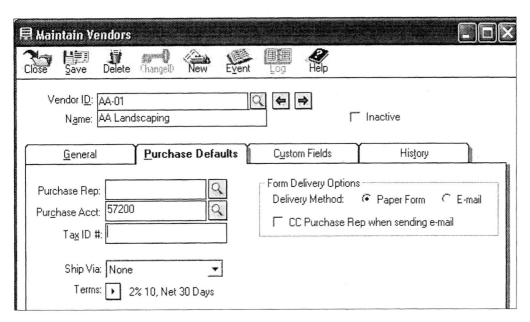

When AA Landscaping is selected as the vendor, Account No. 57200, Materials Cost, will be automatically debited.

10. Click 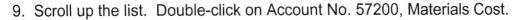 , then return to the Purchases/Receive Inventory window.

Entering a Vendor Invoice

Make sure that the Purchases\Receive Inventory window is displayed and that the cursor is in the Vendor ID field. Follow these steps to enter a vendor invoice.

1. In the Vendor ID field, type **A**. As soon as you type the letter **A**, the vendor list pops up with AA-01, AA Landscaping, highlighted. Press the **<Enter>** key.

2. Observe that the date is Mar 15, 2007. You are *not* going to change the date. Click on the Invoice No. field. In the Invoice # field, type **AA107** and press **<Enter>**.

3. Click on the Quantity field and type **1** and press **<Enter>**.

4. Since you are not purchasing an inventory item, press the **<Enter>** key again.

6. The cursor moves to the Description field. In the Description field, type **Organic Fertilizer** and press **<Enter>**.

6. In the GL Account field press **<Enter>** to accept Account No. 57200, the Materials Cost account.

7. In the Unit Price field, type **45** and press **<Enter>**.

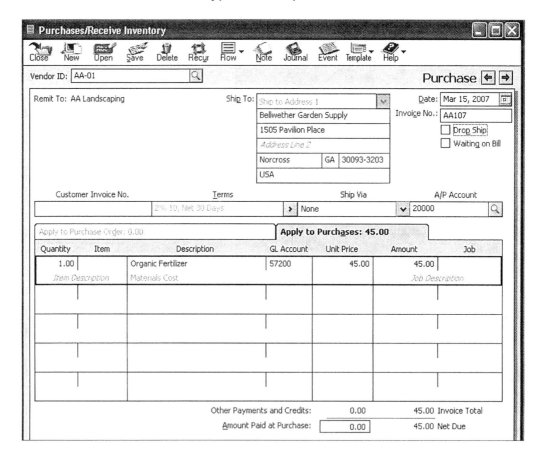

> **Comment**: What if your Purchases/Receive Inventory window does *not* show an A/P Account field or GL Account column?
>
> You should check your settings in the Options/Global selection. Make sure that the boxes in the Hide General Ledger Accounts section are unchecked. These steps were shown on page 56.

Posting a Purchase Transaction

When you make an entry in the Purchases/Receive Inventory window, you are debiting one of the General Ledger Cost of Sales accounts and crediting Accounts Payable/Vendor. In this case, the debit is to Account No. 57200 Materials Cost and the credit to Account No. 20000 Accounts Payable and to the Vendor ID AA-01, AA Landscaping.

Acct. #	Account Description	Debit	Credit
57200	Materials Cost	45.00	
20000/ AA-01	Accounts Payable/ AA Landscaping		45.00

Follow these steps to post this transaction:

1. Make sure the Purchases/Receive Inventory window is displayed as shown on page 68.

2. Click [Save] to post the vendor invoice.

3. Click [Close] or press the **<Esc>** key to return to the menu bar.

PAYMENTS TO VENDORS

When you make a payment to a vendor, you use the Payments window.
The Payments window is the Cash Disbursements Journal.

Follow these steps to pay the AA Landscaping invoice:

1. From the menu bar, select Tasks, then Payments. Compare your
    screen to the one shown below.

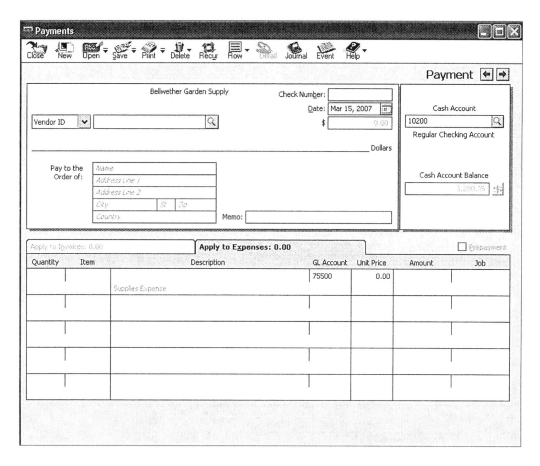

There are two parts to the Payments window: the check section at
the top and the invoice section at the bottom of your screen.

2. The cursor is in the Vendor ID field. Click on the magnifying-glass
    icon, then double-click on AA-01, AA Landscaping. Look at the

invoice section of your screen. The invoice number AA107 is completed with the amount that Bellwether owes AA Landscaping.

3.   Click on the Date field. Type or select **17**.

4.   Click on the Pay box for Invoice AA107. Notice that the check portion of the screen is completed. The amount to be paid is 44.10. This is the amount of the invoice less the discount ($45 -.90 = $44.10).

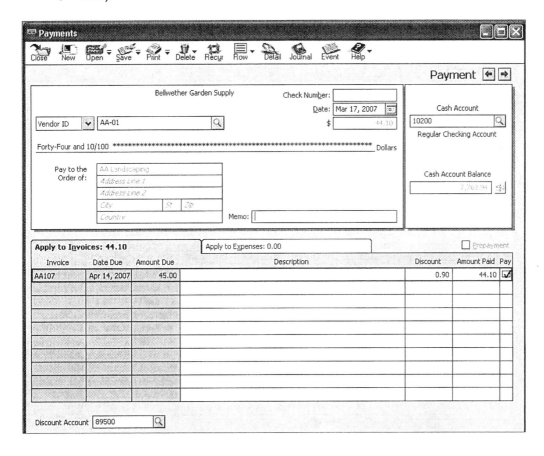

> ➤ **Troubleshooting Tip:** Observe that the Check Number field is blank. The check number is assigned when you print. You only enter a check number if you are *not* going to print checks. You will print checks on pages 72-75

5. Click [Save] to post to the Cash Disbursements Journal.

6. Click [Close] or press **<Esc>** to return to the menu bar.

When you post this payment, the Accounts Payable account is debited for the full invoice amount ($45), which balances the credit created when you entered the invoice. The cash account is decreased (credited) by the amount of the check ($44.10) and the Purchase Discounts account is increased (credited) for the purchase discount ($.90). The Purchase Discounts account was already established for Bellwether Garden Supply.

Acct. #	Account Description	Debit	Credit
20000/ AA-01	Accounts Payable/AA Landscaping Invoice AC701	45.00	
10200	Regular Checking Account		44.10
89500	Purchase Discount		.90

PRINTING CHECKS

You can print a batch of checks or print one check at a time. Since we only have one check to print, you are going to print an individual check. PCA also has special check forms to use for printing checks. These may be purchased from Peachtree Software. Since we do not have check forms, you will print the check on a blank piece of paper.

Follow these steps to print a check:

1. From the menu bar, select Reports, then Accounts Payable.

2. If necessary, scroll down the Report List. Double-click on the Disbursement Checks folder to open it. Click on AP Preprint 1 Stub to highlight it.

Comment

Step 2 instructs you to select AP Preprint 1 Stub as the form to print. If this form does *not* print, select another one. The form you select is tied to the kind of printer you are using. Depending on your printer, you may need to make a different selection.

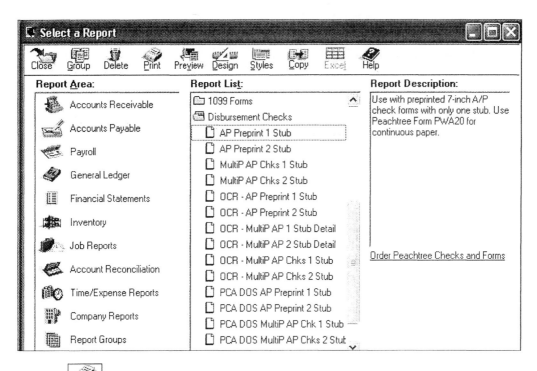

3. Click [Print]. The AP Preprint 1 Stub Filter window appears.

4. Type **10213** in the First check number field.

5. Click on the Calendar icon next to Mar 15, 2007. When the March 2007 calendar pops up, click on 17 to select it. Observe that Mar 17 2007 appears in the date field.

6. In the From and To field, select AA-01 for AA Landscaping. Compare your screen to the one shown on the next page.

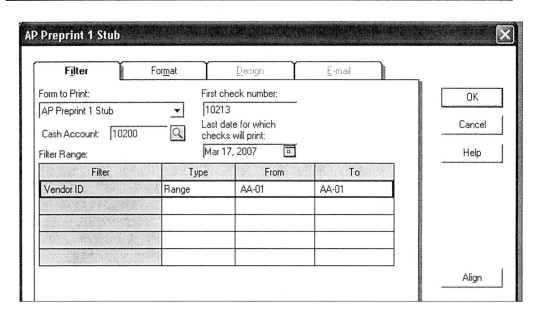

7. Click [OK]. The Print window pops up.

8. Click [OK] and Check No. 10213 starts to print.

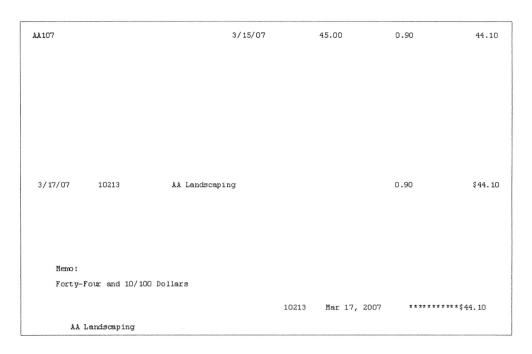

A screen displays asking Did the Checks print properly, and is it OK to assign the check numbers to the checks? Make sure the check printed properly and the amount is correct. (See the Payments screen on page 71.)

9. If not, click [Cancel] and make the necessary corrections. If the check printed properly, click [Yes].

10. Close the Select a Report window.

DISPLAYING THE VENDOR LEDGERS

To display the Vendor Ledgers, follow these steps:

1. From the menu bar, select Reports, then Accounts Payable.

2. In the Report List, highlight Vendor Ledgers.

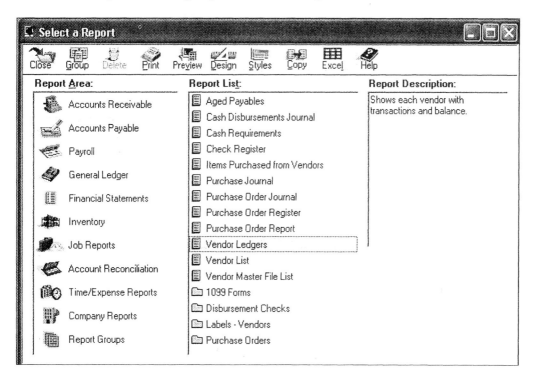

3. Click 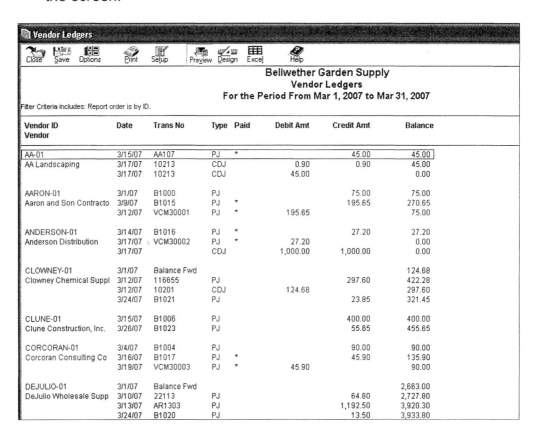 Preview .

4. At the Vendor Ledgers Filter[2] window click ⬚ OK ⬚ .

5. The Vendor Ledgers display on your screen. Compare your screen to the one shown below. To see the entire vendor ledger, scroll down the screen.

Vendor Ledgers

Close Save Options   Print Setup   Preview Design Excel   Help

Bellwether Garden Supply
Vendor Ledgers
For the Period From Mar 1, 2007 to Mar 31, 2007

Filter Criteria includes: Report order is by ID.

Vendor ID Vendor	Date	Trans No	Type	Paid	Debit Amt	Credit Amt	Balance
AA-01	3/15/07	AA107	PJ	*		45.00	45.00
AA Landscaping	3/17/07	10213	CDJ		0.90	0.90	45.00
	3/17/07	10213	CDJ		45.00		0.00
AARON-01	3/1/07	B1000	PJ			75.00	75.00
Aaron and Son Contracto	3/9/07	B1015	PJ	*		195.65	270.65
	3/12/07	VCM30001	PJ	*	195.65		75.00
ANDERSON-01	3/14/07	B1016	PJ	*		27.20	27.20
Anderson Distribution	3/17/07	VCM30002	PJ	*	27.20		0.00
	3/17/07		CDJ		1,000.00	1,000.00	0.00
CLOWNEY-01	3/1/07	Balance Fwd					124.68
Clowney Chemical Suppl	3/12/07	116655	PJ			297.60	422.28
	3/12/07	10201	CDJ		124.68		297.60
	3/24/07	B1021	PJ			23.85	321.45
CLUNE-01	3/15/07	B1006	PJ			400.00	400.00
Clune Construction, Inc.	3/26/07	B1023	PJ			55.65	455.65
CORCORAN-01	3/4/07	B1004	PJ			90.00	90.00
Corcoran Consulting Co	3/16/07	B1017	PJ	*		45.90	135.90
	3/19/07	VCM30003	PJ	*	45.90		90.00
DEJULIO-01	3/1/07	Balance Fwd					2,663.00
DeJulio Wholesale Supp	3/10/07	22113	PJ			64.80	2,727.80
	3/13/07	AR1303	PJ			1,192.50	3,920.30
	3/24/07	B1020	PJ			13.50	3,933.80

The Vendor Ledger is the Accounts Payable subsidiary ledger. The Accounts Payable subsidiary ledger for AA Landscaping was credited for $45 when you entered the vendor invoice in the Purchases/Receive Inventory window (page 68). Once the invoice

---

[2]The Filter tab is the default.

was entered, there was a balance of $45. When you posted the payment (see pages 71 and 72), PCA debited the vendor for the same amount. The balance after posting the payment is zero ($0.00).

VENDOR CREDIT MEMOS

Vendor credit memos are returns to vendors. You can apply vendor credit memos to any existing vendor invoice that has *not* been paid. All entries made on the Vendor Credit Memos window are posted to the general ledger, vendor records, and when applicable, inventory and job records.

The vendor ledger is shown on page 76. Observe that Vendor ID AARON-01, Aaron and Son Contractors, shows three transactions: 1) On 3/1/07, Invoice No. B1000 (Trans No), for $75. This is recorded in the Purchase Journal (PJ). 2) On 3/9/07, Invoice No. B1015, recorded in the purchase journal, for $195.65. 3) On 3/12/07 vendor credit memo 30001 (VCM) recorded in the purchase journal for $195.65. This leaves Aaron and Son Contractors with an original balance of $75. Follow these steps to zoom into these journal entries.

1. Put your cursor over the 3/9/07 vendor ledger entry. Your cursor changes to a magnifying-glass with a Z in it.

AARON-01	3/1/03	B1000	PJ			75.00	75.00
Aaron and Son Contractors	3/9/03	B1015	PJ	*		195.65	270.65
	3/12/03	CM30001	PJ	*	195.65		75.00

2. To zoom in to the 3/9/07 transaction, double-click on it with your left mouse button. The Purchases/Receive Inventory window appears showing the original purchase of inventory items. Compare your screen to the one shown on the next page.

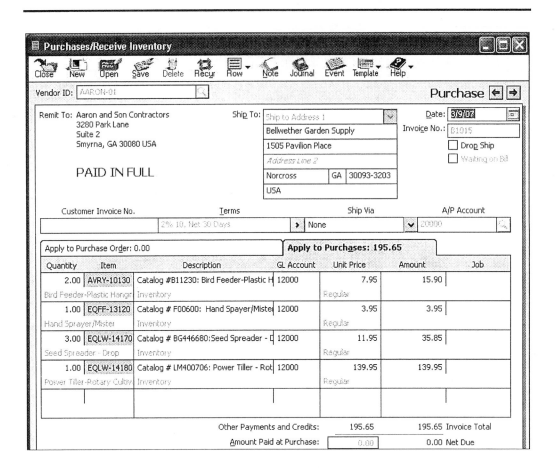

3. Click . You are returned to the Vendor Ledgers.

4. Zoom in to the 3/12/07 vendor credit memo (VCM30001). The Vendor Credit Memos screen appears. Observe that the Apply to Invoice No. tab shows B1015. This is the same merchandise that was purchased on 3/9/07, Invoice No. B1015. (See the Purchases/Receive inventory screen shown on this page.). Compare the two screens. The Vendor Credit Memos screen is shown on the next page.

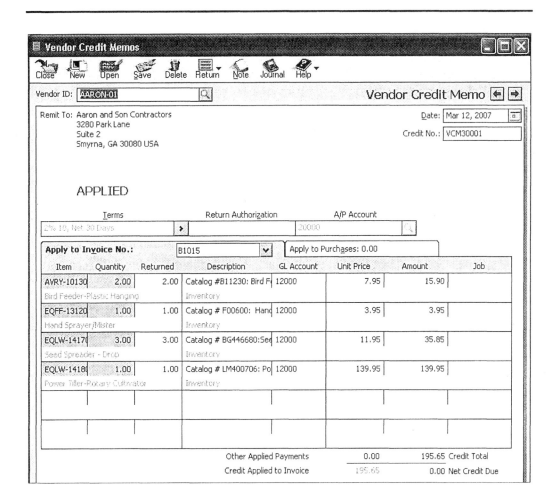

5. Click [Close]. At screen pops up asking if you want to save, click
    [No]. You are returned to the vendor ledgers. Click [Close] two
    times to return to the menu bar.

BACKING UP CHAPTER 2 DATA

Follow these steps to back up Chapter 2 data:

1. Put a blank, formatted disk in drive A.

2. From the menu bar, select File, then Back up.

3. Click [Back Up Now].

4. Click on the down-arrow in the Save in field. If necessary, scroll up the list, then click on 3½ Floppy (A:) to select drive A.

5. Type **Chapter 2** in the File name field.

6. Click [Save].

7. When the screen prompts that This company backup will require approximately 1 diskette, click [OK].

8. When the screen prompts you to insert the first disk, click [OK]. When the Back Up Company scale is 100% completed, you have successfully backed up to the current point in Chapter 2. You are returned to the menu bar.

9. Click on File, Exit to exit Peachtree.

	INTERNET ACTIVITY
1.	From your Internet browser, go to the book's website at http://www.mhhe.com/yacht2004.
2.	In the Student Edition list, link to Internet Activities.
3.	Link to WEB EXERCISES, PART 1.
4.	Scroll down the screen to ACCOUNTING STUDENTS – Chapter 2. Complete steps 1-3.
5.	Using a word processing program, write a summary about the site(s) you selected. Remember to include the website address of each link. Your summary should be no more than 75 words or less than 50 words.

SUMMARY AND REVIEW

SOFTWARE OBJECTIVES: In Chapter 2, you used the software to:

1. Restore data from Exercise 1-2.
2. Enter a purchase order.
3. Enter and post a vendor invoice in the Purchases/Receive Inventory window.
4. Go to the Payments window to pay a vendor.
5. Print a check in payment of the vendor invoice.
6. Analyze payments and vendor credit memos.
7. Make two backups: one blank, formatted disk for Chapter 2; one blank, formatted disk for Exercise 2-2.

WEB OBJECTIVES: In Chapter 2, you did these Internet activities:

1. Used your Internet browser to go to the book's website at http://www.mhhe.com/yacht2004.
2. Completed the Internet activity for Accounting Students.
3. Used a word processing program to write a summary about the website(s) that you visited.

GOING TO THE NET

Access information about domain name statistics at http://www.zooknic.com/Domains/counts.html.

1. gTLD is an abbreviation for what word(s)?

2. What is the number of domain names worldwide?

3. How many .com names are there?

4. List the extensions that are used with domain names.

Multiple Choice Questions: In the space provided write the letter that best answers each question.

_____1. Which menu bar selection do you make to select the Purchases/Receive Inventory window?

    a. File, Backup.
    b. Maintain, Vendors.
    c. Maintain, Default Information.
    d. Tasks, Purchases/Receive Inventory.
    e. None of the above.

_____2. When using Tasks, you can enter information within a lookup field by using one or more of the following keys:

    a. Type the **<+>** symbol.
    b. Double-click with the mouse.
    c. a. or b.
    d. Type the invoice number.
    e. None of the above.

_____3. Cash discounts from vendors in return for early payment of an invoice are called:

    a. Sales discounts.
    b. Returns and allowances.
    c. Purchase discounts.
    d. Markdowns.
    e. None of the above.

_____4. Which menu bar selection do you use to record a payment?

    a. Reports/Accounts Payable/Disbursements Checks.
    b. Maintain, Customers/Prospects.
    c. Options, Global.
    d. Tasks, Payments.
    e. None of the above.

_____5. It is important to use either upper or lowercase letters to identify a vendor because the program:

   a. Is susceptible.
   b. Doesn't recognize numbers.
   c. Doesn't recognize symbols.
   d. Is case-sensitive.
   e. None of the above.

_____6. Why is it important that your coding system for vendors be consistent and logical?

   a. All vendors and customers should be identified by 3 digits.
   b. So that others working in your company can determine a vendor code from the company name.
   c. All the vendors and customer numbers are already set up for Bellwether Garden Supply so you don't have to worry about it.
   d. All customers and vendors should be identified by the first eight letters of a company's name.
   e. None of the above.

_____7. The Internet site for information about accounting students is:

   a. http://www.mhhe.com/business/accounting
   b. http://mhhe.accounting.com
   c. http://www.com
   d. http://accounting.smartpros.com/accountingstudents.xml
   e. None of the above.

_____8. Which of the following tasks do you use to issue a return of merchandise to a vendor?

   a. Purchases/Receive Inventory.
   b. Vendor Credit Memos.
   c. Sales/Invoicing.
   d. Credit Memos.
   e. None of the above.

_____9. When you make an entry in the Purchases/Receive Inventory window for AA Landscaping you are debiting and crediting which accounts:

    a. Dr. Accounts Payable/AA Landscaping
       Cr. Cash in Checking
       Cr. Purchase Discounts
    b. Dr. Cash
       Cr. Accounts Payable
    c. Dr. Cash
       Cr. Sales
    d. Dr. Materials Cost
       Cr. Accounts Payable/AA Landscaping
    e. None of the above.

_____10. Which window do you use to add a new vendor?

    a. Maintain Vendors.
    b. Purchases/Receive Inventory.
    c. Menu bar.
    d. Select a Report.
    e. None of the above.

Exercise 2-1: Follow the instructions below to complete Exercise 2-1.

1. Start Windows, then PCA. Open the sample company, Bellwether Garden Supply.

2. Follow these steps to restore your data from the end of Chapter 2:

    a. Put your Chapter 2 backup disk in drive A. You made this backup on page 80. From the menu bar, click on File, Restore.

    b. From the Select Backup File screen, click | Browse |. The Open Backup File screen pops up.

    c. Click on the down-arrow in the Look in field. Then click on 3½ Floppy (A:) to select drive A (or the appropriate location of your backup file).

d. Click on the Chapter 2.ptb file to highlight it. The File name field displays Chapter 2. Click [Open].

e. Make sure that the Location field shows A:\Chapter 2.ptb (or the appropriate location for your backup file). Click [Next >].

f. From the Select Company screen make sure that the radio button next to An Existing Company is selected. The Company name field shows Bellwether Garden Supply; the Location field shows C:\ProgramFiles\Peachtree\Company\BCS (or the appropriate location on your computer). Click [Next >].

g. The Restore Options screen appears. Make sure that the box next to Company Data is *checked*. Click [Next >].

h. The Confirmation screen appears. Check the From and To fields to make sure they are correct. Click [Finish]. When the Restore Company scale is 100% completed, your data is restored and you are returned to the menu bar.

i. Remove the backup disk.

3. Add the following vendor:

Vendor I<u>D</u>:   VERDE-01
N<u>a</u>me: Verde Office Supplies
Cont<u>a</u>ct: Joe Greene
Vendor Type: OFFICE

P<u>u</u>rchase Defaults:

Pur<u>c</u>hase Acct: Account No. 75500, Supplies Expense

4. Enter the following purchase:

    Vendor ID: VERDE-01
    Invoice#:   V877
    Date: March 15, 2007
    Quantity: 5
    Description: Boxes of file folders
    GL Account: 75500, Supplies Expense
    Unit Price: $10.95

5. Post this purchase.

6. Continue with Exercise 2-2.

Exercise 2-2: Follow the instructions below to complete Exercise 2-2.

1. Enter the following transaction.

Date	*Description of Transaction*
03/17/07	Pay Verde Office Supplies for Invoice V877, $53.65.

2. Post the Cash Disbursements Journal.

3. Print Check No. 10214. (*Hint: On the AP Preprint 1 Stub Filter screen, select the vendor. To do that, select the appropriate vendor in the To and From fields.*)

4. Print the Vendor Ledgers.

5. Follow these steps to back up Exercise 2-2

    a. Put a new blank, formatted disk in drive A.

    b. From the menu bar, select File, then Back up.

    c. Click Back Up Now .

    d. Click on the down-arrow in the Save in field. If necessary, scroll up the list, then click on 3½ Floppy (A:) to select drive A.

e.   Type **Exercise 2-2** in the File name field.

f.   Click [Save].

g.   When the screen prompts that This company backup will require approximately 1 diskette, click [OK].

h.   When the screen prompts you to insert the first disk, click [OK]. When the Back Up Company scale is 100% completed, you have successfully backed up to the current point in Chapter 2. You are returned to the menu bar.

i.   Click on File, Exit to exit Peachtree.

CHAPTER 2 INDEX

Chapter 3 Customer Transactions

SOFTWARE OBJECTIVES: In Chapter 3, you will use the software to:

1. Restore data from Exercise 2-2.
2. Go to the Tasks menu to enter quotes and sales orders.
3. Enter customer terms in the Maintain menu.
4. Go to the Tasks menu to enter a sales invoice.
5. Print a sales invoice.
6. Analyze receipts and customer credit memos.
7. Post a receipt for the previously invoiced amount.
8. Make two backups: one blank, formatted disk for Chapter 3; one blank, formatted disk for Exercise 3-2.[1]

WEB OBJECTIVES: In Chapter 3, you will do these Internet activities:

1. Use your Internet browser to go to the book's website at http://www.mhhe.com/yacht2004.
2. Complete the Internet activity for the American Accounting Association.
3. Use a word processing program to write a summary about the website(s) that you visited.

Chapter 3 introduces you to the basic way that PCA works with customer transactions. First you will learn about quotes and sales orders. Then, you will learn how the information you enter in the Maintain menu is used when posting entries in the Tasks menu. For example, in the Maintain Customers/Prospects window, you set a range of days within which a customer can receive a discount and you set the discount percentage. This information will print on the sales invoices you record. The discount is automatically applied when you enter a receipt within the allotted time. You can see an overview of all outstanding invoices via the Collection Manager in the Analysis menu.

---

[1]Refer to the chart on page 2 for backing up data.

GETTING STARTED

Follow these steps to start PCA:

1. Start Windows and Peachtree in the usual way. Start the sample company, Bellwether Garden Supply.

2. Restore your data from the Exercise 2-2 back up that was made on pages 86 and 87.

    a. Put your Exercise 2-2 backup disk in drive A. You made this backup on pages 86 and 87. From the menu bar, click on File, Restore.

    b. From the Select Backup File screen, click [Browse]. The Open Backup File screen pops up.

    c. Click on the down-arrow in the Look in field. Then click on 3½ Floppy (A:) to select drive A (or the appropriate location of your backup file).

    d. Click on the Exercise 2-2.ptb file to highlight it. The File name field displays Exercise 2-2. Click [Open].

    e. Make sure that the Location field shows A:\Exercise 2-2.ptb (or the appropriate location for your backup file). Click [Next >].

    f. From the Select Company screen make sure that the radio button next to An Existing Company is selected. The Company name field shows Bellwether Garden Supply; the Location field shows C:\ProgramFiles\Peachtree\Company\BCS (or the appropriate location on your computer). Click [Next >].

    g. The Restore Options screen appears. Make sure that the box next to Company Data is *checked*. Click [Next >].

h. The Confirmation screen appears. Check the From and To fields to make sure they are correct. Click [Finish]. When the Restore Company scale is 100% completed, your data is restored and you are returned to the menu bar.

i. Remove the backup disk.

ACCOUNTS RECEIVABLE TASKS

The four basic tasks in Accounts Receivable are:

1. Quotes: This task allows you to enter a quote for a customer.

2. Sales Orders: Sales orders provide you with a means of tracking backorders for your customers.

3. Sales/Invoicing: When you are ready to ship items, the sales/invoicing task is used.

4. Receipts: This task is used for recording receipts from customers. (PCA also includes credit memos.)

Entering a Quote

When you enter a quote for a customer, you are *not* updating any accounting information or inventory amounts. PCA calculates what the total cost of the sale will be for a customer, including sales tax and freight. You can then print the quote for the customer. Follow these steps to enter a sales quote.

1. Click on Tasks, then select Quotes/Sales Orders. A drop-down menu displays. Click on Quotes. The Quotes window displays.

2. Your cursor is in the Customer ID field. Type **F** (use capital F). FOSTER-01 Foster Consulting Technologies displays. Press the **<Enter>** key.

3. Your cursor is in the Ship to Address 1 field. Click on the Date field. Accept the default for the Date and Good thru dates by pressing the **<Enter>** key four times. Observe that the Quote No. field is blank. This is okay. Peachtree will assign a quote number automatically.

> **Comment**
>
> You can also enter a number that you want to print in the Quote # field. If you assign your own number, PCA sorts numbers one digit at a time. Therefore, it is a good idea to assign numbers with the same number of digits. For example, PCA sorts the following numbers in this order:
> 1
> 104
> 12
> 2
> 23

4. Your cursor should be in the Customer PO field. Observe that this field is blank. Since this customer does not have a purchase order number, you are going to leave this field blank. Click on Quantity column. Type **1** and press **<Enter>**. (If the Quantity column shows .01, refer to the steps on page 59 for setting two decimal places.)

5. In the Item column, select EQFF-13110 Fertilizer Compression Sprayer. (*Hint: Scroll down the Item list to make this selection.*) The Description, GL Account, Unit Price, Tax, and Amount columns are automatically completed.

> **Comment**
>
> If the GL Account column is not displayed on the Quotes window, you need to check your global settings. Refer to the steps on page 56 to make sure that the boxes in the Hide General Ledger Accounts section are unchecked (see Options/Global).

6. Click on the Quantity column. Type **4** then select EQWT-15120 Bell-Gro Heavy Duty Garden Hose - 75 ft for the item. Compare your screen to the one shown on the next page.

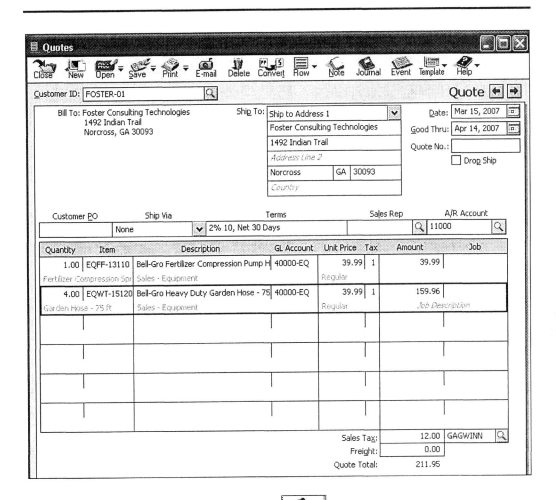

To see the journal entry, click 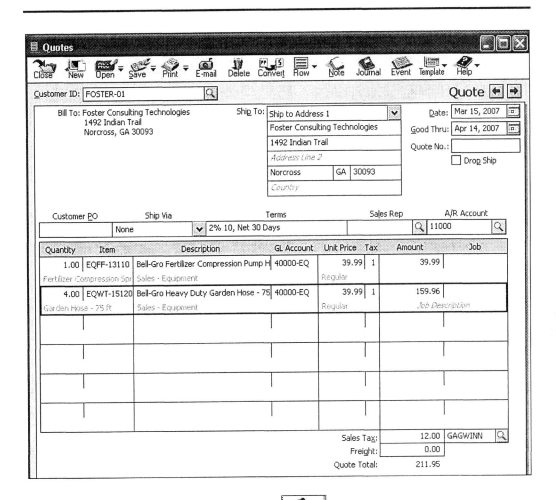. The Quotes Journal lists the sales taxes that are paid for the transaction, the price for each item, and the amount that Bellwether will receive from the customer on this quote.

7. Click [Save] to post this sales quote, then click [Close] to return to the menu bar.

Comment

When a sales quote is posted, you are *not* updating any general ledger accounts. That is handled through the Sales/Invoicing task, which you will work with after you convert the quote and print the sales order.

Converting a Quote to a Sales Order

Let's assume that Foster Consulting Technologies accepts this sales quote. Let's convert the quote to a sales order.

1. Click on Tasks, Quotes/Sales Order, then select Quotes.

2. Click [Open]. The Select Quote window displays.

3. Highlight Foster's quote.

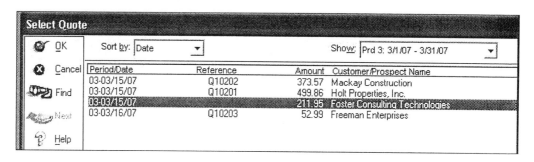

4. Click [OK].

5. The Quotes window displays with Foster's sales quote. Click [Convert]. You have three options: Sales/Invoice; Sales/Invoice and Print Now; Sales Order. Click on the radio button next to Sales Order.

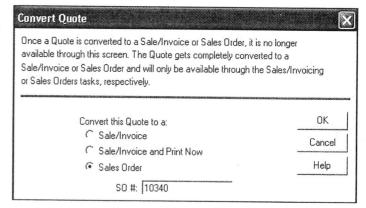

6. Select [OK]. You are returned to the Quote window. Click
    [Close]. You just converted the sales quote to a sales order. Now you
    can invoice the customer for a partial shipment of items.

Entering a Sales Order

The Sales Order task allows you to enter items ordered by your customer
and track backorders. Sales orders also allow you to ship partial
quantities of items, or quantities greater than the originally ordered
quantity.

1. Click on Tasks, then Quotes/Sales Order, then select Sales Orders.
    The Sales Orders window displays.

2. In the Customer ID field, type **H** (use capital H) and press **<Enter>**.
    The Bill To and Ship To fields are completed automatically. The
    customer, Hensley Park Apartments, is selected.

3. The next sales order number is automatically entered in the SO #
    field.

4. Accept the displayed date for the sales order: Mar 15, 2007.

5. Click on the Quantity column, then type **4**.

6. In the Item column, select EQLW-14100 Aerator-Long Spike. The
    Description, GL Account, Unit Price, Tax, and Amounts columns are
    completed automatically. Compare your screen with the one shown
    on the next page.

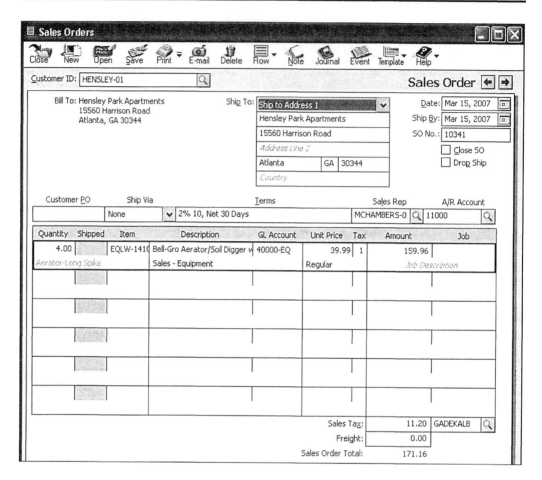

Printing a Sales Order

Printing a sales order gives you the ability to confirm customer orders and fill these orders more efficiently. Your Sales Orders window should be displayed. Follow these steps to print.

1. Click [Print]. The Print Forms: Sales Orders window pops up.

2. Accept the Last used form for Plain Sales Order w/Totals. Click [Print]. The sales order starts to print. Compare your sales order with the one shown on the next page.

Sales Order

Bellwether Garden Supply
1505 Pavilion Place
Norcross, GA 30093-3203
USA

Voice: 770-724-4000
Fax: 770-555-1234

Sales Order Number:
10341

Sales Order Date:
Mar 15, 2007

Ship By:
Mar 15, 2007

Page:
1

Sold To:
Hensley Park Apartments
15560 Harrison Road
Atlanta, GA 30344

Ship To:
Hensley Park Apartments
15560 Harrison Road
Atlanta, GA 30344

Customer ID	PO Number	Sales Rep Name
HENSLEY-01		Mark T. Chambers
Customer Contact	Shipping Method	Payment Terms
Jacob Hensley	None	2% 10, Net 30 Days

Quantity	Item	Description	Unit Price	Extension
4.00	EQLW-14100	Bell-Gro Aerator/Soil Digger w/ long spikes and wood handle	39.99	159.96

			Subtotal	159.96
			Sales Tax	11.20
			Freight	0.00
			TOTAL ORDER AMOUNT	171.16

3. Click Close . You are returned to Bellwether's menu bar.

THE MAINTAIN CUSTOMERS/PROSPECTS WINDOW

The first step is to select the customer you're going to invoice and change one item of information: the discount percentage offered for timely payment.

1. Click on Maintain, then click Customers/Prospects. (Remember, you can use the shortcut keys instead of the mouse: type **<Alt>+<M>**, then type **<C>**.) The Maintain Customers/Prospects window displays. The cursor is in the Customer ID field. Notice the magnifying-glass icon to the right of this field. This icon denotes a Lookup Field or a field with a lookup list attached.

2. Click (the lookup icon) to open the customers/prospects list.[2]

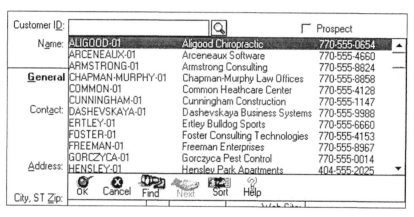

When you click, the customer list dropped down. The magnifying-glass icon works the same way on all PCA windows. For example, when you clicked on the magnifying-glass icon in the Vendor ID field on the Maintain Vendors window on page 58, a list of vendors dropped down.

---

[2]There are three ways to open the list in a lookup field. First, make sure that your cursor is in the text field: 1) Press the right mouse button; 2) type a question mark **<?>**; 3) left-click.

3. The customer file you are going to use is Tidmore Real Estate. Scroll down the customer list, then double-click on **TIDMORE-01 Tidmore Real Estate** to select it from the list. The Maintain Customers/Prospects window shows a completed record for Tidmore Real Estate.

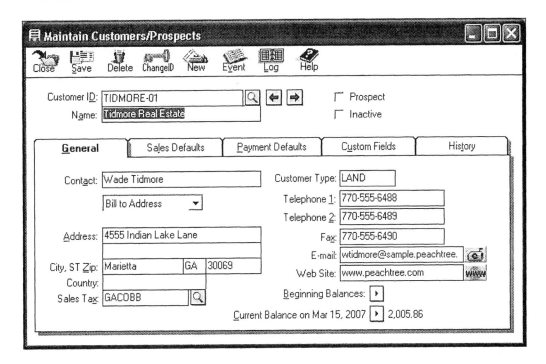

Entering a Discount for a Customer

Because Tidmore Real Estate is such a good customer, we're going to increase their discount from 2% to 5%. As you know from your study of accounting, this is called a *sales discount*. The standard sales discount for Bellwether is 2% if paid within 10 days. Tidmore's new sales discount is 5% if paid within 15 days.

Follow these steps to enter a discount for a customer:

1. Click on the Sales Defaults tab. Compare your screen to the one shown on the next page.

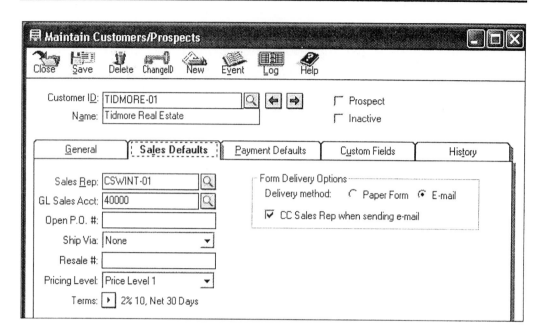

Most of the information in the window changes, but the following items remain the same: the Customer ID, Name, and the Prospect and Inactive check boxes.

2. Click on the Terms arrow button at the bottom of the window. (Remember a diamond shape or arrow button gives you access to an additional dialog box.)

3. Turn off the Use Standard Terms check box by clicking in the box. There should *not* be a check mark in the box.

4. Press the **<Enter>** key five times. The Discount in field is highlighted.

5. Type **15** and press **<Enter>**. The cursor moves to the Discount % field.

6. Type **5** and press **<Enter>**.[3] Compare your screen to the one shown on the next page.

---

[3]You should have set two decimal places in Chapter 2 (see page 54).

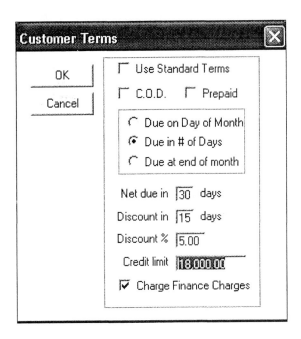

7. Click ⬚ OK ⬚. You are returned to the Maintain Customers/Prospects window. Observe that the Terms have changed to 5% 15, Net 30 Days.

8. Click ⬚ Save ⬚.

9. Click ⬚ Close ⬚. You are returned to the menu bar.

Entering a Sale to a Customer

Let's learn how to invoice Tidmore Real Estate. When you want to print or record an invoice in PCA, you enter a sales invoice for a customer through the Sales/Invoicing window. Like a Sales Journal, the Sales/Invoicing window is reserved for sales from credit customers. The transaction you are going to enter is shown on the next page.

Date   Description of Transaction

03/01/07   Bellwether Garden Supply sold 5 hose-end sprayers to
            Tidmore Real Estate, Customer ID, TIDMORE-01.

Follow these steps to learn how to use the Sales/Invoicing window:

1. From the menu bar, click on Tasks, then Sales/Invoicing.

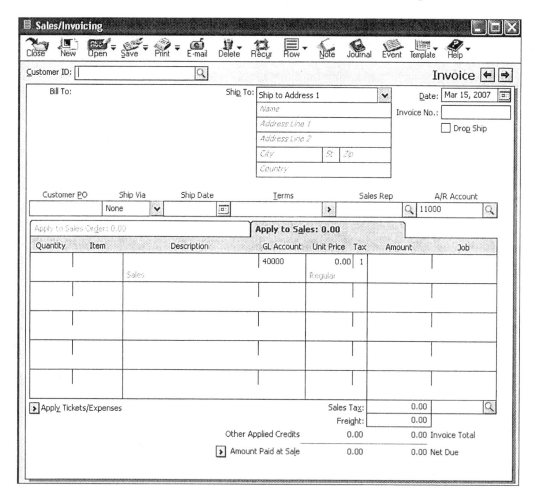

In PCA, much of your work takes place in the Tasks windows:
payments, receipts, purchases, sales, payroll, and the general journal.
This is where you enter the daily transactions for your business.

If you want to enter a cash sale from a customer, you would use the Receipts window, not the Sales/Invoicing window. The Sales/Invoicing window is for credit customers only. Here's a way to remember the difference between Receipts and Sales/Invoicing: if the transaction involves real money (cash or check), enter it in the Receipts window; if the transaction involves a credit sale, enter it in the Sales/Invoicing window. The Sales/Invoicing task is the Sales Journal. The Receipts task is the Cash Receipts Journal.

The Sales/Invoicing window should be displayed on your screen. The cursor is in the Customer ID field. Don't worry if you have forgotten Tidmore's customer ID number because PCA knows it. The Customer ID field has a lookup field.

2. With the cursor in the Customer ID text field, click the right mouse button (or type a question mark, **<?>**). You may also click ⬚.

3. Highlight Tidmore Real Estate, TIDMORE-01.

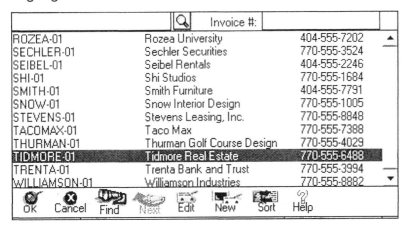

4. Click ⬚. Information for Tidmore Real Estate is automatically completed on the Sales/Invoicing window.

    Observe that the Bill To and Ship To fields are completed automatically. PCA provides an invoice number when the sales invoice is printed so there is no need to enter an invoice number now. Steps for printing the sales invoice are shown on pages 110-113.

You enter an invoice number only when you do *not* wish to print it. If an invoice number is typed, PCA assumes that the invoice has already been prepared. If you type an invoice number on the Sales/Invoicing window, then print it, the sales invoice will show Duplicate on it.

5. Click on the <u>D</u>ate field. The Date field defaults to 3/15/07.

   PCA offers flexibility when entering dates. For example, you can enter March 1, 2007 as 30107 and the program will format the date correctly. You can also enter just the day portion of the date and PCA formats the date in the current period. For example, if you're working in March of 2007, you can type 4 in the date field and the program formats the date as March 4, 2007. You can also use the pop-up calendar to click the date.

6. Type **1** for the date and press **<Enter>**. The cursor moves to the Invoice No. field, which you are going to leave blank.

7. If necessary, click on the Apply to S<u>a</u>les tab.

8. Click on the Quantity column, type **5** and press **<Enter>**. Your cursor goes to the Item lookup field.

9. Click 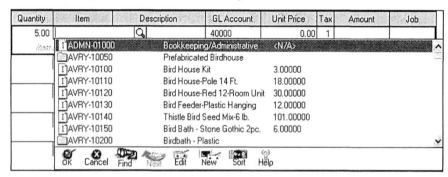 to open the list of inventory items.

Quantity	Item	Description	GL Account	Unit Price	Tax	Amount	Job
5.00			40000	0.00	1		
Item	ADMN-01000	Bookkeeping/Administrative	<N/A>				
	AVRY-10050	Prefabricated Birdhouse					
	AVRY-10100	Bird House Kit		3.00000			
	AVRY-10110	Bird House-Pole 14 Ft.		18.00000			
	AVRY-10120	Bird House-Red 12-Room Unit		30.00000			
	AVRY-10130	Bird Feeder-Plastic Hanging		12.00000			
	AVRY-10140	Thistle Bird Seed Mix-6 lb.		101.00000			
	AVRY-10150	Bird Bath - Stone Gothic 2pc.		6.00000			
	AVRY-10200	Birdbath - Plastic					

OK   Cancel   Find   Next   Edit   New   Sort   Help

There are two ways to enter transaction lines for an invoice:

> By Inventory Item: Because the price of each inventory item is stored in the Maintain Inventory Items file, you only have to enter the quantity supplied. The program will compute the credit amount.

> By Account Number: If there is no line item set up for a particular commodity you sell, or if you don't use the Inventory module, you can distribute directly against the proper General Ledger account.

10. The Inventory Item list should still be open. Let's see what happens if the Sort icon is selected. Click which is located at the bottom of the lookup list on the right side.

    What you have done by selecting Sort is to change the order of the list. The list was sorted by ID number; now the list is sorted alphabetically by name. This feature is available in all lookup lists.

11. Double-click on Hand Sprayer/Mister as the item for this sale. EQFF-13120 displays in the Item field.

12. Your cursor should be in the Description field with the following description highlighted: Bell-Gro Plant All-Purpose Plastic Sprayer/Mister. Since we're not going to add a comment or explanation about this inventory item, press **<Enter>** to move to the GL Account field.

    The default account is Account No. 40000-EQ, Sales – Equipment. The account name is shown below the transaction line. This account will be credited unless you change the account number in this GL Account field. The debit is automatically made to Accounts Receivable–Tidmore Real Estate.

13. Press **<Enter>** to accept Account No. 40000-EQ. The cursor moves to the Unit Price field and 9.99 is automatically completed. Since the price has been set up in the Maintain Inventory Item file, the unit price is automatically completed for you.

14. Press **<Enter>** to go to the tax field. Type a **<?>** to display the lookup list. Inventory Item tax types are set up in the Maintain Inventory Item file. This lookup list lets you specify certain items as exempt or having special tax situations. There is no need to specify any special tax situation.

15. Press **<Enter>** to go to the Amount field. PCA calculates the total, $49.95, and enters it in the field.

16. Press **<Enter>** to go to the Job field. The job field also has a lookup list. You'll learn about Jobs in more detail in Chapter 6.

17. Press **<Enter>** to go to a new transaction line.

➤ **Troubleshooting Tip:** Observe that the Invoice No. field is blank. The invoice number, similar to the check number, is assigned when you print. You only enter an invoice number if you are *not* going to print invoices. You will print the sales invoice on pages 110 – 113.

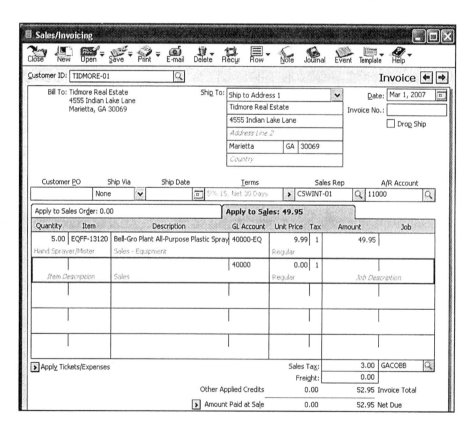

Notice that the Invoice Total and Net Due in the lower right of the screen shows $52.95. The Invoice Total displays a running total of the amount by which the customer's account in the Accounts Receivable subsidiary ledger is increased (debited). When you add the next transaction line, this figure will increase. As you know from your study of accounting, two things happen when the Accounts Receivable subsidiary ledger is used:

a. The Accounts Receivable controlling account in the General Ledger is increased by the amount of the credit sale.

b. The credit to the applicable revenue account is offset by a debit to the Customer's account in the Accounts Receivable ledger.

Distributing Against a Specific Account

In this part of the transaction, Bellwether Garden Supply contracted with Tidmore Real Estate to clean up their back lot for $100. Because no Inventory Item is stored in the maintenance records, this transaction is different than the one you just completed (entering a sale to a customer). In this part of the transaction, you need to distribute the amount ($100.00) directly against the Other Income account.

1. Your cursor is in the Quantity field. Since you don't have a quantity number to enter with this transaction, press **<Enter>**. Your cursor should be in the Item field.

2. Press **<Enter>** to leave the Item text field blank. Your cursor moves to the Description text field.

3. Type **Cleaned back lot** in the Description text field and press **<Enter>**. Your cursor moves to the GL Account field. The default account displays, but it must be changed.

4. Type **41000** (for Other Income) and press **<Enter>**. Now the account description below the current transaction line reads Other Income and your cursor moves to the Unit Price field.

   The account number that automatically displayed, 40000, Sales, was the default account. Since we want to distribute this revenue to a specific account, 41000, Other Income, you must type this account number (41000); otherwise, the program will accept the default account number.

5. Press **<Enter>** to skip the Unit Price field because we don't need a unit price. Your cursor moves to the Tax field.

6. Press **<Enter>** to accept the default tax code. Your cursor moves to the Amount field.

7. Type **100** and press **<Enter>** two times. Notice the screen illustration shows the two amounts entered for this invoice. The Net Due is $158.95.

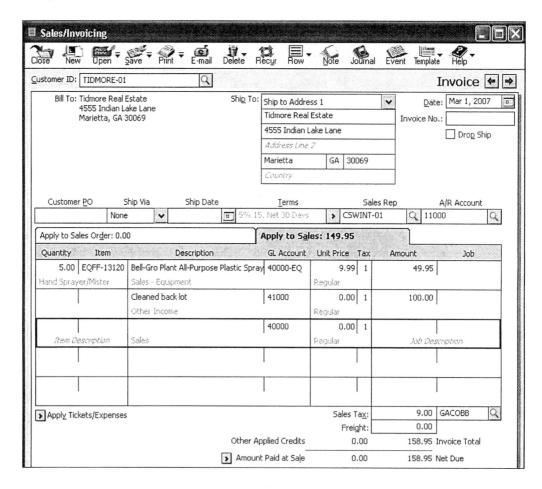

Discount Information

At the beginning of this chapter you changed the sales discount for Tidmore Real Estate. Let's check to make sure that the discount information is current for the invoice you just entered.

1. Click on the arrow 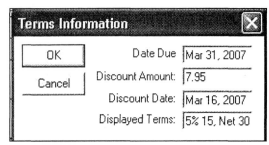 button to the right of <u>T</u>erms. This information is below the Shi<u>p</u> To address. The Terms Information window displays.

   The Date Due, Mar 31, 2007, is the date by which the invoice should be paid. The Discount Amount is the invoice total multiplied by the discount percentage you entered in the Maintain Customer record ($158.95 x 5% = $7.95). (*Hint: Peachtree automatically calculates the Discount Amount on the full sales invoice amount, $158.95. The Discount Amount field can be changed. As you know from your study of accounting, discounts are applied against the sales price of an item* not *the sales price plus tax.*)

2. Since the taxable items add up to $149.95, the five-percent discount should be $7.50 ($149.95 x .05). Type **7.50** in the Discount Amount field, then press **<Enter>**.

   The Discount Date is the date by which the customer must pay to receive the discount. The Displayed Terms are the percentage of discount (5%), the time period in days for receiving the discount (15) and the number of days before the invoice is due (Net 30).

3. Click <u>OK</u> to close the Terms Information window.

POSTING THE INVOICE

The sample company, Bellwether Garden Supply, uses *real-time posting.* When real-time posting is used, the transactions that you enter are posted when you select the [Save] icon.

There is another type of posting included in PCA. It is called *batch posting.* When using batch posting, the transactions you enter are saved to a temporary holding area where you can review them before posting to the general ledger.

Follow these steps to save and post the invoice:

1. Click [Save]. The Sales/Invoicing window is ready for another transaction.

2. Click [Close] or press **<Esc>** to return to the menu bar.

PRINTING INVOICES

Follow these steps to print the invoice for Tidmore Real Estate:

1. Select Reports, then Accounts Receivable.

2. To open the Invoices/Pkg. Slips folder follow these steps.

    b.   Scroll down the Report List and double-click on the Invoices/ Pkg. Slips folder.

    b. Highlight Invoice Plain. Compare your screen with the one shown on the next page.

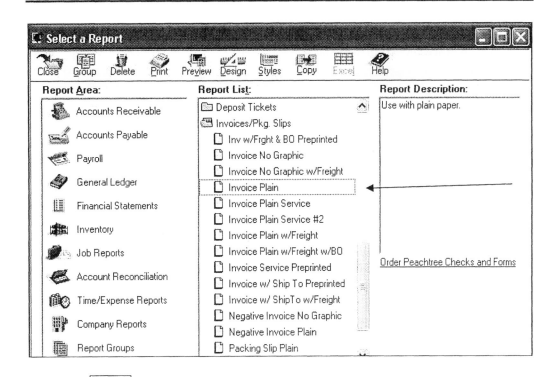

3. Click 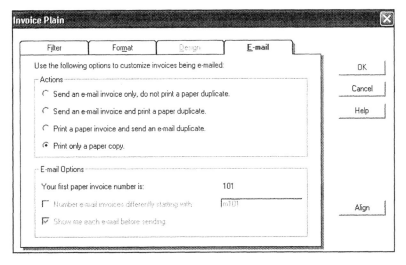.

4. Click on the E-mail tab. Notice that the Actions area has Send an e-mail invoice only, do not print a paper duplicate selected. In order to print invoices you need to change this default. Click on the radio button next to Print only a paper copy to change the default.

5. Click on the Filter tab. The Form to Print field shows Invoice Plain.
    The First Invoice Number field shows 101.

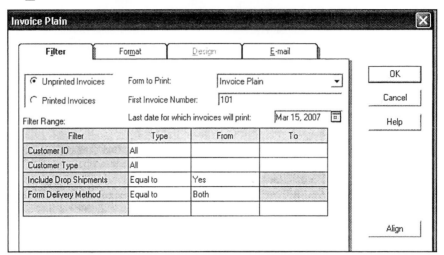

6. Click [OK].

7. The Print window pops up. Click [OK] and the invoice for
    Tidmore Real Estate starts to print. Compare your invoice with the
    one shown on the next page.

Invoice

Bellwether Garden Supply
1505 Pavilion Place
Norcross, GA 30093-3203
USA

Invoice Number:
101

Invoice Date:
Mar 1, 2007

Voice: 770-724-4000
Fax: 770-555-1234

Page:
1

Sold To:
Tidmore Real Estate
4555 Indian Lake Lane
Marietta, GA 30069

Ship to:
Tidmore Real Estate
4555 Indian Lake Lane
Marietta, GA 30069

Customer ID	Customer PO	Payment Terms	
TIDMORE-01		5% 15, Net 30 Days	
Sales Rep ID	Shipping Method	Ship Date	Due Date
CSWINT-01	None		3/31/07

Quantity	Item	Description	Unit Price	Extension
5.00	EQFF-13120	Bell-Gro Plant All-Purpose	9.99	49.95
		Plastic Sprayer/Mister		
		Cleaned back lot		100.00

	Subtotal	149.95
	Sales Tax	9.00
	Total Invoice Amount	158.95
Check/Credit Memo No:	Payment/Credit Applied	
	TOTAL	158.95

Notice the Payment Terms are 5% 15, Net 30 Days. This is the information you entered for Customer Terms on pages 100 and 101.

8. A message box displays asking if the invoice printed properly. When you answer yes, PCA updates invoice numbers and flags the invoice as printed so that it will not print again. Click [Yes].

9. Click [Close] to return to the menu bar.

ENTERING RECEIPTS

Tidmore Real Estate has sent a check in payment of their invoice. Follow these steps to enter the following transaction:

Date   *Description of Transaction*

03/06/07   Received check from Tidmore Real Estate in payment of Invoice No. 101, $151.45.

1. From the menu bar, click on Tasks, then Receipts.

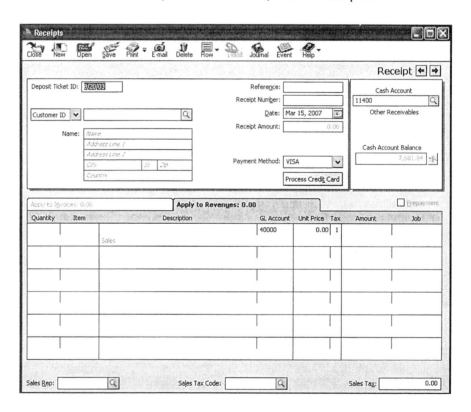

The Receipts window and Payments window look alike. There is a table in the lower half of the window that lists distribution lines for the current transaction. There is an icon bar at the top of the window. The item descriptions and account descriptions appear beneath each transaction line. The title bar identifies the window being used. In this case, the title bar says: Receipts.

2. Your cursor is in the Deposit ticket ID field. Type **999**. This field defaults to today's date and is used to combine receipts for the bank reconciliation. Press **<Enter>**.

3. In the Customer ID field, type the Customer ID for Tidmore: **TIDMORE-01** and press **<Enter>**.

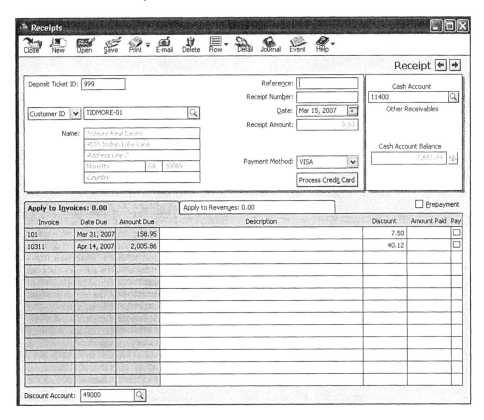

When you enter a Customer ID, the screen shows a list of invoices. When the receipt is to pay for invoiced amounts, you can select an invoice(s) from the list. The invoice amounts, including discounts, fill the receipt's text fields.

4.   Your cursor is in the Refere_n_ce field. Type **8818** for the customer's check number (a Refere_n_ce number must be entered). Press **<Enter>** key two times and the cursor moves to the _D_ate field.

On your screen the _D_ate field displays 3/15/07. This date is important because it is used by PCA to determine if a discount applies. For example, if the transaction date for the invoice was March 1, 2007, and the discount terms were 5% for 10 days, the receipt entered with a date of March 12, 2007 would miss qualifying for a discount. PCA automatically computes and displays the discount amount when one applies.

5.   In the _D_ate field, type **6** (or click on the Calendar icon and select 6), then press **<Enter>**.   Click on the down-arrow in the Payment Method field, then select Check. Press **<Enter>**.

6.   In the Cash Account field, select Account No. 10200, Regular Checking Account. Press **<Enter>**.

7.   If necessary, select the Apply to _I_nvoices tab.

8 .   Select Invoice 101 from the list by clicking on that line. Notice that a magenta line is placed around this selection.

9.   Click on the Pay box. Compare your screen to the one shown on the next page.

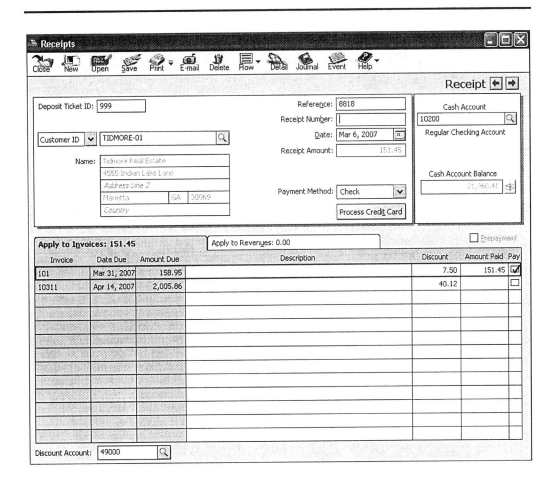

Notice that the Discount column displays the amount of the discount, $7.50. The discount displays because payment was received less than 15 days from the transaction date of the invoice. Therefore, the customer gets the 5% discount and the amount is automatically entered in the Discount field. Then, PCA automatically computes the check for the correct amount of the invoice: $151.45 (149.95 – 7.50 + 9.00 = $151.45). The Receipt Amount in the check portion of the Receipts window shows 151.45, Tidmore's invoice minus the 5% discount, plus sales tax.

10. Click [Save] and the receipt is posted.

11.   Click 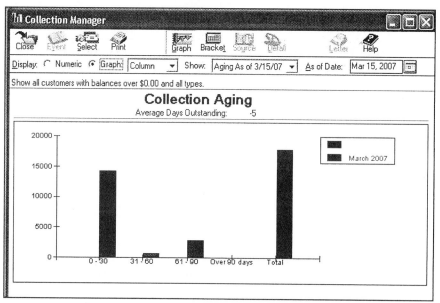 or **<Esc>** to the return to the menu bar.

ANALYZING CUSTOMER PAYMENTS

How well does Bellwether Garden Supply manage its collections of payments from customers? To look at customers and aging amounts, use the Collection Manager. Follow these steps to learn how to use the Collection Manager:

1. From the menu bar, click on Analysis, then Collection Manager. The Collection Aging bar graph appears.

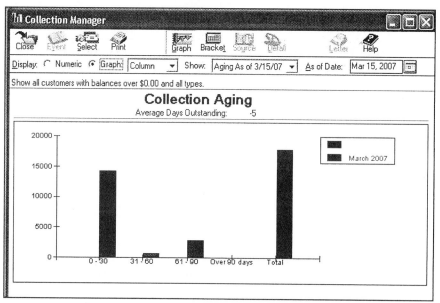

There are four aging brackets along the horizontal or X axis: 0 - 30 days, 31 - 60 days, 61 - 90 days, and over 90 days. The vertical or Y axis shows dollar amounts due.

2.   Click Bracket.

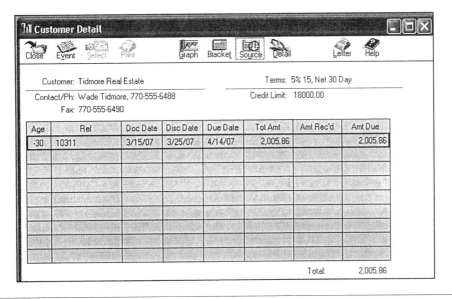

The Total Bracket window shows you the age of the invoice in days, the customer name, the reference (Ref) number, the document date or transaction date, the due date, the total amount due, and whether a letter was sent.

3. Scroll down the screen to highlight the invoice for Tidmore Real Estate (Age, -30; Ref, 10311; Amt Due, 2,005.86). Then, click Source. The Customer Detail screen appears.

At this level you can see all of Tidmore Real Estate's invoices. If you want to send a collection letter you can do that from this window.   By clicking ⌑Letter⌑ on the icon bar you can send a collection letter to Tidmore Real Estate.

4. Click ⌑Close⌑ to exit the Collection Manager and return to the menu bar.

DISPLAYING THE CUSTOMER LEDGERS

To display the Customer Ledgers, follow these steps:

1. From the menu bar, select Reports, then Accounts Receivable. Highlight Customer Ledgers.

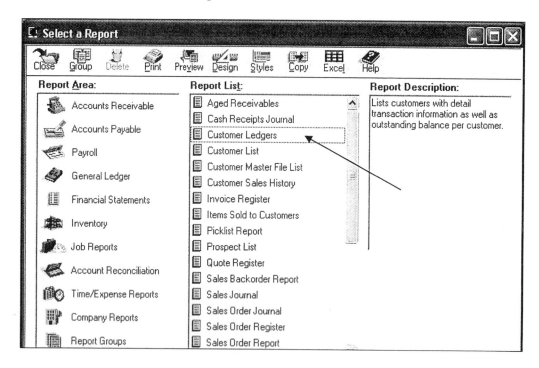

2. Click ⌑Preview⌑.

---

3. At the Customer Ledgers Filter window click OK .

4. The Customer Ledgers appear. To see the rest of the customer ledger, scroll down the screen.

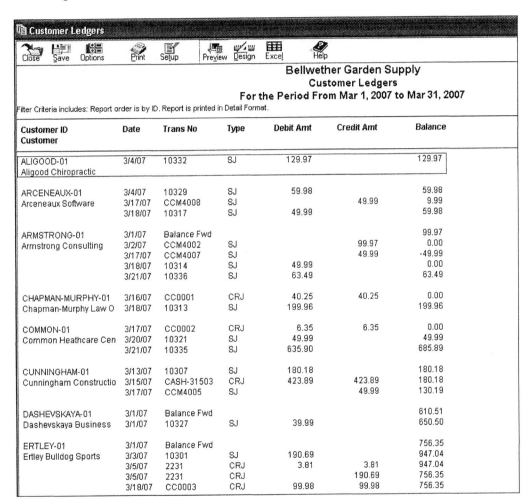

Customer ID Customer	Date	Trans No	Type	Debit Amt	Credit Amt	Balance
ALIGOOD-01 Aligood Chiropractic	3/4/07	10332	SJ	129.97		129.97
ARCENEAUX-01 Arceneaux Software	3/4/07 3/17/07 3/18/07	10329 CCM4008 10317	SJ SJ SJ	59.98 49.99	 49.99 	59.98 9.99 59.98
ARMSTRONG-01 Armstrong Consulting	3/1/07 3/2/07 3/17/07 3/18/07 3/21/07	Balance Fwd CCM4002 CCM4007 10314 10336	 SJ SJ SJ SJ	 49.99 63.49	 99.97 49.99 	99.97 0.00 -49.99 0.00 63.49
CHAPMAN-MURPHY-01 Chapman-Murphy Law O	3/16/07 3/18/07	CC0001 10313	CRJ SJ	40.25 199.96	40.25 	0.00 199.96
COMMON-01 Common Heathcare Cen	3/17/07 3/20/07 3/21/07	CC0002 10321 10335	CRJ SJ SJ	6.35 49.99 635.90	6.35 	0.00 49.99 685.89
CUNNINGHAM-01 Cunningham Constructio	3/13/07 3/15/07 3/17/07	10307 CASH-31503 CCM4005	SJ CRJ SJ	180.18 423.89 	 423.89 49.99	180.18 180.18 130.19
DASHEVSKAYA-01 Dashevskaya Business	3/1/07 3/1/07	Balance Fwd 10327	 SJ	 39.99		610.51 650.50
ERTLEY-01 Ertley Bulldog Sports	3/1/07 3/3/07 3/5/07 3/5/07 3/18/07	Balance Fwd 10301 2231 2231 CC0003	 SJ CRJ CRJ CRJ	 190.69 3.81 99.98	 3.81 190.69 99.98	756.35 947.04 947.04 756.35 756.35

CREDIT MEMOS

Credit Memos are returns to customers. Use the Credit Memos window to enter credit memos for customer returns and credits. You can apply credit memos to any existing customer invoice. All entries made on this window are posted to the General Ledger, customer records, if appropriate, to inventory and job records.

The McGraw-Hill Companies, Inc., *Computer Accounting with Peachtree Complete 2004, 8e*

The customer ledgers should be displayed on your screen. Observe that Armstrong Consulting has a customer credit memo (CCM4002) on 3/2/07. Follow these steps to see how the credit was applied.

1. Observe that on 3/1/07, Armstrong Consulting, shows a balance forward of $99.97. The customer credit memo (CCM4002) on 3/2/07 is a return of that merchandise.

2. Zoom into the 3/2/07 CCM4002 transaction. The Credit Memos screen appears.

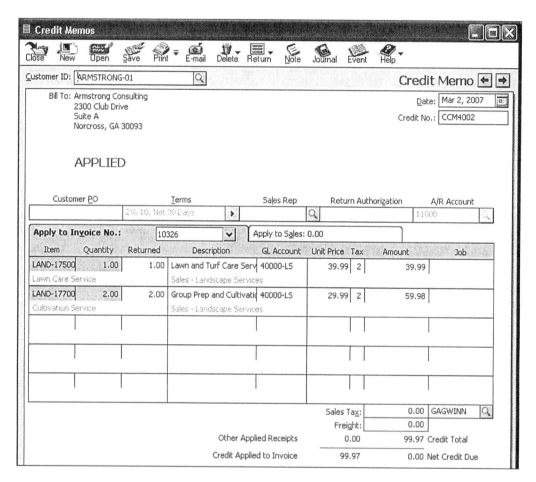

3. This $99.97 credit memo clears the balance forward amount to zero. Close the Credit Memos window, the Customer Ledgers window, and the Select a Report window. You are returned to the menu bar.

BACKING UP CHAPTER 3 DATA

Follow these steps to back up Chapter 3 data:

1. Put a blank, formatted disk in drive A.

2. From the menu bar, select File, then Back up.

3. Click `Back Up Now`.

4. Click on the down-arrow in the Save in field. If necessary, scroll up the list, then click on 3½ Floppy (A) to select drive A.

5. Type **Chapter 3** in the File name field.

6. Click `Save`.

7. When the screen prompts that This company backup will require approximately 1 diskette, click `OK`.

8. When the screen prompts you to insert the first disk, click `OK`. When the Back Up Company scale is 100% completed, you have successfully backed up to the current point in Chapter 3. You are returned to the menu bar.

9. Click on File, Exit to exit Peachtree.

	INTERNET ACTIVITY
1.	From your Internet browser, go to the book's website at http://www.mhhe.com/yacht2004.
2.	In the Student Edition list, link to Internet Activities.
3.	Link to WEB EXERCISES, PART 1.
4.	Scroll down the screen to the AMERICAN ACCOUNTING ASSOCIATION – Chapter 3. Complete steps 1-3.
5.	Using a word processing program, write a summary about the site(s) you selected. Remember to include the website address(es) of each link. Your summaries should be no more than 75 words or less than 50 words.

SUMMARY AND REVIEW

SOFTWARE OBJECTIVES: In Chapter 3, you used the software to:

1. Restore data from Exercise 2-2.

2. Go to the Tasks menu to enter quotes and sales orders.

3. Enter customer terms in the Maintain menu.

4. Go to the Tasks menu to enter a sales invoice.

5. Print a sales invoice.

6. Analyze receipts and customer credit memos.

7. Post a receipt for the previously invoiced amount.

8. Make two backups: one blank, formatted disk for Chapter 3; one blank, formatted disk for Exercise 3-2.

WEB OBJECTIVES: In Chapter 3, you did these Internet activities:

1. Used your Internet browser to go to the book's website at http://www.mhhe.com/yacht2004.

2. Completed the Internet activity for the American Accounting Association.

3. Used a word processing program to write a summary about the website(s) that you visited.

GOING TO THE NET

Access the Financial Accounting Standards Board website at http://raw.rutgers.edu/. Link to FASB. Click on FASB Facts. From the drop-down list, select Board Members/Staff.

1. How many board members serve on the Financial Accounting Standards Board? Do they serve part time or full time?

2. What are the qualifications for the board members?

Short-Answer Questions: In the space provided write an answer to the question.

1. If you want to work with a customer's account, what window do you open? Describe the menu selections.

_____

_____

_____

2. Describe three ways to open a lookup list.

_____

_____

_____

3. What iconic symbol is used to display lookup lists?

_____

_____

_____

4. What is the customer number for Tidmore Real Estate?

_____

_____

5. What is the sales discount for Tidmore Real Estate?

_____

_____

6. What is the default discount for customers?

_____

_____

7. What Internet site is used to go to sites related to the American Accounting Association?

_____

_____

8. When you want to print an invoice in PCA, what are the steps for opening that window?

_____

_____

9. If you receive payment from a customer, what window do you use?

_____

_____

_____

_____

10. Describe what happens when you use the Accounts Receivable subsidiary ledger.

_____

_____

_____

_____

Exercise 3-1: Follow the instructions below to complete Exercise 3-1.

1. Start Windows, then PCA. Start Bellwether Garden Supply.

2. Restore data from the end of Chapter 3. This backup was made on page 123

3. Record the following transaction:

    Date   *Description of Transaction*

    03/02/07   Bellwether Garden Supply sold one rotary mower to
                Tidmore Real Estate, Invoice 102, $299.99. (*Hint:
                Select the Apply to Sales tab. Do not complete the
                Invoice # field. Type 1 in the Quantity field; select
                EQLW-14140 Rotary Mower - Riding 4HP as the Item.*)

4. Post the Invoice.

5. Print Invoice No. 102.

6. Continue with Exercise 3-2.

Exercise 3-2: Follow the instructions below to complete Exercise 3-2.

1. Record the following transaction:

    Date   *Description of Transaction*

    03/10/07   Received Check No. 9915 in the amount of $302.99
                from Tidmore Real Estate in payment of Invoice 102.
                (*Hint: Type 3/10/07 in the Deposit ticket ID field.
                Remember to use the check number in the
                Reference field. Compute the discount and type the
                correct amount in the Discount column. Do not
                include sales tax in the sales discount computation.*)

2. Post the receipt.

3. Print the Customer Ledgers.

4. Back up Exercise 3-2. Use **Exercise 3-2** as the file name.

5. Exit PCA.

CHAPTER 3 INDEX

Chapter 4

Employees

SOFTWARE OBJECTIVES: In Chapter 4, you will use the software to:

1. Restore data from Exercise 3-2.
2. Enter and store information using the Maintain Employees/Sales Rep window.
3. Set up default information for payroll.
4. Store constant information about payroll payment methods.
5. Transfer funds from the regular checking account to the payroll checking account.
6. Enter paychecks in the Payroll Entry window.
7. Print employee paychecks.
8. Make two backups: one blank, formatted disk for Chapter 4; one blank, formatted disk for Exercise 4-2.[1]

WEB OBJECTIVES: In Chapter 4, you will do these Internet activities:

1. Use your Internet browser to go to the book's website.
2. Complete the Internet activity for the American Institute of CPAs.
3. Use a word processing program to write a summary about the website(s) that you visited.

In Chapter 4 you learn how PCA processes payroll. Once default and maintain employee information is set up, payroll is a simple process.

The first step in setting up payroll is to go to the Maintain pull-down menu and select Default Information. The flowchart on the next page explains the steps involved in setting up payroll information.

---

[1]Refer to the chart on page 2 for backing up data.

These steps show you payroll accounting is set up in PCA.

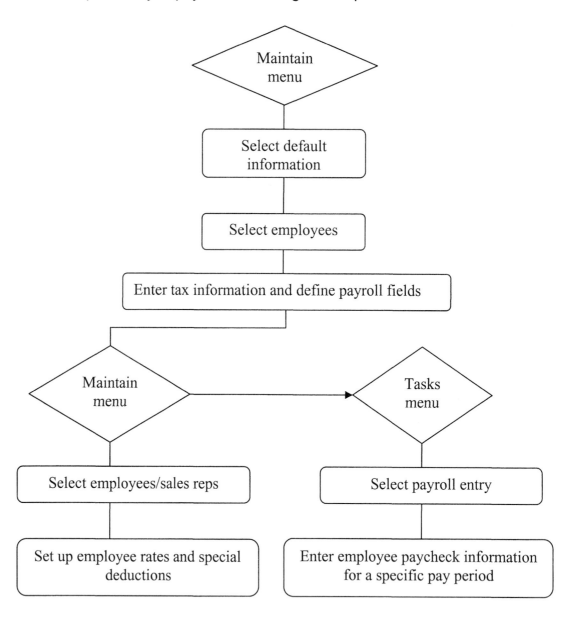

GETTING STARTED

Follow these steps to start PCA:

1. Start Windows and Peachtree in the usual way. Start the sample company, Bellwether Garden Supply.

2. Restore your data from the Exercise 3-2 back up that was made on page 128.

   a.   Put your Exercise 3-2 backup disk in drive A. You made this backup on page 128. From the menu bar, click on File, Restore.

   b.   From the Select Backup File screen, click [Browse]. The Open Backup File screen pops up.

   c.   Click on the down-arrow in the Look in field. Then click on 3½ Floppy (A:) to select drive A (or the appropriate location of your backup file).

   d.   Click on the Exercise 3-2.ptb file to highlight it. The File name field displays Exercise 3-2. Click [Open].

   e.   Make sure that the Location field shows A:\Exercise 3-2.ptb (or the appropriate location for your backup file). Click [Next >].

   f.   From the Select Company screen make sure that the radio button next to An Existing Company is selected. The Company name field shows Bellwether Garden Supply; the Location field shows C:\ProgramFiles\Peachtree\Company\BCS (or the appropriate location on your computer). Click [Next >].

   g.   The Restore Options screen appears. Make sure that the box next to Company Data is *checked*. Click [Next >].

h. The Confirmation screen appears. Check the From and To fields to make sure they are correct. Click [Finish]. When the Restore Company scale is 100% completed, your data is restored and you are returned to the menu bar.

i. Remove the backup disk.

DEFAULT INFORMATION

PCA allows you to set up default information for your business. This information is important for payroll, customer receivables, and vendor payables. Bellwether Garden Supply already has the receivable and payable default information set up. Defaults are not set up for payroll. You will get a chance to do that in this part of the chapter.

Follow these steps to set up payroll Default Information:

1. From the menu bar, click on Maintain, then Default Information. Notice that there is an arrow next to Default Information. This indicates that a pull-down menu exists.

2. Click on Employees.

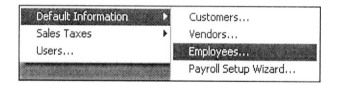

Compare your screen with the one shown on the next page.

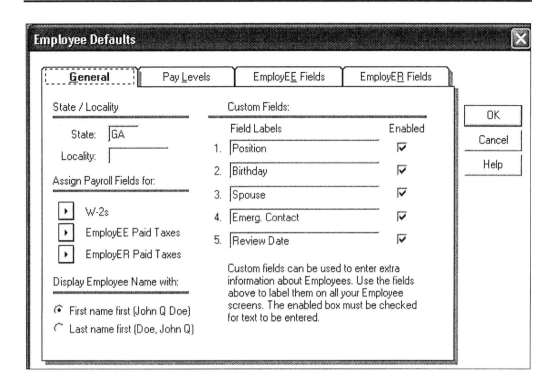

There are four tabs in the Employee Defaults window: General, Pay Levels, EmployEE Fields, and EmployER Fields. You can set up a great deal of information in these tabs. This will make your payroll processing almost automatic.

3. Click on the EmployEE Fields tab.

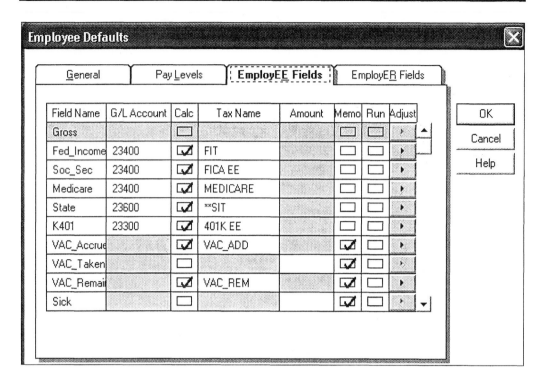

Notice that there are seven items checked in the Calc column: Fed_Income (FIT), Soc_Sec (FICA EE), Medicare (MEDICARE), State (**SIT), K401 (401K EE), VAC_Accrued (VAC_ADD), and VAC_Remaining (VAC_REM). These fields work together with the payroll tax tables to calculate common employee deductions.

The check marks in the Calc and Memo columns indicate common deductions. Bellwether Garden Supply computes Federal Income Tax, Social Security, Medicare, State Income Taxes, 401K, and vacation deductions. These deductions are calculated according to the appropriate tax tables and formulas entered for 401K's and vacation calculations.

The accounts affected by paychecks are liability accounts set up specifically to handle these kinds of deductions. Notice that the GL Account column shows the appropriate account numbers. All the accounts that are checked off are liability accounts. You can also set up voluntary deductions (called allowances in PCA). Voluntary allowances that are individually entered on the employee paycheck could include gas allowances, union dues, and savings bonds.

There is a Memo column with a place to put check marks for amounts that should not be posted to the company's books. The Memo check box is used when you want the employee record to show amounts not on the company's books. An example would be a restaurant business that needed to show employees' tips.

Peachtree Complete Accounting, Release 2004, Educational Version, includes a generic tax table. The payroll tax tables included with the educational version of the software are for example purposes only. In order for the software to calculate the correct payroll tax withholding amounts, you need to subscribe to Peachtree's tax service. Chapter 14, Payroll, goes into more detail about Peachtree's payroll system.

4. Click on the EmployER Fields tab. The tab for EmployER Fields is for the employer's portion of Social Security (Soc_Sec_ER), Medicare (Medicare_ER), Federal Unemployment (FUTA_ER), State Unemployment Insurance (SUI_ER), and 401K (K401_ER).

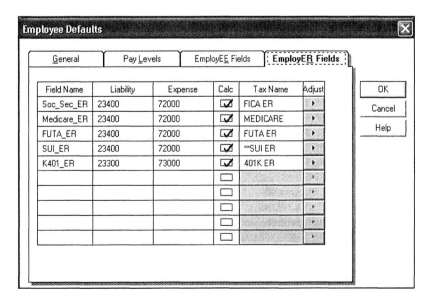

5. Select [OK] or press **<Esc>** to return to the menu bar.

MAINTAIN EMPLOYEES

When default information is completed, PCA sets guidelines for processing the company's payroll. In the Maintain Employees/Sales Reps window, guidelines are specified for individual employees.

1. From the menu bar, click on Maintain, then Employees/Sales Reps.

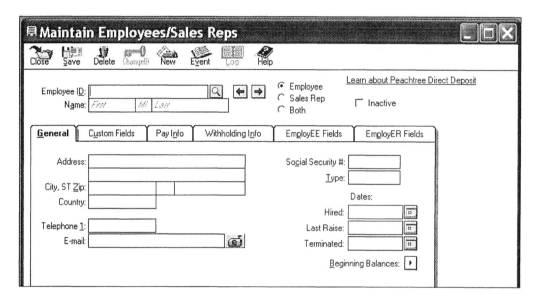

The steps that follow will show you how to look at two employees' records: one salaried employee and one hourly employee.

2. Click 🔍 in the Employee ID field.

3. From the list, double-click on **CLEDUC-01, Charlene M. LeDuc**. (In Chapter 14, you will learn about Peachtree's payroll features in more detail.)

4. Click on the Pay Info tab.

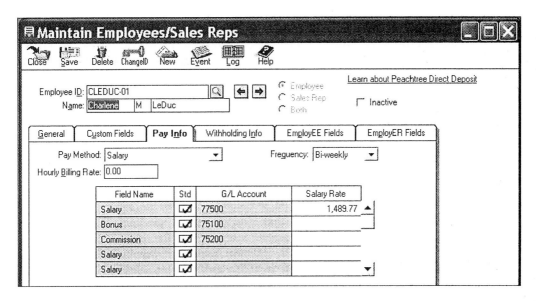

Notice the following about Ms. LeDuc.

a. She is paid a salary of $1,489.77.

b. She is paid bi-weekly (once every two weeks).

5. If your cursor is not in the Employee ID text field, go to that field and click .

6. Select employee **CLIPINSKI-01 Conrad C. Lipinski**. Notice that Mr. Lipinski is paid an hourly wage of $12.00; overtime pay of $18; and that he is paid weekly.

7. Click or press **<Esc>** to return to the menu bar.

PAYROLL TASKS

Once employee default information is set up, PCA automates the payroll process. Now that you have looked at Bellwether's payroll defaults, you will see how easily PCA computes and prints paychecks for hourly and salaried employees.

Transferring Cash to the Payroll Checking Account

Before you make a payroll entry, you will need to transfer $15,000 from Account No. 10200, Regular Checking Account; to Account No. 10300, the Payroll Checking Account. The following transaction will be recorded in the general journal.

Date	*Description of Transaction*
3/28/02	Transfer $15,000 from the regular checking account to the payroll checking account.

Follow these steps to record this transaction in the general journal.

1. From the menu bar, click on Tasks, then select General Journal Entry. The General Journal Entry window appears.

2. Accept 3/15/07 as the date. Click on the Reference field. Type **Transfer** in the Reference field. Press the **<Enter>** key two times.

3. Your cursor is in the Account No. column. Select Account No. 10300, Payroll Checking Account (or you can type **10300**). Press **<Enter>**.

4. Your cursor should be in the Description column. Type **Payroll Checking Account** (or you can type a description) in the Description column. Press **<Enter>**.

5. Type **15000** in the Debit column. Press the **<Enter>** key three times to go to the Account No. column.

6. Your cursor should be in the Account No. column. Select Account No. 10200, Regular Checking Account.

7. Type **Regular Checking Account** in the Description column. Press the **<Enter>** key two times to go to the Credit column.

8. Your cursor is in the Credit column. Type **15000** in the Credit column. Press **<Enter>**. Observe that at the bottom of the General Journal Entry window, the Out of Balance column shows 0.00.

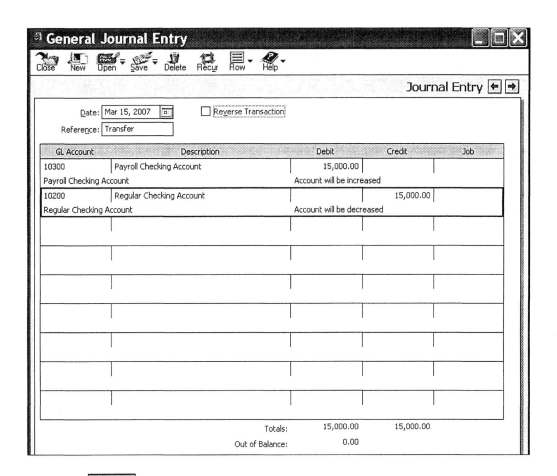

9. Click [Save] to post your entry to the general ledger. Close the general journal entry screen.

Payroll Entry for a Salaried Employee

In the next section you will enter paychecks for these two employees: Charlene M. LeDuc and Conrad C. Lipinski. The information stored in Default Information and in the Maintain Employees file will be important when processing checks. Processing payroll is simple once you have set everything up properly.

Follow these steps to see how a paycheck for a salaried employee is done.

1. From the menu bar, click on Tasks, then Payroll Entry.

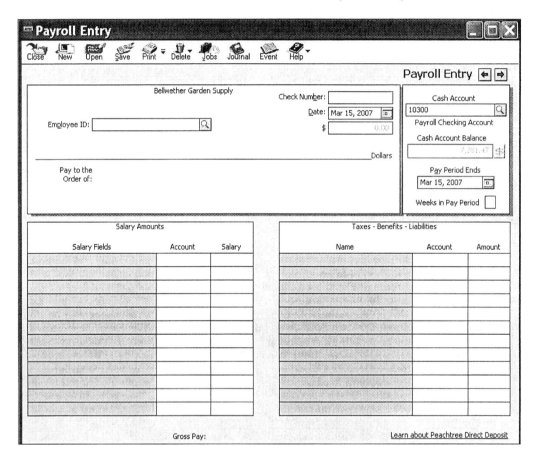

2. In the Employee ID text field, type **CL** for Charlene M. LeDuc and press **<Enter>**.

---

3. To have the program print a check, leave the Check Number field blank by pressing **<Enter>**. If you type a check number, PCA prints Duplicate on the check.

4. Type **29** in the Date field, then press **<Enter>**. (*Remember you can also click on the Calendar icon* 🔲 *and select 29.*) Your cursor goes to the Cash Account field. This check will be charged against the Payroll Checking Account (Account No. 103) which is displayed in the Cash Account field.

5. Press **<Enter>**. Your cursor is in the Pay Period End field. Type **29** then press **<Enter>**. Your cursor goes to the Weeks in Pay Period box. The number 2 is displayed. Ms. LeDuc is on a bi-weekly pay period which means that she has two weeks in her pay period.

    Notice that all the Employee/Employer Fields entered in the Default Information display in a table at the bottom right of the window. All of the Taxes – Benefits – Liabilities fields you asked the program to calculate for you–Fed_ Income, Soc_Sec, Medicare and State tax– have been calculated and display as negative amounts. They display as negative amounts because they decrease the check amount. The amounts shown as positive numbers are *not* deducted from the employee's check.

    Notice that Charlene M. LeDuc has a Salary Amounts table that includes Salary, Bonus, and Commission. If necessary, these amounts can be adjusted.

    Once everything is set up properly in Default Information and Maintain Employees, payroll processing is simple.

    Compare your screen to the one shown on the next page.

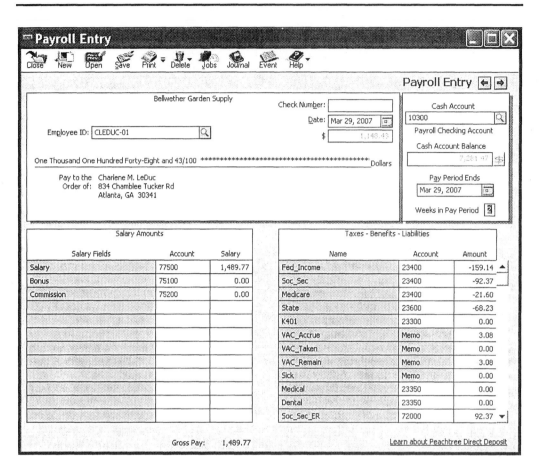

Observe that the Payroll Checking Account Balance in the upper right corner shows a balance of 7,281.47. This is because the default for Peachtree is to recalculate the cash balance automatically for receipts, payments, and payroll entries. From the menu bar, select Options, Global, and notice that a check mark <✓> is placed next to the Recalculate cash balance automatically in Receipts, Payments, and Payroll Entry field. If your balance field does *not* show an amount, then place a check mark in the recalculate cash balance automatically field.

Also notice that Ms. LeDuc's paycheck amount is $1,148.43.

6. Click [Save] to post this payroll entry.

Payroll Entry for an Hourly Employee

1. In the Employee ID field, click 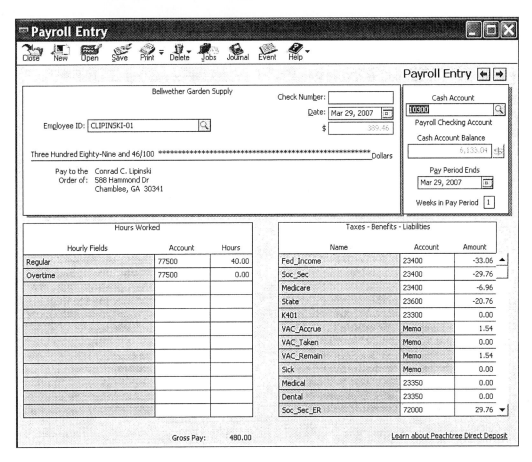. Double-click on Conrad C. Lipinski

2. If necessary, type **29** in the Date field and press **<Enter>** two times.

3. If necessary, type **29** in the Pay Period End field.

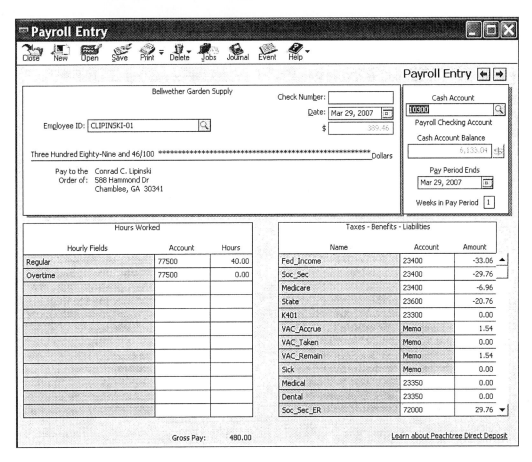

Observe that Mr. Lipinski has one (1) week in his pay period, because he is paid weekly.

Since Conrad C. Lipinski is an hourly employee, the Hours Worked table lists his regular and overtime hours. There are two categories of hours worked for Mr. Lipinski: Regular and Overtime. If necessary, these categories can be adjusted.

4. To see how to adjust the hours that he worked, do the following: in the Hours Worked table, click on Overtime. The Overtime row is highlighted. Make sure your cursor is in the Hours column. Type **3** and press **<Enter>**. Notice how the amounts in the Taxes - Benefits - Liabilities fields are automatically adjusted. The check amount also changed.

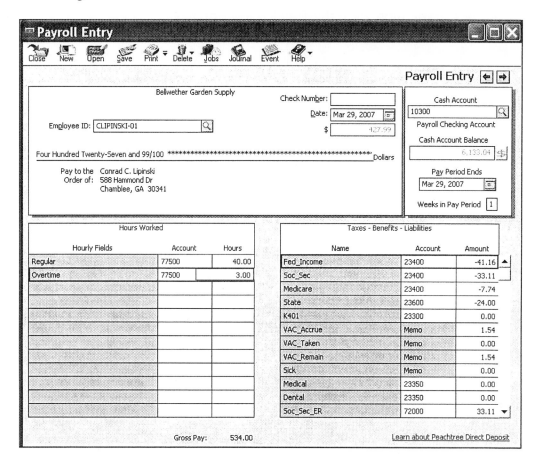

Observe that the Payroll Checking Account Balance in the upper right corner changed to 6,133.04. This is because the default for Peachtree is to recalculate the cash balance automatically for receipts, payments, and payroll entries.

5. Select [Save] to post this paycheck. Close the Payroll Entry screen to return to the menu bar.

Printing Payroll Checks

Similar to vendor disbursements, you have a choice: you may print each check as you enter it in the Payroll Entry window or you may print all checks at once. If you use batch posting, you must print checks before you post. Since you are using real-time posting, you can print checks later.

Follow these steps to print the two checks that you just entered in the Payroll Entry window:

1. From the menu bar, select Reports, then Payroll. The Select a Report window displays.

2. In the Report List, double-click on the Payroll Checks folder to open it.

3. In the Payroll Checks list, double-click on PR Preprint 1 Stub.

Comment

The form you select is tied to the kind of printer you are using. For example, if you are using an HP DeskJet printer, the form that you should select is PR MultiP Chks 2 Stub. You may need to make a different selection depending on your printer.

---

4. If necessary, type **2136** in the First check number field.

5. In the Last date for which checks will print field, click ▦ (calendar). Click once on 29 to select it.

6. Click on the From field, then select Charlene M. LeDuc.

7. In the To field, select Conrad C. Lipinski. Make sure that the First check number field shows 2136.

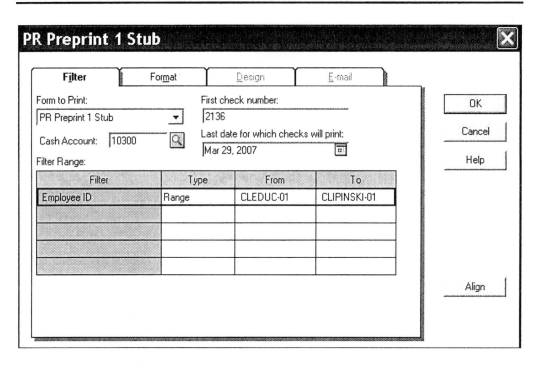

8. Click OK .

9. The Print window pops up. Click OK . The checks for Charlene M. LeDuc and Conrad C. Lipinski start to print. Compare your checks to the ones shown on the next page.

```
    Charlene M. LeDuc                           Employee ID:  CLEDUC-01
                                                Social Sec #  111-32-6555
                    This Check    Year to Date
Gross               1,489.77      2,979.54                                    Total
Fed_Income           -159.14       -318.28  Salary                          1,489.77
Soc_Sec              -92.37        -184.74
Medicare             -21.60        -43.20
State                -68.23        -136.46
VAC_Accrue             3.08          6.16
VAC_Remain             3.08          6.16




Net Check:          $1,148.43               Total                           1,489.77

Pay Period Ending:   3/29/07                          Check Date:   3/29/07
                                                      Check Number: 2136




    One Thousand One Hundred Forty-Eight and 43/100 Dollars


                                               3/29/07      *******$1,148.43


        Charlene M. LeDuc
        834 Chamblee Tucker Rd
        Atlanta, GA  30341
```

```
    Conrad C. Lipinski                          Employee ID:  CLIPINSKI-01
                                                Social Sec #  111-27-2331
                    This Check    Year to Date
Gross                534.00       1,014.00    Hours     Rate      Total
Fed_Income           -41.16        -74.22  Regular  40.00    12.00     480.00
Soc_Sec              -33.11        -62.87  Overtime  3.00    18.00      54.00
Medicare              -7.74        -14.70
State                -24.00        -44.76
VAC_Accrue             1.54          3.08
VAC_Remain             1.54          3.08




Net Check:           $427.99                Total    43.00              534.00

Pay Period Ending:   3/29/07                          Check Date:   3/29/07
                                                      Check Number: 2137




    Four Hundred Twenty-Seven and 99/100 Dollars


                                               3/29/07      ********$427.99


        Conrad C. Lipinski
        588 Hammond Dr
        Chamblee, GA  30341
```

Notice that the employee statement information (also known as the pay stub) is printed first, then the actual check is printed.

10. A window pops up that says Did the checks print properly and is it OK to assign the check numbers to the checks? If your checks are correct, click [Yes].

11. Click [Close] to return to the menu bar.

Comment

In Chapter 14, Payroll, you will learn how to set the defaults for the payroll accounts. Each employee and employer deduction will be set for individual liability accounts and expense accounts. The sample company is used as an example of automatic payroll processing but does *not* reflect correct payroll accounting procedures.

JOURNAL ENTRY FOR PAYROLL

What happens when you post payroll? In the most common case, the Cash Account that you entered in the Payroll Default window is automatically credited for the net paycheck amount when you post payroll checks. The employee salary expense account is debited for the gross amount of the check and any deductions you use are credited. The following table shows you what the payroll journal entry looks like for the hourly employee, Conrad C. Lipinski.

Account Description	Debit	Credit
Wages Expense (Regular Hours)	480.00	
Wages Expense (Overtime Hours)	54.00	
Federal Payroll Taxes Payable (Fed_Income)		41.16
Social Security (Soc_Sec, Employee)		33.11
Medicare (Medicare, Employee)		7.74
State Payroll Taxes Payable (State)		24.00
Payroll Checking Account		427.99

BACKING UP CHAPTER 4 DATA

Follow these steps to back up Chapter 4 data:

1. Put a blank, formatted disk in drive A.

2. From the menu bar, select File, then Back up.

3. Click [Back Up Now]

4. Click on the down-arrow in the Save in field. If necessary, scroll up the list, then click on 3½ Floppy (A:) to select drive A.

5. Type **Chapter 4** in the File name field.

6. Click [Save].

7. When the screen prompts that This company backup will require approximately 1 diskette, click [OK].

8. When the screen prompts you to insert the first disk, click [OK]. When the Back Up Company scale is 100% completed, you have successfully backed up to the current point in Chapter 4. You are returned to the menu bar.

9. Click on File, Exit to exit Peachtree.

	INTERNET ACTIVITY
1.	From your Internet browser, go to the book's website at http://www.mhhe.com/yacht2004.
2.	In the Student Edition list, link to Internet Activities.
3.	Link to WEB EXERCISES, PART 1.
4.	Scroll down the screen to The AMERICAN INSTITUTE OF CPAs – Chapter 4. Complete steps 1-3.
5.	Using a word processing program, write a summary about the site(s) you selected. Remember to include the website address(es) of each link. Your summary should be no more than 75 words or less than 50 words.

SUMMARY AND REVIEW

SOFTWARE OBJECTIVES: In Chapter 4, you used the software to:

1. Restore data from Exercise 3-2.

2. Enter and store information using the Maintain Employees/Sales Rep window.

3. Set up default information for payroll.

4. Store constant information about payroll payment methods.

5. Transfer funds from the regular checking account to the payroll checking account.

6. Enter paychecks in the Payroll Entry window.

7. Print employee paychecks.

8. Make two backups: one blank, formatted disk for Chapter 4; one blank, formatted disk for Exercise 4-2.

WEB OBJECTIVES: In Chapter 4, you did these Internet activities:

1. Used your Internet browser to go to the book's website.

2. Completed the Internet activity for the American Institute of CPAs.

3. Used a word processing program to write a summary about the website(s) that you visited.

GOING TO THE NET

Access the SmartPros website at http://accounting.smartpros.com. Move your cursor over Career Center. From the Career Center drop-down list, select 2003 Career Guide, then link to Accounting Salaries & Trends, then link to Read our overview of the 2003 Salary Guide. Read the article, and then answer the following questions.

1. What industries are expected to have the strongest demand for accountants?

2. What are the specialties and skills most in demand?
3. Who did the research for this article on starting salaries?

Short-Answer Questions: In the space provided, write an answer to the question.

1. Draw the flowchart that shows how payroll accounting is done in PCA.

2. The first step in setting up payroll is to go to the Maintain pull-down menu and select:

   _____

   _____

3. Identify the four tabs in the Employee Defaults window.

   _____

   _____

   _____

4. What do the check marks in the Calc column of the employee defaults indicate? Explain.

_____

_____

_____

_____

5. Why do the employee deductions display as negative amounts on the Payroll Entry window?

_____

_____

_____

_____

6. What is the Maintain Employees window used for?

_____

_____

_____

7. What is the difference in the appearance of the Payroll Entry
    window for an hourly employee and a salaried employee? Explain.

    _____

    _____

8. What are the gross pay amounts for Charlene M. LeDuc and for
    Conrad C. Lipinski?

    _____

    _____

9. What is the net pay for Charlene M. LeDuc and for Conrad C.
    Lipinski?

    _____

    _____

10. What does the American Institute of CPAs do? (*Hint: Refer to the
    Internet Activity to answer this question.*)

    _____

    _____

    _____

Exercise 4-1: Follow the instructions below to complete Exercise 4-1:

1. Start Windows, then PCA. Open Bellwether Garden Supply.

2. Restore data from the end of Chapter 4. This back up was made on page 151.

3. Record the following transaction:

   Date   *Description of Transaction*

   03/29/07   Record paycheck information for Brandee M. Norris.

4. Post the payroll journal.

5. Continue with Exercise 4-2.

Exercise 4-2: Follow the instructions below to complete Exercise 4-2:

1. Record the following transaction:

   Date   *Description of Transaction*

   03/29/07   Record paycheck information for Colista A. Swint. Ms. Swint worked 40 regular hours.

2. Post the payroll journal.

3. Print Check Nos. 2138 and 2139. (*Hint: The First chec*k *number field should display 2138. If not, type* 2138. *In the Last date for which checks will print field, select Mar 29, 2007. Remember to select From Brandee M. Norris To Colista A. Swint.*)

4. Back up Exercise 4-2. Use **Exercise 4-2** as the file name. (*Hint: Use a blank, formatted disk for backing up.*)

5. Exit PCA.

CHAPTER 4 INDEX

Chapter 5 — General Ledger and Inventory

SOFTWARE OBJECTIVES: In Chapter 5, you will use the software to:

1. Restore data from Exercise 4-2.
2. Enter a new account in the Chart of Accounts.
3. Enter a budget amount for an account.
4. Make a General Journal entry to transfer funds.
5. Display the General Ledger Trial Balance.
6. Set up an Inventory Item.
7. Record an inventory adjustment.
8. Make two backups: one blank, formatted disk for Chapter 5; one blank, formatted disk for Exercise 5-2.

WEB OBJECTIVES: In Chapter 5, you will do these Internet activities:

1. Use your Internet browser to go to the book's website.
2. Complete the Internet activity for Ask Jeeves.
3. Complete the steps shown for this activity.

In Chapter 5, you learn how to use the General Ledger Chart of Accounts. This chapter provides you with an explanation of how to set up your own company. When you set up your own company, you need to perform the following steps: set up a chart of accounts and enter any necessary balances or budget amounts.

This chapter also shows you how to use PCA's Inventory system. PCA lets you track inventory items both at the purchasing and the sales level. When you set up an inventory item, you can establish the General Ledger accounts that should be updated by purchases and sales. PCA keeps track of cost of goods sold, stock levels, sales prices, and vendors. PCA uses a *perpetual inventory* system. In a perpetual inventory system, an up-to-date record of inventory is maintained, recording each purchase and each sale that occurs.

CHART OF ACCOUNTS

As you know from your study of accounting, a ***chart of accounts*** is a list of all the accounts used by a company showing the identifying number assigned to each account. PCA includes over 75 sample companies' Charts of Accounts. You can set up your own Chart of Accounts from scratch or select one of the sample companies' Charts of Accounts.

To see the sample companies and their Charts of Accounts, follow these steps:

1. Start Windows and PCA in the usual way. Start the sample company, Bellwether Garden Supply. If necessary, close the Peachtree Today window.

2. Click on Help, then Contents and Index. The Peachtree Help window appears. Peachtree's help is also called online Help. Peachtree Help topics are displayed in the ***HTML*** (Hypertext Markup Language) Help Viewer.

3. If necessary, click on the Contents tab. Double-click on Help about Your Specific Type of Business.

4. Double-click on A-Z List of Business Types.

5. Double-click on List of Sample Charts of Accounts. You can scroll down this list or click on an alphabetic letter to see more companies. Compare your screen to the one shown on the next page.

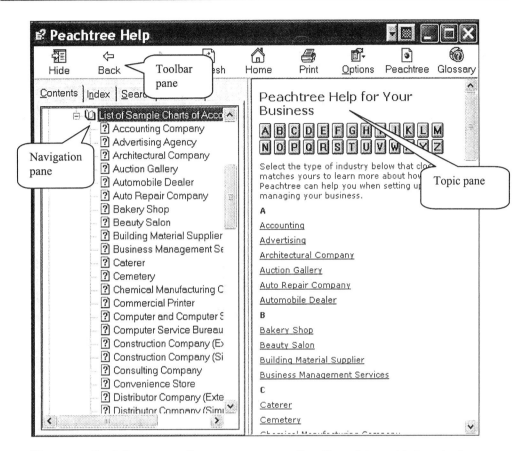

Observe that there are three panes on the Peachtree Help window:

▶ On the left side of the window is the Navigation Pane. It contains four tabs: Contents, Index, Search and Favorites. Use the Navigation pane to browse or search for topics.

▶ On the right side of the window is the Topic pane. The topic pane displays each Help topic or Web page selected in the Navigation pane.

▶ The third pane is the toolbar, located below the Help window title bar. The toolbar is similar to Internet Explorer's toolbar.

6. In the left pane, click on one of the sample charts of accounts to view its contents.

7. Click ☒ in the Peachtree Help title bar to return to the menu bar.

GETTING STARTED

1. PCA 's menu bar should be displayed on your screen.

2. Restore your data from the Exercise 4-2 back up that was made on page 156.

     a.   Put your Exercise 4-2 backup disk in drive A. You made this backup on page 156. From the menu bar, click on File, Restore.

     b.   From the Select Backup File screen, click [Browse]. The Open Backup File screen pops up.

     c.   Click on the down-arrow in the Look in field. Then click on 3½ Floppy (A:) to select drive A (or the appropriate location of your backup file).

     d.   Click on the Exercise 4-2.ptb file to highlight it. The File name field displays Exercise 4-2. Click [Open].

     e.   Make sure that the Location field shows A:\Exercise 4-2.ptb (or the appropriate location for your backup file). Click [Next >].

     f.   From the Select Company screen make sure that the radio button next to An Existing Company is selected. The Company name field shows Bellwether Garden Supply; the Location field shows C:\ProgramFiles\Peachtree\Company\BCS (or the appropriate location on your computer). Click [Next >].

     g.   The Restore Options screen appears. Make sure that the box next to Company Data is *checked*. Click [Next >].

     h.   The Confirmation screen appears. Check the From and To fields to make sure they are correct. Click [Finish]. When the Restore Company scale is 100% completed, your data is restored and you are returned to the menu bar.

     i.   Remove the backup disk.

---

3. From the menu bar, select Maintain, then Chart of Accounts. The Maintain Chart of Accounts window displays.

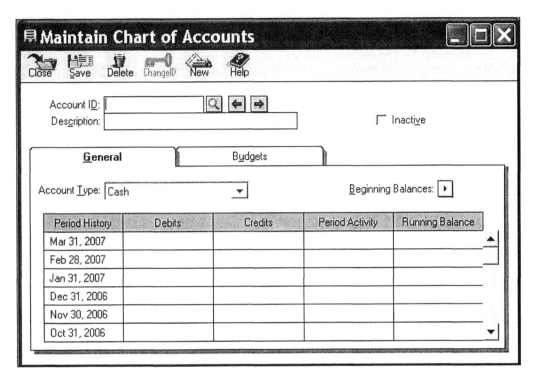

4. To add a new Money Market account, follow these steps:

   a. In the Account ID text field, type **10500** and press **<Enter>**

   b. Your cursor is in the Description field. Type the name of the account **Money-Market Fund**, and press **<Enter>**.

c. Your cursor is in the Account Type list box. There is a drop-down list indicated by a down arrow 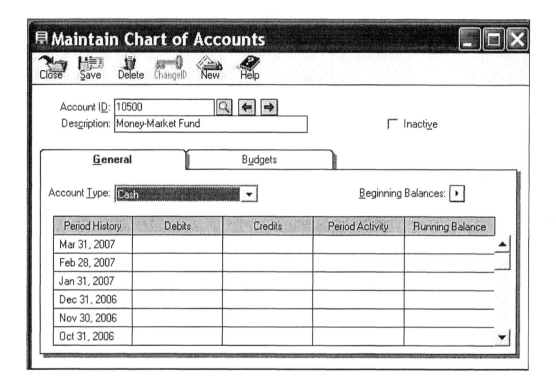 where you can specify the kind of account you are creating, such as, Cash, Cost of Sales, Equity-doesn't close, Equity-gets closed, etc. Select the drop-down list by clicking on the down arrow in the Account Type field to display the list of available account types. Make sure **Cash** is highlighted and press **<Enter>**.

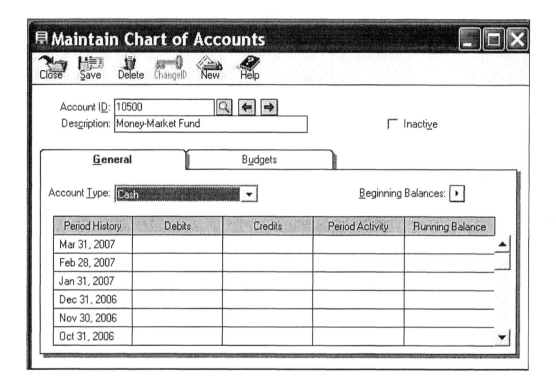

At this point, you may enter beginning balances. In this example, you are transferring funds from one account to another so you will use a General Journal entry. This will be done later in the chapter.

Did you notice that one of the tabs in the Chart of Accounts window says Budgets? Follow these steps to look at the budget features.

1. Select the Budgets tab.

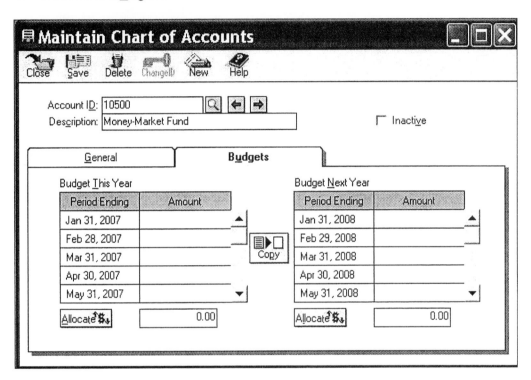

The Budgets tab allows you to budget or allocate amounts for the displayed account for each accounting period. You do not have to enter an amount in each text field. You can have the program apportion equal amounts by using the Allocate button located on the left side under the Budget This Year table.

2. Type **12000** in any Amount field for Budget This Year. Press the **<Enter>** key. (*Hint: If you need to type a decimal point, check your global settings. See page 56, Changing the Global Settings for Accounting Behind the Screens.*)

3. Click 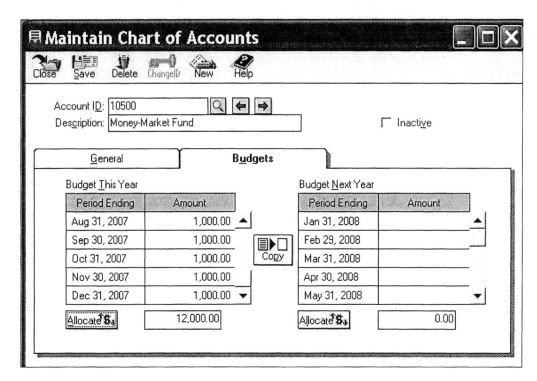 . The $12,000 is allocated over 12 accounting periods at $1,000 for each month. Scroll down the list to see that on December 31, 2007, the amount allocated is $1,000.

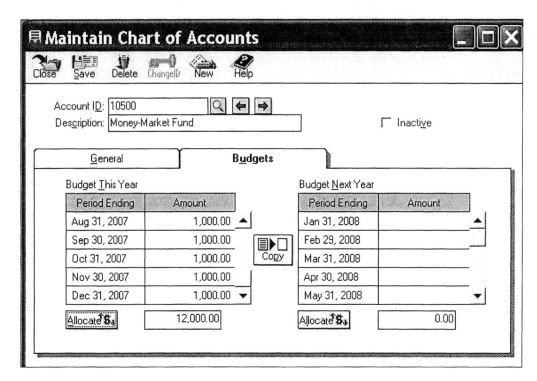

4. Click Save , then Close to return to the menu bar.

GENERAL JOURNAL

To open this Money-Market Fund, you are taking $4,000 from Bellwether's regular checking account and putting $4,000 in the new account (10500, Money-Market Fund). You will also transfer $1,000 from Bellwether's regular checking account to their payroll checking account (10300, Payroll Checking Account). You record this transfer of funds in the General Journal, then post the entry to the General Ledger. Read the transaction on the next page.

Date   Description of Transaction

03/15/07   Transfer $4,000 to the Money-Market Fund and $1,000 to
             the Payroll Checking Account from the Regular Checking
             Account.

Follow these steps to enter the transfer of funds:

1. From the menu bar, select Tasks, then select General Journal Entry.
   The General Journal Entry window appears.

2. Press **<Enter>** to accept the displayed date (3/15/07) in the Date
   field.

3. Your cursor is in the Reference field. Type **Transfer** and press
   <Enter> two times.

4. Your cursor is in the Account No. field. Type the account number for
   the Money-Market Fund account, **10500**, and press the **<Enter>** or
   <Tab> key two times to go to the Debit . Notice that Money-Market
   Fund displays on the line below the account number.

5. You are going to increase this account by $4,000. Type a debit
   amount of **4000** and press **<Enter>** three times. (It doesn't matter
   whether you type the debit or credit part of the entry first.)
   Notice that the Totals field below now displays 4,000.00 beneath the
   Debit column. The Out of Balance amount beneath it totals 4,000.00.

6. Your cursor is in the Account No. column to begin a new line item
   entry. Type **10300** and press **<Enter>** two times which takes you to
   the Debit column. Payroll Checking Account displays on the line
   below the account number.

7. Type **1000** and press **<Enter>** three times.

8. Your cursor is in the Account No. column. Type **10200** and press
   <Enter> three times which takes you to the Credit column.

9. Type **5000** in the Credit column. Notice that the Totals field now displays 5,000.00 beneath the Credit column. The Out of Balance amount now equals zero (0.00). This means that the General Journal is in balance and can be posted.

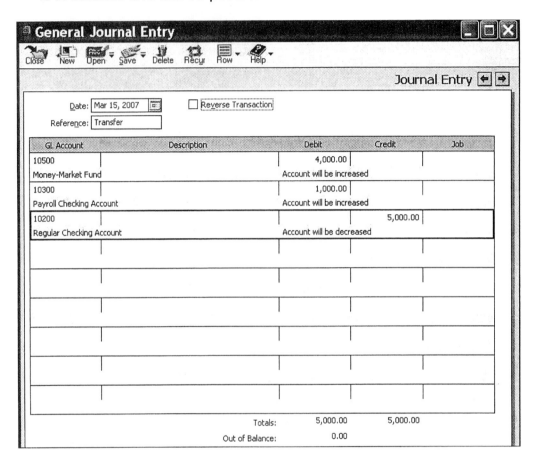

10. Click ![Save] to post to the General Ledger; then ![Close] to return to the menu bar.

The General Journal entry that you just completed transferred $4,000 from Bellwether's Regular Checking Account (Account No. 10200) to their Money-Market Fund (Account No. 10500) and $1,000 to their Payroll Checking Account (Account No. 10300). To check that the account transfers have been made, follow these steps:

1. From the menu bar, select Reports, then General Ledger. The Select a Report window displays.

2.   In the Report List, double-click on General Ledger Trial Balance. A partial General Ledger Trial Balance report appears.

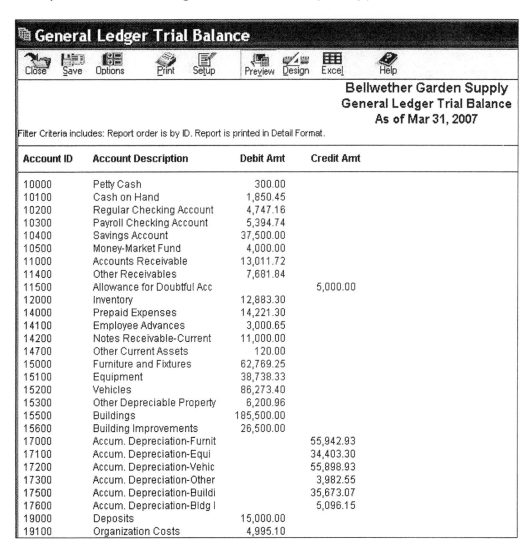

Account ID 10300, Payroll Checking Account, has a debit balance of $5,394.74. and Account ID 10500, Money-Market Fund, has a debit balance of $4,000.00. This shows that the General Journal entry that you just completed is posted correctly. To see the rest of the General Ledger Trial Balance, scroll down the screen.

3.   Click [Close]. You are returned to the Select a Report window.

4. Click 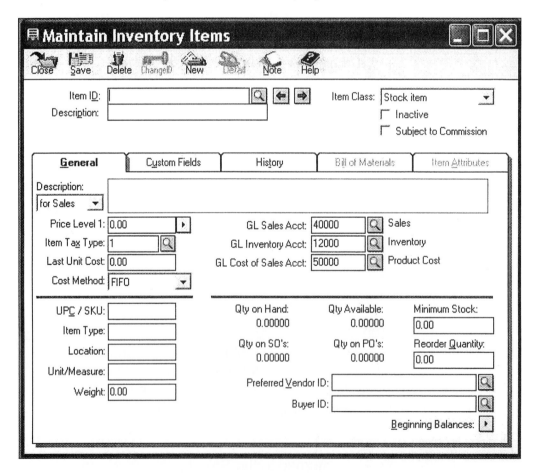 to return to the menu bar.

SETTING UP AN INVENTORY ITEM

This part of Chapter 5 shows you how to implement and use PCA 's Inventory system.

The sample company, Bellwether Garden Supply, has decided to track cleaning supplies as stock inventory items and to bill clients for supplies used. First, you need to enter the cleaning supplies they stock as Inventory Items. Follow these steps to set up an Inventory Item:

1. From the menu bar, click on Maintain, then Inventory Items. The Maintain Inventory Items window displays.

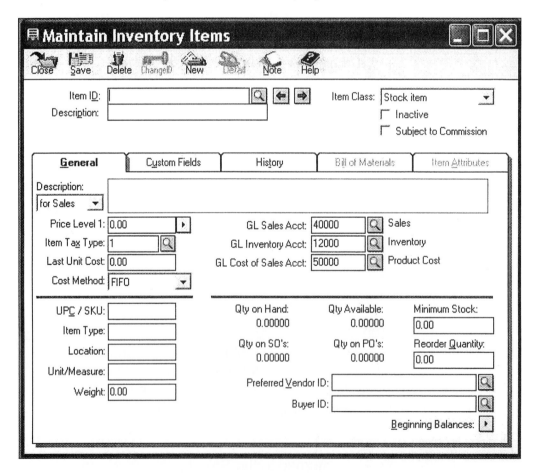

2.   In the Item ID, type **AVRY-10300** (type a capital A because the ID code is case sensitive--the first four characters should in uppercase) and press **<Enter>**.

3.   In the Description text field, type **Oriole Feeder** and press **<Enter>**.

4.   Your cursor is in the Item Class list box. Stock Item displays as the default type.

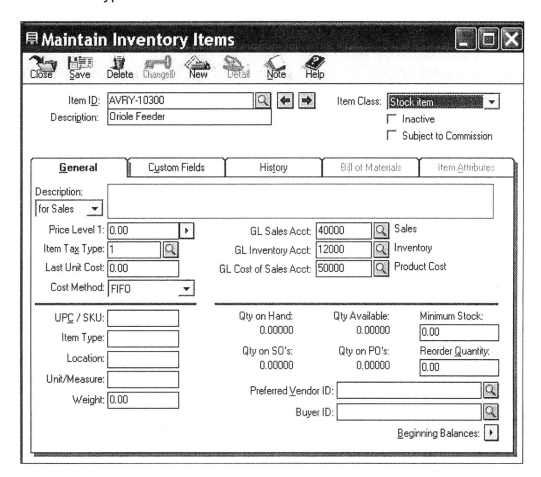

Inventory Types

If you click on the down-arrow next to the Item Class list box, you will notice that there are several types of Inventory Items:

➢   Stock item: This is the default in the Item Class list. It is the traditional inventory item where the program tracks descriptions, unit prices, stock quantities, and cost of goods sold. For stock items, you should complete the entire window. Once an item has been designated as a stock item, the type cannot be changed.

➤ Master Stock Item: A special item that does not represent inventory you stock rather contains information shared with a number of substock items generated from it.

➤ Non-stock item: PCA tracks the description and a unit price for sales. You can also track default accounts. You might use this type for service items such as hours where the unit price is set.

➤ Description only: PCA keeps track of the description of an Inventory Item. This saves time when entering purchases and sales because you don't have to retype the description. You might use this type for service items where the price fluctuates.

➤ Service: This is for services you can apply to your salary and wages account.

➤ Labor: This is for labor you can apply to your salary and wages account. You cannot purchase labor items but you can sell them.

➤ Assembly: You can specify items as assembly items and create a bill of materials for a unit made up of component stock or subassembly items.

➤ Activity item: To indicate how time is spent when performing services for a customer, for a job, or for internal administrative work. Activity items are used with the Time & Billing feature.

➤ Charge item: Expenses recorded by an employee or vendor when company resources are used for a customer or job.

Follow these steps to continue setting up an Inventory Item:

1. Press the **<Enter>** key to accept the Item Class default as Stock item.

2. Your cursor is in the Description for Sales text box. Press the **<Enter>** key to go to the description field. Type **Oriole Feeder** and press **<Enter>**.

3. Your cursor is in the Price Level 1 field. Click on the right arrow button Price Level 1: 0.00 ▶ in this field. The Multiple Price Levels screen pops up. In the Price Level 1 row, click on the Price

column. Type **45** on the Price Level 1 row, then press **<Enter>**. You can set up ten different sales prices per item.

4. Click [OK] to close the Multiple Price Levels window. The Price Level 1 field shows 45.00.

5. Click [Q] in the Item Ta<u>x</u> Type field. Observe that the default, 1, means that this is a regular, taxable item. Press **<Enter>**.

6. Your cursor is on the Last Unit Cost field. Type **15** and press **<Enter>**.

7. Observe that the Cost Method is FIFO. Peachtree includes three inventory cost methods: FIFO, LIFO and Average. Press **<Enter>**.

8. Your cursor is in the GL Sales Account field. Click [Q], then select Account No. 40000-AV, Sales – Aviary, as the sales account. Press **<Enter>**.

9. Accept the default for the GL Inventory Acct, Account No. 12000, Inventory, by pressing **<Enter>**.

10. Your cursor is in the GL Cost of Sales Acct field. Select Account No. 50000-AV, Product Cost – Aviary, as the product cost account. Press **<Enter>**.

11. Your cursor is in the UP<u>C</u>/SKU field. Right click on the field, then select What's This? A box pops up that explains the Universal Price Code/Stock Keeping Unit for an item. Read the information, then click on the box to close it.

12. Click on the Item Type field. The Item Type is a way of classifying similar inventory items for sorting and printing reports. Type **SUPPLY** to classify the Oriole Feeder as an item for which customers will be charged. [Remember: all type fields are case-sensitive. The program reads Supply, SUPPLY, and supply as different types.] Press **<Enter>**.

13.   Your cursor is in the Location field. Type **Aisle 1** and press **<Enter>**.

14.   Your cursor is in the Unit/Measure field. Type **Each** and press **<Enter>** two times.

15.   Your cursor is in the Minimum Stock field. Type **6** and press **<Enter>**.

16.   Your cursor is in the Reorder Quantity field. Type **6** and press **<Enter>**

17.   Select DEJULIO-01, DeJulio Wholesale Suppliers as the Preferred Vendor ID. Compare your screen to the one shown below. Leave the Buyer ID field blank.

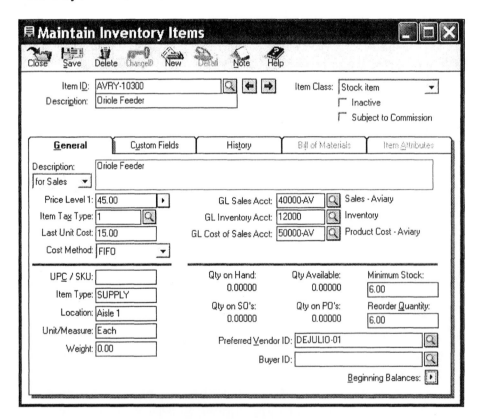

Inventory Default Accounts

When you purchase inventory stock-type items, there is one journal entry: debit the Inventory account and credit Accounts Payable/Vendor account. When you sell Inventory stock-type items, there are two journal entries:

➤ Debit Accounts Receivable, Credit Revenue and Sales Tax Payable.

➤ Debit Costs of Goods Sold, Credit Inventory.

➤ The Maintain Inventory Items window should be displayed. Compare your screen with the one shown on the previous page. Observe that you set the following account defaults for this stock item:

GL Sales Acct	40000-AV	Sales - Aviary
GL Inventory Acct	12000	Inventory
GL Cost of Sales Acct	50000-AV	Product Cost - Aviary

You also selected a preferred vendor. The Preferred <u>V</u>endor ID field should display DEJULIO-01, which is the Vendor ID for DeJulio Wholesale Suppliers. Bellwether purchases Oriole feeders from this vendor.

18. Click  then to return to the menu bar.

INVENTORY AND PURCHASES

In the following transaction, you will journalize and post a purchase of inventory.

Date   *Description of Transaction*

03/17/07   Purchased 6 Oriole feeders from DeJulio Wholesale Suppliers, Invoice No. 44433, at a unit price of $15, for a total of $90.

1. From the menu bar, select Tasks, then Purchases/Receive Inventory. The Purchases/Receive Inventory window displays. If your GL Account column and A/P Account fields are *not* displayed on the Purchases/Receive Inventory window, see the instructions on page 56 for Changing Global Settings for Accounting Behind the Screens.

2. In the Vendor ID field, type **DEJULIO-01** and press **<Enter>** (or use the lookup icon to find DeJulio Wholesale Suppliers).

3. Type or select **17** as the date.

4. In the Invoice # field, type **44433** and press **<Enter>**. This is a required field.

5. If necessary, click on the Apply to Purchases tab.

6. Click on the Quantity field. Type **6** and press **<Enter>**.

7. Your cursor is in the Item field. Type or select the code you just created, **AVRY-10300** and press **<Enter>** three times. The description and the GL Account automatically default to the information you assigned in the Maintain Inventory Items window.

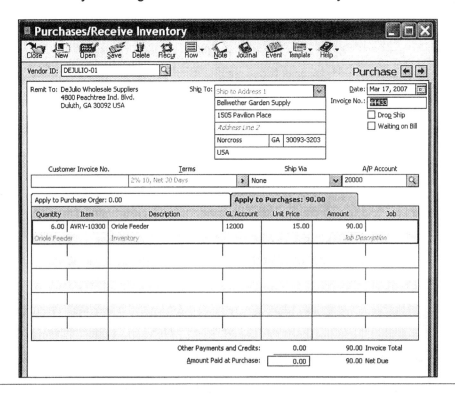

8. Click  to post this purchase. Return to the menu bar.

INVENTORY AND SALES

When you sell a stock-type item, PCA not only updates Accounts Receivable but it computes the Cost of Goods Sold (Product Cost), using one of three costing methods. In the General Ledger, a single entry encompassing all sales in the current period is made to the Product Cost account. This entry is dated the last day of the accounting period.

Hensley Park Apartments wants three Oriole feeders. The following steps show you how to invoice Hensley Park Apartments for three Oriole feeders.

Date   *Description of Transaction*

03/17/07   Sold three Oriole feeders on account to Hensley Park
                    Apartments for $45 each plus sales tax.

1. From the Tasks menu, select Sales/Invoicing. The Sales/Invoicing window displays.

    If the GL Account column and A/R Account field are *not* displayed, refer to the instructions on page 56 for Changing Global Settings for Accounting Behind the Screens.

2. In the Customer ID field, click 🔍 and select **HENSLEY-01, Hensley Park Apartments**.

3. Do not complete the Invoice # field. Type or select **17** as the date.

4. Click on the Apply to Sales tab.

5. Click on the Quantity column. Type **3** and press **<Enter>**.

6. The cursor is in the Item column. Type **AVRY-10300** and press **<Enter>**.

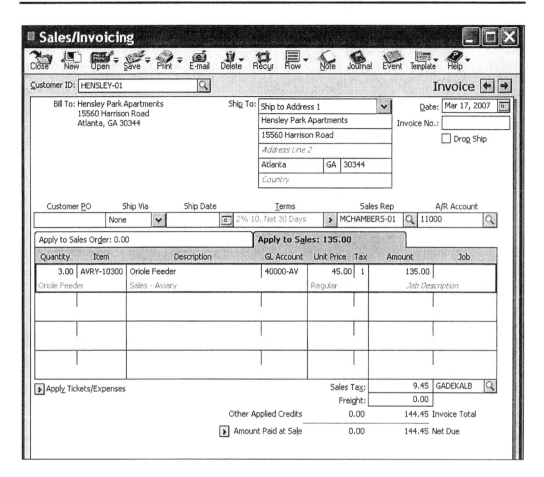

PCA computes the amount based on the quantity times the sales price that was established when setting up the inventory item. All the other lines for this invoice are automatically completed based on the inventory item information.

7. Click [Journal] to see how Peachtree journalizes this entry in the Sales Journal. Scroll down the screen to see the entire entry. Observe that in a perpetual inventory system (Peachtree's default) the sales amount and the cost of sales accounts are represented.

8. Click [Save] to post this sales invoice. Once the entry is posted the cost of sales amount is calculated. Close the window to return to the menu bar.

Let's review the last two sections: Inventory and Purchases and Inventory and Sales. When Bellwether purchased six Oriole Feeders (an inventory stock item) on pages 175-177, the entry in the Purchase Journal was:

Account #	Account Description	Debit	Credit
12000/ AVRY-10300	Inventory	90.00	
20000/ DEJULIO-01	Accounts Payable/DeJulio Wholesale Suppliers		90.00

When three Oriole Feeders were sold on pages 177-178, the entry in the Sales Journal was:

Account #	Account Description	Debit	Credit
11000/ HENSLEY-01	Accts. Rec./Hensley Park Apartments	144.45	
40000-AV	Sales-Aviary		135.00
23100	Sales Tax Payable		9.45
50000-AV	Product Cost-Aviary	45.00	
12000	Inventory		45.00

When three Oriole feeders were sold, they were sold for $45 each, plus tax; therefore, the total sale to Hensley Park Apartments is $135 plus $9.45 in sales tax, for a total of $144.45. When Bellwether Garden Supply bought the Oriole Feeders from the vendor (DeJulio Wholesale Suppliers), they paid $15 each. The second journal entry reflects the cost of the stock items, $15 X 3 = $45.

The journal entries shown above are example of how purchases and sales are recorded in the perpetual inventory system.

INVENTORY ADJUSTMENTS

It may become necessary to adjust the amount of Inventory Items due to faulty records, pilferage or spoilage, or inventory changes. You use the Inventory Adjustment Journal to make inventory adjustment entries.

In the example that follows, one of Bellwether's employees dropped two bird house kits which damaged them beyond repair. Follow these steps to adjust inventory for this loss:

1. From the Tasks menu, select Inventory Adjustments. The Inventory Adjustments window appears.

2. Type **AVRY-10100** (for Bird House Kit) in the Item ID field and the press **<Enter>** key six times. Your cursor is in the Adjust Quantity By field.

3. Type **-2** in the Adjust Quantity By field to decrease the current inventory by two. Press the **<Enter>** key. The New Quantity field shows that you have 1.00 bird house kit.

4. Type **Damaged** as the Reason to Adjust.

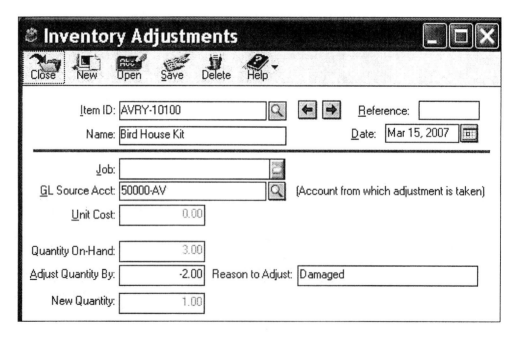

5. Click [Save] to post this adjustment, then close the window to return to the menu bar.

   Adjustments to inventory, like the one you just made, only affect the average cost of the item. For example, let's say you purchased two bird house kits at $30 each and then damaged one. For accounting purposes you now have one bird house kit that cost $30.

BACKING UP CHAPTER 5 DATA

Follow these steps to back up Chapter 5 data:

1. Put a blank, formatted disk in drive A.

2. From the menu bar, select File, then Back up.

3. Click [Back Up Now].

4. Click on the down-arrow in the Save in field. If necessary, scroll up the list, then click on 3½ Floppy (A:) to select drive A.

5. Type **Chapter 5** in the File name field.

6. Click [Save].

7. When the screen prompts that This company backup will require approximately 1 diskette, click [OK].

8. When the screen prompts you to insert the first disk, click [OK]. When the Back Up Company scale is 100% completed, you have successfully backed up to the current point in Chapter 5. You are returned to the menu bar.

	INTERNET ACTIVITY
1.	From your Internet browser, go to the book's website at http://www.mhhe.com/yacht2004
2.	In the Student Edition list, link to Internet Activities.
3.	Link to WEB EXERCISES, PART 1.
4.	Scroll down the screen to the Internet Activity labeled ASK JEEVES – Chapter 5. Read steps 1—4.
5.	Use a word processing program to answer the questions in steps 1-4.

SUMMARY AND REVIEW

SOFTWARE OBJECTIVES: In Chapter 5, you used the software to:

1. Restore data from Exercise 4-2.

2. Enter a new account in the Chart of Accounts.

3. Enter a budget amount for an account.

4. Make a General Journal entry to transfer funds.

5. Display the General Ledger Trial Balance.

6. Set up an Inventory Item.

7. Record an inventory adjustment.

8. Make two backups: one blank, formatted disk for Chapter 5; one blank, formatted disk for Exercise 5-2.

WEB OBJECTIVES: In Chapter 5, you did these Internet activities:

1. Used your Internet browser to go to the book's website.

2. Completed the Internet activity for Ask Jeeves.

3. Completed the steps shown for this activity.

GOING TO THE NET

Access the AccountantsWorld.com website at
http://www.accountsworld.com. Link to About Us. Read the article
"Why Does Accountantsworld Exist?"

1. What does the article say the accounting firm of tomorrow will be like?

2. How will accountantsworld.com serve the needs of the accounting
    community?

Multiple Choice Questions: In the space provided, write the letter that
best answers each question.

_____1.   The account(s) added to Bellwether's Chart of Accounts in this
          chapter is:

          a. Account No. 10200, Regular Checking Account.
          b. Account No. 12000, Inventory.
          c. Account No. 10500, Money-Market Fund.
          d. a. and c.
          e. All of the above.

_____2.   The inventory system used by PCA is called:

          a. Sum-of-the-years digits.
          b. Double-declining balance.
          c. Straight-line.
          d. Perpetual inventory.
          e. None of the above.

_____3. A list of all the accounts used by a company showing an identifying number assigned to each account is called:

   a. A chart of accounts.
   b. Case-sensitive letters.
   c. An account number.
   d. A general ledger.
   e. None of the above.

_____4. Budgeting $12,000 over 12 months means that for each month, the following amount is distributed:

   a. $800.00.
   b. $900.00.
   c. $1,000.00.
   d. $833.37.
   e. None of the above.

_____5. After the March 15, 2007 transfer of funds, the General Ledger Trial Balance shows the following amount in the Money-Market Fund account:

   a. $4,000.00.
   b. $4,747.16.
   c. $37,500.00.
   d. $5,394.74.
   e. None of the above.

_____6. For Stock-Type Inventory Items, PCA tracks the following:

   a. Stock quantities.
   b. Unit prices.
   c. Descriptions.
   d. Cost of goods sold.
   e. All of the above.

____7. For Non-Stock Items, PCA tracks:

a. Description.
b. Unit price.
c. Maximum levels.
d. a. and b.
e. None of the above.

____8. In the Maintain Inventory Items window, the default in the Item Class list is:

a. Labor.
b. Description only.
c. Non stock.
d. Stock item.
e. None of the above.

____9. The journal entry to purchase an inventory stock item is:

a. Debit Accounts Payable/Vendor
   Credit Inventory
b. Debit Inventory
   Credit Accounts Payable/Vendor
c. Debit Account Receivable/Customer
   Credit Sales Tax Payable
d. Debit Product Cost
   Credit Inventory
e. None of the above.

___10.   The journal entry or entries for the sale of an Inventory Item are:

    a. Debit Accounts Receivable/Customer
       Credit Sales
    b. Debit Accounts Receivable/Customer
       Credit Sales
       Credit Sales Tax Payable
       Debit Product Cost
       Credit Inventory
    c. Debit Sales-Retail
       Debit Sales Tax Payable
       Credit Accounts Receivable/Customer
       Debit Product Cost
       Credit Inventory
    d. Debit Inventory
       Credit Product Cost
    e. None of the above.

Exercise 5-1: Follow the instructions below to complete Exercise 5-1.

1.   Start Windows, then PCA. Open Bellwether Garden Supply.

2.   Restore data from the end of Chapter 5. This back up was made on page 181.

3.   Journalize and post the following transactions:

Date	Description of Transaction
03/18/07	Transfer $500 from the Regular Checking Account to the Payroll Checking Account.
03/19/07	Purchased one (1) Oriole Feeder from DeJulio Wholesale Suppliers, Invoice No. 49967, $15.

4.   Continue with Exercise 5-2.

Exercise 5-2: Follow the instructions below to complete Exercise 5-2.

1. Print the General Ledger Trial Balance.

2. Use a blank, formatted disk to back up Exercise 5-2. Use **Exercise 5-2** as the file name.

3. Exit PCA.

CHAPTER 5 INDEX

Chapter 6 — Job Cost

SOFTWARE OBJECTIVES: In Chapter 6, you will use the software to:

1. Restore data from Exercise 5-2.
2. Learn about PCA's Job Cost system.
3. Set up a job.
4. Coordinate job costs with purchases, sales, and payroll.
5. Display a Job Profitability Report.
6. Make two backups: one blank, formatted disk for Chapter 6; one blank, formatted disk for Exercise 6-2.

WEB OBJECTIVES: In Chapter 6, you will do these Internet activities:

1. Use your Internet browser to go to the book's website.
2. Complete the Internet activity for Business Encyclopedia.
3. Complete the steps shown for this activity.

This chapter shows how to use PCA's Job Cost system. PCA lets you assign Job ID codes to purchases, sales, and employee hours. This way, you can track how each of these factors impacts costs for a specific job. The diagram that follows illustrates how this works:

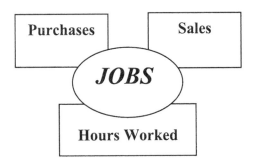

GETTING STARTED

Bellwether Garden Supply has a customer named Cunningham Construction. You need to set up a Job ID for Cunningham Construction so you can track supplies and employee hours charged to this customer.

1. Start Windows and PCA in the usual way. Start the sample company, Bellwether Garden Supply.

2. Restore your data from the Exercise 5-2 back up that was made on page 187.

    a. Put your Exercise 5-2 backup disk in drive A. You made this backup on page 187. From the menu bar, click on File, Restore.

    b. From the Select Backup File screen, click [Browse]. The Open Backup File screen pops up.

    c. Click on the down-arrow in the Look in field. Then click on 3½ Floppy (A:) to select drive A (or the appropriate location of your backup file).

    d. Click on the Exercise 5-2.ptb file to highlight it. The File name field displays Exercise 5-2. Click [Open].

    e. Make sure that the Location field shows A:\Exercise 5-2.ptb (or the appropriate location for your backup file). Click [Next >].

    f. From the Select Company screen make sure that the radio button next to An Existing Company is selected. The Company name field shows Bellwether Garden Supply; the Location field shows C:\ProgramFiles\Peachtree\Company\BCS (or the appropriate location on your computer). Click [Next >].

    g. The Restore Options screen appears. Make sure that the box next to Company Data is *checked*. Click [Next >].

h. The Confirmation screen appears. Check the From and To fields to make sure they are correct. Click [Finish]. When the Restore Company scale is 100% completed, your data is restored and you are returned to the menu bar.

i. Remove the backup disk.

3. From the menu bar, click on Maintain, then Jobs Costs, then Jobs. The Maintain Jobs window appears.

4. In the Job ID text field, type **CUNNINGHAM-01** and press **<Enter>**. (*Hint: Peachtree is case-sensitive: CUNNINGHAM-01 is not the same as cunningham-01.*)

5. In the Description text field, type **Cunningham Construction-Bldg C** and press **<Enter>** three times.

6. Click 🔍 in the For Customer field and select Cunningham Construction. The cursor moves to the Start Date field.

7. Type **3/3/07** in the Start Date field. Press **<Enter>** two times.

8. Your cursor is in the Job Type field. Type **LAND** in the Job Type field.

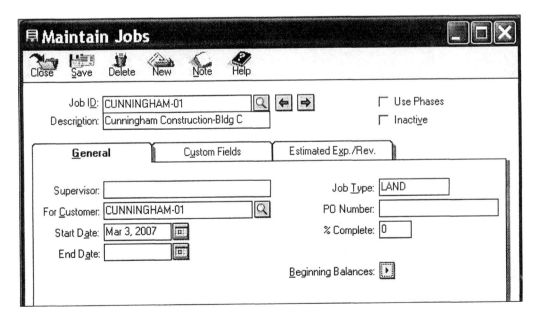

9.   Save this job, then return to the menu bar.

JOB COSTING AND PURCHASING: Purchasing Inventory Items for Jobs

This new job has some special circumstances; namely, Cunningham Construction has a new building overlooking a park. In the park, there are several wooden benches where people can have lunch. According to the terms of the contract with Cunningham Construction, you will purchase and provide a special treatment for the wood to help preserve the wooden benches.

When inventory items are purchased for jobs, you need to do the following:

➢ Record the purchase directly as a job expense. You could indicate a Non-stock or a Description only Inventory Item but not a Stock Item.

➢ Record the purchase into Inventory without entering a Job. When you bill the customer, enter the Item and the Job. The system posts the price as Job revenue and the Cost of Goods Sold as Job Expense.

Let's see how this works:

1.   From the menu bar, click on Tasks, then Purchases/Receive Inventory. The Purchases/Receive Inventory window displays.

2.   Type or select **AA-01** (AA Landscaping) for the Vendor ID.

3.   Select **20** in the Date field. Press **<Enter>**.

4.   Type **8901** for the Invoice #. (This is a *required* field.) Press **<Enter>**.

5.   The Apply to Purchases tab is selected. Type **1** in the Quantity column and press **<Enter>** two times.

6.   In the Description field, type **Special wood treatment** and press **<Enter>** two times.

7. Account No. 57200, Materials Cost, is the default account displayed in the GL Account column. Your cursor is in the Unit Price text field. Type **75** and press **<Enter>** two times.

8. Type or select **CUNNINGHAM-01**, the new Job, in the Job column.

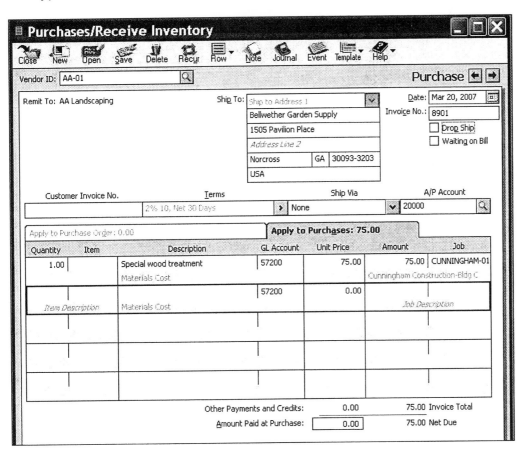

If your GL Account column and A/P Account field are *not* displayed on the Purchases/Receive Inventory window, see the instructions on page 56 for Changing Global Setting for Accounting Behind the Screens.

9. Click ![Save] to post this purchase. Return to the menu bar.

JOB COSTING AND SALES

Follow these steps to invoice Cunningham Construction for a drip-irrigation system and apply this sale to Cunningham Construction-Bldg C, Job ID, CUNNINGHAM-01.

1. From the Tasks pull-down menu, select Sales/Invoicing. The Sales/Invoicing window displays.

2. In the Customer ID text field, click 🔍 and select Cunningham Construction as the Customer. Then, press the **<Enter>** key.

3. Select **21** in the Date field.

4. If necessary, click on the Apply to Sales tab.

5. Click on the Quantity column, type **2** and press **<Enter>**.

6. In the Item column, type **EQWT-15100** (Drip Irrigation System).

7. Press **<Enter>** until you are in the Job column. (You are accepting all of the displayed information when you do this.)

8. Type or select **CUNNINGHAM-01**, the Job ID for Cunningham Construction-Bldg C.

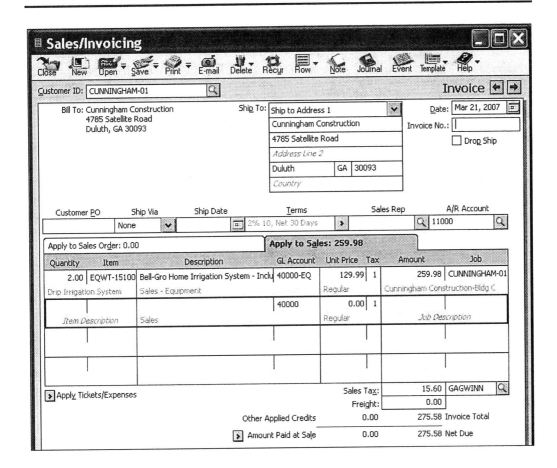

If your GL Account column and A/R Account field are *not* displayed on the Sales/Invoicing window, see the instructions on page 56 for Changing Global Settings for Accounting Behind the Screens.

9. Click ![Save] to post this invoice. Return to the menu bar.

JOB COST AND PAYROLL

In the example that follows, one employee applied the special wood treatment at Cunningham Construction–Bldg C. The employee spent one hour applying the wood treatment.

1. From the menu bar, select Tasks, then Payroll Entry.

2. Click 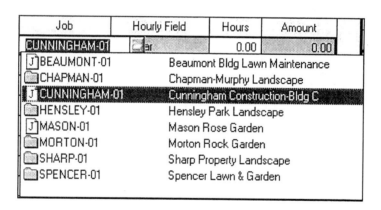 in the Employee ID text field. Select **Brandon A. Hughes** and press **<Enter>**.

3. Type **29** as the Date. Press **<Enter>** three times.

4. Type **29** in the Pay Period End field.

5. On the icon bar, select the Jobs icon. The Labor Distribution to Jobs window pops up.

6. On the Labor Distribution to Jobs icon bar, select the Row icon, then Add to add a distribution line.

7. Select the first empty job row. Then, with the mouse pointer on the empty Job row, click the right mouse button. With your left mouse button, click on CUNNINGHAM-01 to highlight it.

Job	Hourly Field	Hours	Amount
CUNNINGHAM-01	ar	0.00	0.00
J BEAUMONT-01	Beaumont Bldg Lawn Maintenance		
CHAPMAN-01	Chapman-Murphy Landscape		
J CUNNINGHAM-01	Cunningham Construction-Bldg C		
HENSLEY-01	Hensley Park Landscape		
J MASON-01	Mason Rose Garden		
MORTON-01	Morton Rock Garden		
SHARP-01	Sharp Property Landscape		
SPENCER-01	Spencer Lawn & Garden		

8. Press the **<Enter>** key.

9. Type **1** in the Hours column. Press the **<Enter>** key.

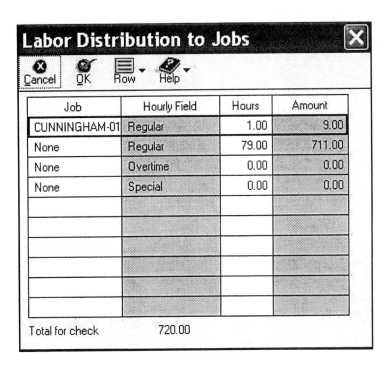

10. Click .

11. Click [Save] to post the paycheck. Close the window and return to the menu bar.

JOB COST REPORTS

Job cost reports tell you how jobs are progressing. Follow these steps to look at Job Cost Reports.

1. From the Reports pull-down menu, select Jobs. The Select A Report window displays.

2. In the Report List, click on Job Profitability Report.

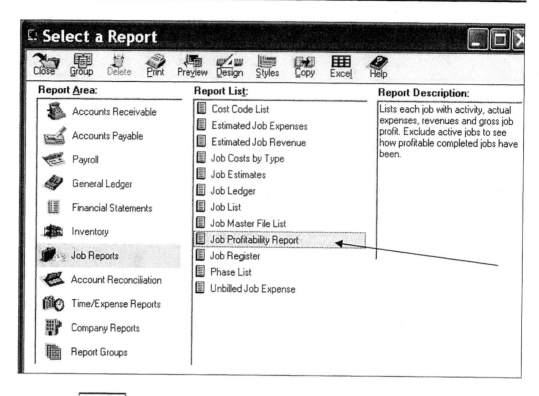

3. Click .

4. Click | OK | at the Job Profitability Report Filter window. Scroll down the screen to Job ID CUNNINGHAM-01.

CUNNINGH		50000-EQ	119.90				
		57200	75.00				
		77500	9.00				
				203.90	259.98		
CUNNINGHA	Total			203.90	259.98	56.08	21.57

The report breaks down each job according to what was spent or earned for each affected general ledger account. It also shows the profit or loss for each job.

5. Close the windows to return to the menu bar.

BACKING UP CHAPTER 6 DATA

Follow these steps to back up Chapter 6 data:

1. Put a blank, formatted disk in drive A.

2. From the menu bar, select File, then Back up.

3. Click Back Up Now .

4. Click on the down-arrow in the Save in field. If necessary, scroll up the list, then click on 3½ Floppy (A:) to select drive A.

5. Type **Chapter 6** in the File name field.

6. Click Save .

7. When the screen prompts that This company backup will require approximately 1 diskette, click OK .

8. When the screen prompts you to insert the first disk, click OK . When the Back Up Company scale is 100% completed, you have successfully backed up to the current point in Chapter 6. You are returned to the menu bar.

9. Click on File, Exit to exit Peachtree.

INTERNET ACTIVITY	
1.	From your Internet browser, go to the book's website at http://www.mhhe.com/yacht2004.
2.	In the Student Edition list, link to Internet Activities.
3.	Link to WEB EXERCISES, PART 1.
4.	Scroll down the screen to BUSINESS ENCYCLOPEDIA – Chapter 6. Read steps 1—3.
5.	Use the Business Encyclopedia website to look up words related to accounting.
6.	Follow the steps shown on the book's website to complete this Internet Activity.

SUMMARY AND REVIEW

SOFTWARE OBJECTIVES: In Chapter 6, you used the software to:

1. Restore data from Exercise 5-2.

2. Learn about PCA's Job Cost system.

3. Set up a job.

4. Coordinate job costs with purchases, sales, and payroll.

5. Display a Job Profitability Report.

6. Make two backups: one blank, formatted disk for Chapter 6; one blank, formatted disk for Exercise 6-2.

WEB OBJECTIVES: In Chapter 6, you did these Internet activities:

1. Used your Internet browser to go to the book's website.

2. Completed the Internet activity for Business Encyclopedia.

3. Completed the steps shown for this activity.

GOING TO THE NET

Access the Sage website at http://www.sage.com. This takes you to The Sage Group website.

1. Is the Sage Group the leading supplier of accounting software around the world?

2. How many customers does the Sage Group have worldwide?

3. Can you go to the Peachtree Software website from the US Small Business link?

Short-Answer Questions: Write a brief answer to each one of the questions.

1. Draw the diagram that shows how the job cost system works.

2. What is the Customer number for Cunningham Construction?

    _____

    _____

3. What is the Job ID for Cunningham Construction-Bldg C for Bellwether's customer, Cunningham Construction?

    _____

    _____

4. How much does Cunningham Construction owe for the two drip irrigation systems (include the sales tax)?

_____

_____

5. What is the GL account (name and number) for the purchase of the wood treatment?

_____

_____

6. What is the name of the report that tells you about Bellwether's jobs?

_____

_____

7. How many hour(s) did Brandon A. Hughes work on Cunningham Construction-Bldg C?

_____

_____

8. What is the website address for the Business Encyclopedia?

_____

_____

Exercise 6-1: Follow the instructions below to complete Exercise 6-1.

1. Start Windows, then PCA. Open Bellwether Garden Supply.

2. Restore data from the end of Chapter 6.

3. Journalize and post the following transactions:

    Date   *Description of Transaction*

    03/26/07   Enter a sales invoice for three impulse sprinklers
                    (EQWT-15160) for Cunningham Construction, $95.37
                    (includes sales tax). Apply to Job ID CUNNINGHAM-
                    01-Bldg C.

    03/26/07   Purchased 1 container of special wood treatment for
                    $75, Invoice No. 9947 from AA Landscaping, Job No.
                    CUNNINGHAM-01. (Debit Materials Cost.)

    03/29/07   Al L. Dunn worked 1 hour on Job CUNNINGHAM-01.
                    Apply his paycheck to this job.

4. Continue with Exercise 6-2.

Exercise 6-2: Follow the instructions below to complete Exercise 6-2.

1. Print a Job Profitability Report.

2. Use a blank, formatted disk to back up Exercise 6-2. Use **Exercise
    6-2** as the file name.

 Read Me

Do *not* reformat the Exercise 6-2 back up disk. You will restore Exercise 6-2 data to
complete the exercises in Chapters 15, 16, 17 and 18.

CHAPTER 6 INDEX

Chapter 7 Financial Statements

SOFTWARE OBJECTIVES: In Chapter 7, you will use the software to:

1. Restore data from Exercise 6-2.
2. Explore Peachtree's Help feature.
3. Print the financial statements.
4. Make an optional backup of Chapter 7. The backups that were made in Chapter 6 include the data for this chapter.

WEB OBJECTIVES: In Chapter 7, you will do these Internet activities:

1. Use your Internet browser to go to the book's website.
2. Complete the Internet activity for Peachtree Software.
3. Complete the steps shown for this activity.

FINANCIAL STATEMENTS

In Chapters 1 through 6, you have explored the sample company, Bellwether Garden Supply. You learned how PCA's graphical user interface works and how to navigate the software. In Chapters 1 through 6, you also journalized and posted various types of transactions. Beginning with Chapter 9, you will learn how to use these features to set up service businesses from scratch.

In Chapter 7, you will learn about PCA's financial statements. Once journal entries have been recorded and posted, Peachtree automatically calculates financial statements. Since business managers and owners have the primary responsibility for the organization, they depend on accounting information in the form of financial statements to understand what is happening.

All the financial statements printed by PCA reflect the current month and year-to-date amounts.

You will print six financial statements in this chapter:

1. Balance Sheet.

2. Gross Profit by Departments.

3. Income Statement.

4. Statement of Cash Flow.

5. Statement of Retained Earnings.

6. Statement of Changes in Financial Position.

Balance Sheet

A balance sheet is a list of assets, liabilities, and capital of a business entity as of a specific date, such as the last day of an accounting period or the last day of the year.

Each financial statement may be modified to fit your needs. PCA includes a Design icon for that purpose. Later in this chapter, you will learn more about how to use PCA's Help feature to design financial statements.

Gross Profit by Departments

A departmentalized accounting system provides information that management can use to evaluate the profitability or cost effectiveness of a department's activities. The Gross Profit by Departments financial statement is a custom report designed for Bellwether that details each department's year-to-date gross profit as of the current month.

Some of Bellwether's chart of account numbers have a dash, then an AV or a BK. For example, Account No. 40000-AV, Sales - Aviary; and Account No. 40000-BK, Sales - Books show this departmental designation.

PCA includes a feature called masking which allows you to organize your business by department. Then, you can design custom forms to accommodate your departmentalized accounting system. The red arrow to the left of some of Bellwether's financial statements indicates that those statements are custom-designed forms.

Income Statement

The income statement is a summary of the revenues and expenses a company accrues over a period of time, such as an accounting period or a year. Only revenue and expense accounts are displayed on the income statement. **Net income** is computed by subtracting total expenses from total revenues. Net income results when revenues exceed expenses. An excess of expenses over revenues results in a **net loss**. Bellwether's net loss for the current month, March 1 through March 31, 2007, is (6,528.02). A net loss is shown on the Net Income line with parentheses around the number. Bellwether's year-to-date net income is also a net loss at (8,247.36).

In addition to dollar figures, the income statement also includes percentage-of-revenue columns for the current month. The percentages shown for each expense, total expenses, and net income (or net loss) indicate the relationship of each item to total revenues.

Statement of Cash Flow

The cash flow from operations is roughly the same as income from operations plus depreciation, depletion, and adjusted for any other operating transactions that had no effect on cash during the period. The statement of cash flow also reports cash transactions associated with the purchase or sale of fixed assets (Investing Activities) and cash paid to or received from creditors and owners (Financing Activities).

The statement of cash flow provides the answers to three questions:

1. From where did cash receipts come?

2. For what were cash payments used?

3. What was the overall change in cash?

Statement of Retained Earnings

The Statement of Retained Earnings shows beginning and ending retained earnings amounts, adjustments made to retained earnings within the report period, and the detail for all Equity-gets closed accounts. The retained earnings balance is the cumulative, lifetime earnings of the company less its cumulative losses and dividends.

Statement of Changes in Financial Position

The statement of changes describes changes in a company's financial position that may not be obvious from other financial statements. The statement of changes shows the change in working capital, assets, and liabilities for a given period of time.

Interrelationship of Financial Statements

The financial statements work together. The net income (or net loss) from the income statement is on the balance sheet's capital section. The net income or net loss is used to update the capital amount: Capital Beginning of the Year - Net Loss (or + Net Income) = Total Capital.

On the statement of retained earnings, the Ending Retained Earnings balance is $180,790.24. On the balance sheet, if you subtract the net loss of (8,247.36) from the retained earnings amount of 189,037.60, this equals the Ending Retained Earnings amount ($189,037.60 – 8,247.36 = $180,790.24).

The total of all the cash accounts on the Balance Sheet (Petty Cash, Cash on Hand, Regular Checking Account, Payroll Checking Account, Savings Account, and Money-Market Fund) is explained in detail on the statement of cash flow. The statement of cash flow uses information from both the balance sheet and income statement.

The statement of changes in financial position uses information from the income statement and balance sheet. The net income is shown on the income statement. Current assets and current liabilities are derived from the balance sheet.

No single financial statement tells the entire story. The income statement indicates how much revenue a business has earned during a specific period of time, but it says nothing about how much of that amount has or has not been received in cash. For information about cash and accounts receivable, we have to look at the balance sheet, statement of cash flow, and statement of changes in financial position.

GETTING STARTED

1. If necessary, start Windows and PCA in the usual way. Start the sample company, Bellwether Garden Supply.

2. If necessary, follow steps a. through i. to restore your data from the Exercise 6-2 back up that was made on page 203.

    a.   Put your Exercise 6-2 backup disk in drive A. You made this backup on page 203. From the menu bar, click on File, Restore.

    b.   From the Select Backup File screen, click | Browse |. The Open Backup File screen pops up.

    c.   Click on the down-arrow in the Look in field. Then click on 3½ Floppy (A:) to select drive A (or the appropriate location of your backup file).

    d.   Click on the Exercise 6-2.ptb file to highlight it. The File name field displays Exercise 6-2. Click | Open |.

    e.   Make sure that the Location field shows A:\Exercise 6-2.ptb (or the appropriate location for your backup file). Click | Next > |.

    f.   From the Select Company screen make sure that the radio button next to An Existing Company is selected. The Company name field shows Bellwether Garden Supply; the Location field shows C:\ProgramFiles\Peachtree\Company\BCS (or the appropriate location on your computer). Click | Next > |.

    g.   The Restore Options screen appears. Make sure that the box next to Company Data is *checked*. Click | Next > |.

    h. The Confirmation screen appears. Check the From and To fields to make sure they are correct. Click | Finish |. When the Restore Company scale is 100% completed, your data is restored and you are returned to the menu bar.

i.   Remove the backup disk.

USING PEACHTREE'S HELP FEATURE

In Chapter 5 you learned how to use PCA's Help pull-down menu to access the sample company's chart of accounts. In this chapter, you will learn how to access Peachtree's Help pull-down menu to learn more about financial statements.

Follow these steps to learn more about Help:

1.   From the menu bar, click on Help, Contents and Index. The Peachtree Help screen displays. If necessary, click on the Index tab.

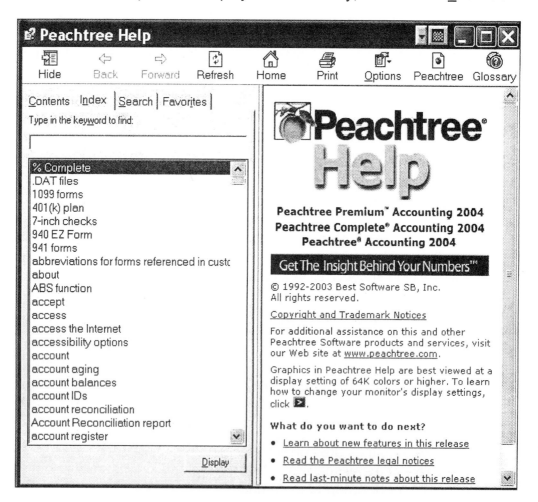

2. Click on the Type in the keyword to find field. Type **balance sheet**. Observe that Balance Sheet is highlighted.

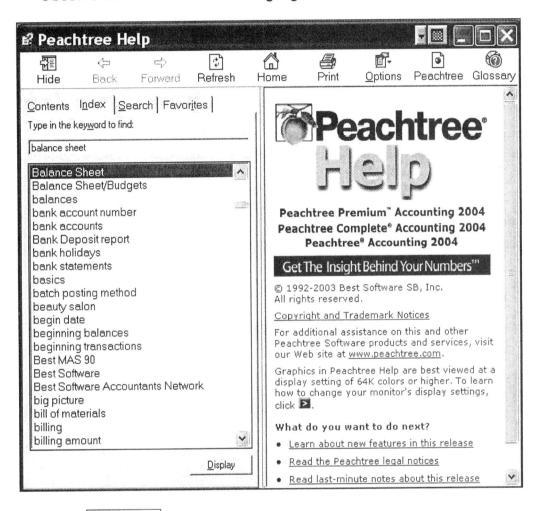

3. Click [Display]. The right pane shows information about the balance sheet. Read the information on this screen.

4. Highlight Balance Sheet (Financial Statement), then click [Display]. Compare your screen to the one shown on the next page.

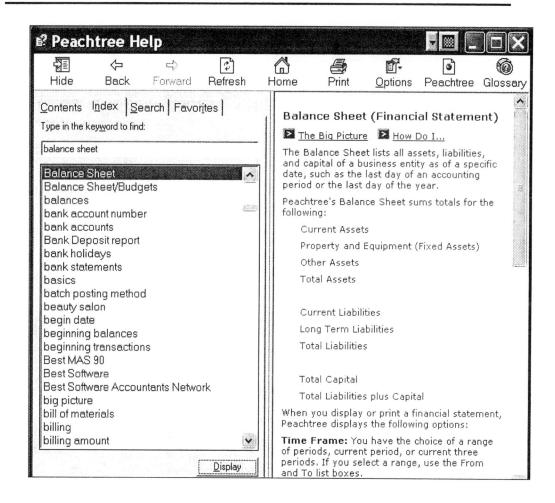

5. You have a couple choices on this screen. You can click on <u>The Big Picture</u>, or click on <u>How Do I...</u>, or you can scroll down this screen and click on other options. Read the information on this screen. If you want to enlarge the screen, click [□] on the title bar.

6. Click [X] Peachtree Help title bar to close the window and return to Bellwether's menu bar.

PRINTING THE FINANCIAL STATEMENTS

You have already used the Reports pull-down menu to print other PCA reports. Using it to print the financial statements is similar to printing other reports.

Follow these steps to print the balance sheet:

1. From the menu bar, click on Reports, Financial Statements. Click on <Standard> Balance Sheet to highlight it. Standard refers to statements that PCA has already set up. As noted in the Help window, Peachtree has a feature that allows you to design financial statements to fit your company's needs. The financial statements with a red arrow next to them are customized forms.

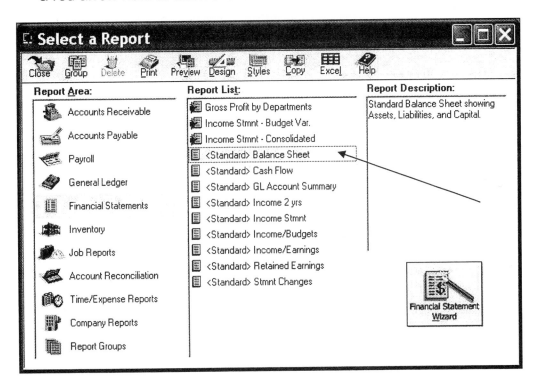

2. Click [Print]. The <Standard> Balance Sheet Options window displays. Click [OK].

---

3. The Print window pops up. Click [OK] and the balance sheet starts to print.

		Bellwether Garden Supply Balance Sheet March 31, 2007
		ASSETS
Current Assets		
Petty Cash	$ 300.00	
Cash on Hand	1,850.45	
Regular Checking Account	4,247.16	
Payroll Checking Account	4,902.49	
Savings Account	37,500.00	
Money-Market Fund	4,000.00	
Accounts Receivable	13,527.12	
Other Receivables	7,681.84	
Allowance for Doubtful Account	(5,000.00)	
Inventory	12,675.75	
Prepaid Expenses	14,221.30	
Employee Advances	3,000.65	
Notes Receivable-Current	11,000.00	
Other Current Assets	120.00	
Total Current Assets		110,026.76
Property and Equipment		
Furniture and Fixtures	62,769.25	
Equipment	38,738.33	
Vehicles	86,273.40	
Other Depreciable Property	6,200.96	
Buildings	185,500.00	
Building Improvements	26,500.00	
Accum. Depreciation-Furniture	(55,942.93)	
Accum. Depreciation-Equipment	(34,403.30)	
Accum. Depreciation-Vehicles	(55,898.93)	
Accum. Depreciation-Other	(3,982.55)	
Accum. Depreciation-Buildings	(35,673.07)	
Accum. Depreciation-Bldg Imp	(5,096.15)	
Total Property and Equipment		214,985.01
Other Assets		
Deposits	15,000.00	
Organization Costs	4,995.10	
Accum Amortiz - Organiz Costs	(2,000.00)	
Notes Receivable- Noncurrent	5,004.90	
Other Noncurrent Assets	3,333.00	
Total Other Assets		26,333.00
Total Assets	$	351,344.77

Balance Sheet concluded

Bellwether Garden Supply
Balance Sheet
March 31, 2007

LIABILITIES AND CAPITAL

Current Liabilities		
Accounts Payable	$ 10,437.16	
Accrued Expenses	3,022.55	
Sales Tax Payable	4,387.68	
Wages Payable	2,320.30	
401 K Deductions Payable	1,099.65	
Health Insurance Payable	(530.64)	
Federal Payroll Taxes Payable	15,984.39	
FUTA Tax Payable	258.20	
State Payroll Taxes Payable	3,096.42	
SUTA Tax Payable	658.67	
Local Payroll Taxes Payable	113.25	
Income Taxes Payable	11,045.75	
Other Taxes Payable	2,590.15	
Current Portion Long-Term Debt	5,167.00	
Contracts Payable- Current	2,000.00	
Other Current Liabilities	(96.00)	
Total Current Liabilities		61,554.53
Long-Term Liabilities		
Notes Payable-Noncurrent	4,000.00	
Total Long-Term Liabilities		4,000.00
Total Liabilities		65,554.53
Capital		
Common Stock	5,000.00	
Paid-in Capital	100,000.00	
Retained Earnings	189,037.60	
Net Income	(8,247.36)	
Total Capital		285,790.24
Total Liabilities & Capital	$	351,344.77

Follow these steps to print the Gross Profit by Departments financial statement for the current period.

1. From the Select a Report window, highlight Gross Profit by Departments. Compare your screen to the one shown on the next page.

2. Click [Print]. The Gross Profit by Departments Options window displays.

3. If the Show Zero Amounts box is checked, click on it once to uncheck it. Click [OK].

4. The Print window appears. Click [Properties...]. Select the Basics tab. (*These instructions may differ for different versions of Windows.*)

5. Select the radio button for Landscape [⦿ Landscape] Click [OK]. You are returned to the Print window.

6. Click [OK].

7. The Gross Profit by Departments report starts to print. Your report should print in landscape orientation.

Bellwether Garden Supply
Departmental Gross Profit Totals
Year To Date Totals For the Month Ending March 31, 2007

	Aviary			Books			Ceramics		Equipment	
Revenues										
Sales	$	6,622.91	100.00	$	3,654.60	100.00	$	0.00	0.00	7,731.28	100.00
Total Revenues		6,622.91	100.00		3,654.60	100.00		0.00	0.00	7,731.28	100.00
Cost of Sales										
Product Cost - Aviary		2,012.00	30.38		0.00	0.00		0.00	0.00	0.00	0.00
Product Cost - Books		0.00	0.00		1,415.37	38.73		0.00	0.00	0.00	0.00
Product Cost - Equipment		0.00	0.00		0.00	0.00		0.00	0.00	3,413.65	44.15
Total Cost of Sales		2,012.00	30.38		1,415.37	38.73		0.00	0.00	3,413.65	44.15
Gross Profit		4,610.91	69.62		2,239.23	61.27		0.00	0.00	4,317.63	55.85

The Gross Profit by Departments report lists the departmental gross profit totals for the following departments: Aviary, Books, Ceramics, and Equipment.

Follow these steps to print the income statement:

1. From the Select a Report window, highlight <Standard> Income Stmnt.

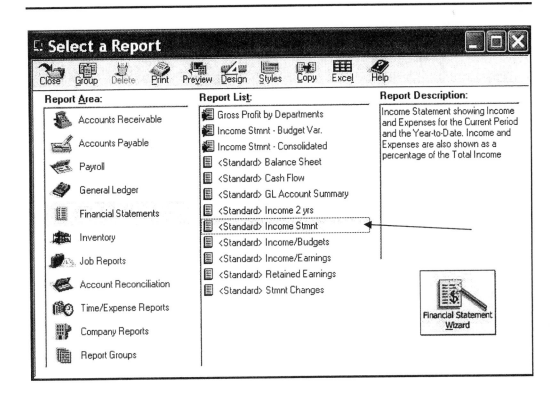

2. Click .

3. The <Standard Income Stmnt> window pops us. Click on the box next to Show Zero Amounts to uncheck it.

4. Click [OK]. The Print window pops up.

5. Click [OK]. The income statement starts to print. Compare it to the one shown on the next page.

Bellwether Garden Supply
Income Statement
For the Three Months Ending March 31, 2007

	Current Month			Year to Date	
Revenues					
Sales	$ 5,175.00	7.73	$	8,250.95	10.05
Sales - Aviary	5,523.13	8.25		6,622.91	8.07
Sales - Books	149.75	0.22		3,654.60	4.45
Sales - Equipment	2,969.66	4.43		7,731.28	9.42
Sales - Food/Fert	367.60	0.55		697.24	0.85
Sales - Furniture	30,000.00	44.79		30,000.00	36.55
Sales - Hand Tools	199.92	0.30		801.64	0.98
Sales - Landscape Services	2,059.53	3.07		2,939.34	3.58
Sales - Miscellaneous	18,199.98	27.17		18,199.98	22.17
Sales - Nursery	1,182.48	1.77		1,420.34	1.73
Sales - Pots	510.58	0.76		580.53	0.71
Sales - Seeds	223.17	0.33		766.24	0.93
Sales - Soil	351.48	0.52		365.46	0.45
Other Income	100.00	0.15		100.00	0.12
Sales Discounts	(28.30)	(0.04)		(42.02)	(0.05)
Total Revenues	66,983.98	100.00		82,088.49	100.00
Cost of Sales					
Product Cost	394.50	0.59		394.50	0.48
Product Cost - Aviary	1,573.10	2.35		2,012.00	2.45
Product Cost - Books	14.27	0.02		1,415.37	1.72
Product Cost - Equipment	1,350.45	2.02		3,413.65	4.16
Product Cost - Food/Fert	146.00	0.22		278.40	0.34
Product Cost - Hand Tools	76.40	0.11		316.45	0.39
Product Cost - Pots	209.35	0.31		237.10	0.29
Product Cost - Seeds	89.15	0.13		305.30	0.37
Product Cost - Soil	148.92	0.22		156.42	0.19
Materials Cost	1,547.45	2.31		1,547.45	1.89
Materials Cost - Nursery	198.90	0.30		270.30	0.33
Subcontractors - Landscaping	335.50	0.50		335.50	0.41
Total Cost of Sales	6,083.99	9.08		10,682.44	13.01
Gross Profit	60,899.99	90.92		71,406.05	86.99
Expenses					
Freight	0.00	0.00		50.00	0.06
Advertising Expense	1,325.00	1.98		1,325.00	1.61
Auto Expenses	274.56	0.41		274.56	0.33
Bank Charges	18.00	0.03		18.00	0.02
Depreciation Expense	5,522.60	8.24		16,788.00	20.45
Legal and Professional Expense	150.00	0.22		510.00	0.62
Licenses Expense	150.00	0.22		150.00	0.18
Maintenance Expense	75.00	0.11		75.00	0.09
Office Expense	479.89	0.72		479.89	0.58
Payroll Tax Exp	5,684.21	8.49		5,684.21	6.92
Rent or Lease Expense	550.00	0.82		1,100.00	1.34
Repairs Expense	75.00	0.11		75.00	0.09
Supplies Expense	2,722.07	4.06		2,722.07	3.32
Utilities Expense	303.45	0.45		303.45	0.37
Wages Expense	49,643.54	74.11		49,643.54	60.48
Other Expense	464.80	0.69		464.80	0.57
Purchase Disc- Expense Items	(10.11)	(0.02)		(10.11)	(0.01)
Total Expenses	67,428.01	100.66		79,653.41	97.03
Net Income	$ (6,528.02)	(9.75)	$	(8,247.36)	(10.05)

Follow these steps to print the Statement of Cash Flow.

1. From the Select a Report window, highlight <Standard> Cash Flow.

2. Click [Print]. The <Standard> Cash Flow Options window displays.

3. Click on the Show Zero Amounts box to uncheck it. Click [OK].

4. The Print window pops up. Click [OK]. The statement of cash flow starts to print.

		Bellwether Garden Supply Statement of Cash Flow For the three Months Ended March 31, 2007	
		Current Month	Year to Date
Cash Flows from operating activities			
Net Income	$	(6,528.02) $	(8,247.36)
Adjustments to reconcile net income to net cash provided by operating activities			
Accum. Depreciation-Furniture		841.60	2,524.80
Accum. Depreciation-Equipment		770.10	2,530.50
Accum. Depreciation-Vehicles		2,875.78	8,627.34
Accum. Depreciation-Other		129.14	387.42
Accum. Depreciation-Buildings		792.74	2,378.22
Accum. Depreciation-Bldg Imp		113.26	339.74
Accounts Receivable		(7,677.52)	(10,428.68)
Other Receivables		0.00	(3,672.24)
Inventory		2,704.77	5,922.44
Accounts Payable		4,193.63	6,534.41
Sales Tax Payable		1,007.70	1,927.13
401 K Deductions Payable		654.95	654.95
Health Insurance Payable		(530.64)	(530.64)
Federal Payroll Taxes Payable		14,397.54	14,397.54
State Payroll Taxes Payable		2,111.09	2,111.09
Total Adjustments		22,384.14	33,704.02
Net Cash provided by Operations		15,856.12	25,456.66
Cash Flows from investing activities Used For			
Net cash used in investing		0.00	0.00
Cash Flows from financing activities Proceeds From Used For			
Net cash used in financing		0.00	0.00
Net increase <decrease> in cash	$	15,856.12 $	25,456.66
Summary			
Cash Balance at End of Period	$	52,800.10 $	52,800.10
Cash Balance at Beg of Period		(36,944.20)	(27,343.66)
Net Increase <Decrease> in Cash	$	15,855.90 $	25,456.44

Follow these steps to print the Statement of Retained Earnings:

1. From the Select a Report window, highlight <Standard> Retained Earnings.

2. Click [Print]. The <Standard> Retained Earnings Options window displays.

3. Click on the Show Zero Amounts box to uncheck it. Click [OK].

4. The Print window pops up. Click [OK]. The statement of retained earnings starts to print.

		Bellwether Garden Supply
		Statement of Retained Earnings
		For the Three Months Ending March 31, 2007
Beginning Retained Earnings	$	189,037.60
Adjustments To Date		0.00
Net Income		(8,247.36)
Subtotal		180,790.24
Ending Retained Earnings	$	180,790.24

Follow these steps to print the Statement of Changes in Financial Position:

1. From the Select a Report window, highlight <Standard> Stmnt Changes.

2. Click [Print]. The <Standard> Stmnt Changes Options window displays.

3. Click on the Show Zero Amounts box to uncheck it. Click [OK].

4. The Print window pops up. Click [OK].

	Bellwether Garden Supply	
	Statement of Changes in Financial Position	
	For the three months ended March 31, 2007	
	Current Month	Year To Date
Sources of Working Capital		
Net Income	$ (6,528.02) $	(8,247.36)
Add back items not requiring		
working capital		
Accum. Depreciation-Furniture	841.52	2,524.72
Accum. Depreciation-Equipment	769.98	2,530.38
Accum. Depreciation-Vehicles	2,875.78	8,627.34
Accum. Depreciation-Other	129.14	387.42
Accum. Depreciation-Buildings	792.72	2,378.20
Accum. Depreciation-Bldg Imp	113.26	339.74
Working capital from operations	(1,005.62)	8,540.44
Other sources		
Total sources	(1,005.62)	8,540.44
Uses of working capital		
Total uses	0.00	0.00
Net change	$ (1,005.62) $	8,540.44
Analysis of componants of changes		
Increase <Decrease> in Current Assets		
Petty Cash	$ 200.00 $	200.00
Regular Checking Account	(16,679.93)	(7,079.39)
Payroll Checking Account	(1,664.17)	(1,664.17)
Savings Account	30,000.00	30,000.00
Money-Market Fund	4,000.00	4,000.00
Accounts Receivable	7,677.52	10,428.68
Other Receivables	0.00	3,672.24
Inventory	(2,704.77)	(5,922.44)
<Increase> Decrease in Current Liabilities		
Accounts Payable	(4,193.63)	(6,534.41)
Sales Tax Payable	(1,007.70)	(1,927.13)
401 K Deductions Payable	(654.95)	(654.95)
Health Insurance Payable	530.64	530.64
Federal Payroll Taxes Payable	(14,397.54)	(14,397.54)
State Payroll Taxes Payable	(2,111.09)	(2,111.09)
Net change	$ (1,005.62) $	8,540.44

5. Close all windows to return to the menu bar.

BACKING UP CHAPTER 7 DATA (Optional Backup)

You have not added any new data in Chapter 7. If you would prefer to have another backup disk, follow these steps to back up Chapter 7:

1. Put your backup disk in drive A.

2. From the menu bar, select File, then Back up.

3. Click Back Up Now .

4. Click on the down-arrow in the Save in field. If necessary, scroll up the list, then click on 3½ Floppy (A:) to select drive A.

5. Type **Chapter 7** in the File name field.

6. Click Save .

7. When the screen prompts that This company backup will require approximately 1 diskette, click OK .

8. When the screen prompts you to insert the first disk, click OK . When the Back Up Company scale is 100% completed, you have successfully backed up to the current point in Chapter 7. You are returned to the menu bar.

	INTERNET ACTIVITY
1.	From your Internet browser, go to the book's website at http://www.mhhe.com/yacht2004.
2.	In the Student Edition list, link to Internet Activities.
3.	Link to WEB EXERCISES, PART 1.
4.	Scroll down the screen to PEACHTREE SOFTWARE – Chapter 7. Read steps 1 and 2.
5.	Follow the steps shown on the textbook's website to complete this Internet activity.
6.	Use a word processing program to write a summary for each website visited. Your summaries should be no more than 75 words.

SUMMARY AND REVIEW

SOFTWARE OBJECTIVES: In Chapter 7, you used the software to:

1. Restore data from Exercise 6-2.

2. Explore Peachtree's Help feature.

3. Print the financial statements.

4. Make an optional backup of Chapter 7. The backups that were made in Chapter 6 include the data for this chapter.

WEB OBJECTIVES: In Chapter 7, you did these Internet activities:

1. Used your Internet browser to go to the book's website

2. Completed the Internet activity for Peachtree Software.

3. Completed the steps shown for this activity.

GOING TO THE NET

Access the article How to Read a Balance Sheet: Introduction at http://www.fool.com/school/valuation/howtoreadabalancesheet.htm. Read the article. Answer the following questions.

1. What are liquid assets?

2. What are the liquid assets called on the balance sheet?

3. In the How to Read a Balance Sheet: Introduction list, link to two other sites. Define each link; include the website address(es) in your answer.

True/Make True: Write the word True in the space provided if the statement is true. If the statement is not true, write the correct answer.

1. In Chapter 7, you printed three financial statements.

_____

_____

_____

_____

2. Peachtree automatically calculates financial statements once journal entries have been journalized and posted.

_____

_____

3. The balance sheet lists the revenues and expenses of the business.

_____

_____

4. The statement of cash flow is roughly the same thing as a balance sheet.

_____

_____

5. The income statement is a summary of the revenue and expenses of a company for a period of time, such as an accounting period or a year.

_____

_____

6. The financial statements printed by Peachtree reflect month-to-date amounts only.

_____

7. The term standard refers to financial statements that are designed by the company.

    _____

    _____

8. The financial statements are interrelated.

    _____

    _____

9. Bellwether Garden Supply showed a net loss for the current month, March 31, 2007.

    _____

    _____

    _____

10. The statement of changes in financial position derives its information from the income statement.

    _____

    _____

Exercise 7-1: Answer the following questions about the balance sheet and income statement:

1. The total assets are: _____

2. The total capital is: _____

3. Indicate the amount of the net income or (net loss) for the month of March: _____

4. The current month's gross profit is: _____

5. The current month's total expenses are: _____

Exercise 7-2: Answer the following questions about the statement of cash flow and the statement of retained earnings:

1. The current month's net cash provided by operations is: _____

2. The year-to-date's net cash provided by operations is: _____

3. The cash balance at end of period for the current month is: _____

4. The beginning Retained Earnings balance is: _____

5. The ending Retained Earnings balance is: _____

CHAPTER 7 INDEX

Chapter 8

Pavilion Design Group: Time & Billing

SOFTWARE OBJECTIVES: In Chapter 8, you will use the software to:

1. Start the sample company, Pavilion Design Group.
2. Explore Peachtree's time and billing feature.
3. Make one backup: one blank, formatted disk for Chapter 8.

WEB OBJECTIVES: In Chapter 8, you will do these Internet activities:

1. Use your Internet browser to go to the book's website.
2. Complete the Internet activity for Search Engines.
3. Complete the steps shown for this activity.

PAVILION DESIGN GROUP

When you installed Peachtree Complete Accounting 2004, two sample companies were included with the software: Bellwether Garden Supply and Pavilion Design Group. In Chapters 1–7 you worked with Bellwether Garden Supply. In this chapter, you will focus on how the second sample company, Pavilion Design Group, uses PCA's time and billing feature.

TIME & BILLING

Time & Billing gives you a way to track expenses and time when working with your customers. For example, there are daily services that you perform for your customers like making copies, designing a proposal, and out-of-pocket expenses. These expenses can be tracked and documented using PCA's time and billing feature. The purpose of PCA's time and billing feature is to give you the tools to record customer-related work or expenses.

To track time and expenses, PCA uses two forms or tickets: the time ticket and the expense ticket. Each ticket type can be specific to a customer, job, or non-billable administrative tasks (miscellaneous items). Each ticket has its own special type of inventory item: the activity item for time tickets and the charge item for expense tickets.

Time Tickets

Time tickets are used to record time-based activities such as research or consultations. They record the activities of either an employee or a vendor. The two methods of entering time ticket information are weekly or daily.

The billing rate used for a recorded activity can be based on the employee who records the ticket or one of the five billing rates assigned to the activity item. Or, you can record the billing at the time you enter the time ticket.

Expense Tickets

Expense tickets are used to track and aid in the recovery of customer-related expenses. These expenses are *not* based on time. Expenses can be based on the various charges related to the service being offered. For example, if you were an accountant, you might charge your client for copying fees or faxing fees.

Both time and expense tickets can be used in the Sales/Invoicing window to bill your customers. The Sales/Invoicing window includes a feature called Apply Tickets/Reimbursable Expenses which takes you to the time and billing feature. The rate for expense tickets is determined by the unit price of the charge item multiplied by the quantity.

The chart below shows how time and billing works:

Time & Billing Ticket Types			
Ticket Type	Inventory Item Class	Examples	Billing Amount Equals
Time Ticket	Activity Item	Research Consultants Writing Reports	Billing Rate Times Activity Divisions
Expense Ticket	Charge Item	Copying Faxing Court Fees	Unit Price of the Charge Item Times Quantity

GETTING STARTED

1. Start Windows and PCA in the usual way. From the startup menu, select Explore a sample company. (*Hint: Pavilion Design Group will be listed in the Company Name box after the first time it is opened.*)

2. The Explore a Sample Company window appears. Select Pavilion Design Group.

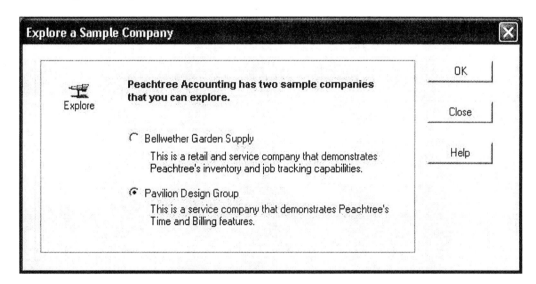

3. Click   OK .

4. Close Peachtree Today. The menu bar for Peachtree Accounting: Pavilion Design Group appears.

USING TIME & BILLING

Let's look at how Pavilion Design Group has set up time and billing. First, they set up how they are going to invoice for their services. There are two special inventory item classes for Time & Billing: *activity items* and *charge items*. Activity items are used on time tickets. Charge items are used on expense tickets. These inventory items must be set up prior to entering a time or expense ticket.

There are four steps to complete PCA's Time & Billing:

Step 1:   Set up the inventory item
Step 2:   Enter the time ticket
Step 3:   Record the sales invoice
Step 4:   Payroll

Inventory Item Maintenance

You use maintenance windows to set up defaults. Follow these steps to look at the inventory maintenance information for Pavilion.

1. From the menu bar, click on Maintain, then Inventory Items. The Maintain Inventory Items window appears.

2. In the Item ID field, select CONC01, Layout Concept.

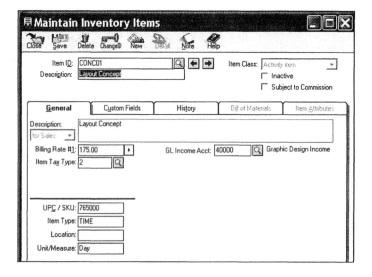

Review the information on this screen. Observe that $175.00 per hour is shown in the Billing Rate #1 field (click on the right-arrow to see other billing rates); the Item Ta_x_ Type is 2 (for exempt); and the GL Income Acct is Account No. 40000, Graphic Design Income. This maintenance window is similar to ones that you have set up before. *Remember, maintenance windows are where you set up defaults for PCA.*

3. Close the Maintain Inventory Items window.

Time Ticket

The Time Ticket shows how much was billed to the customer. To see how time is billed, you are going to look at a job that Jeff Henderson has already completed. This means you will need to use the Abc Open icon to select one of the time ticket records.

1. Select Tasks, Time/Expense, then Time Tickets.

2. The Time Tickets window appears. Make sure that the Daily tab is selected. Click 【Open】.

3. In the Sho_w_ field, click on the down arrow, scroll up, and then select All Transactions. Click on Reference 18 for Jeff Henderson.

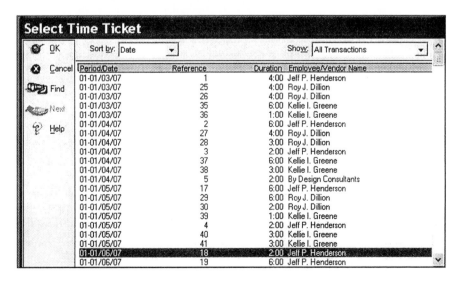

4. Click [OK]. The Time Tickets window appears. The <u>D</u>aily tab should be selected. If it is not, select it. Notice that the Activity Item is for CONC01, Layout Concept, and that the customer is Merchant's Bank. Mr. Henderson worked for two hours and Merchant's Bank was billed $350.

5. Click on the Week<u>l</u>y tab.

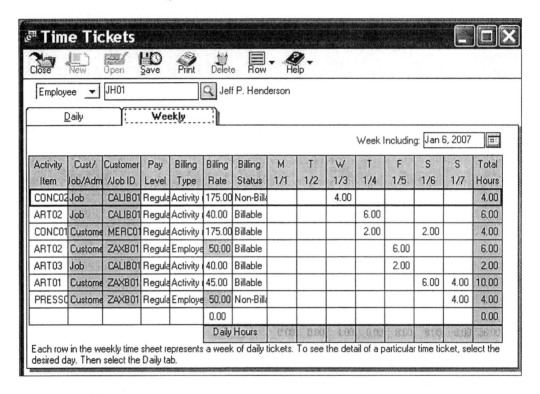

This screen shows the weekly time ticket for Pavilion's employee, Jeff P. Henderson. Notice that the Layout Concept activity, CONC01 is shown for Tuesday, 1/4, for two hours and Saturday 1/6 for two hours for a total of 4 hours.

6. Close the Week<u>l</u>y Time Tickets window to return to the menu bar.

Sales Invoice

In order to see how Mr. Henderson's charges were billed to a customer, you will need to use the 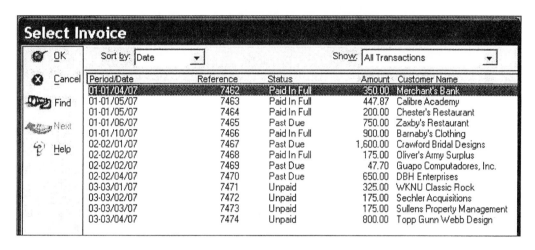 Open feature on the Sales/Invoicing window.

1. Select Tasks, then Sales/Invoicing. Click Open.

2. The Select Invoice window appears. In the Show field, select All Transactions.

3. Highlight Reference 7462 for Merchant's Bank.

Select Invoice

Period/Date	Reference	Status	Amount	Customer Name
01-01/04/07	7462	Paid In Full	350.00	Merchant's Bank
01-01/05/07	7463	Paid In Full	447.87	Calibre Academy
01-01/05/07	7464	Paid In Full	200.00	Chester's Restaurant
01-01/06/07	7465	Past Due	750.00	Zaxby's Restaurant
01-01/10/07	7466	Paid In Full	900.00	Barnaby's Clothing
02-02/01/07	7467	Past Due	1,600.00	Crawford Bridal Designs
02-02/02/07	7468	Paid In Full	175.00	Oliver's Army Surplus
02-02/02/07	7469	Past Due	47.70	Guapo Computadores, Inc.
02-02/04/07	7470	Past Due	650.00	DBH Enterprises
03-03/01/07	7471	Unpaid	325.00	WKNU Classic Rock
03-03/02/07	7472	Unpaid	175.00	Sechler Acquisitions
03-03/03/07	7473	Unpaid	175.00	Sullens Property Management
03-03/04/07	7474	Unpaid	800.00	Topp Gunn Webb Design

Sort by: Date   Show: All Transactions

OK   Cancel   Find   Next   Help

4. Click OK.

5. The Sales/Invoicing window appears for Invoice No. 7462 for January 4, 2007.

6. Click on the arrow next to Apply Tickets/Expenses Apply Tickets/Expenses. (*Hint: This is located in the lower left of the screen.*)

7. The Apply Tickets/Reimbursable Expenses window pops up. Compare your screen to the one shown on the next page.

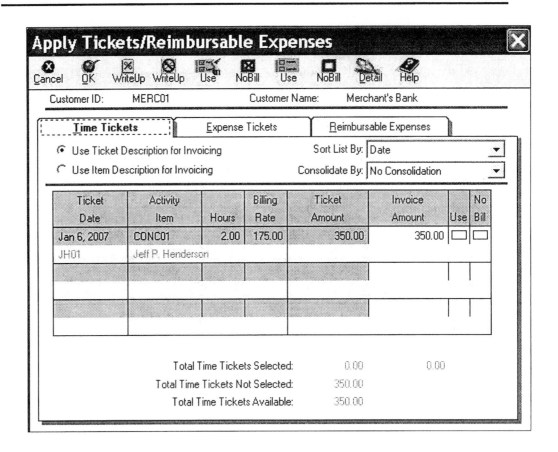

Observe that this time ticket shows that Jeff Henderson has invoiced $350 for this job.

8. Click [OK] to close the Apply Tickets/Reimbursable Expenses window. You are returned to the Merchant Bank's sales invoice.

9. Click [Close]. You are returned to the menu bar.

Payroll

You also need to set up information in Payroll. You do this by selecting Hourly-Time Ticket Hours for employees. Let's see how Pavilion sets this up.

1. From the menu bar, select Maintain, then Employees/Sales Reps. The Maintain Employees/Sales Reps window appears.

2. Select the Pay Info tab.

3. In the Employee ID field, select Jeff P. Henderson (JH01).

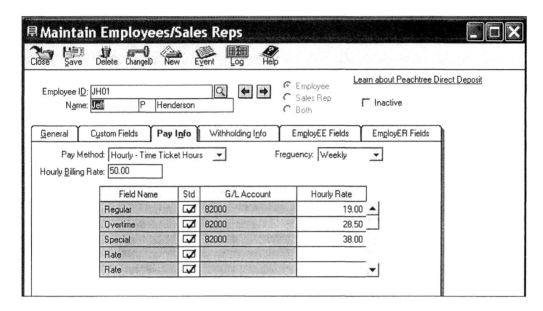

Observe that Mr. Henderson's Pay Method is Hourly – Time Ticket Hours.

4. Click Close.

You use the Payroll Entry task to issue Mr. Henderson a paycheck for the work completed at Merchant's Bank.

BACKING UP CHAPTER 8 DATA

Use one blank, formatted disk for the Chapter 8 back up. Refer to the chart on page 2 for backing up data.

1. Put your backup disk in drive A.

2. From the menu bar, select File, then Back up. When the Back Up Company window pops up, click on the box next to Include the company name in the backup file name to *uncheck* it.

3. Click [Back Up Now].

4. Click on the down-arrow in the Save in field. If necessary, scroll up the list, then click on 3½ Floppy (A:) to select drive A.

5. Type **Chapter 8** in the File name field.

6. Click [Save].

7. When the screen prompts that This company backup will require approximately 1 diskette, click [OK].

8. When the screen prompts you to insert the first disk, click [OK]. When the Back Up Company scale is 100% completed, you have successfully backed up to the current point in Chapter 8. You are returned to the menu bar.

	INTERNET ACTIVITY
1.	From your Internet browser, go to the book's website at http://www.mhhe.com/yacht2004.
2.	In the Student Edition list, link to Internet Activities.
3.	Link to WEB EXERCISES, PART 1.
4.	Scroll down the screen to SEARCH ENGINES. Read steps 1and 2.
5.	Follow the steps shown on the book's website to complete this Internet activity.
6.	Use a word processing program to write a short summary of what you found. Your summary should be no more than 75 words.

SUMMARY AND REVIEW

SOFTWARE OBJECTIVES: In Chapter 8, you used the software to:

1. Start the sample company, Pavilion Design Group.

2. Explore Peachtree's time and billing feature.

3. Make one backup: one blank, formatted disk for Chapter 8.

WEB OBJECTIVES: In Chapter 8, you did these Internet activities:

1. Used your Internet browser to go to the book's website.

2. Completed the Internet activity for Search Engines.

3. Completed the steps shown for this activity.

GOING TO THE NET

Access the Peachtree Complete Accounting 2004, Frequently Asked Questions and Answers website at http://www.peachtree.com/peachtreeaccountingline/complete/frequently_asked_questions.cfm. Answer the following questions.

1. What are the differences between the Peachtree 2004 products? Link to the Compare Products chart.

2. What features are available in Peachtree 2004 to get me started quickly?

Multiple Choice Questions: In the space provided, write the letter that best answers each question.

_____1. In Chapter 8, you work with the sample company called:

        a. Bellwether Garden Supply.
        b. Pavilion Graphic Design.
        c. Merchant's Bank.
        d. Jeff Henderson, Graphics.
        e. None of the above.

_____2. The focus of Chapter 8 is to:

        a. Complete a sales invoice.
        b. Complete a payroll entry.
        c. Complete defaults.
        d. Look at PCA's time and billing features.
        e. None of the above.

_____3. The purpose of PCA's time and billing feature is to:

    a. Give you the tools to record customer-related work or expenses.
    b. Track how much an employee earns.
    c. Track how many sales invoices are completed in a month.
    d. Record employee payroll.
    e. None of the above.

_____4. Time tickets are used to:

    a. Record weekly or monthly information.
    b. Record payroll.
    c. Record time-based activities.
    d. Track sales invoices.
    e. None of the above.

_____5. Expense tickets are used to:

    a. Track and aid in the recovery of customer-related expenses.
    b. Record time-based activities such as research or consultants.
    c. Track sales invoices.
    d. Record payroll.
    e. None of the above.

_____6. Examples of time ticket activity items are:

    a. Copying, faxing, court fees.
    b. Research, consultants, writing reports.
    c. Inventory accounts.
    d. Fixed asset accounts.
    e. None of the above.

_____7. Examples of expense ticket charge items are:

     a. Fixed asset accounts.
     b. Inventory accounts.
     c. Copying, faxing, court fees.
     d. Research, consultants, writing reports.
     e. None of the above.

_____8. You use maintenance windows to set up:

     a. Payroll entries.
     b. Sales/Invoicing tasks.
     c. Defaults.
     d. Tasks for time tickets.
     e. None of the above.

_____9. The time ticket shows:

     a. How much was billed to a vendor.
     b. How much was billed to a customer.
     c. How much was billed to an employee.
     d. Expenses minus revenue.
     e. None of the above.

_____10. How many hours did Mr. Henderson work completing the Layout Concept for Merchant's Bank?

     a. Three hours.
     b. Four hours.
     c. Five hours.
     d. Six hours.
     e. None of the above.

Exercise 8-1: Answer the following questions about time and billing.

1. Jeff Henderson's hourly billing rate is?   _____

2. The billing rate for Layout Concept is?   _____

3. The tax status for Layout Concept is?   _____

4. The general ledger account used for layout
    concept is: _____

5. The item identification for Layout Concept is: _____

Exercise 8-2: Answer the following questions.

1. Merchant Bank's 1/4/07 sales invoice is in the
    amount of?   _____

2. The unit price of Merchant Bank's 1/4/07 sales
    invoice is?

3. The G/L account number for Jeff Henderson's
    regular pay is?   _____

3. Peachtree classifies Jeff Henderson's pay
    method as?   _____

4. How many hours did Jeff Henderson work on
    the layout concept for Merchant Bank?   _____

CHAPTER 8 INDEX

Part 2

Peachtree Complete Accounting 2004 for Service Businesses

In Part 2 of *Computer Accounting with Peachtree Complete 2004, Eighth Edition,* you are the owner of an accounting practice. Your accounting business does monthly record keeping for local service businesses. In Part 2, you will record entries in the Cash Receipts Journal (receipts task) and Cash Disbursements Journal (write checks task) You will also use the General Journal for adjusting entries. At the end of each month, you will reconcile the bank statement and print the general ledger trial balance and financial statements. At the end of the fourth quarter, you will use Peachtree to complete end-of-quarter adjusting entries, print the adjusted trial balance, print financial statements, close the fiscal year, and print a post-closing trial balance.

After you record journal entries, the next step is to post them to the General Ledger. One of the best features of a computerized accounting system is how quickly *posting* is done. Once journal entries are recorded and checked for accuracy, posting is a click of the mouse. All entries are posted to the correct accounts in the ledger and account balances are calculated–fast, easy, and accurate. Of course, the accuracy of your records will depend on the accuracy of your journal entries. An added feature in PCA is that once your entries are posted, the bank reconciliation can also be completed.

Part 2 includes two chapters and two projects: Chapters 9 and 10 and Projects 1 and 1A. In Chapters 9 and 10, you maintain the accounting records for Taylor Rinaldi, Graphic Artist. You complete accounting tasks for the fourth quarter–October, November and December 2004. You also complete end-of-quarter adjusting entries for Mr. Rinaldi. At the end of Chapter 9, you start an exercise for a new service business that is completed in Chapter 10.

In Project 1 you complete the Computer Accounting Cycle for Lena Becker, Consultant. This project gives you an opportunity to apply what you have learned in Chapters 9 and 10. At the end of Project 1, there is a Check Your Progress assessment.

Project 1A gives you a chance to design a service business of your own. You select a chart of accounts, write and journalize transactions, reconcile the bank statement, and complete the computer accounting cycle for your business.

The chart below shows that you will use six blank, formatted disks to back up the data in Part 2–Chapters 9, 10, and Project 1. The author suggests that you reformat the disks used in Part 1 (Chapters 1-8) *except* the Exercise 6-2, disk 6 of 7.

Disk Label	Chapter	Backup Name	Kilobytes	Page Nos.
Disk 1 of 6	9	a:\Chapter 9 Begin	441 KB	271-273
		a:\Chapter 9 Check Register October[1]	*449 KB*	*285*
		a:\Chapter 9 October	452 KB	299
Disk 2 of 6		a:\Exercise 9-1	432 KB	305
		a:\Exercise 9-2	440 KB	308
Disk 3 of 6	10	a:\Chapter 10 November	458 KB	322-323
		a:\Chapter 10 December UTB	461 KB	329-330
		a:\Chapter 10 December	465 KB	339-340
Disk 4 of 6		a:\Chapter 10 EOY	465 KB	346-347
		a:\Exercise 10-1	449 KB	354
		a:\Exercise 10-2	449 KB	355
Disk 5 of 6	Project 1	a:\Lena Becker Begin	440 KB	360
		a:\Lena Becker UTB	464 KB	362
		a:\Lena Becker December	457 KB	363
Disk 6 of 6		a:\Lena Becker EOY	456 KB	363

The size of your backup files may differ from the amounts shown on the chart. This is okay. The differences are insignificant.

Part 2 shows you how you would computerize record keeping for three service businesses: 1) Taylor Rinaldi, Graphic Artist; 2) Your Name, Artist; 3) Project 1, Lena Becker, Consultant.

---

[1]This is an optional back up.

SOFTWARE OBJECTIVES: In Chapter 9, you will use the software to:

1. Set up company information for Taylor Rinaldi, Graphic Artist.
2. Select a sample company.
3. Edit the chart of accounts.
4. Enter chart of accounts beginning balances.
5. Use Windows Explorer to see the company's file size.
6. Record and post transactions in the cash receipts and cash disbursements journals.
7. Complete account reconciliation.
8. Preview the general ledger trial balance.
9. Preview the cash account register.
10. Print financial statements.
11. Make four backups using two blank, formatted disks: Use one disk to back up Chapter 9 beginning data and October data. Use the second disk to back up Exercise 9-1 and Exercise 9-2.[1]

WEB OBJECTIVES: In Chapter 9, you will do these Internet activities:

1. Use your Internet browser to go to the book's website. (Go online to www.mhhe.com/yacht2004).
2. Go to the Internet Activity link on the book's website. Then, select WEB EXERCISES, PART 2. Complete the first web exercise in Part 2, Starting a Business.
3. Use a word processing program to write summaries of the websites that you visited.

Chapter 9 begins Part 2 of the book–Peachtree Complete Accounting 2004 for Service Businesses. In this part of the book you are the owner of an accounting practice that does the monthly record keeping for

---

[1]You may reformat the disks you used in Part 1, Chapters 1–8, for making the backups in Part 2 (Chapters 9, 10, and Project 1). *Remember, do not reformat the Exercise 6-2 backup disk. You will use this data again in Part 4.* To see how many disks you need for backing up, refer to the chart on page 246.

several service businesses. In this chapter you will maintain the accounting records for a graphic artist, Taylor Rinaldi. You will set up a business using one of the sample companies included in PCA. Then, you will complete the computer accounting cycle for the month of October using your client's checkbook register and bank statement as *source documents*. In your study of accounting, you learned that source documents are used to show written evidence of a business transaction. For Taylor Rinaldi, the source documents used are his checkbook register and bank statement.

GETTING STARTED

Taylor Rinaldi is a graphic artist and educator. His sources of income are: graphic design work, book royalties, and part-time teaching for Glendale Community College. He is single and has no dependents.

Follow these steps to select a sample chart of accounts for your client, Taylor Rinaldi:

1. Start Windows and Peachtree in the usual way.

2. At the Peachtree Accounting startup screen, click on <u>S</u>et up a new company. The New Company Setup - Introduction screen appears. Read the information on this screen.

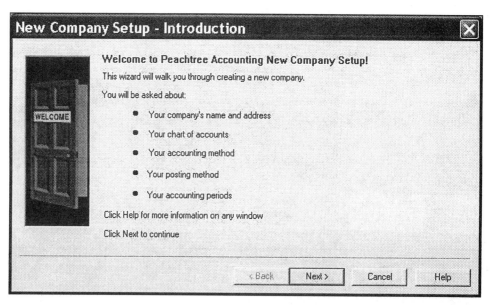

 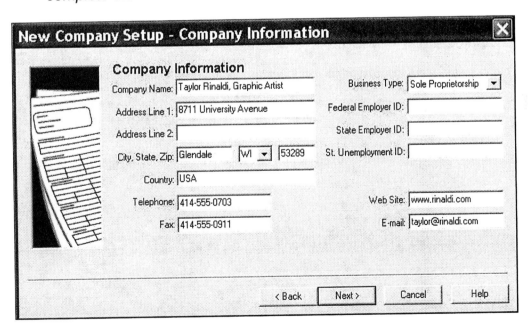

3. Click [Next >]. Type the following information in each field. Press the **<Tab>** key between each field.

Company Information

Company Name:	**Taylor Rinaldi, Graphic Artist (use your name)**[2]
Address Line 1:	**8711 University Avenue**
City, State, Zip:	**Glendale, WI 53289**
Country:	**USA**
Telephone:	**414-555-0703**
Fax:	**414-555-0911**
Business Type:	Select Sole Proprietorship
Web Site:	www.rinaldi.com
E-Mail:	taylor@rinaldi.com

Compare your screen to the one below. *The company name field should show your first and last name, Graphic Artist. Do not complete the ID fields.*

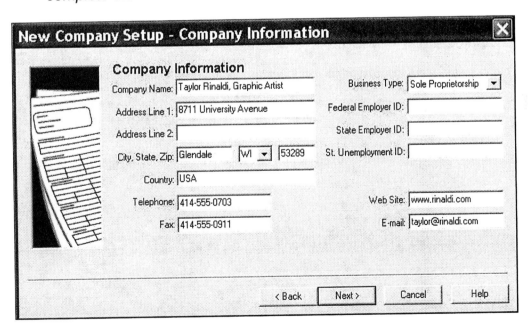

---

[2]Boldface indicates information that you type. If you use your name as the company name then your Peachtree printouts will have your name on them.

4. Check the information you just typed, then click [Next >]. The Chart of Accounts screen appears.

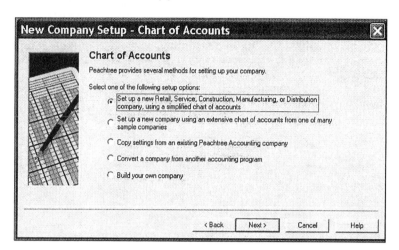

5. Accept the default for Set up a new Retail, Service, Construction, Manufacturing, or Distribution company using a simplified chart of accounts by clicking on [Next >].

6. Read the information about selecting a chart of accounts. The Available Charts of Accounts list shows five business types. Click on Service Company to highlight it.

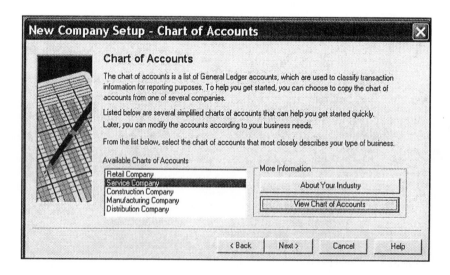

7. Make sure that Service Company is highlighted, then click .

8. Read the information on the Accounting Method screen.

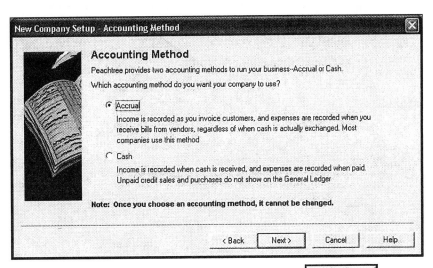

9. Accept the default for Accrual by clicking on Next >.

10. Read the information about the Posting Method. Peachtree Software recommends real-time posting for networked computers.

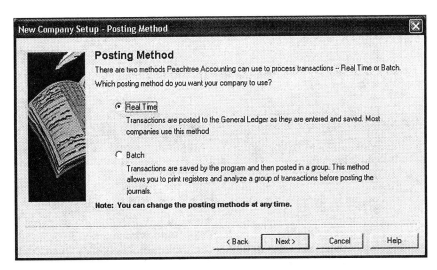

11. Accept the default for real-time posting by clicking on Next >.

12. Read the information about Accounting Periods.

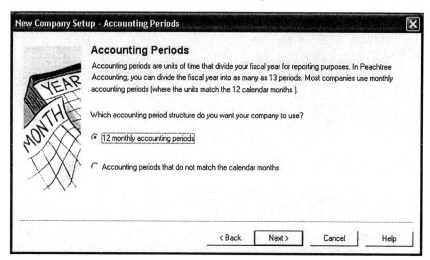

13. Accept the default for 12 monthly accounting periods by clicking on
    Next >.

14. Read the information about Monthly Accounting Periods. Use this
    information to complete the fields.

	Month	Year
When do you want your frist fiscal year to start?	January	**2004**
When is the first month you will be entering data?	**October**	2004
What is the first year you will be entering payroll?[3]		2004

Make sure the year 2004 is selected. Compare your screen to the
one shown on the next page.

---

[3]You will work with Peachtree's payroll features in Part 3, Chapters 11-14.

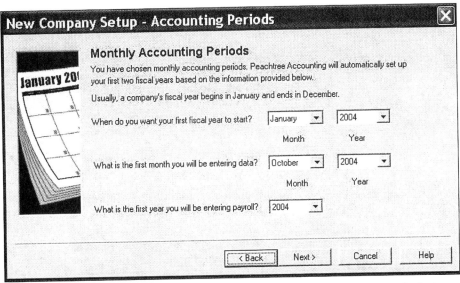

Check this screen carefully. You cannot change it later.

15. Click 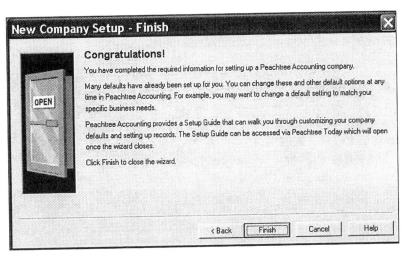 . The Defaults screen appears.

16. The Defaults screen will be explained in greater detail in Chapter 11. Since you are not concerned with payment and credit terms in Chapters 9 and 10, click Next > to accept the defaults.

17. Read the information on the Congratulations screen.

18. Click 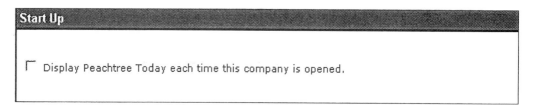. The Welcome to Peachtree Today! screen and menu bar for your company appears. (Your name will appear on the title bar if you used your name as the company name.)

Follow these steps to close the Peachtree Today screen.

1. On the left side of the Peachtree Today screen, select **● Preferences**.

2. If necessary, scroll down the screen to the Start Up area. Click on the field next to Display Peachtree Today each time this company is opened to uncheck the field.

Start Up

☐ Display Peachtree Today each time this company is opened.

3. Click ☒ on Peachtree Today's title bar to close the screen. The menu bar for your company appears.

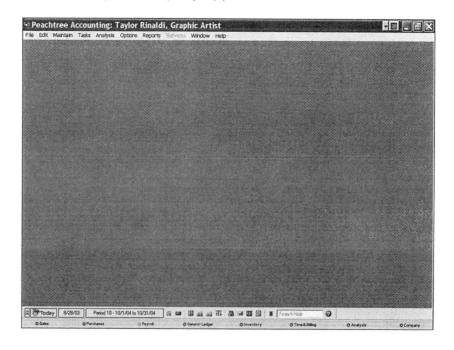

Observe that the toolbar at the bottom of the shows Period 10 - 10/1/04 to 10/31/04. October 1 through 31, 2004 is the first month that you will be entering data.

The New Company Setup is complete. A data path is set up on your hard drive for Taylor Rinaldi, Graphic Artist. That default program and data path is C:\Program Files\Peachtree\Company\tayringr. The subfolder for Taylor Rinaldi, Graphic Artist is tayringr.

You can see this subfolder by going to Windows Explorer. To review the steps for using Windows Explorer, see pages 20-22.

Company Maintenance Information

Follow these steps to see information about your company.

1. From Peachtree's menu bar, select Maintain, then Company Information.

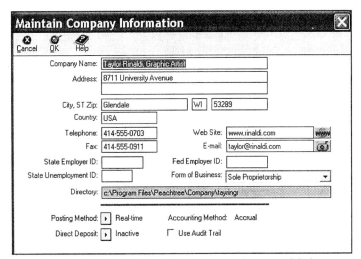

2. Compare these fields to the company information set up on page 249. They should agree. Notice that the Directory field also shows you the program and data path shown above. Make any needed corrections. Click [OK] to return to the menu bar.

3. Continue with the next section, Chart of Accounts.

CHART OF ACCOUNTS

The chart of accounts is a list of all the accounts in the general ledger. When you selected Service Company from the list of business types, a chart of accounts was included. Follow the steps that follow to edit PCA's sample chart of accounts for Taylor Rinaldi, Graphic Artist.

Delete Accounts

1. From the menu bar, click on Maintain, then Chart of Accounts. The Maintain Chart of Accounts window displays.

2. In the Account ID field, click 🔍. The Chart of Accounts list drops down.

3. Double-click on Account No. 1150, Allowance for Doubtful Account.

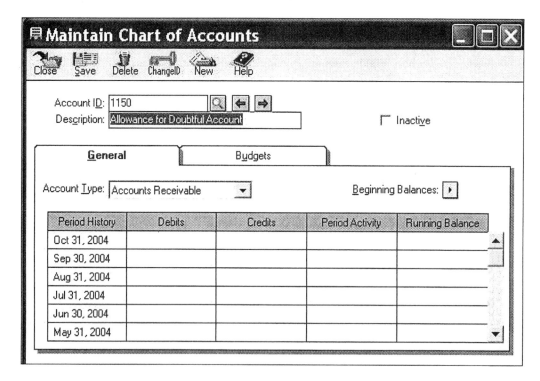

4. Click Delete.

5. The Peachtree Accounting - Are you sure you want to delete this record? window pops up.

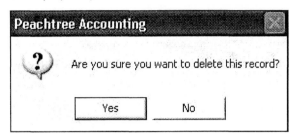

6. Click [Yes].

(*Hint: To delete the accounts, you can type in the account number in the Account ID field or click* [🔍]*, and then double-click on the account.*)

Delete the following accounts:

Acct. ID	Account Description
2310	Sales Tax Payable
2320	Deductions Payable
2330	Federal Payroll Taxes Payable
2340	FUTA Tax Payable
2350	State Payroll Taxes Payable
2360	SUTA Payable
2370	Local Taxes Payable
2500	Current Portion Long-Term Debt
2700	Long-Term Debt - Noncurrent
4300	Other Income
5900	Inventory Adjustments
6050	Employee Benefit Programs Expense
6250	Other Taxes Expense
6650	Commissions and Fees Expense
7100	Gain/Loss on Sale of Assets

Change Accounts

To change the name of an account, follow these steps:

1. Double-click on Account No. 3920, Owner's Contribution.

2. In the Description field, type **Taylor Rinaldi, Capital** (use your name, Capital).

3. In the Account Type field, click on the down arrow. Scroll up and select Equity-doesn't close. (When you change the Account Description of the accounts shown on page 259, you do *not* have to change the Account Type.)

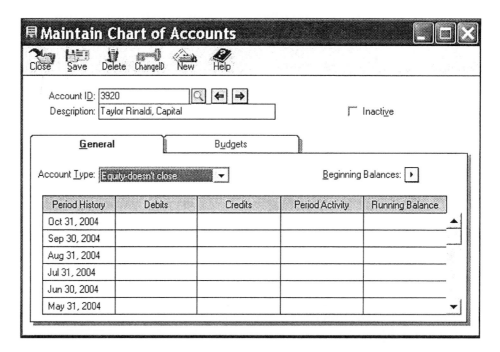

4. Click [Save].

Change the names of these accounts:

Acct. ID	Account Description	New Account Description
1010	Cash on Hand	**Money Market Account**
1400	Prepaid Expense	**Prepaid Rent**
1500	Property and Equipment	**Computer Equipment**
1900	Accum. Depreciation – Prop&Eqt	**Accum. Depreciation – Comp Eq**
2000	Accounts Payable	**VISA Payable**
2400	Customer Deposits	**Publisher Advances**
3930	Owner's Draw	**Taylor Rinaldi, Draw** (your name, Draw)
4000	Professional Fees	**Teaching Income**
4050	Sales of Materials	**Royalty Income**
6100	Payroll Tax Expense	**Dues and Subscriptions**
6150	Bad Debt Expense	**Auto Registration**
6550	Other Office Expense	**My Long Distance**
6850	Service Charge Expense	**Bank Service Charge**
7050	Depreciation Expense	**Deprec. Exp. – Comp Eq**

Add Accounts

To add an account to the Chart of Accounts, follow these steps:

1. In the Maintain Chart of Accounts window, click ⬚New .

2. In the Account ID field, type **1040** and press **<Enter>**.

3. In the Description field, type **IRA Savings Account** and press **<Enter>**.

4. In the Account Type field, click on the down arrow. A list of account types drops down. Make sure that Cash is highlighted. If not, click once on Cash to select it.

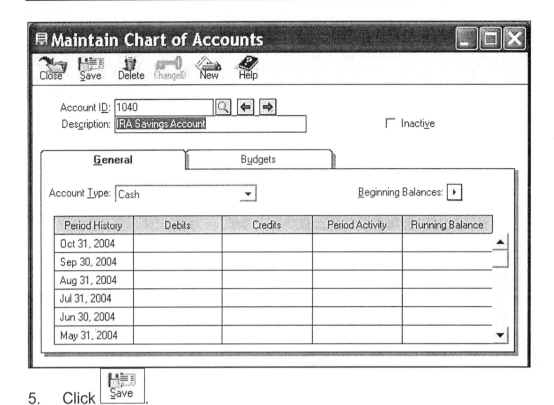

5. Click .

Add the following accounts:

Acct. ID	Account Description	Account Type
1045	WI State Retirement	Cash
1300	Prepaid Insurance	Other Current Assets
1450	Supplies	Other Current Assets
1510	Furniture	Fixed Assets
1520	Automobile	Fixed Assets
1910	Accum. Depreciation – Furnitur	Accumulated Depreciation
1920	Accum. Depreciation – Automobi	Accumulated Depreciation
6560	Internet Service Provider	Expenses
7060	Deprec. Exp. - Furniture	Expenses
7070	Deprec. Exp. - Automobile	Expenses

6.   Click 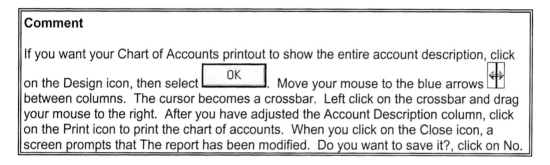 when you are through with the Chart of Accounts. You are returned to the menu bar.

Printing the Chart of Accounts

1.   From the menu bar, click on Reports, then General Ledger.

2.   At the Select a Report window, click on the Chart of Accounts to highlight it.

Comment

If you want your Chart of Accounts printout to show the entire account description, click on the Design icon, then select | OK |. Move your mouse to the blue arrows ⟷ between columns. The cursor becomes a crossbar. Left click on the crossbar and drag your mouse to the right. After you have adjusted the Account Description column, click on the Print icon to print the chart of accounts. When you click on the Close icon, a screen prompts that The report has been modified. Do you want to save it?, click on No.

---

3.   Click | Print |, then at the Chart of Accounts Filter window, click | OK |.

4.   At the Print window, click | OK | and the Chart of Accounts will start to print.

Taylor Rinaldi, Graphic Artist
Chart of Accounts
As of Oct 31, 2004

Filter Criteria includes: Report order is by ID. Report is printed with Accounts having Zero Amounts and in Detail Format.

Account ID	Account Description	Active?	Account Type
1010	Money Market Account	Yes	Cash
1020	Checking Account	Yes	Cash
1040	IRA Savings Account	Yes	Cash
1045	WI State Retirement	Yes	Cash
1100	Accounts Receivable	Yes	Accounts Receivable
1200	Inventory	Yes	Inventory
1300	Prepaid Insurance	Yes	Other Current Assets
1400	Prepaid Rent	Yes	Other Current Assets
1450	Supplies	Yes	Other Current Assets
1500	Computer Equipment	Yes	Fixed Assets
1510	Furniture	Yes	Fixed Assets
1520	Automobile	Yes	Fixed Assets
1900	Accum. Depreciation - Comp Eq	Yes	Accumulated Depreciation
1910	Accum. Depreciation - Furnitur	Yes	Accumulated Depreciation
1920	Accum. Depreciation - Automobi	Yes	Accumulated Depreciation
2000	VISA Payable	Yes	Accounts Payable
2380	Income Taxes Payable	Yes	Other Current Liabilities
2400	Publisher Advances	Yes	Other Current Liabilities
3910	Retained Earnings	Yes	Equity-Retained Earnings
3920	Taylor Rinaldi, Capital	Yes	Equity-doesn't close
3930	Taylor Rinaldi, Draw	Yes	Equity-gets closed
4000	Teaching Income	Yes	Income
4050	Royalty Income	Yes	Income
4100	Interest Income	Yes	Income
4200	Finance Charge Income	Yes	Income
4900	Sales/Fees Discounts	Yes	Income
5000	Cost of Sales	Yes	Cost of Sales
5400	Cost of Sales-Salary & Wage	Yes	Cost of Sales
6000	Wages Expense	Yes	Expenses
6100	Dues and Subscriptions	Yes	Expenses
6150	Auto Registration	Yes	Expenses
6200	Income Tax Expense	Yes	Expenses
6300	Rent or Lease Expense	Yes	Expenses
6350	Maintenance & Repairs Expense	Yes	Expenses
6400	Utilities Expense	Yes	Expenses
6450	Office Supplies Expense	Yes	Expenses
6500	Telephone Expense	Yes	Expenses
6550	My Long Distance	Yes	Expenses
6560	Internet Service Provider	Yes	Expenses
6600	Advertising Expense	Yes	Expenses
6800	Freight Expense	Yes	Expenses
6850	Bank Service Charge	Yes	Expenses
6900	Purchase Disc-Expense Items	Yes	Expenses
6950	Insurance Expense	Yes	Expenses
7050	Deprec. Exp. - Comp Eq	Yes	Expenses
7060	Deprec. Exp. - Furniture	Yes	Expenses
7070	Deprec. Exp. - Automobile	Yes	Expenses

Observe that the chart of accounts is dated As of Oct 31, 2004. Since Peachtree posts on the last day of the month, your reports will show October 31, 2004 as the date.

Notice that Taylor Rinaldi's chart of accounts includes Account No. 3910, Retained Earnings. At the end of every fiscal year, the temporary owner's equity accounts (revenues, expenses, and drawing) are closed to a permanent owner's equity account. In PCA, there are two permanent owner's equity accounts: the owner's capital account and the Retained Earnings account. PCA closes the temporary accounts to the Retained Earnings account. This will be discussed in more detail in Chapter 10 when you close the fiscal year.

5. Click to return to the menu bar. Check your Chart of Accounts to make sure that you have deleted accounts and made the necessary changes and additions. If you need to edit your Chart, select Maintain, then Chart of Accounts.

The next section describes how to enter the chart of accounts beginning balances. After entering the beginning balances and using Windows Explorer (pages 269 and 270) to see the size of Taylor Rinaldi's company file, you will back up the company's data.

ENTERING CHART OF ACCOUNTS BEGINNING BALANCES

Mr. Rinaldi has hired you to do his monthly record keeping. In order to begin accounting tasks for Mr. Rinaldi, you asked him for a *Balance Sheet*. As you know from your study of accounting, a Balance Sheet lists the types and amounts of assets, liabilities, and equity as of a specific date. A balance sheet is also called a *statement of financial position*.

Taylor Rinaldi, Graphic Artist Balance Sheet **October 1, 2004**		
ASSETS		
Current Assets		
Money Market Account	$ 4,370.85	
Checking Account	6,949.78	
IRA Savings Account	25,750.32	
WI State Retirement	32,411.75	
Prepaid Insurance	2,100.00	
Prepaid Rent	600.00	
Supplies	<u>1,771.83</u>	
Total Current Assets		$ 73,954.53
Property and Equipment		
Computer Equipment	$ 6,800.00	
Furniture	5,000.00	
Automobile	<u>19,000.00</u>	
Total Property and Equipment		<u>30,800.00</u>
Total Assets		$ 104,754.53
LIABILITIES AND CAPITAL		
Current Liabilities		
VISA Payable	$ 6,243.85	
Total Current Liabilities		$ 6,243.85
Capital		
Taylor Rinaldi, Capital		<u>98,510.68</u>
Total Liabilities and Capital		$ 104,754.53

The information in this Balance Sheet will be the basis for recording Mr. Rinaldi's beginning balances.

Follow these steps to record Taylor Rinaldi's opening entry.

1. Click on Maintain, then Chart of Accounts.

2. Click on the arrow 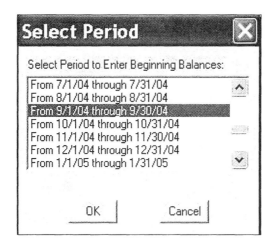 next to Beginning Balances.

   Observe that the balance sheet on page 264 is for October 1, 2004. In step 3, you will set beginning balances. **Beginning balances must be set for the preceding month–September 1 through 30, 2004**. You select September 1 through 30, 2004, because Peachtree posts on the last day of the month (September 30). When you select September 1 through 30, 2004, as your chart of accounts beginning balance period, your journals will start on October 1, 2004, and your reports will be dated October 31, 2004. *The September 30 ending balance is the October 1 beginning balance.*

   In Chapter 10, you will print end-of-year financial statements. In order for your end-of-year financial statements to show the correct current month and year-to-date amounts, you *must* set your beginning balances for the preceding month. *Remember, you must select September 1 through 30, 2004, as the period for setting beginning balances. The beginning balance period cannot be changed later.*

3. Scroll down the Select Period list. Click on From 9/1/04 through 9/30/04 to highlight it.

Select Period

Select Period to Enter Beginning Balances:

From 7/1/04 through 7/31/04
From 8/1/04 through 8/31/04
From 9/1/04 through 9/30/04
From 10/1/04 through 10/31/04
From 11/1/04 through 11/30/04
From 12/1/04 through 12/31/04
From 1/1/05 through 1/31/05

OK   Cancel

Double-check this screen. The period you select is very important –From 9/1/04 through 9/30/04.

4. Check that you have selected the correct period: **From 9/1/04 through 9/30/04**. You cannot change this period later. *Make sure the period is correct*, then click [OK].

5. The Chart of Accounts Beginning Balances window appears. The Assets, Expenses column is highlighted. Account No. 1010, Money Market Account is selected. A magenta line is placed around the row. Type **4370.85** in the Assets, Expenses column. Press **<Enter>**.

6. Account No. 1020, Checking Account is selected. Type **6949.78** and press **<Enter>**.

   Continue entering the beginning balances using the Balance Sheet on page 264. For credit balances, if necessary, click on the Liabilities, Equity, Income column. When you are finished, the Assets, Expenses column equals the Liabilities, Equity, Income column. This indicates that there are equal debits and credits.

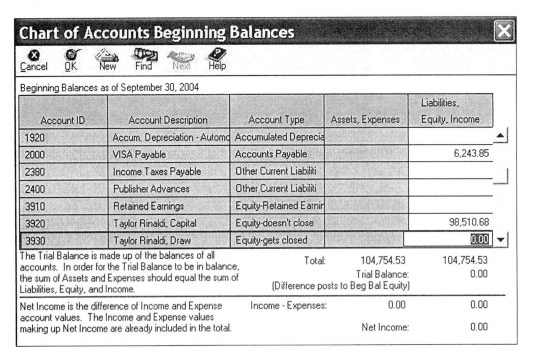

Comment

What if your Trial Balance does *not* show 0.00? Make sure that debit balances for assets and credit balances for liabilities and capital accounts were entered correctly.

Make sure that your beginning balances are as of September 30, 2004. If you enter your balances for the wrong month (period), your financial statements will not show the current month and year-to-date amounts correctly. To check your chart of accounts beginning balances, select Maintain, Chart of Accounts, Beginning Balances; then select the month shown on your Chart of Accounts Beginning Balances screen. Make any needed corrections. Refer to pages 263-267 for setting the chart of accounts beginning balances correctly.

7. Click [OK]. A window pops up briefly that says Creating Journal Entries.

8. At the Maintain Chart of Accounts window, click [Close]. You are returned to the menu bar.

Follow these steps to print a Balance Sheet:

1. From the menu bar, select Reports, then Financial Statements. The

   <Standard> Balance Sheet is highlighted. Click [Print].

2. The <Standard> Balance Sheet Options window pops up. Click [OK].

3. At the Print window, click [OK]. The Balance Sheet starts to print. Compare your balance sheet to the one shown on the next page. Your account balances should match the ones shown on page 264.

		Taylor Rinaldi, Graphic Artist
		Balance Sheet
		October 31, 2004

ASSETS

Current Assets		
Money Market Account	$ 4,370.85	
Checking Account	6,949.78	
IRA Savings Account	25,750.32	
WI State Retirement	32,411.75	
Prepaid Insurance	2,100.00	
Prepaid Rent	600.00	
Supplies	1,771.83	
Total Current Assets		73,954.53
Property and Equipment		
Computer Equipment	6,800.00	
Furniture	5,000.00	
Automobile	19,000.00	
Total Property and Equipment		30,800.00
Other Assets		
Total Other Assets		0.00
Total Assets		$ 104,754.53

LIABILITIES AND CAPITAL

Current Liabilities		
VISA Payable	$ 6,243.85	
Total Current Liabilities		6,243.85
Long-Term Liabilities		
Total Long-Term Liabilities		0.00
Total Liabilities		6,243.85
Capital		
Taylor Rinaldi, Capital	98,510.68	
Net Income	0.00	
Total Capital		98,510.68
Total Liabilities & Capital		$ 104,754.53

The Preview icon (Preview) was used to display the balance sheet shown above.

4. Click Close to return to the menu bar.

USING WINDOWS EXPLORER TO SEE THE FILE SIZE

To see the size of your Taylor Rinaldi, Graphic Artist file, following these steps.

1. Go to Windows Explorer.

2. Double-click on the folder for Peachtree. The default program and data path is C:\Program Files\Peachtree\Company.

3. Right-click on the subfolder for tayringr.

4. Left-click on Properties. (Your screen may differ.)

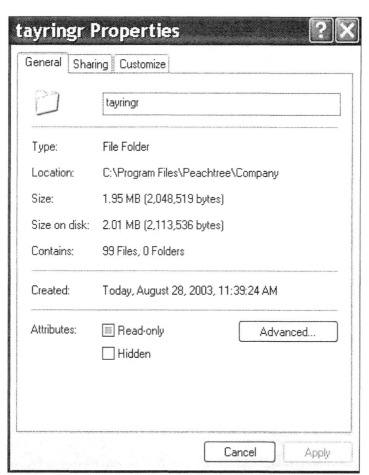

Observe that the size of the file is 1.95 MB (1,950,000 bytes) and that 2,048,519 bytes are used. That means if you want to save all the data contained in Taylor Rinaldi's file, you should use Windows Explorer to copy, then paste the tayringr subfolder from drive C to either a Zip disk or CD. The tayringr folder is too large for a floppy disk. If you use Windows Explorer to copy/paste, you will need a Zip disk or CD because of the size of the Taylor Rinaldi, Graphic Artist subfolder. (Your file size may differ from the tayringr Properties screen shown on page 269. This is okay.)

When you are finished comparing your properties screen, click 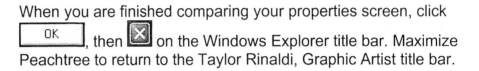, then ☒ on the Windows Explorer title bar. Maximize Peachtree to return to the Taylor Rinaldi, Graphic Artist title bar.

BACKING UP COMPANY DATA

At this point you should back up your data. When using PCA, information is automatically saved to the hard drive of the computer. In a classroom setting, a number of students may be using the same computer. This means that when you return to the computer lab, your data will be gone. Backing up your data simply means saving it to a floppy disk, so that it will be available when you want to work again.

You will back up all your data to a floppy disk in drive A. You may reformat the disks used in Part 1 of the book. The chart on page 246 shows you that you can use two blank, formatted disks to back up the data in Chapter 9, including the end-of-chapter exercises.

When you make this back up, you are saving the new company set up information, the revised chart of accounts, and the chart of accounts beginning balances.

Comment

The author suggests using two blank, formatted disks to make the four backups in Chapter 9. Since PCA compresses the backup file, you can use two disks to back up data in Chapter 9 and the end-of-chapter work (Exercises 9-1 and 9-2).

When you back up, you are saving the current point in Peachtree. Each time you make a backup, you should type a different backup name (file name) to distinguish between them. In this way, if you need to restore to an earlier backup, you have the data for that purpose.

When you begin Chapter 10, you will use another blank, formatted disk to back up. Remember, you can Restore if you need to go back to an earlier point in the company's data. Without a backup disk, you cannot go back to an earlier point in the data. Since Chapters 9 and 10 work together, your back up disks are important. They should be stored in a safe place.

In the business world, backups are unique to each business: daily, weekly, monthly. *Remember, back up before you leave the computer lab!*

Follow these steps to back up Taylor Rinaldi's company:

1. Put a blank, formatted disk in drive A. The text directions that follow assume you are using drive A for backing up. (You may also back up to the hard drive or network.)

2. From the menu bar, select File, then Back up. The Back Up Company window appears. Read the information on this screen.

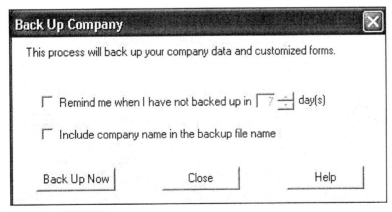

3. Click [Back Up Now].

---

4. Click on the down-arrow in the Save in field. If necessary, scroll up the list, then click on 3½ Floppy (A:) to select drive A.

 Read Me: *What if you do* not *want to back up to a floppy disk?*

The instructions that follow show you how to back up to a floppy disk in drive A. You may also accept the default location and back up to drive C; for example, c:\Program Files\Peachtree\Company\tayringr. If you used a unique company name, your subfolder (or data path) location will differ. Or, select the appropriate location to back up to the network.

5. Type **Chapter 9 Begin** in the File name field.

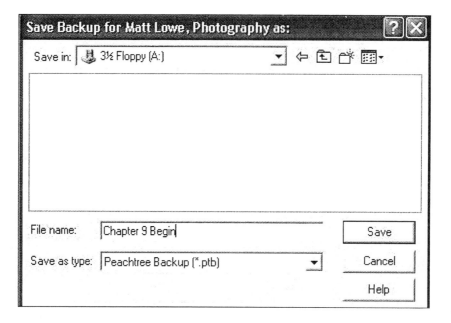

Observe that the Save as type field shows that you are making a Peachtree Backup (*.ptb), which is abbreviated ptb. This is the standard default for Peachtree backups.

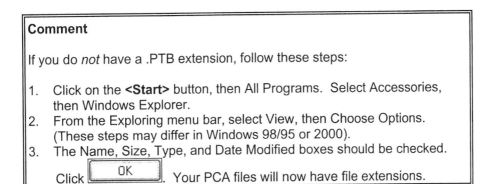

6. Click [Save].

7. When the screen prompts that This company backup will require approximately 1 diskette, click [OK].

8. When the screen prompts you to insert the first disk, click [OK]. When the Back Up Company scale is 100% completed, you have successfully backed up to the current point in Chapter 9. You are returned to the menu bar.

9. Click on File, Exit to exit Peachtree.

Follow these steps to see the size of the backup file.

1. Go to Windows Explorer.

2. From Windows Explorer, go to drive A. Compare your screen to the one shown below. You may need to click on View, then Details to see drive A displayed similarly.

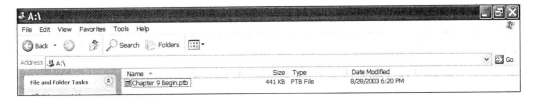

The Name of the file is Chapter 9 Begin.ptb; the Size of the file is 441 KB (441 kilobytes or 441,000 bytes); the Type is PTB File; and the Date Modified shows the date and time of the back up. Your date and time will differ. Since the backup file is 441 KB, and a disk holds 1.44MB of data, you will be able to save all of Chapter 9 on one blank, formatted disk. *(Your file size may differ slightly.)*

RESTORING COMPANY DATA

After completing new company setup, editing the chart of accounts, and entering beginning balances you backed up (saved) Taylor Rinaldi, Graphic Artist company information. In order to start where you left off the last time you backed up, you use the Restore command.

In the steps that follow you are shown how to restore the Peachtree backup file (.ptb extension). You made this backup on pages 270-273. Peachtree backups are compressed files.

1. Start Windows and Peachtree in the usual way.

2. On the startup screen, click on Open an existing company. (You can also click File, New Company from the menu bar.)

3. When the Open an Existing Company window appears, select Taylor Rinaldi, Graphic Artist.

> **Troubleshooting: What if Taylor Rinaldi, Graphic Artist (or another name, Graphic Artist) is not shown on the Open an Existing Company screen; Company Name list?**

  a. Click [Browse] to open another existing company. The Open Company window pops up.

  b. If Taylor Rinaldi, Graphic Artist (or, other name Graphic Artist) is shown select it, and then click [OK]. Go to page 275, step 4, and follow the steps to restore your data.

  c. If no Graphic Artist company is shown, click [Cancel]. Then, select [Close]; Close this window. There are three menu bar options: File, Options and Help. Click File; Restore.

d. The Select Backup File window appears. Click Browse . Put
    your backup disk in drive A. In the Look in field, select drive A or
    the location of your backup file.

e. Select the file you just backed up, Chapter 9 Begin.ptb; click
    Open .

f. Make sure the Location field shows the correct path for your file
    (A:\Chapter 9 Begin.ptb; *or* the location where your backup file
    resides.) Click Next > .

g. The Select Company screen appears. Click on the radio button
    next to A New Company.

 Read Me

Observe that there are two options on the Select Company screen: An Existing
Company *and* A New Company. If you select A New Company, then the company will
be named exactly as the backup file you selected. You can restore to an existing
company—one that is previously set up—*or* you can restore to a new company,
bypassing the process of setting up a new company.

Let's say you wanted to restore a backup file for a company that was *not* set up in
Peachtree. Some computer labs delete subdirectories from the hard drive; for example,
you have a back up file but the company, in this case Taylor Rinaldi, Graphic Artist, is
not listed as a Peachtree company.

If you start Peachtree and you *cannot* select the appropriate company, use the Restore
Wizard to select A New Company. Using your backup file, and the selection for A New
Company, you are able to start where you left off the last time you used Peachtree.

---

h. The Company Name field shows Taylor Rinaldi, Graphic Artist.
    The Location field shows C:\Program Files\Peachtree\
    Company\tayringr. (If you used your first and last name the
    Company Name field and Location field will differ.) Click
    Next > . Continue with step 11 on page 276.

4. Put your Chapter 9 Begin.ptb backup disk in drive A. You made this
    backup on pages 271-273.

---

5. From the menu bar, click File, Restore. The Restore Wizard – Select Backup File screen appears. Click | Browse |.

6. Click on the down-arrow in the Look in field. Then click on 3½ Floppy (A:) to select drive A (or the appropriate location of your backup file).

7. Click on the Chapter 9 Begin.ptb file to highlight it. The File name field displays Chapter 9 Begin.

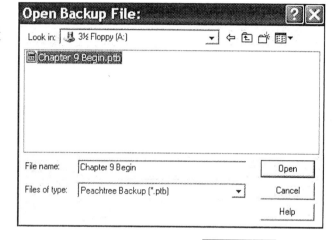

8. Click | Open |.

9. Make sure that the Location field shows A:\Chapter 9 Begin.ptb

(or the appropriate location for your backup file). Click | Next > |.

10. From the Select Company screen make sure that the radio button next to An Existing Company is selected. The Company name field shows your first and last name, Graphic Artist; the Location field shows C:\ProgramFiles\Peachtree\Company\tayringr (or the appropriate location on your computer). Click | Next > |.

11. The Restore Options screen appears. Make sure that the box next to Company Data is *checked*. Click | Next > |.

12. The Confirmation screen appears. Check the From and To fields to make sure they are correct. Click | Finish |. When the Restore Company scale is 100% completed, your data is restored and you are returned to the menu bar.

13. Remove the backup disk.

Now that you have restored Taylor Rinaldi's data, you are ready to continue. *Remember before you exit PCA, make a backup of your work.*

> **Comment**
>
> In Chapter 2 on page 59, you were instructed to make sure that manual was selected for 2 decimal places. If you did *not* do this on page 59, follow these steps:
>
> 1. From the menu bar, click on Options, then Global.
> 2. In the Decimal Entry field, click on Manual. When Manual is selected, a black circle is placed within a circle (radio button).
> 3. In the Number of decimal places field, make sure the number **2** is selected.
> 4. Click OK .
>
> You should also check the Global Settings shown on page 56. In order for your task screens to look like the ones shown in this textbook, you need to have the *same* global settings as the ones shown in Chapter 2. When global options are selected, this feature is in effect for all companies.

You just learned how to use information from a Balance Sheet for an opening entry and then you saved your beginning or starting data. Now you are going to see how Mr. Rinaldi's check register can provide information for Cash Receipts Journal entries and Cash Disbursements Journal entries for the month of October 2004.

RECORDING ENTRIES IN THE CASH RECEIPTS JOURNAL AND CASH DISBURSEMENTS JOURNAL

In PCA, the Receipts window is used to record deposits. When you save a receipt, PCA automatically journalizes the entry in the Cash Receipts Journal. When Mr. Rinaldi writes a check, this disbursement is recorded in the Write Checks window. When you save the recorded check, PCA automatically journalizes the entry in the Cash Disbursements Journal.

Peachtree's write checks task is a simplified version of the Payments window. Like the Payments window, Write Checks lets you write a check for expenses, assets, or owner's draw. Unlike Payments, the Write Checks task does *not* let you pay vendor invoices (making vendor payments will be shown in Chapter 11, Accounts Payable). Write Checks is your choice whenever you want to make payments for expenses or assets that do *not* involve invoices or the need to track inventory.

Mr. Rinaldi's check register will supply the information necessary to record entries for the month of October. Since Mr. Rinaldi is a new client, information from his Balance Sheet was used for an opening entry. Now his check register will supply financial information for the rest of the month.

Follow these steps to show the cash balance on the Receipts window and Payments window.

1. From the menu bar, click on Options, Global.

2. Make sure the box next to Recalculate cash balance automatically in Receipts, Payments,

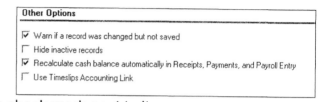

    and Payroll Entry has a check mark next to it.

3. Click [OK]. When you use the Receipts window or Write Checks window, you will see that your check register's balance agrees with the cash balance in these screens.

Mr. Rinaldi's check register shows an October 2 deposit of $12,000. A section of Mr. Rinaldi's check register is shown below.

Check Number	Date	Description of Transaction	Payment	Deposit	Balance
					6,949.78
	10/1	Deposit (publisher's advance)		12,000.00	18,949.78

Follow these steps to record the October 2 deposit from Mr. Rinaldi's check register:

1. From the menu bar, select Tasks, then Receipts. The Select a Cash Account window displays. If necessary click on the down arrow to select the Checking Account.

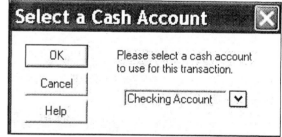

2. Click [OK]. The Receipts window displays.

3. Your cursor is in the Deposit ticket ID field. Type **10/01/04**. (*Hint: Use the date of the deposit for the Deposit ticket ID field.*)

4. Click on the Name field. Type **Deposit** in the Name field.

5. Click on the Reference field. Type **Advance** in the Reference field. Press **<Enter>** two times.

6. Accept the default for Oct 1, 2004 in the Date field by pressing **<Enter>**.

7. Verify that the Payment Method is Check and that Account No. 1020, Checking Account, is displayed in the Cash Account lookup field.

8. The Balance field displays $6,949.78. This agrees with the partial check register balance shown on page 278.

9. Make sure that the Apply to Revenues tab is selected. Click once on the Quantity column. Type **1** in the Quantity column. Press the **<Enter>** key two times.

10. Type **Publisher's advance** in the Description column. Press **<Enter>**.

11. Click 🔍 in the GL Account column. Select Account No. 2400, Publisher Advances.

12. Type **12000** in the Unit Price column.

Comment

When you enter **12000** does 120.00 display in the Unit Price field rather than 12,000.00? To change the global settings for two decimal places, follow these steps. (These steps are also shown on page 59.)

1. From the menu bar, click on Options, then Global.
2. In the Decimal Entry field, click on Manual. When Manual is selected, a black circle is placed within a circle (radio button).
3. In the Number of decimal places field, make sure the number **2** is selected.
4. Click [OK].

When global options are selected, this feature is in effect for all companies.

---

13. Press the **<Enter>** key two times. If your screen looks different, refer to the global settings, page 56.

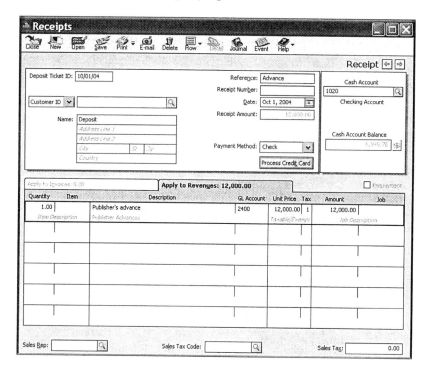

14. Click ![Save] to post this entry. After you post, the Balance field shows the same balance, $18,949.78, as the partial check register shown on page 278. The Receipts window is ready for another transaction and the transaction is posted to the Cash Receipts Journal.

15. Click ![Close] to close the Receipts window. Or, you can minimize the Receipts window by clicking on the minimize button ![minimize] on the Receipts window title bar.

You will use the Write Checks task for Check No. 5001. A section of the check register is shown.

Check Number	Date	Description of Transaction	Payment	Deposit	Balance
					6,949.78
	10/1	*Deposit (publisher's advance)*		*12,000.00*	*18,949.78*
5001	**10/2**	**Transfer to Money Market Account**	**6,000.00**		**12,949.78**

Follow these steps to enter Check No. 5001 and post it to the Cash Disbursements Journal.

1. From the menu bar, click on Tasks, then Write Checks. The Select a Cash Account window displays. If necessary, click on the down arrow to select the Checking Account.

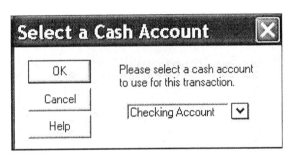

2. Click [OK] .

3. The Write Check window displays. Click on the Pay to the Order of field. Type **Money Market Account**.

4. Click 🔍 in the Expense Account field. The Chart of Accounts list is displayed. Even though you are *not* charging Check No. 5001 against an expense account, you use the Expense Account field to select the appropriate account. Select Account No.1010, Money Market Account. The Description field is automatically completed with Money Market Account.

5. Click on the Check Number field. Type **5001** in the Check Number field and press **<Enter>**.

6. Type **2** in the Date field and press **<Enter>**.

7. Verify that the Balance field displays $18,949.78. This agrees with the partial check register above (beginning balance plus publisher's advance). If the Balance field does not agree with your check register, see the instructions on page 277 for setting the global option for recalculating the cash balance for receipts, payments, and payroll.

8. Type **6000** in the $ field. Press **<Enter>**. Observe that the check is completed.

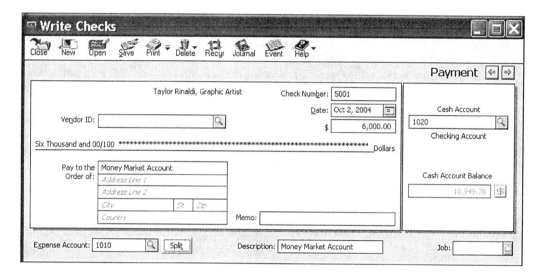

9. Click [Save] to post your entry to the Cash Disbursements Journal. Verify that your Balance field displays the October 2 balance (this is the same balance, $12,949.78, as the partial check register on page 281). You are ready for your next transaction. (*Hint: you may need to change the date to 10/2/04 to see the correct cash balance.*)

10. Click [Close] to return to the menu bar. Or, minimize the Write Checks window.

Comment

PCA automatically completes the Check Number field once the first number is typed. After you type another reference in the Check Number field (for example, ATM), then you will have to type the appropriate check number.

In your study of accounting, you have learned that source documents are used to show written evidence of a business transaction. Examples of source documents are sales invoices, purchase invoices, and in this case, Mr. Rinaldi's check register for his checking account.

Starting with the ATM withdrawal on October 3 for $200, record the transactions shown in the check register on pages 284 and 285 in the Cash Disbursements Journal (Tasks/Write Checks) or Cash Receipts Journal (Tasks/Receipts). Assign each transaction in the check register an appropriate account number from Mr. Rinaldi's Chart of Accounts. Some of the transactions listed in Mr. Rinaldi's check register are for the same date. Record individual journal entries for each check number, deposit, or ATM transaction.

Each deposit (cash or check received) is a debit to Account No. 1020, Checking Account, and is recorded in the Cash Receipts Journal using the Receipts task. On the Receipts window, you select the appropriate general ledger account for the credit part of the entry. The debit part of the entry is automatically entered for Account No. 1020, Checking Account.

Each payment (check issued and ATM withdrawal) listed on the check register is a credit to Account No. 1020, Checking Account, and is recorded in the Cash Disbursements Journal using the Write Checks task. On the Write Checks window, you select the appropriate general ledger account for the debit part of the entry. The credit part of the entry is automatically entered for Account No. 1020, Checking Account.

After recording each check, deposit, or ATM, you should verify that the Balance field on the Write Checks and Receipts window agrees with the check register balances on pages 284-285. You have already entered the first two transactions for October 1 and October 2. Continue recording entries with the October 3 ATM transaction.

Remember to click [Save] *to post each transaction in the check register. Each saved entry in the check register is a transaction.*

Read Me: *Why should I use the Write Checks task instead of the Payments task?*

The Write Checks window is a simplified version of the Payments window. Both the Write Checks task and the Payments task post to the Cash Disbursements Journal. In Chapters 9 and 10, you will use the Write Checks window for checks and ATM withdrawals. You could use the Payments task for checks and ATMs but it is quicker to use the Write Checks task.

Check Number	Date	Description of Transaction	Payment	Deposit	Balance
					6,949.78
	10/1	Deposit (publisher's advance)		12,000.00	18,949.78
5001	10/2	Transfer to Money Market Fund	6,000.00		12,949.78
	10/3	ATM[4]	200.00		12,749.78
	10/4	Deposit (book royalty)		3,950.95	16,700.73
5002	10/4	Office Equipment & More (hardware upgrade; computer equipment)	1,235.79		15,464.94
5003	10/9	U.S. Post Office (stamps)[5]	37.00		15,427.94
5004	10/9	The Journal (newspaper subscription)[6]	53.00		15,374.94
5005	10/9	Midwest Gas (utilities)	42.89		15,332.05
5006	10/10	Dept. of Water and Power[7]	85.50		15,246.55
5007	10/10	The Telephone Co. (telephone expense)	43.20		15,203.35

[4]For each ATM transaction use Account No. 3930, Taylor Rinaldi, Draw. Type **ATM** in the Check Number field and Pay to the Order of field. For the next check, you will need to type the check number in the Check Number field.

[5]Add account No. 7400, Postage Expense. (*Hint: On the toolbar, click* to add *an account on the fly.*)

[6]Debit Account No. 6100, Dues and Subscriptions.

[7]Add Account No. 6420, Water and Power Expense.

5008	10/10	My Long Distance	62.75		15,140.60
	10/11	ATM[8]	400.00		14,740.60
	10/14	Deposit (Glendale Community College)		2,635.80	17,376.40
5009	10/14	Clarke Parts (car headlight - auto expenses)[9]	214.00		17,162.40
5010	10/14	Veronica Hughes (install headlight)	105.00		17,057.40
5011	10/29	Dept. of Motor Vehicles (car registration)	185.00		16,872.40
5012	10/29	The Office Place (letterhead and envelopes)[10]	219.65		16,652.75
5013	10/30	Internet Service Provider	25.95		16,626.80

You may want to back up your data before you do account reconciliation. A suggested file name for this optional back up is a:\Chapter 9 Check Register October.

ACCOUNT RECONCILIATION

Taylor Rinaldi receives a bank statement every month for his checking account (Account No. 1020) from Merchant's Bank. The bank statement shows which checks and deposits have cleared the bank. PCA's Account Reconciliation feature allows you to reconcile his bank statement. Mr. Rinaldi's bank statement for his Checking Account is shown on the next page.

---

[8]If you typed ATM in the Check Number field for the October 3 withdrawal, a WARNING! That reference number has already been entered for this Cash Account displays. Click OK.

[9]Add Account No. 6180, Automobile Expense.

[10]Debit, Account No. 1450, Supplies.

Statement of Account			Taylor Rinaldi, Graphic Artist
Merchant's Bank			8711 University Avenue
October 1 to October 31, 2004		Account # 93244-9123	Glendale, WI 53239
REGULAR CHECKING			
Previous Balance		$ 6,949.78	
3 Deposits (+)		18,586.75	
9 checks (-)		7,836.24	
2 Other Deductions (-)		600.00	
Service Charges (-)	10/31/04	8.00	
Ending Balance	10/31/04	**$17,092.29**	
DEPOSITS			
	10/4/04	12,000.00	
	10/7/04	3,950.95	
	10/17/04	2,635.80	
CHECKS (Asterisk * indicates break in check number sequence)			
	10/2/04	5001	6,000.00	
	10/6/04	5002	1,235.79	
	10/15/04	5003	37.00	
	10/16/04	5004	53.00	
	10/16/04	5006*	85.50	
	10/17/04	5007	43.20	
	10/20/04	5008	62.75	
	10/23/04	5009	214.00	
	10/30/04	5010	105.00	
OTHER DEDUCTIONS (ATM's)			
	10/3/04	ATM	200.00	
	10/13/04	ATM	400.00	

Follow these steps to reconcile your bank statement balance to Account No. 1020, Checking Account.

1. From the menu bar, select Tasks, then Account Reconciliation.

2. In the Account to Reconcile field, select Account No. 1020, Checking Account.

3. Did you notice that the bank statement shows a service charge of $8? In the Service charges field type **8** on the Account Reconciliation screen. The Date defaults to October 31, 2004. In the Account field, select Account No. 6850, Bank Service Charge.

4. In the Statement Ending Balance field (at the bottom of the screen), type **17092.29**. (This is the ending balance on Mr. Rinaldi's bank statement.)

5. In the Checks and Credits table, place a check mark <✓> in the Clear column for the bank service charge and each check and ATM transaction that is listed on the bank statement.   Do not check off the outstanding checks: 5005, 5011, 5012, 5013.

6. In the Deposits & Debits table, place a check mark <✓> in the Clear column for each deposit that is listed on the bank statement. Compare your screen to the one shown on the next page.

Comment
Observe that the Unreconciled Difference is zero (0.00). This zero balance is proof that Account No. 1020, Checking Account, is reconciled.
The GL (System) Balance is $16,618.80. The check register on pages 284-285 shows an ending balance of $16,626.80. When you subtract the service charge of $8, the check register balance (16,626.80 – 8 = 16,618.80), agrees with the GL (System) Balance.

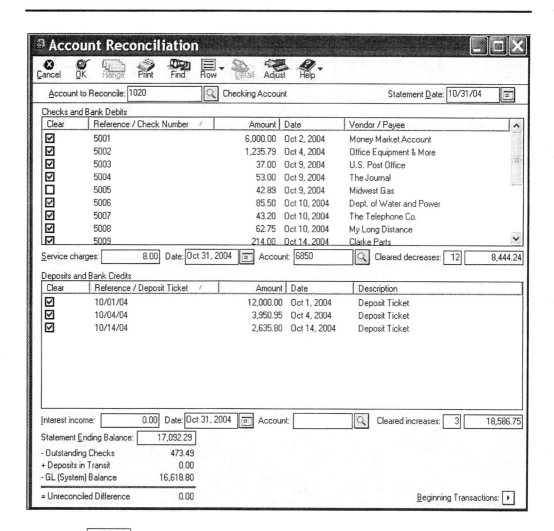

7. Click OK when you are finished.

The Account Reconciliation feature allows you to adjust Mr. Rinaldi's bank statement. Another name for this is *bank reconciliation* – the process of bringing the balance of the bank statement and the balance of the cash account into agreement. The Account Reconciliation feature applies to other accounts, too.

DISPLAYING THE CASH ACCOUNT REGISTER

Entries for Write Checks and the Receipts task, are also placed in PCA's Account Register. To see the Account Register follow these steps.

1. From the menu bar, select Tasks; then Account Register.

2. Compare your Account Register screen to your check register on pages 284 and 285. Click ▣ to enlarge your screen. If necessary, scroll down the Account Register screen to see all of the entries.

Edit	Date	Type	Payee/Paid By		Payment	Receipt	Balance
		Reference	GL Account	Memo		Sales Tax	
	Oct 1, 2004		Opening Balance			6,949.78	6,949.78
	Oct 1, 2004	Receipt	Deposit			12,000.00	18,949.78
		Advance	2400	10/01/04			
	Oct 2, 2004	Wrt. Chks.	Money Market Account		6,000.00		12,949.78
		5001	1010				
	Oct 3, 2004	Wrt. Chks.	ATM		200.00		12,749.78
		ATM	3930				
	Oct 4, 2004	Receipt	Deposit			3,950.95	16,700.73
		Book royalty	4050	10/04/04			
	Oct 4, 2004	Wrt. Chks.	Office Equipment & M		1,235.79		15,464.94
		5002	1500				
	Oct 9, 2004	Wrt. Chks.	U.S. Post Office		37.00		15,427.94
		5003	7400				
	Oct 9, 2004	Wrt. Chks.	The Journal		53.00		15,374.94
		5004	6100				
	Oct 9, 2004	Wrt. Chks.	Midwest Gas		42.89		15,332.05
		5005	6400				
	Oct 10, 2004	Wrt. Chks.	Dept. of Water and P		85.50		15,246.55
		5006	6420				
	Oct 10, 2004	Wrt. Chks.	The Telephone Co.		43.20		15,203.35
		5007	6500				
	Oct 10, 2004	Wrt. Chks.	My Long Distance		62.75		15,140.60
		5008	6550				
	Oct 11, 2004	Wrt. Chks.	ATM		400.00		14,740.60
		ATM	3930				
	Oct 14, 2004	Receipt	Deposit: Glendale Co			2,635.80	17,376.40
		Deposit	4000	10/14/04			
	Oct 14, 2004	Wrt. Chks.	Clarke Parts		214.00		17,162.40
		5009	6180				
	Oct 14, 2004	Wrt. Chks.	Veronica Hughes		105.00		17,057.40
		5010	6180				
	Oct 29, 2004	Wrt. Chks.	Dept. of Motor Vehic		185.00		16,872.40
		5011	6150				
	Oct 29, 2004	Wrt. Chks.	The Office Place		219.65		16,652.75
		5012	1450				
	Oct 30, 2004	Wrt. Chks.	Internet Service Pro		25.95		16,626.80
		5013	6560				
	Oct 31, 2004	Gen. Jrnl.			8.00		16,618.80
		10/31/04	6850				

(Cash Account: 1020 — Checking Account. Show transactions for: This Period)

PCA's Account Register lists your payments and receipts similarly to the check register on pages 284-285. If you notice a discrepancy use **drill down** to follow the path of the transaction's origin. Follow these steps to use drill down.

a. Double-click on the first Oct. 4, 2004 transaction (Receipt for $3,950.95). Notice that your cursor turns into a magnifying glass with a Z in the center

Oct 4, 2004	Receipt
	Book royalty

.

b. The Receipts window appears with the October 4, 2004 deposit shown.

c. If there is no need to make a correction, close the Receipts window. You are returned to the Account Register screen.

Notice that the Account Register screen includes a Reconcile icon . This is another way to perform account reconciliation. In the preceding section, you selected Account Reconciliation from the Tasks menu.

3. Click on the down arrow next to the Print icon; then click 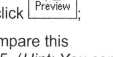; OK . The Cash Account Register appears. Compare this information with the check register on pages 284-285. (*Hint: You can also display the Cash Account Register from the Reports menu; select General Ledger, then Cash Account Register.*)

Observe that the register shows the Opening Balance; deposits (Receipt Amt); Checks, ATMs, bank service charge (Gen. Jrnl.). Compare your screen to the one shown on the next page. It is okay if the deposit explanations in the Reference columns differ. Notice that the Memo column displays the information that you typed in the Deposit ID box.

You can also drill down from the Cash Account Register to the Write Checks, Receipts, or General Journal windows. Drill down allows you to show the origin of your entry. For example, if you double-click on the check number, you will go to the Write Checks window; if you double-click on the 10/31/04 entry for the bank service charge (8.00) you will go to the General Journal Entry window.

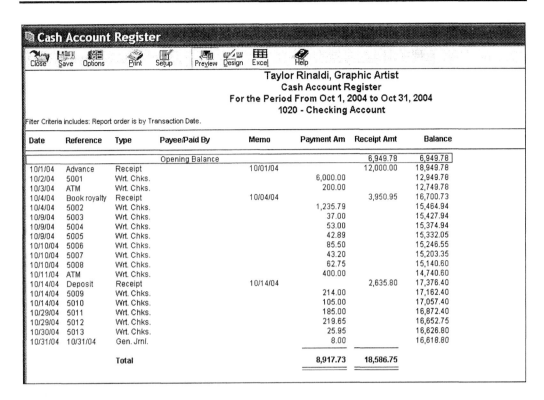

4. Close the Cash Account Register screen. Close the Account Register.

5. Follow these steps to display the General Journal.

   a. From the menu bar, click Reports, and then select General Ledger.

   b. Click on General Journal; then click [Preview], [OK].

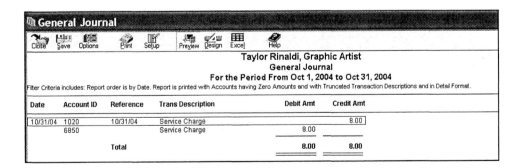

PRINTING THE CASH RECEIPTS JOURNAL

Follow these steps to print the Cash Receipts Journal:

1. From the menu bar, click on Reports, and then select Accounts Receivable.

2. Highlight Cash Receipts Journal.

3. Click [Print]. The Cash Receipts Journal Filter window displays. Click [OK].

4. The Print window pops up. Click [OK].

Page: 1

Taylor Rinaldi, Graphic Artist
Cash Receipts Journal
For the Period From Oct 1, 2004 to Oct 31, 2004
Filter Criteria includes: Report order is by Check Date. Report is printed in Detail Format.

Date	Account ID	Transaction Ref	Line Description	Debit Amnt	Credit Amnt
10/1/04	2400	Advance	Publisher's advance		12,000.00
	1020		Deposit	12,000.00	
10/4/04	4050	Book royalty	Royalty Income		3,950.95
	1020		Deposit	3,950.95	
10/14/0	4000	Deposit	Teaching Income		2,635.80
	1020		Deposit: Glendale Community Co	2,635.80	
				18,586.75	18,586.75

Comment

The information in the Transaction Ref column may differ. The information in this column is the same as what you typed in the Reference column of the Receipts window (Cash Receipts Journal).

PRINTING THE CASH DISBURSEMENTS JOURNAL

1. The Select a Report window should be displayed. In the Report Area, highlight Accounts Payable.

2. Highlight the Cash Disbursements Journal.

---

3. Click [Print]. The Cash Disbursements Journal Filter window displays. Click [OK].

4. The Print window pops up. Click [OK]

			Taylor Rinaldi, Graphic Artist		
			Cash Disbursements Journal		
			For the Period From Oct 1, 2004 to Oct 31, 2004		
Filter Criteria includes: Report order is by Date. Report is printed in Detail Format.					
Date	**Check #**	**Account ID**	**Line Description**	**Debit Amount**	**Credit Amount**
10/2/04	5001	1010	Money Market Account	6,000.00	
		1020	Money Market Account		6,000.00
10/3/04	ATM	3930	Taylor Rinaldi, Draw	200.00	
		1020	ATM		200.00
10/4/04	5002	1500	Computer Equipment	1,235.79	
		1020	Office Equipment & More		1,235.79
10/9/04	5003	7400	Postage Expense	37.00	
		1020	U.S. Post Office		37.00
10/9/04	5004	6100	Dues and Subscriptions	53.00	
		1020	The Journal		53.00
10/9/04	5005	6400	Utilities Expense	42.89	
		1020	Midwest Gas		42.89
10/10/04	5006	6420	Water and Power Expense	85.50	
		1020	Dept. of Water and Power		85.50
10/10/04	5007	6500	Telephone Expense	43.20	
		1020	The Telephone Co.		43.20
10/10/04	5008	6550	My Long Distance	62.75	
		1020	My Long Distance		62.75
10/11/04	ATM	3930	Taylor Rinaldi, Draw	400.00	
		1020	ATM		400.00
10/14/04	5009	6180	Automobile Expense	214.00	
		1020	Clarke Parts		214.00
10/14/04	5010	6180	Automobile Expense	105.00	
		1020	Veronica Hughes		105.00
10/29/04	5011	6150	Auto Registration	185.00	
		1020	Dept. of Motor Vehicles		185.00
10/29/04	5012	1450	Supplies	219.65	
		1020	The Office Place		219.65
10/30/04	5013	6560	Internet Service Provider	25.95	
		1020	Internet Service Provider		25.95
	Total			8,909.73	8,909.73

5. Return to the menu bar.

EDITING JOURNAL TRANSACTIONS

Compare your journal entries to the ones shown on pages 293 and 294. Some of the Line Descriptions may vary. That is okay. If your dates, check numbers, or account numbers are different, you should edit the journal entry. Follow these steps to edit the Cash Receipts Journal:

1. From the menu bar, click on Tasks, Receipts. The Receipts window displays.

2. Click [Open]. The Select Receipt window displays.

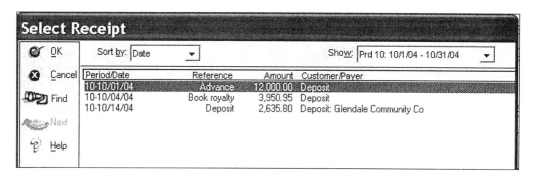

3. Highlight the journal entry that you want to edit, then click [OK].

4. This takes you to the Receipts window. Make any necessary corrections, then click [Save] to post.

5. If necessary, click [Close] to return to the menu bar.

6. Editing the Cash Disbursements Journal is similar. Go to the Write Checks task, and then click [Open]. Select the journal entry you want to change, make your changes, then click [Save] to post.

PREVIEWING THE GENERAL LEDGER TRIAL BALANCE

Follow these steps to preview (display) the General Ledger Trial Balance:

1. From the menu bar, click on Reports, General Ledger, then General Ledger Trial Balance.

2. Click `Preview` icon, then `OK`. Compare your General Ledger Trial Balance with the one shown.

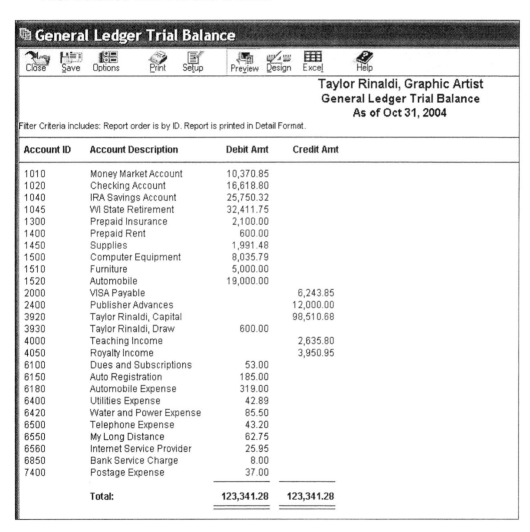

Account ID	Account Description	Debit Amt	Credit Amt
1010	Money Market Account	10,370.85	
1020	Checking Account	16,618.80	
1040	IRA Savings Account	25,750.32	
1045	WI State Retirement	32,411.75	
1300	Prepaid Insurance	2,100.00	
1400	Prepaid Rent	600.00	
1450	Supplies	1,991.48	
1500	Computer Equipment	8,035.79	
1510	Furniture	5,000.00	
1520	Automobile	19,000.00	
2000	VISA Payable		6,243.85
2400	Publisher Advances		12,000.00
3920	Taylor Rinaldi, Capital		98,510.68
3930	Taylor Rinaldi, Draw	600.00	
4000	Teaching Income		2,635.80
4050	Royalty Income		3,950.95
6100	Dues and Subscriptions	53.00	
6150	Auto Registration	185.00	
6180	Automobile Expense	319.00	
6400	Utilities Expense	42.89	
6420	Water and Power Expense	85.50	
6500	Telephone Expense	43.20	
6550	My Long Distance	62.75	
6560	Internet Service Provider	25.95	
6850	Bank Service Charge	8.00	
7400	Postage Expense	37.00	
	Total:	**123,341.28**	**123,341.28**

Taylor Rinaldi, Graphic Artist
General Ledger Trial Balance
As of Oct 31, 2004

Filter Criteria includes: Report order is by ID. Report is printed in Detail Format.

3. To print the general ledger trial balance, select `Print`, then make the selections to print.

Notice that the Checking Account (Account No. 1020) balance on the General Ledger Trial Balance and the GL (System) Balance on the Account Reconciliation screen illustration on page 288 are the same: $16,618.80.

PRINTING FINANCIAL STATEMENTS

The Computer Accounting Cycle shows that adjusting entries are needed at this point. (See the Computer Accounting Cycle on page 43.) There is no need to complete adjusting entries at the end of October since quarterly adjusting entries are done on December 31, 2004. Instead, you will print Mr. Rinaldi's financial statements.

Print the following financial statements:

1. <Standard> Balance Sheet.

2. <Standard> Income Stmnt (Income Statement).

You will print the other financial statements at the end of the quarter. Compare your balance sheet to the one shown on the next page.

		Taylor Rinaldi, Graphic Artist
		Balance Sheet
		October 31, 2004

ASSETS

Current Assets		
Money Market Account	$ 10,370.85	
Checking Account	16,618.80	
IRA Savings Account	25,750.32	
WI State Retirement	32,411.75	
Prepaid Insurance	2,100.00	
Prepaid Rent	600.00	
Supplies	1,991.48	
Total Current Assets		89,843.20
Property and Equipment		
Computer Equipment	8,035.79	
Furniture	5,000.00	
Automobile	19,000.00	
Total Property and Equipment		32,035.79
Other Assets		
Total Other Assets		0.00
Total Assets		$ 121,878.99

LIABILITIES AND CAPITAL

Current Liabilities		
VISA Payable	$ 6,243.85	
Publisher Advances	12,000.00	
Total Current Liabilities		18,243.85
Long-Term Liabilities		
Total Long-Term Liabilities		0.00
Total Liabilities		18,243.85
Capital		
Taylor Rinaldi, Capital	98,510.68	
Taylor Rinaldi, Draw	(600.00)	
Net Income	5,724.46	
Total Capital		103,635.14
Total Liabilities & Capital		$ 121,878.99

Compare your income statement to the one shown below.

	Taylor Rinaldi, Graphic Artist				
	Income Statement				
	For the Ten Months Ending October 31, 2004				
	Current Month			Year to Date	
Revenues					
Teaching Income	$	2,635.80	40.02	$ 2,635.80	40.02
Royalty Income		3,950.95	59.98	3,950.95	59.98
Total Revenues		6,586.75	100.00	6,586.75	100.00
Cost of Sales					
Total Cost of Sales		0.00	0.00	0.00	0.00
Gross Profit		6,586.75	100.00	6,586.75	100.00
Expenses					
Dues and Subscriptions		53.00	0.80	53.00	0.80
Auto Registration		185.00	2.81	185.00	2.81
Automobile Expense		319.00	4.84	319.00	4.84
Utilities Expense		42.89	0.65	42.89	0.65
Water and Power Expense		85.50	1.30	85.50	1.30
Telephone Expense		43.20	0.66	43.20	0.66
My Long Distance		62.75	0.95	62.75	0.95
Internet Service Provider		25.95	0.39	25.95	0.39
Bank Service Charge		8.00	0.12	8.00	0.12
Postage Expense		37.00	0.56	37.00	0.56
Total Expenses		862.29	13.09	862.29	13.09
Net Income	$	5,724.46	86.91	$ 5,724.46	86.91

Comment

To print an Income Statement without zero balances, uncheck the Show Zero Amounts box on the <Standard> Income Statement Options window.

In addition to dollar figures, you will observe that the income statement also includes percentage of revenue columns for both the current month and the year to date. The percentages shown for each expense, total expenses, and net income indicate the relationship of each item to total revenues.

BACKING UP CHAPTER 9 DATA

Follow these steps to back up Chapter 9 data:

1. Put your backup disk in drive A. You may use the same disk that you used to back up data on pages 270-273.

2. From the menu bar, select File, then Back up.

3. Click [Back Up Now].

4. Click on the down-arrow in the Save in field. If necessary, scroll up the list, then click on 3½ Floppy (A:) to select drive A. *Or*, back up to the network or hard drive.

5. Type **Chapter 9 October** in the File name field.

6. Click [Save].

7. When the screen prompts that This company backup will require approximately 1 diskette, click [OK].

8. When the screen prompts you to insert the first disk, click [OK]. When the Back Up Company scale is 100% completed, you have successfully backed up to the current point in Chapter 9. You are returned to the menu bar.

9. Click on File, Exit to exit Peachtree.

INTERNET ACTIVITY	
1.	From your Internet browser, go to the book's website at http://www.mhhe.com/yacht2004
2.	In the Student Edition list, link to Internet Activities.
3.	Link to WEB EXERCISES, PART 2.
4.	Scroll down the screen to STARTING A BUSINESS – Chapter 9. Read steps 1 – 7.
5.	Follow the steps shown on the book's website to complete this Internet activity.
6.	Use a word processing program to write a summary for each website visited. Your summaries should be no more than 75 words.

SUMMARY AND REVIEW

SOFTWARE OBJECTIVES: In Chapter 9, you used the software to:

1. Set up company information for Taylor Rinaldi, Graphic Artist.

2. Select a sample company.

3. Edit the chart of accounts.

4. Enter chart of accounts beginning balances.

5. Use Windows Explorer to see the company's file size.

6. Record and post transactions in the cash receipts and cash disbursements journals.

7. Complete account reconciliation.

8. Preview the general ledger trial balance.

9. Preview the cash account register.

10. Print financial statements.

11. Make four backups using two blank, formatted disks: 1) Use one disk to back up Chapter 9 beginning data and October data. Use the second disk to back up Exercise 9-1 and Exercise 9-2.

WEB OBJECTIVES: In Chapter 9, you did these Internet activities:

1. Used your Internet browser to go to the book's website. (Go online to www.mhhe.com/yacht2004.)

2. Went to the Internet Activity link on the book's website. Then, selected WEB EXERCISES, PART 2. Completed the first web exercise in Part 2, Starting a Business.

3. Used a word processing program to write summaries of the websites that you visited.

GOING TO THE NET

Comment
The textbook website at www.mhhe.com/yacht2004 has a link to Textbook Updates. Check this link for updated Going to the Net exercises.

Access the information about the chart of accounts at http://www.allianceonline.org. In the site search field, type **chart of accounts**, then press <Enter>. Link to <u>What Should Our Chart of Accounts Include?</u>, and then link to <u>What are the Features of a Simple Chart of Accounts?</u>.

1. List the standard order that accounts are presented on the balance sheet and income statement.
2. How are account numbers organized? Why are they organized that way?

Multiple Choice Questions: In the space provided, write the letter that best answers each question.

_____1. Which type of accounting method does Mr. Rinaldi use?

   a. Cash basis accounting.
   b. Accrual accounting.
   c. PCA does not require you to make a choice.
   d. There is no difference between cash basis and accrual accounting.
   e. None of the above.

_____2. In Part 2 of the book, you complete monthly accounting for which type of business?

   a. Corporate form of business.
   b. Merchandising business.
   c. Manufacturing business.
   d. Service business.
   e. None of the above.

_____3. Taylor Rinaldi's type of business is:

   a. A corporation.
   b. A partnership.
   c. A sole proprietorship.
   d. A non-profit.
   e. None of the above.

_____4. What chart of accounts did you pick for Mr. Rinaldi's chart of accounts?

   a. Accounting firm.
   b. Merchandising Company.
   c. Non-profit business.
   d. Service Company.
   e. None of the above.

_____5. Mr. Rinaldi uses which type of posting method?

   a. Batch posting.
   b. Real-time posting.
   c. There is no need to post his books.
   d. PCA does not require you to make a posting choice.
   e. None of the above.

_____6. You can restore data by making which menu bar selection?

   a. File, Restore
   b. Tasks, Backup
   c. Maintain, Restore
   d. Maintain, Backup
   e. None of the above.

_____7. The correct file name for backing up Chapter 9 data for the month of October to a disk in drive A is:

   a. Chapter 9 October
   b. Chapter 9 Begin
   c. chap6
   d. chap7
   e. None of the above.

_____8.   Another term for the Balance Sheet is:

     a. Income statement.
     b. Assets and liabilities.
     c. Statement of financial position.
     d. Statement of cash flow.
     e. None of the above.

_____9.   Taylor Rinaldi's Balance Sheet at the end of October 2004 shows the following total assets:

     a. $89,843.20
     b. $98,510.68
     c. $121,878.99
     d. $18,243.85
     e. None of the above.

_____10. Taylor Rinaldi's net income for the month of October is:

     a. $6,586.75
     b. $5,274.46
     c. $2,519.50
     d. $6,724.46
     e. None of the above.

Exercise 9-1: Follow the instructions below to complete Exercise 9-1:

1.   Start Windows and Peachtree.

2.   Set up a new company. Type the following company information:

Company Name:	Your Name, Artist (*Use your own name*)
Address Line 1:	Your address
City, State, Zip	Your city, Your State, Your Zip code
Country:	USA
Telephone:	Your telephone number
Fax:	Your fax number (if any)
Business Type:	Sole Proprietorship
E-mail:	Type your email address

Leave the Tax ID Numbers fields blank.

3.   At the New Company Setup - Chart of Accounts window, select Copy settings from an existing Peachtree Accounting company.

4.   Highlight Taylor Rinaldi, Graphic Artist, then click | Next > |.

5.   At the Copy Company Information window click | Next > |.

6.   Accept the default for accrual accounting.

7.   Accept the default for Real Time posting.

8.   At the Congratulations window, click | Finish |. The menu bar for your company appears. (Close the Peachtree Today window; or refer to page 254 to remove it.)

9.   Make the following changes to the Chart of Accounts:

     a. Change the name of the following accounts:

         •   Account No. 1020, Checking Account to Bank One
         •   Account No. 2000, VISA Payable to Accounts Payable
         •   Account No. 3920, Taylor Rinaldi, Capital to Your Name, Capital
         •   Account No. 3930, Taylor Rinaldi, Draw to Your Name, Draw
         •   Account No. 4050, Royalty Income to Art Income
         •   Account No. 6550 My Long Distance to MCA Long Distance
         •   Account No. 6800 Freight Expense to Conference Fees

     b. Delete the following accounts:

         •   Account No. 1010, Money Market Fund
         •   Account No. 1040, IRA Savings Account
         •   Account No. 1045, WI State Retirement
         •   Account No. 2400, Publisher Advances

10. Print the chart of accounts.

11. Follow these steps to back up Exercise 9-1.

a. Put a blank, formatted disk in drive A. (Or, back up to the hard drive, network drive or other media.)

b. From the menu bar, select File, then Back up.

c. Click Back Up Now .

d. Click on the down-arrow in the Save in field. If necessary, scroll up the list, then click on 3½ Floppy (A:) to select drive A. Or, back up to the network or hard drive.

e. Type **Exercise 9-1** in the File name field.

f. Click Save .

g. When the screen prompts that This company backup will require approximately 1 diskette, click OK .

h. When the screen prompts you to insert the first disk, click OK . When the Back Up Company scale is 100% completed, you have successfully backed up to the current point in Exercise 9-1. You are returned to the menu bar.

i. Click on File, Exit to exit Peachtree.

Exercise 9-2: Follow the instructions below to complete Exercise 9-2. Exercise 9-1 *must* be completed before starting Exercise 9-2.

1. Start Windows, then PCA. Open the company that you set up in Exercise 9-1.

2. Follow these steps to restore Exercise 9-1.[11]

---

[11]You can restore from your back up file even if *no* Peachtree company exists. Close Peachtree's start up screen. Select File; Restore. Select the location of your backup file. On the Restore Wizard's Select Company screen, select A New Company. The *A New Company* selection allows you to restore your backup data, bypassing the process of new company set up. For more information, refer to Troubleshooting on pages 274 and 275.

a. Put your Exercise 9-1 backup disk in drive A. From the menu bar, click on File, Restore.

b. From the Select Backup File screen, click [Browse]. The Open Backup File screen pops up.

c. Click on the down-arrow in the Look in field. Then click on 3½ Floppy (A:) to select drive A (or the appropriate location of your backup file).

d. Click on the Exercise 9-1.ptb file to highlight it. The File name field displays Exercise 9-1. Click [Open].

e. Make sure that the Location field shows A:\Exercise 9-1.ptb (or the appropriate location for your backup file). Click [Next >].

f. From the Select Company screen make sure that the radio button next to An Existing Company is selected. The Company name field shows your first and last name, Artist; the Location field shows C:\ProgramFiles\Peachtree\Company\xxxxxxar (the x's represent your subdirectory; or restore from the appropriate location on your computer). Click [Next >].

g. The Restore Options screen appears. Make sure that the box next to Company Data is *checked*. Click [Next >].

h. The Confirmation screen appears. Check the From and To fields to make sure they are correct. Click [Finish]. When the Restore Company scale is 100% completed, your data is restored and you are returned to the menu bar.

i. Remove the backup disk.

3. Use the Balance Sheet on the next page to record the Chart of Accounts Beginning Balances. (*Hint: Remember to select* **9/1/04 through 9/30/04** *as the period for entering chart of accounts beginning balances. You should enter beginning balances of September 30, 2004.*)

Your Name, Artist Balance Sheet October 1, 2004		
ASSETS		
Current Assets		
Bank One	$8,500.00	
Prepaid Insurance	1,000.00	
Prepaid Rent	700.00	
Supplies	850.00	
Total Current Assets		$11,050.00
Property and Equipment		
Computer Equipment	6,500.00	
Furniture	3,500.00	
Automobile	19,000.00	
Total Property and Equipment		29,000.00
Total Assets		$ 40,050.00
LIABILITIES AND CAPITAL		
Current Liabilities		
Accounts Payable	$1,570.00	
Total Current Liabilities		$1,570.00
Total Liabilities		
Student Name, Capital		
Your Name, Capital		38,480.00
Total Liabilities and Capital		$ 40,050.00

4. Print a Balance Sheet.

5. Follow these steps to back up Exercise 9-2.

    a. Put your backup disk in drive A. You may use the same disk that you used to back up Exercise 9-1 on page 306.

    b. From the menu bar, select File, then Back up.

    c. Click Back Up Now .

    d. Click on the down-arrow in the Save in field. If necessary, scroll up the list, then click on 3½ Floppy (A:) to select drive A. Or, back up to the network or hard drive.

    e. Type **Exercise 9-2** in the File name field.

    f. Click Save .

    g. When the screen prompts that This company backup will require approximately 1 diskette, click OK .

    h. When the screen prompts you to insert the first disk, click OK . When the Back Up Company scale is 100% completed, you have successfully backed up to the current point in Exercise 9-2. You are returned to the menu bar.

    i. Click on File, Exit to exit Peachtree.

CHAPTER 9 INDEX

Chapter 10 — Completing Quarterly Activities and Closing the Fiscal Year

SOFTWARE OBJECTIVES: In Chapter 10, you will use the software to:

1. Restore data from Chapter 9.[1]
2. Change accounting periods.
3. Journalize and post transactions for Taylor Rinaldi, Graphic Artist, for the months of November and December.
4. Complete account reconciliation.
5. Print a General Ledger Trial Balance (unadjusted).
6. Journalize and post quarterly adjusting entries in the General Journal.
7. Print financial statements.
8. Close the fiscal year.
9. Print a Post-Closing Trial Balance.
10. Make six backups using two blank, formatted disks: four backups of Taylor Rinaldi, Graphic Artist data; one backup of Exercise 10-1; and one backup of Exercise 10-2.[2]

WEB OBJECTIVES: In Chapter 10, you will do these Internet activities:

1. Use your Internet browser to go to the book's website.
2. Go to the Internet Activity link on the book's website. Then, select WEB EXERCISES PART 2. Complete the second web exercise in Part 2, Understanding Accounting Terms.
3. Use a word processing program to write summaries of the websites that you visited.

Chapters 9 and 10 work together. In Chapter 10 you continue recording financial information for Taylor Rinaldi, Graphic Artist. You will complete the Computer Accounting Cycle for November and December. Mr. Rinaldi's checkbook registers and bank statements will be used as source documents. At the end of December, which is also the end of the fourth quarter, you will complete adjusting entries for Mr. Rinaldi, print financial statements, and close the fiscal year.

---

[1]All activities in Chapter 9 must be completed before starting Chapter 10.

[2]You may also back up to the hard drive, network, or other media.

The steps of the Computer Accounting Cycle that will be completed in Chapter 10 are:

PCA's Computer Accounting Cycle
1.   Change accounting periods.
2.   Journalize entries.
3.   Post entries to the General Ledger.
4.   Account Reconciliation.
5.   Print the General Ledger Trial Balance (unadjusted).
6.   Journalize and post adjusting entries.
7.   Print the General Ledger Trial Balance (adjusted).
8.   Print depreciation report.
9.   Print the financial statements: Balance Sheet, Income Statement, Statement of Retained Earnings, Statement of Cash Flow, Statement of Changes in Financial Position.
10.   Close the fiscal year.
11.   Interpret accounting information.

GETTING STARTED

Follow these steps to continue using Taylor Rinaldi's company data.

1. Start Windows and Peachtree in the usual way. Open an existing company, Taylor Rinaldi, Graphic Artist (or your name, Graphic Artist).[3]

2. To restore Taylor Rinaldi's data from Chapter 9, do the following:

   a. Put your Chapter 9 October backup disk in drive A. You made this backup on page 299. From the menu bar, click on File, Restore.

   b. From the Select Backup File screen, click [Browse]. The Open

---

[3]You can restore from your back up file even if *no* graphic artist company exists. Close Peachtree's start up screen. Select File; Restore. Select the location of your backup file. On the Restore Wizard's Select Company screen, select A New Company. *The A New Company* selection allows you to restore your backup data, bypassing the process of new company set up. For more information, refer to Troubleshooting on pages 274 and 275.

c. Click on the down-arrow in the Look in field. Then click on 3½ Floppy (A:) to select drive A (or the appropriate location of your backup file).

d. Click on the Chapter 9 October.ptb file to highlight it. The File name field displays Chapter 9 October. Click | Open |.

e. Make sure that the Location field shows A:\Chapter 9 October.ptb (or the appropriate location for your backup file). Click | Next > |.

f. From the Select Company screen make sure that the radio button next to An Existing Company is selected. The Company name field shows your first and last name, Graphic Artist; the Location field shows C:\ProgramFiles\Peachtree\Company\xxxxxxxx (the x's represent your subdirectory; or restore from the appropriate location on your computer). Click | Next > |.

g. The Restore Options screen appears. Make sure that the box next to Company Data is *checked*. Click | Next > |.

h. The Confirmation screen appears. Check the From and To fields to make sure they are correct. Click | Finish |. When the Restore Company scale is 100% completed, your data is restored and you are returned to the menu bar.

i. Remove the backup disk.

3. To make sure you are starting in the right place, display your general ledger trial balance and compare it to the one shown on page 295. Close the windows to return to the menu bar.

4. Follow these steps to change accounting periods:

a. From the menu bar, select Tasks, then System.

b. From the System pull-down menu, select Change Accounting Period.

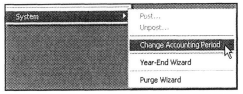

c. From the drop-down list, select 11-Nov 01, 2004 to Nov 30, 2004.

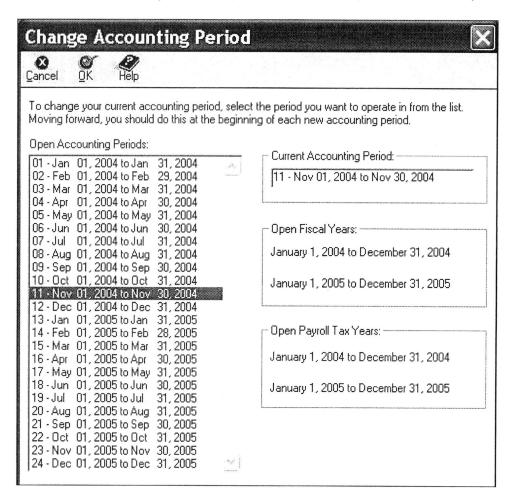

d. Make sure you have selected period 11 - Nov 01, 2004 to Nov 30, 2004. Click [OK]. If necessary, click [No] when the Would you like to print your invoices or checks before continuing? window pops up. At the Would you like to print your reports before continuing? screen, click [No]. You are returned to the menu bar. Observe that the toolbar shows Period 11 - 11/1/04 to 11/30/04.

When you changed accounting periods, you prepared Peachtree to record November's journal entries.

CHECKBOOK REGISTER AND BANK STATEMENT: NOVEMBER 2004

Use Mr. Rinaldi's checkbook register to journalize and post transactions for the month of November. (*Hint: Use the Write Checks window for recording checks and ATMs.*)

Comment
Before you start journalizing entries, you should make sure that you are starting with correct data. To do that, display the General Ledger Trial Balance and compare it to the one shown on page 295 in Chapter 9. Since you changed accounting periods on pages 313 and 314, your trial balance will be dated November 30, 2004.
Verify that Account No. 1020, Checking Account, shows a balance of $16,618.80 which is the same as the starting balance on the check register below.

Check Number	Date	Description of Transaction	Payment	Deposit	Balance
	10/31	*Bank Service Charge*	*8.00*		*16,618.80*
	11/3	Deposit (book royalty)		2,402.75	19,021.55
	11/5	ATM	200.00		18,821.55
	11/6	Deposit (Glendale CC)		2,635.80	21,457.35
5014	11/10	Dept. of Water and Power	81.60		21,375.75
5015	11/10	Midwest Gas (utilities)	63.90		21,311.85
5016	11/12	The Telephone Co.	43.28		21,268.57
5017	11/14	My Long Distance	100.60		21,167.97
	11/16	ATM	200.00		20,967.97
5018	11/27	VISA card payment	6,243.85		14,724.12
5019	11/28	Internet Service Provider	25.95		14,698.17
	11/28	ATM	200.00		14,498.17

Follow the steps below to complete the Computer Accounting Cycle.

1. Journalize and post the Cash Receipts and Cash Disbursements Journals. (*Hint: Start your journal entries with the November 3 deposit. Remember to record each transaction--checks, deposits, ATM withdrawals--as a separate journal entry. Post after each transaction*).

2. Use Mr. Rinaldi's bank statement to complete account reconciliation for Account No. 1020, Checking Account.

Remember to record the bank service charge (Account No. 6850) on the Account Reconciliation screen.

Statement of Account			Taylor Rinaldi, Graphic Artist	
Merchant's Bank			8711 University Avenue	
November 1 to November 30, 2004		Account # 93244-9123	Glendale, WI 53289	
REGULAR CHECKING				
Previous Balance	10/31/04	17,092.29		
2 Deposits(+)		5,038.55		
8 checks (-)		762.87		
3 Other deduction (-)		600.00		
Service Charges (-)	11/30/04	8.00		
Ending Balance	11/30/04	**20,759.97**		
DEPOSITS				
	11/3/04	2,402.75		
	11/8/04	2,635.80		
CHECKS (Asterisk * indicates break in check number sequence)				
	11/3/04	5005*	42.89	
	11/3/04	5011*	185.00	
	11/3/04	5012	219.65	
	11/5/04	5013	25.95	
	11/17/04	5014	81.60	
	11/27/04	5015	63.90	
	11/28/04	5016	43.28	
	11/28/04	5017	100.60	
OTHER DEDUCTIONS (ATM's)				
	11/5/04	200.00		
	11/14/04	200.00		
	11/28/04	200.00		

3. Follow these steps to display the Cash Account Register.

   a. From the menu bar, select Tasks; Account Register. Click 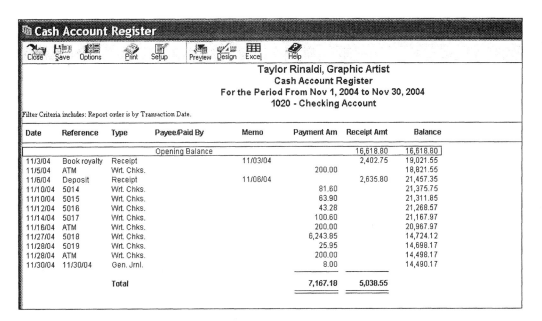 to enlarge your screen.

   b. Click on the down arrow next to the Print icon (); then click Preview, OK.

   c. Compare your Cash Account Register to the one shown below and to the check register on page 315. If necessary, drill down to make corrections.

Cash Account Register

Close Save Options Print Setup Preview Design Excel Help

Taylor Rinaldi, Graphic Artist
Cash Account Register
For the Period From Nov 1, 2004 to Nov 30, 2004
1020 - Checking Account

Filter Criteria includes: Report order is by Transaction Date.

Date	Reference	Type	Payee/Paid By	Memo	Payment Am	Receipt Amt	Balance
			Opening Balance			16,618.80	16,618.80
11/3/04	Book royalty	Receipt		11/03/04		2,402.75	19,021.55
11/5/04	ATM	Wrt. Chks.			200.00		18,821.55
11/6/04	Deposit	Receipt		11/06/04		2,635.80	21,457.35
11/10/04	5014	Wrt. Chks.			81.60		21,375.75
11/10/04	5015	Wrt. Chks.			63.90		21,311.85
11/12/04	5016	Wrt. Chks.			43.28		21,268.57
11/14/04	5017	Wrt. Chks.			100.60		21,167.97
11/16/04	ATM	Wrt. Chks.			200.00		20,967.97
11/27/04	5018	Wrt. Chks.			6,243.85		14,724.12
11/28/04	5019	Wrt. Chks.			25.95		14,698.17
11/28/04	ATM	Wrt. Chks.			200.00		14,498.17
11/30/04	11/30/04	Gen. Jrnl.			8.00		14,490.17
		Total			7,167.18	5,038.55	

4. Close the windows and return to the menu bar.

5. Follow these steps to print an Account Reconciliation report:

   a. From the menu bar, click on Reports, then Account Reconciliation.

   b. At the Select a Report window, highlight Account Reconciliation.

   c. Click .

d. The Account Reconciliation Filter window displays. If necessary, in the GL Account ID field, select Account No. 1020, Checking Account. Click [OK].

e. At the Print window, click [OK].

	Taylor Rinaldi, Graphic Artist		
	Account Reconciliation		
	As of Nov 30, 2004		
	1020 - Checking Account		
	Bank Statement Date: November 30, 2004		

Filter Criteria includes: Report is printed in Detail Format.

Beginning GL Balance		16,618.80	
Add: Cash Receipts		5,038.55	
Less: Cash Disbursement		(7,159.18)	
Add (Less) Other		(8.00)	
Ending GL Balance		14,490.17	
Ending Bank Balance		20,759.97	
Add back deposits in transi			
Total deposits in transit			
(Less) outstanding checks			
	Nov 27, 20 5018	(6,243.85)	
	Nov 28, 20 5019	(25.95)	
Total outstanding checks		(6,269.80)	
Add (Less) Other			
	Sep 1, 20 BEGBAL	6,949.78	
Total other		6,949.78	
Unreconciled difference		(6,949.78)	
Ending GL Balance		14,490.17	

6. Close the account reconciliation report.[4]

---

[4]The Unreconciled difference is the October 1 beginning balance for Account No. 1020, Checking Account. This amount showed as 0.00 (zero) on the Tasks; Account Reconciliation screen.

7. Print or display your Cash Receipts Journal and compare it to the one shown.

Taylor Rinaldi, Graphic Artist
Cash Receipts Journal
For the Period From Nov 1, 2004 to Nov 30, 2004

Filter Criteria includes: Report order is by Check Date. Report is printed in Detail Format.

Date	Account ID	Transaction Ref	Line Description	Debit Amnt	Credit Amnt
11/3/04	4050	Book royalty	Royalty Income		2,402.75
	1020		Deposit	2,402.75	
11/6/04	4000	Deposit	Teaching Income		2,635.80
	1020		Deposit: Glendale Community Co	2,635.80	
				5,038.55	5,038.55

8. Print or display your Cash Disbursements Journal and compare it to the one shown.

Taylor Rinaldi, Graphic Artist
Cash Disbursements Journal
For the Period From Nov 1, 2004 to Nov 30, 2004

Filter Criteria includes: Report order is by Date. Report is printed in Detail Format.

Date	Check #	Account ID	Line Description	Debit Amount	Credit Amount
11/5/04	ATM	3930	Taylor Rinaldi, Draw	200.00	
		1020	ATM		200.00
11/10/04	5014	6420	Water and Power Expense	81.60	
		1020	Dept. of Water and Power		81.60
11/10/04	5015	6400	Utilities Expense	63.90	
		1020	Midwest Gas		63.90
11/12/04	5016	6500	Telephone Expense	43.28	
		1020	The Telephone Co.		43.28
11/14/04	5017	6550	My Long Distance	100.60	
		1020	My Long Distance		100.60
11/16/04	ATM	3930	Taylor Rinaldi, Draw	200.00	
		1020	ATM		200.00
11/27/04	5018	2000	VISA Payable	6,243.85	
		1020	VISA card		6,243.85
11/28/04	5019	6560	Internet Service Provider	25.95	
		1020	Internet Service Provider		25.95
11/28/04	ATM	3930	Taylor Rinaldi, Draw	200.00	
		1020	ATM		200.00
	Total			7,159.18	7,159.18

9. Print or display the general journal to see the bank service charge.

			Taylor Rinaldi, Graphic Artist			
			General Journal			
			For the Period From Nov 1, 2004 to Nov 30, 2004			

Filter Criteria includes: Report order is by Date. Report is printed with Accounts having Zero Amounts and with Truncated Transaction Descriptions and in Detail Format.

Date	Account ID	Reference	Trans Description	Debit Amt	Credit Amt
11/30/04	1020	11/30/04	Service Charge		8.00
	6850		Service Charge	8.00	
		Total		8.00	8.00

If your journals do not agree with the ones shown, edit the journals and post again. (Refer to page 294 Editing Journal Transactions.)

10. Print or display the General Ledger Trial Balance.

		Taylor Rinaldi, Graphic Artist	
		General Ledger Trial Balance	
		As of Nov 30, 2004	

Filter Criteria includes: Report order is by ID. Report is printed in Detail Format.

Account ID	Account Description	Debit Amt	Credit Amt
1010	Money Market Account	10,370.85	
1020	Checking Account	14,490.17	
1040	IRA Savings Account	25,750.32	
1045	WI State Retirement	32,411.75	
1300	Prepaid Insurance	2,100.00	
1400	Prepaid Rent	600.00	
1450	Supplies	1,991.48	
1500	Computer Equipment	8,035.79	
1510	Furniture	5,000.00	
1520	Automobile	19,000.00	
2400	Publisher Advances		12,000.00
3920	Taylor Rinaldi, Capital		98,510.68
3930	Taylor Rinaldi, Draw	1,200.00	
4000	Teaching Income		5,271.60
4050	Royalty Income		6,353.70
6100	Dues and Subscriptions	53.00	
6150	Auto Registration	185.00	
6180	Automobile Expense	319.00	
6400	Utilities Expense	106.79	
6420	Water and Power Expense	167.10	
6500	Telephone Expense	86.48	
6550	My Long Distance	163.35	
6560	Internet Service Provider	51.90	
6850	Bank Service Charge	16.00	
7400	Postage Expense	37.00	
	Total:	122,135.98	122,135.98

11. Print or display the Balance Sheet.

Taylor Rinaldi, Graphic Artist
Balance Sheet
November 30, 2004

ASSETS

Current Assets		
Money Market Account	$ 10,370.85	
Checking Account	14,490.17	
IRA Savings Account	25,750.32	
WI State Retirement	32,411.75	
Prepaid Insurance	2,100.00	
Prepaid Rent	600.00	
Supplies	1,991.48	
Total Current Assets		87,714.57
Property and Equipment		
Computer Equipment	8,035.79	
Furniture	5,000.00	
Automobile	19,000.00	
Total Property and Equipment		32,035.79
Other Assets		
Total Other Assets		0.00
Total Assets		$ 119,750.36

LIABILITIES AND CAPITAL

Current Liabilities		
Publisher Advances	$ 12,000.00	
Total Current Liabilities		12,000.00
Long-Term Liabilities		
Total Long-Term Liabilities		0.00
Total Liabilities		12,000.00
Capital		
Taylor Rinaldi, Capital	98,510.68	
Taylor Rinaldi, Draw	(1,200.00)	
Net Income	10,439.68	
Total Capital		107,750.36
Total Liabilities & Capital		$ 119,750.36

12. Print or display the Income Statement.

	Taylor Rinaldi, Graphic Artist				
	Income Statement				
	For the Eleven Months Ending November 30, 2004				
	Current Month			Year to Date	
Revenues					
Teaching Income	$ 2,635.80	52.31	$	5,271.60	45.35
Royalty Income	2,402.75	47.69		6,353.70	54.65
Total Revenues	5,038.55	100.00		11,625.30	100.00
Cost of Sales					
Total Cost of Sales	0.00	0.00		0.00	0.00
Gross Profit	5,038.55	100.00		11,625.30	100.00
Expenses					
Dues and Subscriptions	0.00	0.00		53.00	0.46
Auto Registration	0.00	0.00		185.00	1.59
Automobile Expense	0.00	0.00		319.00	2.74
Utilities Expense	63.90	1.27		106.79	0.92
Water and Power Expense	81.60	1.62		167.10	1.44
Telephone Expense	43.28	0.86		86.48	0.74
My Long Distance	100.60	2.00		163.35	1.41
Internet Service Provider	25.95	0.52		51.90	0.45
Bank Service Charge	8.00	0.16		16.00	0.14
Postage Expense	0.00	0.00		37.00	0.32
Total Expenses	323.33	6.42		1,185.62	10.20
Net Income	$ 4,715.22	93.58	$	10,439.68	89.80

BACKING UP NOVEMBER DATA

Follow these steps to back up Chapter 10 data:

1. Put a blank, formatted disk in drive A. Or, back up to the hard drive, network, or other media.

2. From the menu bar, select File, then Back up.

3. Click [Back Up Now].

4. Click on the down-arrow in the Save in field. If necessary, scroll up the list, then click on 3½ Floppy (A:) to select drive A. *Or*, back up to the network, hard drive, or other media.

5. Type **Chapter 10 November** in the File name field.

6. Click [Save].

7. When the screen prompts that This company backup will require approximately 1 diskette, click [OK].

8. When the screen prompts you to insert the first disk, click [OK]. When the Back Up Company scale is 100% completed, you have successfully backed up to the current point in Chapter 10. You are returned to the menu bar.

DATA FILE STATISTICS

To display information about your company data files, follow these steps.

1. From the menu bar, click on Help, Customer Support and Service, then select File Statistics.

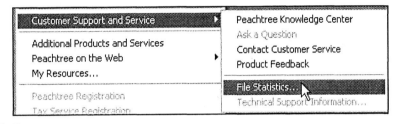

The Data File Statistics screen lists the number of records and sizes in kilobytes for each data file for the company that is open. It also provides a grand total (scroll down).

Peachtree displays the company's shortened name (tayringr) on the title bar.[5] This represents the name of the directory (subfolder) where the opened company resides. Observe that the Directory field shows where the company resides on your hard drive.

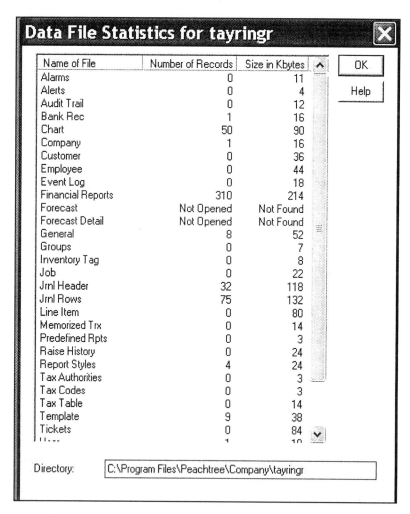

Data File Statistics for tayringr

Name of File	Number of Records	Size in Kbytes
Alarms	0	11
Alerts	0	4
Audit Trail	0	12
Bank Rec	1	16
Chart	50	90
Company	1	16
Customer	0	36
Employee	0	44
Event Log	0	18
Financial Reports	310	214
Forecast	Not Opened	Not Found
Forecast Detail	Not Opened	Not Found
General	8	52
Groups	0	7
Inventory Tag	0	8
Job	0	22
Jrnl Header	32	118
Jrnl Rows	75	132
Line Item	0	80
Memorized Trx	0	14
Predefined Rpts	0	3
Raise History	0	24
Report Styles	4	24
Tax Authorities	0	3
Tax Codes	0	3
Tax Table	0	14
Template	9	38
Tickets	0	84
I I....	1	10

Directory: C:\Program Files\Peachtree\Company\tayringr

2. To close the Date File Statistics window, click ‎ OK ‎.

---

[5]If you used your name, your company's shortened name will differ.

CHANGING ACCOUNTING PERIODS

Follow these steps to change accounting periods:

1. From the menu bar, select Tasks, then System.

2. From the System pull-down menu, select Change Accounting Period.

9. From the drop-down list, select period 12 - Dec 01, 2004 to Dec 31, 2004.

10. Click OK. If necessary, click No when the Would you like to print your invoices or checks before continuing? window pops up. At the Would you like to print your reports before continuing? window, click No. Observe that your toolbar shows Period 12 - 12/1/04 to 12/31/04.

CHECKBOOK REGISTER AND BANK STATEMENT: DECEMBER 2004

1. Use Mr. Rinaldi's checkbook register to journalize and post transactions for the month of December. His checkbook register is shown below.

> **Comment**
>
> Before you start journalizing entries, make sure that you are starting with correct data. To do that, display the General Ledger Trial Balance and compare it to the one shown on page 320.

Check Number	Date	Description of Transaction	Payment	Deposit	Balance
	11/30	Bank Service Charge	8.00		14,490.17
	12/3[6]	ATM	400.00		14,090.17
	12/8	Deposit (Glendale CC)		2,635.80	16,725.97
5020	12/10	Dept. of Water and Power	65.50		16,660.47
5021	12/11	Midwest Gas (utilities)	93.82		16,566.65
5022	12/12	The Telephone Co.	45.90		16,520.75

---

[6]Start your journal transactions with the December 3 ATM transaction.

5023	12/15	Z-Gallery (business cards - debit, Supplies)	115.25		16,405.50
5024	12/18	My Long Distance	80.39		16,325.11
5025	12/18	Internet Service Provider	25.95		16,299.16
	12/19	ATM	400.00		15,899.16
	12/29	ATM	400.00		15,499.16

2. Use Mr. Rinaldi's bank statement to complete the account reconciliation. (*Remember to record the bank service charge on the Account Reconciliation screen.*)

Statement of Account				Taylor Rinaldi, Graphic Artist	
Merchant's Bank				8711 University Avenue	
December 1 to December 31, 2004		Account # 93244-9123		Glendale, WI 53239	
		REGULAR CHECKING			
Previous Balance	11/30/04	20,759.97			
1 Deposit(+)		2,635.80			
6 Checks (-)		6,670.66			
2 Other Deduction (-)		1,200.00			
Service Charges (-)	12/31/04	8.00			
Ending Balance	12/31/04	**15,517.11**			
	12/8/04	2,635.80			
	CHECKS (Asterisk * indicates break in check number sequence)				
	12/8/04	5018		6,243.85	
	12/8/04	5019		25.95	
	12/22/04	5020		65.50	
	12/29/04	5021		93.82	
	12/29/04	5022		45.90	
	12/31/04	5023		115.25	
	12/31/04	5024		80.39	
	OTHER DEDUCTIONS (ATM's)				
	12/3/04	400.00			
	12/19/04	400.00			
	12/29/04	400.00			

3. Display the Cash Account Register (Reports; General Ledger, Cash Account Register; Preview). Compare the registers to the check register on pages 325 and 326. Use drill down to make any needed corrections.

Taylor Rinaldi, Graphic Artist
Cash Account Register
For the Period From Dec 1, 2004 to Dec 31, 2004
1020 - Checking Account

Filter Criteria includes: Report order is by Transaction Date.

Date	Reference	Type	Payee/Paid By	Memo	Payment Am	Receipt Amt	Balance
			Opening Balance			14,490.17	14,490.17
12/3/04	ATM	Wrt. Chks.			400.00		14,090.17
12/8/04	Deposit	Receipt		12/08/04		2,635.80	16,725.97
12/10/04	5020	Wrt. Chks.			65.50		16,660.47
12/11/04	5021	Wrt. Chks.			93.82		16,566.65
12/12/04	5022	Wrt. Chks.			45.90		16,520.75
12/15/04	5023	Wrt. Chks.			115.25		16,405.50
12/18/04	5024	Wrt. Chks.			80.39		16,325.11
12/18/04	5025	Wrt. Chks.			25.95		16,299.16
12/19/04	ATM	Wrt. Chks.			400.00		15,899.16
12/29/04	ATM	Wrt. Chks.			400.00		15,499.16
12/31/04	12/31/04	Gen. Jrnl.			8.00		15,491.16
		Total			1,634.81	2,635.80	

4. Print or display the Account Reconciliation report.

Taylor Rinaldi, Graphic Artist
Account Reconciliation
As of Dec 31, 2004
1020 - Checking Account
Bank Statement Date: December 31, 2004

Filter Criteria includes: Report is printed in Detail Format.

Beginning GL Balance				14,490.17
Add: Cash Receipts				2,635.80
Less: Cash Disbursement				(1,626.81)
Add (Less) Other				(8.00)
Ending GL Balance				15,491.16
Ending Bank Balance				15,517.11
Add back deposits in transi				
Total deposits in transit				
(Less) outstanding checks	Dec 18, 2	5025	(25.95)	
Total outstanding checks				(25.95)
Add (Less) Other	Sep 1, 20	BEGBAL	6,949.78	
Total other				6,949.78
Unreconciled difference				(6,949.78)
Ending GL Balance				15,491.16

5. Print or display the Cash Receipts Journal.

		Taylor Rinaldi, Graphic Artist			
		Cash Receipts Journal			
		For the Period From Dec 1, 2004 to Dec 31, 2004			

Filter Criteria includes: Report order is by Check Date. Report is printed in Detail Format.

Date	Account ID	Transaction Ref	Line Description	Debit Amnt	Credit Amnt
12/8/04	4000	Deposit	Teaching Income		2,635.80
	1020		Deposit: Glendale Community Co	2,635.80	
				2,635.80	2,635.80

11. Print or display the Cash Disbursements Journal.

			Taylor Rinaldi, Graphic Artist		
			Cash Disbursements Journal		
			For the Period From Dec 1, 2004 to Dec 31, 2004		

Filter Criteria includes: Report order is by Date. Report is printed in Detail Format.

Date	Check #	Account ID	Line Description	Debit Amount	Credit Amount
12/3/04	ATM	3930	Taylor Rinaldi, Draw	400.00	
		1020	ATM		400.00
12/10/04	5020	6420	Water and Power Expense	65.50	
		1020	Dept. of Water and Power		65.50
12/11/04	5021	6400	Utilities Expense	93.82	
		1020	Midwest Gas		93.82
12/12/04	5022	6500	Telephone Expense	45.90	
		1020	The Telephone Co.		45.90
12/15/04	5023	1450	Supplies	115.25	
		1020	Z-Gallery		115.25
12/18/04	5024	6550	My Long Distance	80.39	
		1020	My Long Distance		80.39
12/18/04	5025	6560	Internet Service Provider	25.95	
		1020	Internet Service Provider		25.95
12/19/04	ATM	3930	Taylor Rinaldi, Draw	400.00	
		1020	ATM		400.00
12/29/04	ATM	3930	Taylor Rinaldi, Draw	400.00	
		1020	ATM		400.00
	Total			1,626.81	1,626.81

If your journals do not agree with the ones shown, edit your records and post again.

7. Display or print a General Ledger Trial Balance (unadjusted).

Taylor Rinaldi, Graphic Artist			
General Ledger Trial Balance			
As of Dec 31, 2004			

Filter Criteria includes: Report order is by ID. Report is printed in Detail Format.

Account ID	Account Description	Debit Amt	Credit Amt
1010	Money Market Account	10,370.85	
1020	Checking Account	15,491.16	
1040	IRA Savings Account	25,750.32	
1045	WI State Retirement	32,411.75	
1300	Prepaid Insurance	2,100.00	
1400	Prepaid Rent	600.00	
1450	Supplies	2,106.73	
1500	Computer Equipment	8,035.79	
1510	Furniture	5,000.00	
1520	Automobile	19,000.00	
2400	Publisher Advances		12,000.00
3920	Taylor Rinaldi, Capital		98,510.68
3930	Taylor Rinaldi, Draw	2,400.00	
4000	Teaching Income		7,907.40
4050	Royalty Income		6,353.70
6100	Dues and Subscriptions	53.00	
6150	Auto Registration	185.00	
6180	Automobile Expense	319.00	
6400	Utilities Expense	200.61	
6420	Water and Power Expense	232.60	
6500	Telephone Expense	132.38	
6550	My Long Distance	243.74	
6560	Internet Service Provider	77.85	
6850	Bank Service Charge	24.00	
7400	Postage Expense	37.00	
	Total:	**124,771.78**	**124,771.78**

BACKING UP THE UNDADJUSTED TRIAL BALANCE

Follow these steps to back up Chapter 10 data:

1. Put your backup disk in drive A. You may use the same disk that you used to back up November data on pages 322-323.

2. From the menu bar, select File, then Back up.

3. Click [Back Up Now].

4. Click on the down-arrow in the Save in field. If necessary, scroll up the list, then click on 3½ Floppy (A:) to select drive A. *Or*, back up to the network, hard drive, or other media.

5. Type **Chapter 10 December UTB** in the File name field. (UTB is an abbreviation for unadjusted trial balance.)

6. Click [Save].

7. When the screen prompts that This company backup will require approximately 1 diskette, click [OK].

8. When the screen prompts you to insert the first disk, click [OK]. When the Back Up Company scale is 100% completed, you have successfully backed up to the current point in Chapter 10. You are returned to the menu bar.

9. Click on File, Exit to exit Peachtree. Or, continue with the next section, End-of-Quarter Adjusting Entries.

You will print the financial statements after you journalize and post the end-of-quarter adjusting entries.

END-OF-QUARTER ADJUSTING ENTRIES

It is the policy of your accounting firm to record adjusting entries at the end of the quarter. Mr. Rinaldi's accounting records are complete through December 31, 2004. The following adjusting entries need to be recorded in the General Journal.

Follow these steps to journalize and post the adjusting entries in the general journal.

1. From the menu bar, click on Tasks, then General Journal Entry.

2. Type **31** in the Date text field. Press **<Enter>**.

3. In the Account No. column, select the appropriate account to debit. Type the account name in the Description column. Press the **<Enter>** key once to go to the Debit column. Type the debit amount, then press the **<Enter>** key three times.

4. In the Account No. column, select the appropriate account to credit. Type the account name in the Description column. Press the **<Enter>** key two times to go to the Credit column. Type the credit amount. Press the **<Enter>** key.

5. Click [Save] to post each adjusting entry.

Journalize and post the following December 31, 2004 adjusting entries:

1. Office supplies on hand are $1,500.00

Acct. #	Account Name	Debit	Credit
6450	Office Supplies Expense	606.73	
1450	Supplies		606.73

Computation: Supplies $2,106.73
                 Office supplies on hand   - 1,500.00
                 Adjustment $ 606.73

Hint: To post your transaction to the general ledger, click [Save] after each general journal entry.

2. Adjust three months of prepaid insurance ($2,100 X 3/12 = $525). Mr. Rinaldi paid a one year insurance premium on 10/1/04.

Acct. #	Account Name	Debit	Credit
6950	Insurance Expense	525.00	
1300	Prepaid Insurance		525.00

3. Adjust three months of prepaid rent ($200 X 3 = $600.)

Acct. #	Account Name	Debit	Credit
6300	Rent or Lease Expense	600.00	
1400	Prepaid Rent		600.00

4. Use straight-line depreciation for Mr. Rinaldi's computer equipment. His computer equipment has a three-year service life and a $1,000 salvage value. To depreciate computer equipment for the fourth quarter, use this calculation:

$8,035.79 - $1,000 ÷ 3 years X 3/12 = $586.32

Computer Equipment, 10/1/04	$6,800.00	
Hardware Upgrade, 10/3/04	1,235.79	
Total computer equipment, 12/31/04	$8,035.79	

Acct. #	Account Name	Debit	Credit
7050	Deprec. Exp.-Comp Eq	586.32	
1900	Accum. Depreciation - Comp Eq		586.32

5. Use straight-line depreciation to depreciate Mr. Rinaldi's furniture. His furniture has a 5-year service life and a $500 salvage value. To depreciate furniture for the fourth quarter, use this calculation:

$5,000 - $500 ÷ 5 X 3/12 = $225.00

Acct. #	Account Name	Debit	Credit
7060	Deprec. Exp.- Furniture	225.00	
1910	Accum. Depreciation - Furniture		225.00

6. Mr. Rinaldi purchased his automobile on October 1, 2004. Use the following adjusting entry. The computation is:

$19,000 X 20% X 3/12 = $950.00

Acct. #	Account Name	Debit	Credit
7070	Deprec. Exp. - Automobile	950.00	
1920	Accum. Depreciation - Automobile		950.00

7. Mr. Rinaldi received a $12,000 advance from his publisher. This was recorded as **unearned revenue** on October 2, 2004. Unearned revenue is a liability account used to report advance collections from customers or clients. The amount of this adjusting entry is based on Mr. Rinaldi's royalty statement.

Acct. #	Account Name	Debit	Credit
2400	Publisher Advances	3,000.00	
4050	Royalty Income		3,000.00

8. After journalizing and posting the end-of-quarter adjusting entries, print the General Journal for December 31, 2004. Follow these steps to print your December 31, 2004 General Journal:

a. From the menu bar, click on Reports, then General Ledger.

b. Highlight General Journal.

c. Click [Print].

d. In the From field, click on the Calendar icon. A December calendar pops up. Click on 31.

e. Click [OK], then [OK] again. The December 31 general journal starts to print. (Since the bank service charge posts to the general journal, December's service charge is also shown.)

Taylor Rinaldi, Graphic Artist
General Journal
For the Period From Dec 1, 2004 to Dec 31, 2004

Filter Criteria includes: Report order is by Date. Report is printed with Accounts having Zero Amounts and with Truncated Transaction Descriptions and in Detail Format.

Date	Account ID	Reference	Trans Description	Debit Amt	Credit Amt
12/31/04	6450		Office Supplies Expense	606.73	
	1450		Supplies		606.73
	6950		Insurance Expense	525.00	
	1300		Prepaid Insurance		525.00
	6300		Rent or Lease Expense	600.00	
	1400		Prepaid Rent		600.00
	7050		Deprec. Exp. - Comp Eq	586.32	
	1900		Accum. Depreciation - Comp Eq		586.32
	7060		Deprec. Exp. - Furniture	225.00	
	1910		Accum. Depreciation - Furniture		225.00
	7070		Deprec. Exp. - Automobile	950.00	
	1920		Accum. Depreciation - Automobile		950.00
	2400		Publisher Advances	3,000.00	
	4050		Royalty Income		3,000.00
12/31/04	1020	12/31/04	Service Charge		8.00
	6850		Service Charge	8.00	
		Total		6,501.05	6,501.05

If any of your general journal entries are incorrect, click [icon] to drill down to the General Journal Entry window. Make the appropriate corrections, and then post your revised general journal entry. Display or print the general journal report.

9. Print the General Ledger Trial Balance (adjusted).

Taylor Rinaldi, Graphic Artist
General Ledger Trial Balance
As of Dec 31, 2004

Filter Criteria includes: Report order is by ID. Report is printed in Detail Format.

Account ID	Account Description	Debit Amt	Credit Amt
1010	Money Market Account	10,370.85	
1020	Checking Account	15,491.16	
1040	IRA Savings Account	25,750.32	
1045	WI State Retirement	32,411.75	
1300	Prepaid Insurance	1,575.00	
1450	Supplies	1,500.00	
1500	Computer Equipment	8,035.79	
1510	Furniture	5,000.00	
1520	Automobile	19,000.00	
1900	Accum. Depreciation - Co		586.32
1910	Accum. Depreciation - Furn		225.00
1920	Accum. Depreciation - Auto		950.00
2400	Publisher Advances		9,000.00
3920	Taylor Rinaldi, Capital		98,510.68
3930	Taylor Rinaldi, Draw	2,400.00	
4000	Teaching Income		7,907.40
4050	Royalty Income		9,353.70
6100	Dues and Subscriptions	53.00	
6150	Auto Registration	185.00	
6180	Automobile Expense	319.00	
6300	Rent or Lease Expense	600.00	
6400	Utilities Expense	200.61	
6420	Water and Power Expense	232.60	
6450	Office Supplies Expense	606.73	
6500	Telephone Expense	132.38	
6550	My Long Distance	243.74	
6560	Internet Service Provider	77.85	
6850	Bank Service Charge	24.00	
6950	Insurance Expense	525.00	
7050	Deprec. Exp. - Comp Eq	586.32	
7060	Deprec. Exp. - Furniture	225.00	
7070	Deprec. Exp. - Automobile	950.00	
7400	Postage Expense	37.00	
	Total:	**126,533.10**	**126,533.10**

10.   Print the Balance Sheet.

Taylor Rinaldi, Graphic Artist
Balance Sheet
December 31, 2004

ASSETS

Current Assets		
Money Market Account	$ 10,370.85	
Checking Account	15,491.16	
IRA Savings Account	25,750.32	
WI State Retirement	32,411.75	
Prepaid Insurance	1,575.00	
Supplies	1,500.00	
Total Current Assets		87,099.08
Property and Equipment		
Computer Equipment	8,035.79	
Furniture	5,000.00	
Automobile	19,000.00	
Accum. Depreciation - Comp Eq	(586.32)	
Accum. Depreciation - Furnitur	(225.00)	
Accum. Depreciation - Automobi	(950.00)	
Total Property and Equipment		30,274.47
Other Assets		
Total Other Assets		0.00
Total Assets		$ 117,373.55

LIABILITIES AND CAPITAL

Current Liabilities		
Publisher Advances	$ 9,000.00	
Total Current Liabilities		9,000.00
Long-Term Liabilities		
Total Long-Term Liabilities		0.00
Total Liabilities		9,000.00
Capital		
Taylor Rinaldi, Capital	98,510.68	
Taylor Rinaldi, Draw	(2,400.00)	
Net Income	12,262.87	
Total Capital		108,373.55
Total Liabilities & Capital		$ 117,373.55

11. Print the Income Statement.

	Taylor Rinaldi, Graphic Artist Income Statement For the Twelve Months Ending December 31, 2004				
	Current Month			Year to Date	
Revenues					
Teaching Income	$ 2,635.80	46.77	$	7,907.40	45.81
Royalty Income	3,000.00	53.23		9,353.70	54.19
Total Revenues	5,635.80	100.00		17,261.10	100.00
Cost of Sales					
Total Cost of Sales	0.00	0.00		0.00	0.00
Gross Profit	5,635.80	100.00		17,261.10	100.00
Expenses					
Dues and Subscriptions	0.00	0.00		53.00	0.31
Auto Registration	0.00	0.00		185.00	1.07
Automobile Expense	0.00	0.00		319.00	1.85
Rent or Lease Expense	600.00	10.65		600.00	3.48
Utilities Expense	93.82	1.66		200.61	1.16
Water and Power Expense	65.50	1.16		232.60	1.35
Office Supplies Expense	606.73	10.77		606.73	3.52
Telephone Expense	45.90	0.81		132.38	0.77
My Long Distance	80.39	1.43		243.74	1.41
Internet Service Provider	25.95	0.46		77.85	0.45
Bank Service Charge	8.00	0.14		24.00	0.14
Insurance Expense	525.00	9.32		525.00	3.04
Deprec. Exp. - Comp Eq	586.32	10.40		586.32	3.40
Deprec. Exp. - Furniture	225.00	3.99		225.00	1.30
Deprec. Exp. - Automobile	950.00	16.86		950.00	5.50
Postage Expense	0.00	0.00		37.00	0.21
Total Expenses	3,812.61	67.65		4,998.23	28.96
Net Income	$ 1,823.19	32.35	$	12,262.87	71.04

12. Follow these steps to print the Statement of Retained Earnings.

    a. In the Financial Statement list, click on <Standard> Retained Earnings to highlight it.

    b. Click .

    c. Uncheck Show Zero Amounts. Make the selections to print. Compare your Statement of Retained Earnings to the one shown below.

		Taylor Rinaldi, Graphic Artist
		Statement of Retained Earnings
		For the Twelve Months Ending December 31, 2004
Beginning Retained Earnings	$	0.00
Adjustments To Date		0.00
Net Income		12,262.87
Subtotal		12,262.87
Taylor Rinaldi, Draw		(2,400.00)
Ending Retained Earnings	$	9,862.87

The Statement of Retained Earnings shows the net income at the end of the Quarter, $12,262.87, minus Mr. Rinaldi's drawing, $2,400. When you close the fiscal year, the Ending Retained Earnings amount, $9,862.87, will be shown on the post-closing trial balance.

Comment

If your financial statements *do not agree* with the printouts, edit your journals, post, then reprint your reports. If your Year to Date column *does not agree* with what is shown on the Statement of Cash Flow (p. 338) and the Statement of Changes in Financial Position (p. 339), refer to Entering Chart of Accounts Beginning Balances in Chapter 9 on pages 263- 267. Correct year-to-date balances depend on setting the beginning balances correctly for 9/1/04 through 9/30/04 (see the screen illustration on p. 265).

---

13. Print the Statement of Cash Flow. Compare it to the one shown on the next page.

	Current Month	Year to Date
Taylor Rinaldi, Graphic Artist		
Statement of Cash Flow		
For the twelve Months Ended December 31, 2004		
Cash Flows from operating activities		
Net Income	$ 1,823.19	$ 12,262.87
Adjustments to reconcile net income to net cash provided by operating activities		
Accum. Depreciation - Comp Eq	586.32	586.32
Accum. Depreciation - Furnitur	225.00	225.00
Accum. Depreciation - Automobi	950.00	950.00
Prepaid Insurance	525.00	(1,575.00)
Prepaid Rent	600.00	0.00
Supplies	491.48	(1,500.00)
Publisher Advances	(3,000.00)	9,000.00
Total Adjustments	377.80	7,686.32
Net Cash provided by Operations	2,200.99	19,949.19
Cash Flows from investing activities		
Used For		
Computer Equipment	0.00	(8,035.79)
Furniture	0.00	(5,000.00)
Automobile	0.00	(19,000.00)
Net cash used in investing	0.00	(32,035.79)
Cash Flows from financing activities		
Proceeds From		
Taylor Rinaldi, Capital	0.00	98,510.68
Used For		
Taylor Rinaldi, Draw	(1,200.00)	(2,400.00)
Net cash used in financing	(1,200.00)	96,110.68
Net increase <decrease> in cash	$ 1,000.99	$ 84,024.08
Summary		
Cash Balance at End of Period	$ 84,024.08	$ 84,024.08
Cash Balance at Beg of Period	(83,023.09)	0.00
Net Increase <Decrease> in Cash	$ 1,000.99	$ 84,024.08

14. Print the Statement of Changes in Financial Position (<Standard> Stmnt Changes).

	Current Month	Year To Date
Taylor Rinaldi, Graphic Artist		
Statement of Changes in Financial Position		
For the twelve months ended December 31, 2004		
Sources of Working Capital		
Net Income	$ 1,823.19	$ 12,262.87
Add back items not requiring		
working capital		
Accum. Depreciation - Comp Eq	586.32	586.32
Accum. Depreciation - Furnitur	225.00	225.00
Accum. Depreciation - Automobi	950.00	950.00
Working capital from operations	3,584.51	14,024.19
Other sources		
Taylor Rinaldi, Capital	0.00	98,510.68
Total sources	3,584.51	112,534.87
Uses of working capital		
Computer Equipment	0.00	(8,035.79)
Furniture	0.00	(5,000.00)
Automobile	0.00	(19,000.00)
Total uses	0.00	(32,035.79)
Net change	$ 3,584.51	$ 80,499.08
Analysis of componants of changes		
Increase <Decrease> in Current Assets		
Money Market Account	$ 0.00	$ 10,370.85
Checking Account	1,000.99	15,491.16
IRA Savings Account	0.00	25,750.32
WI State Retirement	0.00	32,411.75
Prepaid Insurance	(525.00)	1,575.00
Prepaid Rent	(600.00)	0.00
Supplies	(491.48)	1,500.00
<Increase> Decrease in Current Liabilities		
Publisher Advances	3,000.00	(9,000.00)
Net change	$ 2,384.51	$ 78,099.08

BACKING UP DECEMBER DATA

Follow these steps to back up Taylor Rinaldi's December data:

1. Put your backup disk in drive A. You may use the same disk that you used to back up November data on pages 329 and 330.

2. From the menu bar, select File, then Back up.

3. Click [Back Up Now].

4. Click on the down-arrow in the Save in field. If necessary, scroll up the list, then click on 3½ Floppy (A:) to select drive A. *Or*, back up to the network or hard drive.

5. Type **Chapter 10 December** in the File name field.

6. Click [Save].

7. When the screen prompts that This company backup will require approximately 1 diskette, click [OK].

8. When the screen prompts you to insert the first disk, click [OK]. When the Back Up Company scale is 100% completed, you have successfully backed up to the current point in Chapter 10. You are returned to the menu bar.

9. Click on File, Exit to exit Peachtree or continue with the next section, Closing the Fiscal Year.

CLOSING THE FISCAL YEAR

At the end of the year, PCA automatically completes the closing procedure. Follow these steps to close Taylor Rinaldi's fiscal year:

1. If necessary, start Windows and Peachtree in the usual way, then open Taylor Rinaldi, Graphic Artist. From the menu bar, select Tasks, System, Year-End Wizard.[7]

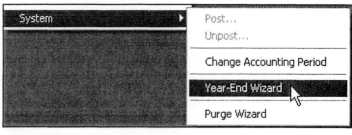

[7] If a Peachtree Accounting screen pops up that asks if you still want to open the Year-End Wizard, click on Yes.

2. The Year-End Wizard - Welcome window appears. Read the information on this screen.

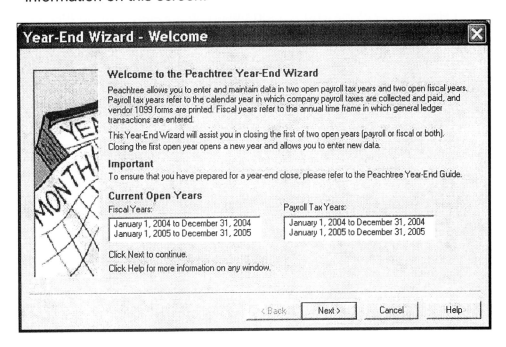

3. Click ⌊ Next > ⌋ .

4. The Close Options window appears. In the Years to Close list, Fiscal and Payroll Tax Years is the default. Read the information on this screen.

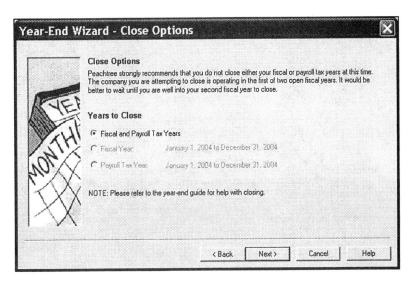

5. Click [Next >] .

6. The Print Fiscal Year-End Reports window appears. Read the information on this screen. Since you have already printed reports, click on the checkmarks in the print column to uncheck them.

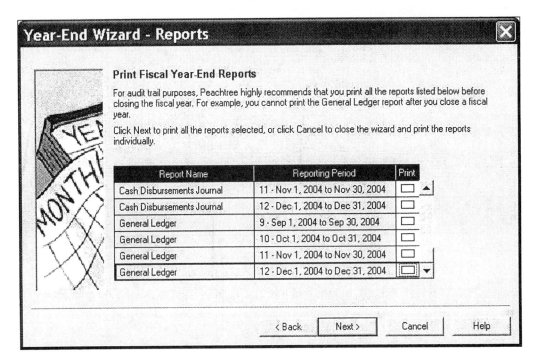

Hint: If you do not *uncheck the boxes, the general ledger prints.*

7. Click [Next >] .

8. The Back Up Company Data window appears. You already made a back up on page 339 but you may want to make another one. Read the information on this screen. Click [Back Up] . The Back Up Company window appears.

---

9. Observe that the box next to Include company name in the backup file name is checked. Click Back Up Now.

10. The Save Backup for Taylor Rinaldi, Graphic Artist as window appears. Observe that the File name field includes the name of the company and today's date. Put a disk in drive A.

11. In the Save in field, select drive A.

12. Click Save. Make the selections to back up.

13. After the back up is made, you are returned to the Back Up Company Data window. Click Next >.

14. The New Open Fiscal Years window appears. Read the information on this screen.

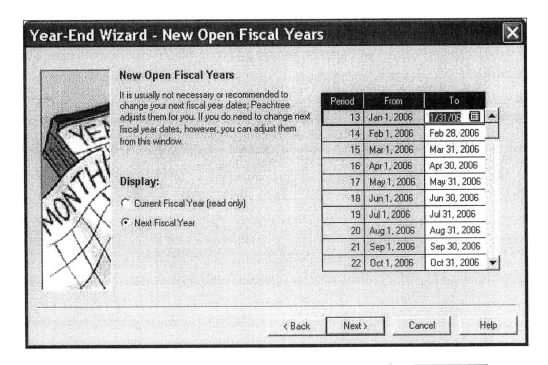

15. Accept the default for Next Fiscal Year by clicking on Next >.

---

16. The Important - Confirm Year-End Close window appears. Read the information on this screen.

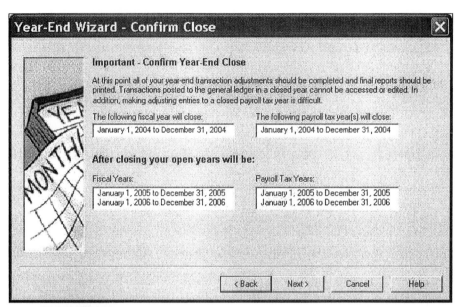

17. Click [Next >].

18. The Begin Close-Year Process window appears. Read the information on this screen.

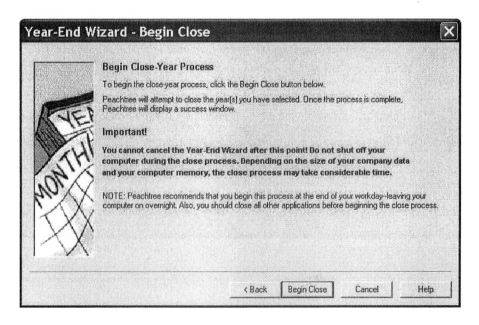

19. Click Begin Close.

20. The Congratulations! window appears. Read the information on this
     screen.

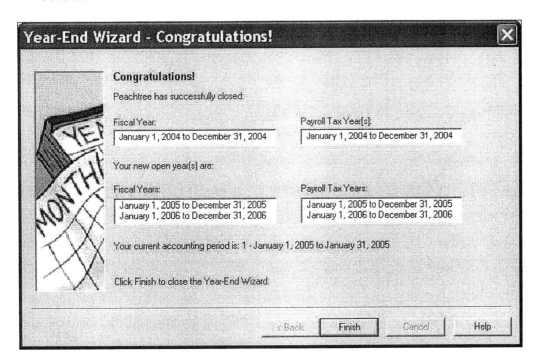

21. Click Finish. You are returned to Taylor Rinaldi, Graphic Artist
     menu bar.

PRINTING THE POST-CLOSING TRIAL BALANCE

After the fiscal year is closed, a post-closing trial balance is printed. Only
permanent accounts appear on the post-closing trial balance. All
temporary accounts (revenues and expenses) have been closed.
This completes the computer accounting cycle.

Follow these steps to print Taylor Rinaldi's post-closing trial balance:

1. From the menu bar, select Reports, General Ledger, General Ledger
    Trial Balance.

2. Make the selections to print the post-closing trial balance.

	Taylor Rinaldi, Graphic Artist		
	General Ledger Trial Balance		
	As of Jan 31, 2005		

Filter Criteria includes: Report order is by ID. Report is printed in Detail Format.

Account ID	Account Description	Debit Amt	Credit Amt
1010	Money Market Account	10,370.85	
1020	Checking Account	15,491.16	
1040	IRA Savings Account	25,750.32	
1045	WI State Retirement	32,411.75	
1300	Prepaid Insurance	1,575.00	
1450	Supplies	1,500.00	
1500	Computer Equipment	8,035.79	
1510	Furniture	5,000.00	
1520	Automobile	19,000.00	
1900	Accum. Depreciation - Co		586.32
1910	Accum. Depreciation - Furn		225.00
1920	Accum. Depreciation - Auto		950.00
2400	Publisher Advances		9,000.00
3910	Retained Earnings		9,862.87
3920	Taylor Rinaldi, Capital		98,510.68
	Total:	**119,134.87**	**119,134.87**

Observe that the post-closing trial balance is dated January 31, 2005. The balance in retained earnings (Account No. 3910) is Mr. Rinaldi's year-to-date net income minus the total of his drawing accounts (12,262.87 − 2,400 = 9,862.87).

BACKING UP YEAR-END DATA

Follow these steps to back up Taylor Rinaldi's year-end data:

1. Put a blank, formatted disk in drive A. You may use the same disk that you used to back up December data on page 341.

2. From the menu bar, select File, then Back up. If necessary, uncheck the box next to Include company name in the backup file name.

3. Click Back Up Now. Remember to uncheck the box next to Include company name in the backup file name.

4. Click on the down-arrow in the Save in field. If necessary, scroll up the list, then click on 3½ Floppy (A:) to select drive A. *Or*, back up to the network or hard drive.

5. Type **Chapter 10 EOY** in the File name field.

6.   Click [Save].

7.   When the screen prompts that This company backup will require approximately 1 diskette, click [OK].

8.   When the screen prompts you to insert the first disk, click [OK]. When the Back Up Company scale is 100% completed, you have successfully backed up to the current point in Chapter 10. You are returned to the menu bar.

9.   Click on File, Exit to exit Peachtree.

	INTERNET ACTIVITY
1.	From your Internet browser, go to the book's website at http://www.mhhe.com/yacht2004.
2.	In the Student Edition list, link to Internet Activities.
3.	Link to WEB EXERCISES PART 2.
4.	Scroll down the screen to UNDERSTANDING ACCOUNTING TERMS – Chapter 10. Read steps 1 – 5.
5.	Follow the steps shown on the book's website to complete this Internet activity.
6.	Use a word processing program to write a summary for each website visited. Your summaries should be no more than 75 words or less than 50 words.

SUMMARY AND REVIEW

SOFTWARE OBJECTIVES: In Chapter 10, you used the software to:

1.   Restore data from Chapter 9.

2.   Change accounting periods.

3.   Journalize and post transactions for Taylor Rinaldi, Graphic Artist, for the months of November and December.

4.   Complete account reconciliation.

5.   Print a General Ledger Trial Balance (unadjusted).

6.   Journalize and post quarterly adjusting entries in the General Journal.

7. Print financial statements.

8. Close the fiscal year.

9. Print a Post-Closing Trial Balance.

10. Make six backups using two blank, formatted disks: four backups of Taylor Rinaldi, Graphic Artist data; one backup of Exercise 10-1; and one backup of Exercise 10-2.

WEB OBJECTIVES: In Chapter 10, you did these Internet activities:

1. Used your Internet browser to go to the book's website.

2. Went to the Internet Activity link on the book's website. Then, selected WEB EXERCISES PART 2. Completed the second web exercise in Part 2, Understanding Accounting Terms.

3. Used a word processing program to write summaries of the websites that you visited.

GOING TO THE NET

Access the depreciation calculator at http://www.fixedassetinfo.com/calculator.asp. This takes you to the Fixed AssetsInfo.com depreciation calculator. Read the How to Use information for completing the calculation for depreciation.

1. Complete the following fields:

   Property Type: Select Furn. and Equipment
   Placed in Service date: 6/1/2002
   Cost: 6000.00

2. Click Next >

3. Read the information on this page. Accept the defaults for Straight Line as the Depreciation Method, Half-Year as the Averaging Convention, and 7 as the Depreciable Life (yrs.).

4. Click Depreciate.

5.   Click to print the depreciation table.

True/Make True: Write the word True in the space provided if the statement is true. If the statement is not true, write the correct answer.

1.   You can complete the activities in Chapter 10 without completing Chapter 9.

_____

_____

2.   Step 4 of PCA's Computer Accounting Cycle is reconciling the bank statement.

_____

_____

3.   To change an accounting period, use the Maintain pull-down menu.

_____

_____

4. Taylor Rinaldi's checkbook register and bank statement are used as source documents for recording journal entries.

_____

_____

_____

5. The account reconciliation feature can reconcile the cash account only.

_____

_____

_____

6. The accounting periods used in Chapter 10 are November 1 - 30 and December 1 - 31, 2004.

_____

_____

7. PCA includes an editing feature so that records can be corrected.

_____

_____

_____

8. For the two months ending November 30, 2004, Mr. Rinaldi's net income is $4,715.22.

_____

_____

9. At the end of the quarter, Mr. Rinaldi's total assets are $117,373.55.

_____

_____

10. On the post-closing trial balance, Mr. Rinaldi's retained earnings are $9,862.87.

_____

_____

_____

Exercise 10-1: Follow the instructions below to complete Exercise 10-1. You must complete Exercises 9-1 and 9-2 before you can do Exercise 10-1.

1. Start Windows and Peachtree in the usual way. Open the company that you started in Exercise 9-1. The company name was Your Name, Artist.

2. Restore your data from Exercise 9-2.[8] The suggested file name was **Exercise 9-2.ptb**. *(Hint: You must use the same file name that you used to back up Exercise 9-2 on page 308. To make sure you are starting in the right place, display the balance sheet and compare it to the one shown on page 307.)*

3. Use the check register on this page and page 353 to journalize and post cash receipts journal and cash disbursement journal transactions. (*Hint: Use the Write Checks task for checks and ATMs.*)

Check Number	Date	Description of Transaction	Payment/ Dr (-)	Deposit/ Cr. (+)	Balance
					8,500.00
	10/2/04	ATM	100.00		8,400.00
	10/3/04	Deposit (Art Income)		2,307.55	10,707.55
2001	10/3/04	Accounts Payable	1,570.00		9,137.55
	10/8/04	Deposit (Teaching Income)		2,105.00	11,242.55
2002	10/9/04	Utilities Co.	35.80		11,206.75
2003	10/10/04	Mattson Advertising, Inc.	105.00		11,101.75
2004	10/13/04	U.S. Post Office	37.00		11,064.75
2005	10/13/04	Artist's Workshop (conference)[9]	175.00		10,889.75

---

[8]You can restore from your back up file even if *no* Peachtree company exists. Close Peachtree's start up screen. Select File; Restore. Select the location of your backup file. On the Restore Wizard's Select Company screen, select A New Company. The *A New Company* selection allows you to restore your backup data, bypassing the process of new company set up. For more information, refer to Troubleshooting on pages 274 and 275.

[9]Debit Account No. 6800, Conference Fees.

2006	10/15/04	Area Telephone	35.15		10,854.60
2007	10/16/04	Internet Service	20.95		10,833.65
	10/20/04	ATM	100.00		10,733.65
2008	10/28/04	Wheaton Office Supplies[10]	47.80		10,685.85
	10/30/04	ATM	200.00		10,485.85

4. Use the Bank Statement below to complete Account Reconciliation. (*Hint: Remember to record the bank service charge on the Account Reconciliation screen.*)

Statement of Account Bank One October 1 to October 31, 2004		Account No. 41904-783-9	Your Name Your Address Your city, state, Zip	
		REGULAR CHECKING		
Previous Balance	9/30/04	8,500.00		
2 Deposits(+)		4,412.55		
6 Checks (-)		1,943.75		
2 Other Deductions (-)		400.00		
Service Charges (-)	10/31/04	12.00		
Ending Balance	10/31/04	**10,556.80**		
		DEPOSITS		
	10/6/04	2,307.55		
	10/8/04	2,105.00		
	CHECKS (Asterisk * indicates break in check number sequence)			
	10/10/04	2001	1,570.00	
	10/10/04	2002	35.80	
	10/24/04	2003	105.00	
	10/24/04	2004	37.00	
	10/27/04	2005	175.00	
	10/30/04	2007*	20.95	
				continued

---

[10]Debit Account No. 1450, Supplies.

	OTHER DEDUCTIONS (ATM's)			
	10/2103	100.00		
	10/17/04	100.00		
	10/30/04	200.00		

5. Print an Account Reconciliation report.

6. Print the Cash Account Register.

7. Print the Cash Receipts Journal.

8. Print the Cash Disbursements Journal.

9. Print the General Ledger Trial Balance.

10. Make a backup of Exercise 10-1:

   a. Put your backup disk in drive A. You may use the same disk that you used to back up data on pages 339-340.

   b. From the menu bar, select File, then Back up.

   c. Click Back Up Now .

   d. Click on the down-arrow in the Save in field. If necessary, scroll up the list, then click on 3½ Floppy (A:) to select drive A. *Or*, back up to the network or hard drive.

   e. Type **Exercise 10-1** in the File name field.

   f. Click Save .

   g. When the screen prompts that This company backup will require approximately 1 diskette, click OK .

   h. When the screen prompts you to insert the first disk, click OK . When the Back Up Company scale is 100% completed, you have successfully backed up to the current point in Exercise 10-1. You are returned to the menu bar.

   i. Click on File, Exit to exit Peachtree.

Exercise 10-2: Follow the directions below to complete Exercise 10-2.

1. Start Windows, then PCA. Open your company from Exercise 10-1.

2. Restore your data from Exercise 10-1.

3. Print the Balance Sheet.

4. Print the Income Statement.

5. Print the Statement of Retained Earnings.

6. Print the Statement of Cash Flow.

7. Print the Statement of Changes in Financial Position.

8. Back up Exercise 10-2. Use **Exercise 10-2.ptb** as the backup name.
    You may use the same disk that you used to back up Exercise 10-1
    on page 354.

CHAPTER 10 INDEX

Project 1

Lena Becker, Consultant

In Project 1, you will complete the Computer Accounting Cycle for Lena Becker, Consultant. Ms. Becker started her consulting business on December 1, 2004 in Mesa, AZ. Ms. Becker employs two consulting technicians and one administrative assistant. Ms. Becker's employees are independent contractors. Further study of payroll accounting will be done in Chapter 14.

In this project you will complete the accounting cycle for the month of December 2004. Lena Becker's balance sheet, checkbook register, and bank statement are provided as source documents.

At the end of this project, a checklist is shown listing the printed reports you should have. The step-by-step instructions also remind you to print reports at certain intervals. Your instructor may require these printouts for grading purposes. Remember to make backups at periodic intervals.

Follow these steps to complete Project 1:

Step 1: Start Windows and Peachtree in the usual way.

Step 2: At the startup screen, select Set up a new company.

Step 3: Type the following company information:

Company Name:	**Lena Becker, Consultant** (*use your name*)
Address Line 1:	**200 Broadway**
City, State, Zip	**Mesa, AZ 85032**
Country:	**USA**
Telephone:	**480-555-9132**
Fax:	**480-555-9133**
Business Type:	Select Sole Proprietorship
Leave the Tax ID Numbers fields blank.	
Web Site:	www.becker.com
E-mail:	lena@becker.com

Step 4:   At the New Company Setup - Chart of Accounts window, accept the default for Set up a new Retail, Service, Construction, Manufacturing, or Distribution company using a simplified chart of accounts.

Step 5:   Select Service Company.

Step 6:   Accept the default for Accrual accounting.

Step 7:   Accept the default for Real Time posting.

Step 8:   At the Accounting Periods screen, accept the default for 12 monthly accounting periods.

Step 9:   On the Monthly Accounting Periods screen, make the following selections:

When do you want your first fiscal year to start?   Month: **January**   Year   **2004**
What is the first month you will be entering data?   Month: **December** Year   2004
What is the first year you will be entering payroll? 2004

Step 10:   Accept the defaults for payment terms and credit limits.

Step 11:   At the Congratulations screen [Finish]. When the Peachtree Today window appears, disable it.

Step 12:   Make the following changes to the Chart of Accounts:

Delete these accounts:

1010	Cash on Hand
1150	Allowance for Doubtful Account
2310	Sales Tax Payable
2320	Deductions Payable
2330	Federal Payroll Taxes Payable
2340	FUTA Tax Payable
2350	State Payroll Taxes Payable
2360	SUTA Payable
2370	Local Payroll Taxes Payable
2400	Customer Deposits
2700	Long-Term Debt – Noncurrent

4300   Other Income
5900   Inventory Adjustments
6250   Other Taxes Expense
6650   Commissions and Fees Expense
7100   Gain/Loss – Sale of Assets Exp

Change these accounts:[1]

1020	Checking Account	**Mesa Bank**
1400	Prepaid Expenses	**Prepaid Rent**
1500	Property and Equipment	**Computer Equipment**
1900	Accum. Depreciation-Prop&Eqt	**Accum. Depreciation-Comp Eq**
2500	Current Portion Long-Term Debt	**Notes Payable**
3920	Owner's Contribution	**Lena Becker, Capital** (*Account Type: Equity-doesn't close*)
3930	Owner's Draw	**Lena Becker, Draw**
4000	Professional Fees	**Consulting Fees**
6000	Wages Expense	**Wages Expense - Adm Asst**
6050	Employee Benefit Programs Exp.	**Wages Expense - Cons Tech**
6150	Bad Debts Expense	**Subscriptions Expense**
6450	Office Supplies Expense	**Supplies Expense**
6550	Other Office Expense	**Internet Service Provider**
7050	Depreciation Expense	**Deprec Exp – Comp Eq**

Add these accounts:

1450	**Supplies**	Other Current Assets
1510	**Furniture and Fixtures**	Fixed Assets
1520	**Automobile**	Fixed Assets
1910	**Accum. Depreciation – Furn&Fix**	Accum. Depreciation
1920	**Accum. Depreciation – Automobi**	Accum. Depreciation
7060	**Deprec. Exp.- Furn&Fix**	Expenses

---

[1]New account names are shown in boldface.

| 7070 | **Deprec. Exp.- Automobile** | Expenses |
| 7400 | **Postage Expense** | Expenses |

Step 13: Print the Chart of Accounts.

Step 14: Use Lena Becker's Balance Sheet to enter the beginning balances. Remember when selecting the period, use 11/1/04 through 11/30/04.

Lena Becker, Consultant, Balance Sheet December 1, 2004		
ASSETS		
Current Assets		
Mesa Bank	$29,500.00	
Accounts Receivable	11,500.00	
Prepaid Rent	4,000.00	
Supplies	3,300.00	
Total Current Assets		$48,300.00
Property and Equipment		
Computer Equipment	12,600.00	
Furniture and Fixtures	15,000.00	
Automobile	21,500.00	
Total Property and Equipment		49,100.00
Total Assets		$ 97,400.00
LIABILITIES AND CAPITAL		
Current Liabilities		
Accounts Payable	$11,200.00	
Notes Payable	8,400.00	
Total Current Liabilities		19,600.00
Capital		
Lena Becker, Capital		77,800.00
Total Liabilities and Capital		$ 97,400.00

Step 15: Back up Ms. Becker's beginning data. The suggested file name is Lena Becker Begin.

Step 16: The checkbook register on the next page provides you with the information necessary for December's journal entries. Remember to post between each transaction.

Check Number	Date	Description of Transaction	Payment/ Dr. (-)	Deposit/ Cr. (+)	Balance
					29,500.00
	12/1	Deposit (consulting fees)		3,950.00	33,450.00
8001	12/1	Bank Corp. (Notes Payable)	2,500.00		30,950.00
8002	12/1	Office Place - laser printer (computer equipment)	620.32		30,329.68
8003	12/6	Administrative Asst.	1,250.00		29,079.68
8004	12/6	Consulting Technician	690.00		28,389.68
8005	12/11	Mesa Office Supplies (letterhead - supplies)	115.85		28,273.83
8006	12/13	Administrative Asst.	1,250.00		27,023.83
8007	12/13	Consulting Technician	690.00		26,333.83
	12/15	Deposit (consulting fees)		4,000.00	30,333.83
8008	12/17	Southwestern Telephone Service (telephone bill)	74.99		30,258.84
8009	12/19	U.S. Post Office (stamps)	37.00		30,221.84
8010	12/19	Consultant's Journal (subscription)	505.00		29,716.84
8011	12/20	Administrative Asst.	1,250.00		28,466.84
8012	12/20	Consulting Technician	620.00		27,846.84
	12/23	Deposit (consulting fees)		3,950.00	31,796.84
8013	12/24	Maricopa Electric Co. (utilities bill)	145.20		31,651.64
	12/26	Deposit (consulting fees)		3,500.00	35,151.64
8014	12/27	Administrative Asst.	1,250.00		33,901.64
8015	12/27	Consulting Technician	750.00		33,151.64
	12/29	Deposit (payment received from client on account)		1,500.00	34,651.64
8016	12/29	Internet Service Provider	68.66		34,582.98

Step 17: Lena Becker' bank statement is shown below. (*Hint:* Remember to record the bank service charge.)

Statement of Account Mesa Bank December 1 to December 31, 2004		Account #4753-05-234	Lena Becker, Consultant 200 Broadway Mesa, AZ 85032	
REGULAR CHECKING				
Previous Balance	11/30/04	29,500.00		
4 Deposits(+)		15,400.00		
12 Checks (-)		10,456.36		
Service Charges (-)	12/31/04	25.00		
Ending Balance	12/31/04	**34,418.64**		
DEPOSITS				
	12/3/04	3,950.00	12/26/04	3,950.00
	12/17/04	4,000.00	12/30/04	3,500.00
CHECKS (Asterisk * indicates break in check number sequence)				
	12/10/04	8001	2,500.00	
	12/11/04	8002	620.32	
	12/15/04	8003	1,250.00	
	12/15/04	8004	690.00	
	12/15/04	8005	115.85	
	12/15/04	8006	1,250.00	
	12/15/04	8007	690.00	
	12/21/04	8008	74.99	
	12/21/04	8011*	1,250.00	
	12/19/04	8012	620.00	
	12/29/04	8013	145.20	
	12/30/04	8014	1,250.00	

Step 18: Print an Account Reconciliation report.

Step 19: Print a Cash Account Register.

Step 20: Print a General Ledger Trial Balance (unadjusted).

Step 21: Back up. The suggested file name is Lena Becker UTB. (UTB is an abbreviation for unadjusted trial balance.)

Step 22:   Complete these adjusting entries:

    a. Supplies on hand: $2,600.00.
    b. Depreciation for Computer Equipment: $336.11.
    c. Depreciation for Furniture and Fixtures: $166.67.
    d. Depreciation for the Automobile: $358.33.
    e. Rent was paid for two months on November 30, 2004. Adjust one month's rent.[2]

Step 23:   Print the December 31, 2004 General Journal, Cash Receipts Journal, and Cash Disbursements Journal.

Step 24:   Print the General Ledger Trial Balance (adjusted).

Step 25:   Print the General Ledger. (*Hint: Select Reports, General Ledger, highlight General Ledger, make the selections to print.*)

Step 26:   Print the financial statements: balance sheet, income statement, statement of retained earnings, statement of cash flow, statement of changes in financial position.

Step 27:   Back up December data. The suggested file name is Lena Becker December.

Step 28:   Close the fiscal year.

Step 29:   Print the Post-Closing Trial Balance.

Step 30:   Back up year-end data. The suggested file name is Lena Becker EOY.

---

[2]Refer to the December 1, 2004, Balance Sheet for the account balance in the Prepaid Rent account.

Your instructor may want to collect this project. A Checklist of Printouts is shown below.

Checklist of Printouts, Project 1: Lena Becker, Consultant	
	Chart of Accounts
	Account Reconciliation
	Cash Account Register
	General Ledger Trial Balance (unadjusted)
	December 31, 2004 General Journal
	Cash Receipts Journal
	Cash Disbursements Journal
	General Ledger Trial Balance (adjusted)
	General Ledger
	Balance Sheet
	Income Statement
	Statement of Retained Earnings
	Statement of Cash Flow
	Statement of Changes in Financial Position
	Post-Closing Trial Balance

Student Name_____ **Date**_____

CHECK YOUR PROGRESS: PROJECT 1, Lena Becker, Consultant

1. What are the total debit and credit balances on your unadjusted trial balance? _____

2. What are the total debit and credit balances on your adjusted trial balance? _____

3. According to your account reconciliation report, what is the Ending GL Balance? _____

4. What is the depreciation expense for furniture and fixtures on December 31? _____

5. What is the depreciation expense for computer equipment on December 31? _____

6. What is the amount of total revenues as of December 31? _____

7. How much net income <or net loss> is reported on December 31? _____

8. What is the account balance in the Supplies account on December 31? _____

9. What is the account balance in the Accounts Payable account on December 31? _____

10. What is the account balance in the Capital account on December 31? _____

11. Is there an Increase or Decrease in cash for the the month of December? _____

12. Were any Accounts Payable incurred during the month of December? (Circle your answer).   YES   NO

Project

1A

Student-Designed Service Business

In Chapters 9, 10 and Project 1, you learned how to complete the Computer Accounting Cycle for a service business. Project 1A gives you a chance to design a service business of your own.

You will select the type of service business you want, edit your business's Chart of Accounts, create source documents, and complete PCA's Computer Accounting Cycle. Project 1A also gives you an opportunity to review the software features learned so far.

You should think about the kind of business you want to create. Since you have been working on sole proprietorship service businesses in Part 2, you might want to design a business similar to these. Service businesses include: accountants, beauty salons, architects, hotels, airlines, cleaning stores, doctors, artists, etc. If you have a checking account and receive a monthly bank statement, you could use your own records for this project.

Before you begin you should design your business. You will need the following:

1. Company information that includes business name, address, and telephone number. (*Hint: Set your company up for Period 12, December 1 - 31, so that you can close the fiscal year.*)

2. One of PCA's sample companies.

3. A Chart of Accounts: 25 accounts minimum; 30 maximum.

4. One month's transactions for your business. You will need a Balance Sheet, checkbook register, and bank statement. Your checkbook register should include a minimum of 15 transactions and a maximum of 25. You should have at least four adjusting entries.

If you don't want to use a checkbook register and bank statement, you could write 15 to 25 narrative transactions.

After you have designed your business, you should follow the steps of PCA's Computer Accounting Cycle to complete Project 1A.

For grading purposes, Project 1A should include the following printouts:

Checklist of Printouts **Project 1A** **Student-Designed Project**
Chart of Accounts
Account Reconciliation
Cash Account Register
General Ledger Trial Balance (unadjusted)
Cash Receipts Journal
Cash Disbursements Journal
December 31, 200X General Journal
General Ledger
General Ledger Trial Balance (adjusted)
Balance Sheet
Income Statement
Statement of Retained Earnings
Statement of Cash Flow
Statement of Changes in Financial Position
Post-Closing Trial Balance

Part	**Peachtree Complete Accounting 2004 for Merchandising Businesses**
3	

In Part 3 of *Computer Accounting with Peachtree Complete 2004, Eighth Edition*, your accounting business is hired to do the monthly record keeping for three merchandising businesses: Matt's Service Merchandise, the end-of-chapter exercise (Student Name Sales & Service), and Copper Bicycles.

Part 3 includes four chapters and two projects.

Chapter 11: Accounts Payable

Chapter 12: Accounts Receivable

Chapter 13: Merchandise Inventory

Chapter 14: Payroll

Project 2: Copper Bicycles

Project 2A: Student-Designed Merchandising Business

As you know from your study of accounting, merchandising businesses purchase products ready-made from a vendor and then resell these ready-made products to their customers. Units purchased by a merchandising business for resale are referred to as merchandise. A merchandising business earns revenue from buying and selling goods. Items such as office supplies or computer equipment are *not* merchandise because they are *not* purchased for resale but are to be used by the business.

In Part 1 you were shown how the sample company, Bellwether Garden Supply, used Peachtree's customer, vendor, payroll, and inventory features. The chapters that follow will illustrate these features in more detail.

Chapters 11 through 14 are cumulative. This means that the businesses you set up in Chapter 11, Matt's Service Merchandise and the end-of-chapter business, are continued in Chapters 12, 13, and 14.
At the end of Part 3, you will complete Project 2, Copper Bicycles, which

reviews all the features of PCA that apply to merchandising businesses. At the end of Project 2, there is a Check Your Progress assessment that your instructor may want you to turn in. Project 2A, Student-Designed Merchandising Business, gives you an opportunity to design your own merchandising business.

The chart below shows that you need nine blank, formatted disks to back up all the data in Chapters 11-14 and Project 2. You may also back up to the hard drive, network, or other media. If you are using floppy disks, the author suggests that you reformat disks used in earlier chapters. *Remember: do not reformat the Exercise 6-2 backup. Exercise 6-2 will be used in Part 4 of the textbook.*

Disk Label	Chapter	Backup Name	Kilobytes	Page Nos.
Disk 1 of 9	11	a:\Chapter 11 Begin	451 KB	392-393
		a:\Chapter 11	464 KB	414-415
Disk 2 of 9		a:\Exercise 11-1	450 KB	424-425
		a:\Exercise 11-2	460 KB	428
Disk 3 of 9	12	a:\Chapter 12 Begin	471 KB	449-450
		a:\Chapter 12	479 KB	470-471
Disk 4 of 9		a:\Exercise 12-1	462 KB	477
		a:\Exercise 12-2	467 KB	478
Disk 5 of 9	13	a:\Chapter 13 Begin	481 KB	491-492
		a:\Chapter 13	494 KB	500-501
Disk 6 of 9		a:\Exercise 13-1	473 KB	505
Disk 7 of 9	14	a:\Chapter 14 Begin	494 KB	525
		a:\Chapter 14	512 KB	539
Disk 8 of 9		a:\Exercise 14-1	474 KB	545
		a:\Exercise 14-2	494 KB	546
Disk 9 of 9	Project 2	a:\Copper Bicycles Begin	456 KB	560
		a:\Copper Bicycles January	501 KB	563

The size of your backup files may differ from the amounts shown on the chart. This is okay.

Chapter

11 Accounts Payable

SOFTWARE OBJECTIVES: In Chapter 11, you will use the software to:

1. Set up company information for Matt's Service Merchandise.
2. Enter the following general ledger information: chart of accounts and beginning balances.
3. Enter the following accounts payable information: vendor defaults and vendor records.
4. Enter the following inventory information: inventory defaults, inventory items, and inventory beginning balances.
5. Record accounts payable transactions: merchandise purchases, purchase orders, cash purchases, and purchase returns.
6. Make four backups using two blank, formatted disks: two backups for Matt's Service Merchandise data; one backup for Exercise 11-1; one backup for Exercise 11-2.[1]

WEB OBJECTIVES: In Chapter 11, you will do these Internet activities:

1. Use your Internet browser to go to the book's website. (Go online to www.mhhe.com/yacht2004.)
2. Go to the Internet Activity link on the book's website. Then, select WEB EXERCISES PART 3. Complete the first web exercise in Part 3—Accounting List.
3. Use a word processing program to write summaries of the websites that you visited.

Chapter 11 begins Part 3 of the book: Peachtree Complete Accounting 2004 for Merchandising Businesses. Merchandising businesses are retail stores that resell goods and services. In this chapter, you will set up a merchandising business called Matt's Service Merchandise. Matt's Service Merchandise is a partnership owned by Matt Lowe and Sharon Albert. Mr. Lowe and Ms. Albert divide their income equally.

---

[1]The chart on page 366 shows you how many disks you need for the Part 3 (Chapters 11 - 14 and Project 2) backups. You may also reformat the disks you used in Part 2 (Chapters 9, 10, and Project 1) for making the backups in Chapters 11 - 14 and Project 2.

Merchandising businesses purchase the merchandise they sell from suppliers known as *vendors*. Vendors are the businesses that offer Matt's Service Merchandise credit to buy merchandise and/or assets, or credit for expenses incurred. When Matt's Service Merchandise makes purchases on account from vendors, the transactions are known as *accounts payable transactions*.

PCA organizes and monitors Matt's Service Merchandise's *accounts payable*. Accounts Payable is the amount of money the business owes to suppliers or vendors.

When entering a purchase, you first enter the vendor's code. The vendor's name and address information, the standard payment terms, and the general ledger purchase account are automatically entered in the appropriate places. Of course, this information can be edited if any changes are needed. This works similarly for accounts receivable.

Once you have entered purchase information, printing a check to pay for a purchase is simple. When you enter the vendor's code, a list of purchases displays. You simply select the ones you want to pay and click on the Pay box. You can print the check or wait to print a batch of checks later. You can even pay a whole batch of vendors at one time, using the Select for Payment option on the Tasks pull-down menu.

The flowchart below illustrates how vendors are paid.

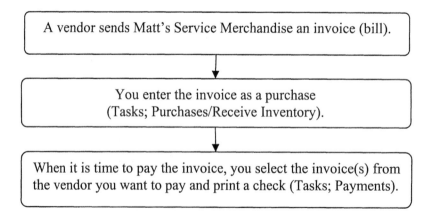

A vendor sends Matt's Service Merchandise an invoice (bill).

You enter the invoice as a purchase
(Tasks; Purchases/Receive Inventory).

When it is time to pay the invoice, you select the invoice(s) from the vendor you want to pay and print a check (Tasks; Payments).

In Chapter 11, the businesses that you set up are continued in Chapters 12, 13, and 14.

GETTING STARTED

Matt's Service Merchandise started operations on January 1, 2004. Matt's Service Merchandise is a partnership owned by Matt Lowe and Sharon Albert and is located in La Jolla, CA. Follow these steps to set up a Sales & Service company.

1. Start Windows and Peachtree in the usual way.

2. At the Peachtree Accounting startup screen, click on <u>S</u>et up a new company. The New Company Setup - Introduction screen appears. Read the information on this screen.

3. Click [Next >]. In each text field, type the Company Information and Tax ID Information shown below. Press the **<Tab>** key between each field.

Company Information

Company Name:	**Matt's Service Merchandise** *(use your first name then Service Merchandise)*
Address Line 1:	**1801 University Drive**
City, State, Zip:	**La Jolla, CA 95331**
Country:	**USA**
Telephone:	**858-555-9213**
Fax:	**858-555-9215**
Business Type:	Select Partnership

Tax ID Information

Federal Employer ID:	**26-1255314**
State Employer ID:	**16-9988456**
State Unemployment ID:	**168921-3**
Web Site:	**www.mattservicemdse.com**
E-mail:	**matt@mattservicemdse.com**

> **Comment**
>
> If you use a your name in the Company Name field, the name of your company will appear on all printouts.

4. Check the information you just typed, then click [Next >]. The New Company Setup - Chart of Accounts screen appears.

5. Click on Set up a new company using an extensive chart of accounts from one of many sample companies.

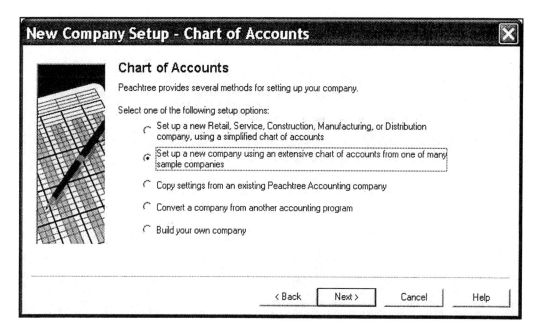

6. Click [Next >].

7. Read the information about selecting a chart of accounts. The Available Chart of Accounts list shows numerous sample companies. Scroll down the list. Click on Sales & Service Company to highlight it.

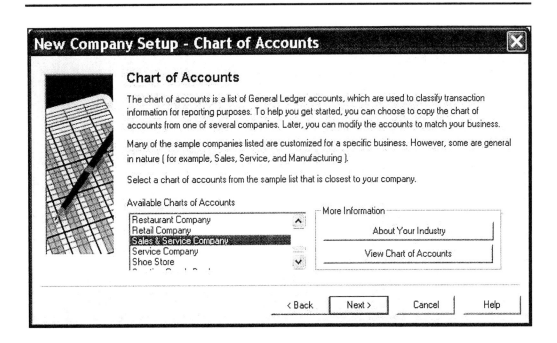

8. Make sure that Sales & Service Company is highlighted, then click Next >.

9. Read the information about the Accounting Method. Accept the default for Accrual by clicking on Next >.

10. Read the information about Posting Method. Peachtree Software recommends real-time posting for networked computers. Accept the default for real-time posting by clicking on Next >.

11. At the Accounting Periods screen, accept the default for 12 monthly accounting periods by clicking on Next >.

12. Read the information about Monthly Accounting Periods. Use this information to complete the fields.

	Month	Year
When do you want your fiscal year to start?	January	**2004**
When is the first month you will be entering data?	**January**	2004
What is the first year you will be entering payroll?[2]		2004

Make sure the year 2004 is selected. Compare your screen to the one shown below.

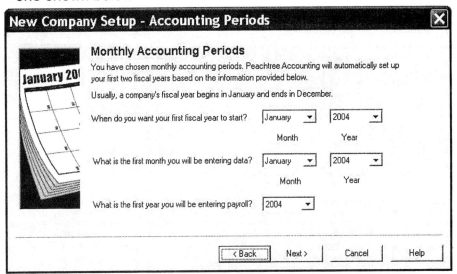

Check this screen carefully. You cannot change it later.

13. Click [Next >]. The Defaults screen appears.

14. Read the information about Defaults, then click [Next >].

15. The New Company Setup - Finish, Congratulations! screen appears. Read the information on this screen. Click [Finish].

16. Verify that your toolbar shows Period 1 - 1/1/04 to 1/31/04
[Period 1 - 1/1/04 to 1/31/04].

---

[2]You will work with Peachtree's payroll features in Part 3, Chapters 11-14.

Once your company is set up, the Peachtree Today window appears. You could use the Setup Guide to set defaults or set your company's defaults through the Maintain menu. Either way, the results are the same. Since the instructions that follow show you how to set up your defaults through the Maintain menu, close the Peachtree Today window.

To permanently disable Peachtree Today, follow these steps.

1. Select <u>Preferences</u>.

2. Scroll down the screen to the Start Up area.

3. Click on the box next to Display Peachtree Today each time this company is opened. The box should be *unchecked*.

4. Click on Peachtree Today's title bar to close the window.

GENERAL LEDGER

Follow these steps to record general ledger information.

1. From the menu bar, click on Maintain; Chart of Accounts.

   Delete the following accounts:

Comment
Detailed steps for deleting, adding, and changing accounts was shown in Chapter 9, pages 256-261.

10000	Petty Cash
10100	Cash on Hand
11400	Other Receivables
14100	Employee Advances
14200	Notes Receivable-Current
14700	Other Current Assets
15200	Automobiles
15300	Other Depreciable Property
15400	Leasehold Improvements
15600	Building Improvements
16900	Land
17200	Accum. Depreciation-Automobi

17300 Accum. Depreciation-Other
17400 Accum. Depreciation-Leasehol
17600 Accum. Depreciation-Bldg Imp
19000 Deposits
19100 Organization Costs
19150 Accum. Amortiz -Org. Costs
19200 Notes Receivable-Noncurrent
19900 Other Noncurrent Assets
23300 Deductions Payable
23800 Local Payroll Taxes Payable
24800 Other Current Liabilities
24900 Suspense-Clearing Account
58000 Cost of Sales-Other
60500 Amortization Expense
61000 Auto Expenses
62500 Cash Over and Short
63000 Charitable Contributions Exp
63500 Commissions and Fees Exp
65000 Employee Benefit Programs Exp
68000 Laundry and Cleaning Exp
73000 Other Taxes
74000 Rent or Lease Expense
76500 Travel Expense
77000 Salaries Expense

Change the following accounts:

10200	Regular Checking Account	**La Jolla Bank**
10400	Savings Account	**Stockmen's Savings & Loan**
12000	Inventory	**Merchandise Inventory**
14000	Prepaid Expenses	**Prepaid Insurance**
15100	Equipment	**Computers & Equipment**
17000	Accum. Depreciation-Furniture	**Accum. Depreciation - Furn&Fix**
17100	Accum. Depreciation-Equipment	**Accum. Depreciation - Comp&Eq**
24000	Other Taxes Payable	**FICA Employee Taxes Payable**
24100	Employee Benefits Payable	**FICA Employer Taxes Payable**
24200	Current Portion Long-Term Debt	**Medicare Employee Taxes Payabl**
24400	Customer Deposits	**Medicare Employer Taxes Payabl**
27000	Notes Payable-Noncurrent	**Long-Term Notes Payable**
27400	Other Long Term-Liabilities	**Mortgage Payable**

39006	Partner's Contribution	**Matt Lowe, Capital** *(Note: Scroll up the Account Type field, select Equity-doesn't close)*
39007	Partner's Draw	**Matt Lowe, Drawing**
40200	Sales #1	**Sales-Hardware**
40400	Sales #2	**Sales-Wall**
40600	Sales #3	**Sales-Floor**
50000	Cost of Goods Sold #1	**Cost of Goods Sold-Hardware**
50500	Cost of Goods Sold #2	**Cost of Goods Sold-Wall**
51000	Cost of Goods Sold #3	**Cost of Goods Sold-Floor**
64000	Depreciation Expense	**Deprec Exp-Furn & Fixtures**
64500	Dues and Subscription Exp	**Deprec Exp-Computers & Equip**

Add the following accounts: *Account Type:*

13000	**Supplies**	Other Current Assets
39008	**Sharon Albert, Capital**	Equity-doesn't close
39009	**Sharon Albert, Drawing**	Equity- gets closed
64600	**Deprec Exp-Building**	Expenses
72510	**FICA Expense**	Expenses
72530	**FUTA Expense**	Expenses
72540	**SUTA Expense**	Expenses
77600	**Overtime Expense**	Expenses

2. Click Beginning Balances.

3. The Select Period window pops up. Highlight From 12/1/03 through 12/31/03. Beginning balances *must* be set for the preceding month. The starting balance sheet on page 381 is dated January 1, 2004. This means that the period for entering beginning balances must be from December 1 through December 31, 2003 the month *before* the starting balances.

Comment

Select December 1 - 31, 2003 as your Chart of Accounts Beginning Balance period so that your journals will start on January 1, 2004. Your reports will be dated January 31, 2004. Remember, Peachtree posts on the last day of the month. The December 31, 2003 balance is January 1, 2004's starting balance.

Compare your screen to the one shown on the next page.

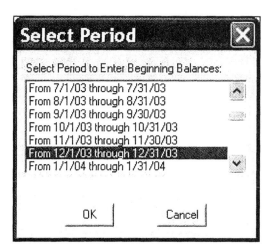

Check this screen carefully. You cannot change the period for entering beginning balances later.

4. Click [OK]. The Chart of Accounts Beginning Balances screen appears.

5. Matt Lowe and Sharon Albert purchased Matt's Service Merchandise in December 2003. Use the Balance Sheet shown on the next page to record the Chart of Accounts Beginning Balances. If you need to review how to record beginning balances, see Chapter 9 pages 266-267. The January 1, 2004 balance sheet is shown on the next page.

Matt's Service Merchandise		
Balance Sheet		
January 1, 2004		
ASSETS		
Current Assets:		
La Jolla Bank	$50,700.00	
Stockmen's Savings & Loan	22,000.00	
Merchandise Inventory	27,740.00	
Supplies	1,750.00	
Prepaid Insurance	2,400.00	
Total Current Assets		$104,590.00
Property and Equipment:		
Furniture and Fixtures	5,000.00	
Computers & Equipment	7,500.00	
Building	100,000.00	
Total Property and Equipment		112,500.00
Total Assets		$217,090.00
LIABILITIES AND CAPITAL		
Long-Term Liabilities:		
Long-Term Notes Payable	20,500.00	
Mortgage Payable	75,000.00	
Total Long-Term Liabilities		$95,500.00
Capital:		
Matt Lowe, Capital	60,795.00	
Sharon Albert, Capital	60,795.00	
Total Capital		121,590.00
Total Liabilities and Capital		$217,090.00

6.   When you are finished entering the beginning balances, click

 .

7.   Close the Maintain Chart of Account window.

ACCOUNTS PAYABLE

The next section shows you how to set up Accounts Payable defaults. This is where you will set up information about the vendors who offer credit to Matt's Service Merchandise. Vendors offer Matt's Service Merchandise a 2 percent discount for invoices paid within 10 days (2% 10, Net 30 Days).

Follow these steps to enter vendor default information.

1.   Click on Maintain; Default Information; Vendors. The Vendor Defaults window appears.

2.   Due in number of days is selected in the Standard Terms list. If necessary, type **2** in the Discount % field, then press the **<Tab>** key two times.

3.   In the Purchase Account field, click 🔍. Scroll up the chart of accounts list. Double click on Account No. 12000, Merchandise Inventory.

4.   In the Discount GL Account field, click 🔍. Double click on Account No. 59500, Purchase Discounts.

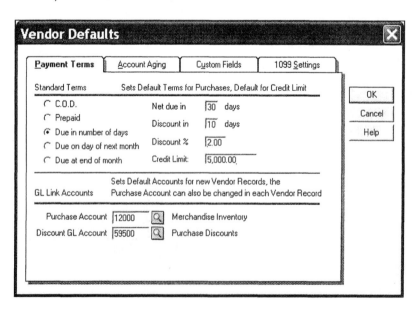

Make sure that the Purchase Account field shows Account No. 12000, Merchandise Inventory; and that the Discount GL field shows Account No. 59500, Purchase Discounts. This sets up the default accounts for merchandise purchases and vendor discounts.

In PCA, the Merchandise Inventory account contains summary information about the total cost of the merchandise on hand and available for sale. In addition, PCA tracks vendor discounts in Account No. 59500, Purchase Discounts. PCA also keeps a detailed inventory record for each item of merchandise in stock. PCA automatically updates subsidiary records every time there is a change in the Merchandise Inventory account caused by a purchase, sale, or return of merchandise.

5. Click [OK]. You are returned to the menu bar.

6. Click on Maintain; Vendors. The Maintain Vendors window displays. Follow these steps to enter vendor information:

   a. In the Vendor ID field, type **JJH06** (use a zero) then press the **<Enter>** key.

   b. In the Name field, type **Jessica Johnson Hardware** then press the **<Enter>** key three times.

   c. In the Address field, type **1103 North Alvarado Street** then press the **<Enter>** key two times.

   d. In the City, ST Zip field, type **Los Angeles** then press the **<Enter>** key. Click on the down arrow ▼ then select CA from the list of states. Press the **<Enter>** key. Type **90004** as the Zip code, press **<Enter>**.

   e. In the Country field, type **USA** then press **<Enter>**.

   f. In the Vendor Type field, type **hardware** then press **<Enter>**.

   g. In the 1099 Type field, click on the down arrow ▼ and select Independent Contractor. Press the **<Enter>** key.

h. In the Telephone 1 field, type **213-555-1288** then press **<Enter>** two times.

i. In the Fax field, type **213-555-2189** then press **<Enter>**.

j. In the E-mail field, type **jes@johnsonhardware.com** and then press **<Enter>**.

k. Type **www.johnsonhardware.com** in the Web Site field.

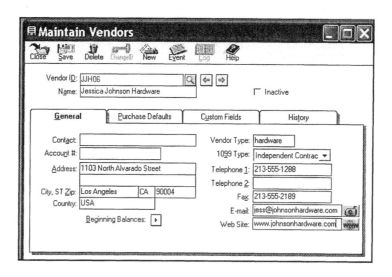

7. Click on the Purchase Defaults tab. Follow these steps to complete the fields:

a. Type **16-7833212** in the Tax ID # field.

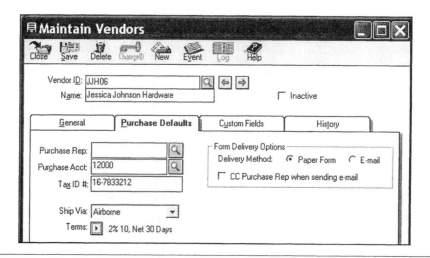

> **Comment**
>
> The Ship Via field on this screen shows Airborne. You complete shipping information when you set the defaults for inventory.

b. Click .

c. Click on the <u>G</u>eneral tab. The screen displays vendor information for Jessica Johnson Hardware.

d. Click ⌊New⌋. The Maintain Vendors window is ready for the next vendor. Complete the vendor and purchase default information:

1) Vendor ID: **LLP07**
   Name: **Linda Lucks Products**
   Address: **706 East Broadway**
   City, ST Zip   **San Diego, CA 90011**
   Country: **USA**
   Vendor Type: **floor**
   1099 Type: **Independent Contractor**
   Telephone 1:   **619-555-9244**
   Fax: **619-555-8866**
   E-mail: **Linda@llproducts.net**
   Web Site: **www.llproducts.net**

   Purchase Defaults:

   Tax ID #:   **16-6953412**

2) Vendor ID: **RBF08**
   Name: **Robert Barton Fabrics**
   Address: **8702 Sepulveda Blvd.**
   City, ST Zip   **Los Angeles, CA 90068**
   Country: **USA**
   Vendor Type: **wall**
   1099 Type: **Independent Contractor**
   Telephone 1:   **323-555-1988**
   Fax: **323-555-1989**
   E-mail: **Robert@bartonfabrics.biz**
   Web Site: **www.bartonfabrics.biz**

Purchase Defaults:

    Tax ID #:   **16-0984579**

8. Check your vendor information carefully. When you are finished entering vendor default information, close the Maintain Vendors window.

   How does vendor information work in PCA? The flowchart below shows how vendor maintenance information, vendor default information and purchases and payments work together.

Vendor Maintenance Information	*Vendor Default Information*
Terms: 2% 10, Net 30 Days *Purchase Account*: Merchandise Inventory	*Accounts*: Accounts Payable; Merchandise Inventory (purchase account); Purchase Discounts (discount GL account); La Jolla Bank (cash disbursed)

Purchases/Receive Inventory and Payments (Tasks)
Purchase Order
↓
Check to Vendor

INVENTORY ITEMS

In the next section you will complete default information for inventory items. Because the Merchandise Inventory account is increased or decreased for every purchase, sale or return, its balance in the general ledger is current.

1. Click on Maintain; Default Information, Inventory Items.

2. Click on the G<u>L</u> Accts/Costing tab. In the Stock item row, click on the down arrow ☑ next to FIFO in the Costing column. Select Average.

> **Comment**
>
> Further study of inventory costing methods will be done in Chapter 13, Merchandise Inventory.

3. On the Master Stock item row, change FIFO to Average.

4. On the Assembly row, change FIFO to Average.

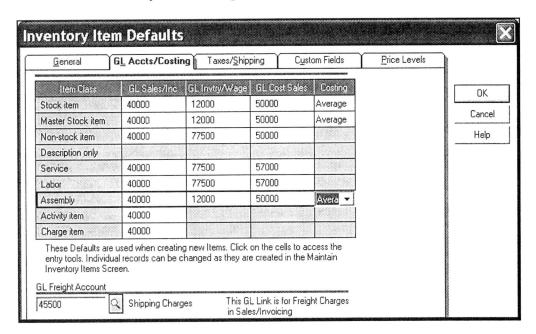

5. Click [OK].

6. Click on Maintain; Inventory Items. The Maintain Inventory Items window displays. Follow the steps on the next page to complete inventory information.

a. In the Item ID field, type **001hardware**, then press the **<Enter>** key.

b. In the Description field, type **hardware** then press **<Enter>**.

c. Accept the default for Stock item by pressing the **<Enter>** key two times.

d. In the Description: for Sales field, type **hardware--restoration** then press **<Enter>**.

e. Click on the right arrow ▸ in the Price Level 1 field. The Multiple Price Levels window appears. Type **150** in the Price column of Price Level 1, then press **<Enter>**.

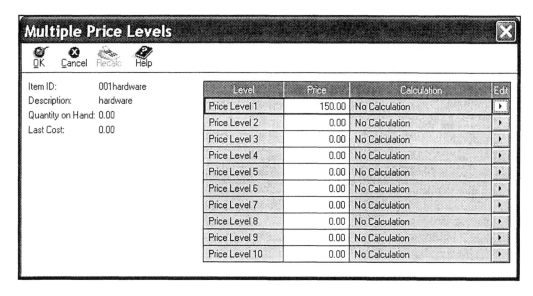

f. Click [OK].

Comment

What if your Price Level 1 field does not display 150.00 but 1.50? Follow these steps to set the decimal point:

1. Close the Inventory and Setup Checklist screens. From the menu bar, click on Options, then Global.
2. In the Decimal Entry field, click on Manual. Make sure that the number 2 is shown in the Number of decimal places field.
3. Click ⬚OK⬚. This sets your decimal place globally. That means from now on all numbers with decimal places will be set automatically; for example, 150 will display as 150.00.

Click on Maintain, select Setup Checklist, then Inventory Items and Assembly Records. In the Item ID field, select 001hardware.

---

g. Type **50** in the Last Unit Cost field. Press **<Enter>**.

h. Select Account No. 40200, Sales-Hardware as the GL Sales Acct.

i. Accept the default for Account No. 12000, Merchandise Inventory, as the GL Inventory Acct by pressing **<Enter>**

j. Accept the default for Account No. 50000, Cost of Goods Sold-Hardware as the GL Cost of Sales Acct by pressing **<Enter>** two times

k. In the Item Type field, type **hardware** then press **<Enter>** two times.

l. In the Unit/Measure field, type **each** then press **<Enter>** two times.

m. In the Minimum Stock field, type **10** then press **<Enter>**.

n. In the Reorder Quantity field, type **4** then press **<Enter>**.

o. In the Preferred Vendor ID field, click 🔍. Select Jessica Johnson Hardware, JJH06, as the vendor. Compare your screen with the one shown on the next page.

Maintain Inventory Items

Close Save Delete Change New Detail Note Help

Item ID: 001hardware | Item Class: Stock item
Description: hardware

☐ Inactive
☐ Subject to Commission

| **General** | Custom Fields | History | Bill of Materials | Item Attributes |

Description: hardware--restoration
for Sales ▼

Price Level 1: 150.00 ▸   GL Sales Acct: 40200 🔍 Sales-Hardware
Item Tax Type: 1 🔍   GL Inventory Acct: 12000 🔍 Merchandise Inventory
Last Unit Cost: 50.00   GL Cost of Sales Acct: 50000 🔍 Cost of Goods
Cost Method: Average ▼

UPC / SKU: [ ]   Qty on Hand: Qty Available: Minimum Stock:
Item Type: hardware   0.00000   0.00000   10.00
Location: [ ]   Qty on SO's: Qty on PO's: Reorder Quantity:
Unit/Measure: each   0.00000   0.00000   4.00
Weight: 0.00

                              Preferred Vendor ID: JJH06 🔍
                                        Buyer ID: [ ] 🔍

                                        Beginning Balances: ▸

p. Click **Save**.

q. Click **New**.

Enter the following stock items:

1) Item ID: **002wall**
   Description: **wall**
   Description for Sales: **wall coverings**
   Price Level 1:   **100**
   Last Unit Cost: **30**
   GL Sales Acct: **40400 Sales-Wall**
   GL Inventory Acct: **12000 Merchandise Inventory**

	GL Cost of Sales Acct:	**50500 Cost of Goods Sold-Wall**
	Item Type:	**wall**
	Unit/Measure:	**each**
	Minimum Stock:	**10**
	Reorder Quantity:	**4**
	Preferred Vendor ID:	**RBF08**

2)	Item ID:	**003floor**
	Description:	**floor**
	Description for Sales:	**flooring**
	Price Level 1:	**160**
	Last Unit Cost:	**54**
	GL Sales Acct:	**40600 Sales-Floor**
	GL Inventory Acct:	**12000 Merchandise Inventory**
	GL Cost of Sales Acct:	**51000 Cost of Goods Sold-Floor**
	Item Type:	**floor**
	Unit/Measure:	**each**
	Minimum Stock:	**25**
	Reorder Quantity:	**10**
	Preferred Vendor ID:	**LLP07**

7. Click on Beginning Balances. The Inventory Beginning Balances window displays. Follow these steps to record beginning balances.

   a. In the Item ID column, click on 001hardware. Press the **<Tab>** key.

   b. In the Quantity field, type **90** then press **<Enter>**.

   c. In the Unit Cost field, type **50** then press **<Enter>**.

   d. The Total Cost field displays 4,500.00. Press the **<Enter>** key.

   e. Enter the beginning balances for walls and floors:

Item ID	Description	Quantity	Unit Cost	Total Cost
002wall	wall	148	30	4,440.00
003floor	floor	200	54	10,800.00

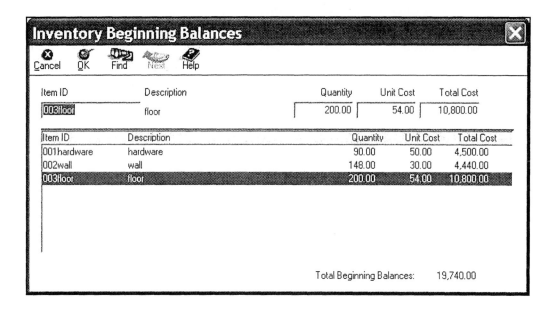

f. Click [OK]. A window pops up that says Updating Inventory Totals.

g. Close the Maintain Inventory Items window.

BACKING UP YOUR DATA

Follow these steps to make a backup:

1. Put your backup disk in drive A.

2. From the menu bar, select File, then Back up.

3. Make sure that the box next to Include company name in the backup file name is *unchecked*. Click [Back Up Now].

4. Click on the down-arrow in the Save in field. If necessary, scroll up the list, then click on 3½ Floppy (A:) to select drive A. *Or,* back up to your hard drive, network location, or other media. Peachtree's default location for backups is your company's hard drive location; for example, c:\Program Files\Peachtree\Company\matserme. If you used a unique company name, your data path will differ.

5. Type **Chapter 11 Begin** in the File name field.

6. Click [Save].

7. When the screen prompts that This company backup will require approximately 1 diskette, click [OK].

8. When the screen prompts you to insert the first disk, click [OK]. When the Back Up Company scale is 100% completed, you have successfully backed up to the current point in Chapter 11. You are returned to the menu bar.

9. Continue or click on File, Exit to exit Peachtree.

ACCOUNTS PAYABLE TASKS: PURCHASES/RECEIVE INVENTORY

The Tasks pull-down menu includes a selection for Purchases/Receive Inventory. In PCA, all information about a purchase is recorded in a Purchases/Receive Inventory window. Then, PCA takes the necessary information from the screen and automatically journalizes the transaction in the Purchase Journal.

The Tasks, Purchases/Receive Inventory selection takes you to the Purchases/Receive Inventory window. This is also the ***Purchase Journal***. In the Purchases/Receive Inventory window, you enter invoices received from vendors or enter purchase orders. As you know from your study of accounting, purchase orders are the business forms used by the purchasing department to place orders with vendors. Purchase Orders authorize the vendor to ship the ordered merchandise at the stated price and terms.

After recording vendor purchases in the Purchases/Receive Inventory window, you can display or print the Purchase Journal by selecting Reports, then Accounts Payable and highlighting the Purchase Journal. These steps are included in this chapter. Just remember, each time you use the Purchases/Receive Inventory window you are also journalizing in the Purchase Journal.

Purchases are posted both to the General Ledger and to the **_Vendor Ledger_** or **_Accounts Payable Ledger_**. You can also apply purchases to Inventory Items or Jobs.

Purchases work hand in hand with Payments. Payments is also one of the selections in the Tasks menu. Once you have entered and posted a purchase (vendor invoice), that invoice is available when you enter the Vendor's ID code in Payments. You can select the invoice, then save (post) the payment; PCA distributes the proper amounts.

Using the Purchase Journal: Purchases/Receive Inventory Window

1. If you exited Peachtree on page 393 start Windows and Peachtree in the usual way. Then, open Matt's Service Merchandise and restore the Chapter 11 Begin.ptb backup file.

2. From the Tasks menu, click on Purchases/Receive Inventory. The Purchases/Receive Inventory window displays. Check that *both* the A/P Account lookup field and GL Account column are shown on your Purchases/Receive Inventory window.

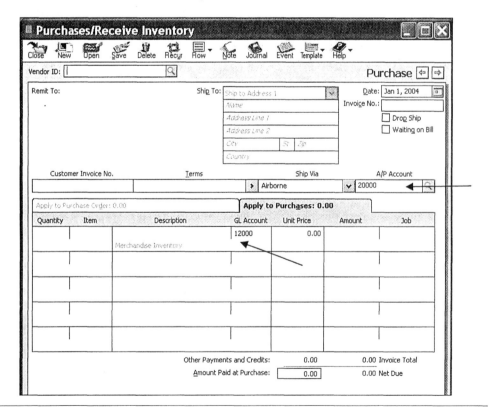

If the A/P Account lookup field and GL Account column are not shown, you should check your global settings. To do that, click on Options, Global. The boxes in the Hide General Ledger Accounts section *must* be unchecked. (See page 56, Changing Global Settings for Accounting Behind the Screens.)

On the Purchases/Receive Inventory window, your cursor is in the Vendor ID lookup field. There are three ways to select a vendor or add a new vendor:

➤ Type a question mark **<?>** in the text field and the vendor list displays.

➤ With the mouse pointer in the text field field, click on the right mouse button. The vendor list displays.

➤ Click [🔍] icon and the vendor list displays. The transaction that you are going to work with is:

Date   *Description of Transaction*

01/02/04   Invoice No. 64JR was received from Jessica Johnson
                Hardware for the purchase of six curtain rods for a unit
                cost of $50.00 each, and a total of $300.00. (Matt's
                Service Merchandise classifies curtain rods as
                hardware.)

3. Select JJH06, Jessica Johnson Hardware as the vendor.

The name and address information is automatically completed when you select an existing vendor. Observe that when you select Jessica Johnson Hardware, the Ship To, Ship Via, Terms, and A/P Account[3] field are automatically completed.

4. In the Date field type **2** (or select 2).

---

[3]If the A/P Account lookup field does not display, click on Options, Global. The boxes in the Hide General Ledger Accounts section *must* be unchecked. (See page 56, Changing Global Settings for Accounting Behind the Screens.)

5. In the Invoice # field, type **64JR** and press the **<Enter>** key.

6. Click on the Quantity column and type **6** then press the **<Enter>** key.

7. In the Item column, click 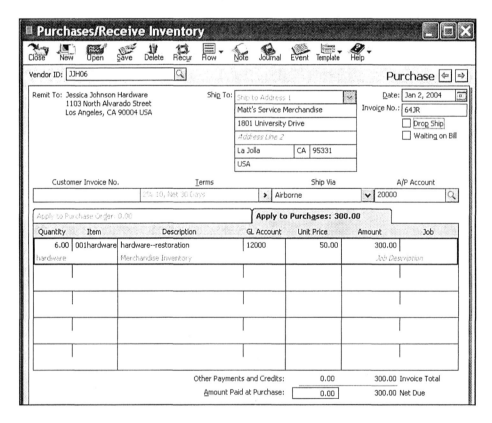 and select 001hardware. Accept the description. Press the **<Tab>** key. Observe that the following purchase information was automatically completed:

    a. Description column, hardware--restoration.

    b. GL Account 12000, Merchandise Inventory.

    c. Unit Price 50.00.

    d. Amount 300.00.

    e. Invoice Total and Net Due, 300.00

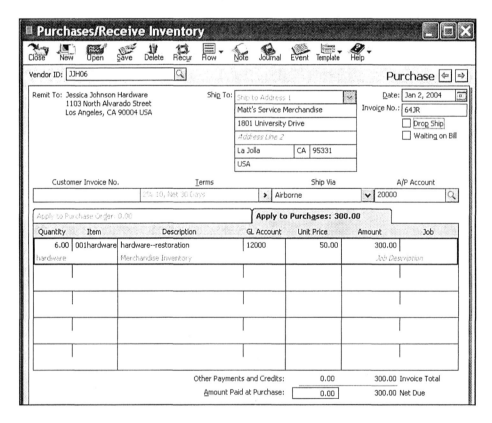

The Invoice Total: The Invoice Total keeps a running total of the entry lines you have added to the Purchase Journal. Before you post a Purchase Journal entry, you should check to see that the amount column is the same as the total invoice amount (Net Due) on the vendor invoice.

The total that shows in the Amount column is automatically credited to the accounts payable account (Account No. 20000, Accounts Payable and the vendor account). The information entered on the Purchases/Receive Inventory window will be recorded in the Purchase Journal.

8. Click [Journal] to see this entry in the Purchases Journal.

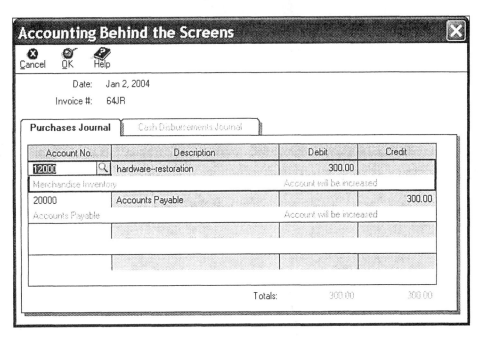

Inventory Items and Purchases: Since you entered an Inventory Item (hardware), the debit amount is shown in the merchandise inventory account (Account No. 12000) that you specified when you set up this inventory item. (On page 382, step 4, you set up the Purchase Account default for Account No. 12000, Merchandise Inventory.)

9. Click [OK] to return to the Purchases/Receive Inventory window.

10. Click [Save] to post this entry. The Purchases/Receive Inventory window is ready for another entry.

When you enter and post purchases of inventory items, three things happen:

a. The amount or stock level of the item is updated.

b. The **Average Cost** is updated based on the Unit Price entered. Average cost is computed using the **weighted-average method** for inventory. The Average Cost is used by PCA to compute Cost of Goods Sold when these Inventory Items are entered as Sales.

c. For Stock-Type items, the Inventory account is debited and Accounts Payable is credited (debit, Account No. 12000, Merchandise Inventory; credit, Account No. 20000, Accounts Payable/Vendor.)

Additional Purchases

The following transactions need to be entered in the Purchases Journal. Remember to click [Save] after each transaction to post.

Date	Description of Transaction
01/20/04	Invoice RB710 was received from Linda Lucks Products for the purchase of eight rolls of vinyl flooring at $54 each, for a total of $432. (*Hint: Select 003floor as the inventory item.*)
01/20/04	Invoice 201 was received from Robert Barton Fabrics for four pairs of curtains at $30 each, for a total vendor invoice of $120. (*Hint: Select 002wall as the inventory item.*)
01/20/04	Invoice 150JR was received from Jessica Johnson Hardware for the purchase of 10 curtain rods at $50 each, for a total of $500. (*Hint: Select 001hardware as the inventory item.*)

CASH PURCHASES: Write Checks Window

Matt's Service Merchandise pays cash for some purchases. Usually these cash disbursements are for expenses. All payments of cash are recorded in the **cash disbursements journal**. Follow these steps to see how cash purchases are entered.

 Read Me:

The Write Checks window is a simplified version of the Payments window. Both the Write Checks task and the Payments task post to the Cash Disbursements Journal. You will use the Payments window for Vendor Payments, page 406.

---

1. From the Tasks menu, select Write Checks. When the Select a Cash Account window appears, make sure La Jolla Bank is selected. Then, click [OK]. The Write Checks window displays.

    Date   *Description of Transaction*

    01/23/04   Matt's Service Merchandise issued check 2030 in the amount of $130 to Jack Guth for cleaning (debit Account No. 70000, Maintenance Expense). Print Check No. 2030.

Comment

Your Write Checks window will show a cash account balance in the Balance field (see page 400). Your Cash Account Balance field should show the same amount as the January 1, 2004 balance sheet, page 381, La Jolla Bank.

---

2. Click on the Pay to the Order of field and type **Jack Guth**.

3. Type **2030** in the Check Number field. Press **<Enter>**.

4. Type **23** in the Date field and press **<Enter>**.

5. Type **130** in the $ field.

---

6. In the Expense Account field, select Account No. 70000, Maintenance Expense.

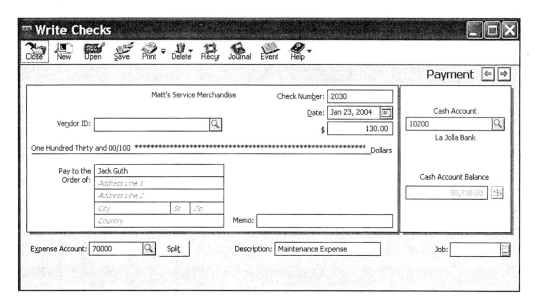

Printing the Check

Follow these steps to print the check:

1. The Write Checks window with Jack Guth's check should be displayed on your screen.

2. Click .

> **Comment**
>
> Step 3 instructs you to select AP Preprint 1 Stub as the form to print. If this form does *not* print, select another one. The form you select is tied to the kind of printer you are using. Depending on your printer, you may need to make a different selection.

3. The Print Forms: Disbursement Checks window pops up. Click Change Form. Then click on AP Preprint 1 Stub to highlight it.

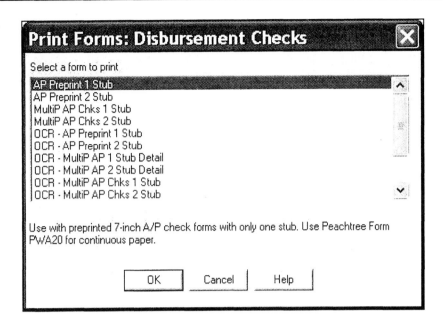

4. Click [OK].

5. The Print Forms: Disbursements window appears. The Last used form shows AP Preprint 1 Stub; the First Check Number shows 2030.

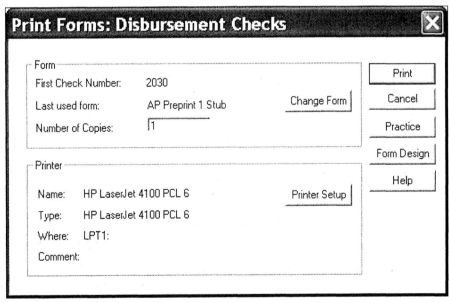

6. Peachtree automatically sequences check numbers after the first one is entered. Click [Print]. The check starts to print.

```
          Maintenance Expense                                                    130.00
```

```
1/23/04      2030           Jack Guth                                          $130.00
```

```
    Memo:
    One Hundred Thirty and 00/100 Dollars
                                                    2030    Jan 23, 2004    **********$130.00
        Jack Guth
```

Comment

If your check does not show the same amount, go back to the Write Checks window and click [Open]. Select January 23, Jack Guth. Make the necessary corrections. When you reprint Check No. 2030, Duplicate will be shown on the printout.

After you print a check, the Write Checks window is ready for another payment. Remember, the check form that you select is tied to the kind of printer you are using. If necessary, select a different form to print.

7. Record the additional payments listed. Since you are *not* going to print Check Nos. 2031-2035, type the appropriate check number in the Check Number field on the Write Checks window.

Date	Description of Transaction
Date	*Description of Transaction*

01/23/04   Matt's Service Merchandise issued Check No. 2031 in the amount of $37.00 to the U.S. Post Office for stamps. (*Hint: Since your are not going to print checks, type Check No.* **2031** *in the Check Num_ber field. Click _Save after each entry.*)

01/23/04   Issued Check No. 2032 in the amount of $110.82 to La Jolla Office Supplies for letterhead paper, envelopes, and note pads. (Debit Account No. 75500, Supplies Expense.)

01/24/04   Issued Check No. 2033 in the amount of $73.60 to MCA Phone Service.

01/24/04   Issued Check No. 2034 to Matt Lowe for $500.

01/24/04   Issued Check No. 2035 to Sharon Albert for $500.

8. Click ⟦Open⟧ to see if you have issued Check Nos. 2030 through 2035.

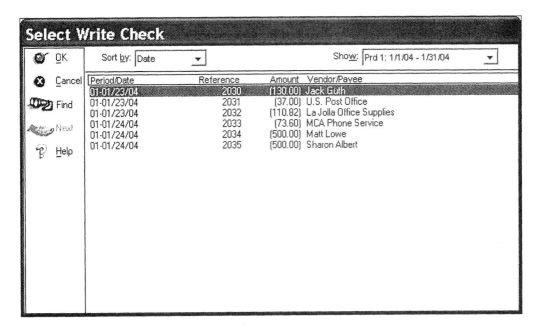

9. If you have any transactions to edit, highlight the line. Then, click ![OK]. When the screen displays, make the necessary corrections. Otherwise, click on Cancel. Remember to click Save for any revised transactions.

10. To close the Write Check window, click ![Close].

PURCHASE RETURNS: VENDOR CREDIT MEMOS

Sometimes it is necessary to return merchandise that has been purchased. When entering a purchase return, you need to record it as a vendor credit memo.

The following transaction is for merchandise returned to a vendor:

Date   *Description of Transaction*

01/24/04   Returned one roll of vinyl flooring to Linda Lucks Products, Invoice RB710 and paid the invoice on the same day.

Follow these steps to enter a purchase return:

1. From the Tasks menu, select Vendor Credit Memos.

2. In the Vendor ID field, select Linda Lucks Products.

3. Type **24** in the Date field.

4. Type **VCMRB710** in the Credit No field. For the credit number you are using the abbreviation VCM for Vendor Credit Memo, then the invoice number.

5. The Apply to Invoice No. tab is selected. Click on the down-arrow to select RB710. Observe that the Item, Quantity, Description, GL Account, and Unit Price columns are completed.

6. Type **1** in the Returned column. After you type 1 in the Returned column, the Amount column shows 54.00. Also, notice that the Credit Applied to Invoice shows 54.00. This agrees with the Credit Total.

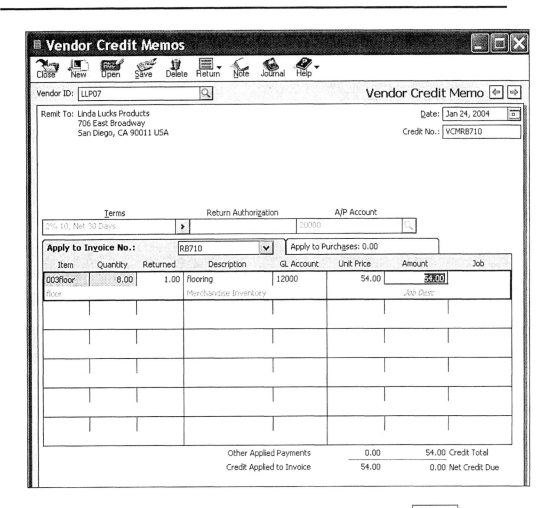

7. To see how the vendor credit memo is journalized, click 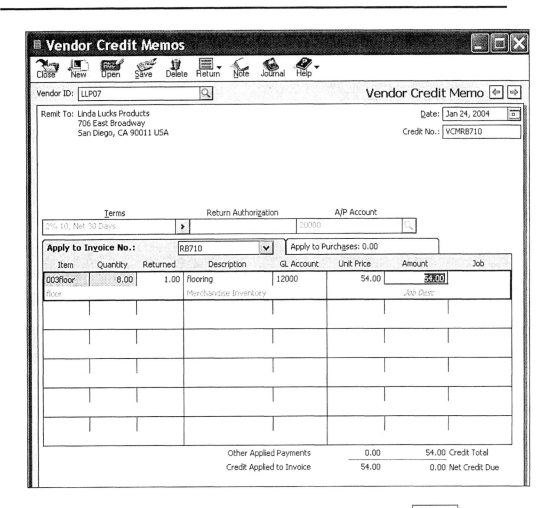. Notice that Account No. 12000, Merchandise Inventory, is credited for $54 and Account No. 20000, Account Payable, is debited for $54.

8. Click to post, then .

Paying a Vendor, Minus a Return of Merchandise

How does the return of merchandise affect the payment to the vendor?
Follow these steps to pay Invoice No. RB710 less the return.

1. From the menu bar, select Tasks, then Payments.

   Date   *Description of Transaction*

   01/24/04   Matt's Service Merchandise issued Check No. 2036 to
   Linda Lucks Products in payment of Invoice No.
   RB710 (less the return of merchandise). Print Check
   No. 2036.

2. In the Vendor ID lookup field, select Linda Lucks Products.

3. Type **24** in the Date field. Observe that the Apply to Invoices tab is
   selected and that the Invoice, RB710; Date Due and Amount Due
   columns are completed. Matt's Service Merchandise owes Linda
   Lucks Products $378 ($432, original invoice amount, less the $54
   return). Linda Lucks Products extends a 2% vendor discount to Matt's
   Service Merchandise. Type **7.56** in the Discount column (.02 x 378 =
   7.56). Observe that the Pay box is checked.

   The payment was calculated as follows:

Jan. 20	Invoice RB710	$432.00
Jan. 24	Less, VCMRB710	54.00
Jan. 24	Less, Purchase discount	7.56
Total Paid		$370.44

   Compare your screen to the one shown on the next page. Make sure
   that Discount column is shows 7.56 and that the Discount Account
   field shows Account No. 59500, Purchase Discounts.

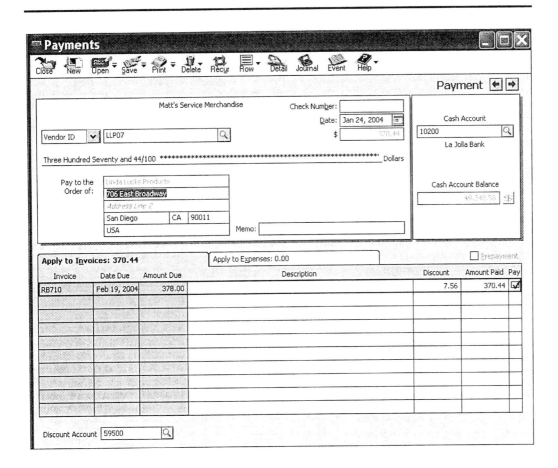

> ➤ **Troubleshooting Tip:** What if your Balance field does not show an amount? Close the Payments window without saving. Then, from the menu bar, go to Options/Global. A checkmark should be placed next to Recalculate cash balance automatically in Receipts, Payments, and Payroll Entry. If necessary, click on the appropriate field, then OK. Go back to step 1 on page 406.

4. Click .

5. The Print Forms: Disbursement Checks window displays. Type **2036** in the First Check Number field.

6. The Last used form shows AP Preprint 1 Stub. If this selection is *not* made, click Change Form , then select AP Preprint 1 Stub. Click

| Print |. Check No. 2036 starts to print. Make sure the check amount is $370.44.

7. Close the Payments window.

8. Record the following purchase return and payment:

    Date   *Description of Transaction*

    01/27/04   Returned two curtain rods (001hardware) to Jessica
                    Johnson Hardware, Invoice No. 150JR. Matt's Service
                    Merchandise paid $50 each for the two curtain rods.

    01/28/04   Issued Check No. 2037 to pay Jessica Johnson
                    Hardware for Invoice No. 150JR (minus returned
                    merchandise). (*Hint: Type the check number in the
                    Check Number field instead of printing it. The discount
                    is 8.00*)

PAYING SPECIFIC VENDOR INVOICES

Once you have entered a vendor invoice in the Purchases/Receive
Inventory window, you can apply payments to specific invoices. You
enter the vendor invoice using the Purchases/Receive Inventory task;
then when you post, the purchase journal is updated. To pay for the
merchandise purchased, you select the specific invoice from the vendor's
transaction list. When you print a check, you are also posting to the cash
disbursements journal. The journal entry below shows a specific vendor
payment.

Account Name	Debit	Credit
Accounts Payable/Robert Barton Fabrics	$120.00	
Purchase Discounts		$2.40
La Jolla Bank		$117.60

You should take advantage of both the Purchases/Receive Inventory and
Payments Tasks. Because amounts are disbursed and discounts are
tracked automatically, your job is made easier. This also provides a
detailed and complete **audit trail**. An audit trail is the path from the
source document to the accounts.

The flowchart below shows how the Purchases and Payments Tasks work together with Payments.

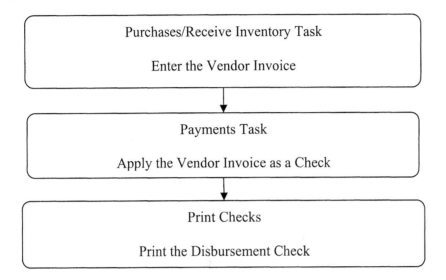

| Purchases/Receive Inventory Task |
| Enter the Vendor Invoice |

| Payments Task |
| Apply the Vendor Invoice as a Check |

| Print Checks |
| Print the Disbursement Check |

Date   *Description of Transaction*

01/28/04   Issued Check No. 2038 to Robert Barton Fabrics in payment of Invoice No. 201.

Follow these steps to pay vendor invoice 201:

1. From the Tasks menu, select Payments. The Payments window displays.

2. Select Robert Barton Fabrics as the vendor.

3. If necessary, type **2038** in the Check Num<u>b</u>er field.

4. Type **28** in the <u>D</u>ate field.

5. The Apply to <u>I</u>nvoices tab should already be selected. For Invoice No. 201, click on the Pay box.

6. Click 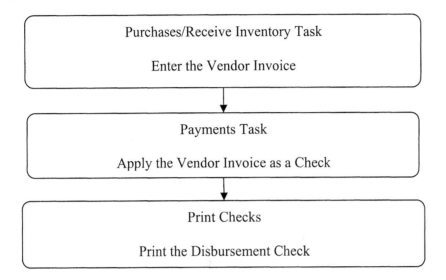 to post.

Editing Payments

If you have already paid a vendor, you can edit payments. Follow these steps to see what vendors have been paid:

1. Display the Payments window.

2. Click 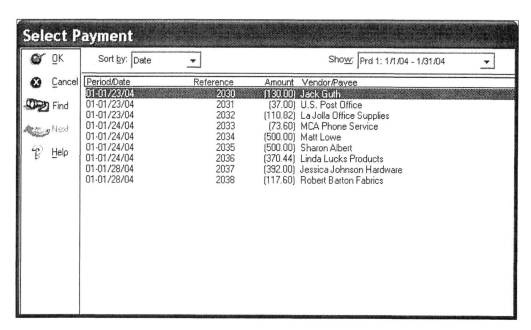 .

3. If you want to edit, highlight one of the payments. Then click [OK]. Or, click on Cancel if all payments listed are correct.

4. Make any necessary changes, then post.

5. When you are finished close the Payments window.

PRINTING THE PURCHASE JOURNAL AND CASH DISBURSEMENTS JOURNAL

Complete the following steps to print the Purchase Journal and the Cash Disbursements Journal:

1. From the Reports menu, select Accounts Payable.

2. Highlight Purchase Journal.

3. Click [Print]. The Purchase Journal Filter window pops up. Click [OK].

4. The Print window pops up. Click [OK]. Compare your purchase journal to the one shown below.

Page: 1

Matt's Service Merchandise
Purchase Journal
For the Period From Jan 1, 2004 to Jan 31, 2004
Filter Criteria includes: Report order is by Date. Report is printed in Detail Format.

Date	Account ID Account Description	Invoice/CM #	Line Description	Debit Amoun	Credit Amount
1/2/04	12000 Merchandise Inventory 20000 Accounts Payable	64JR	hardware--restoration Jessica Johnson Hardware	300.00	300.00
1/20/04	12000 Merchandise Inventory 20000 Accounts Payable	150JR	hardware--restoration Jessica Johnson Hardware	500.00	500.00
1/20/04	12000 Merchandise Inventory 20000 Accounts Payable	201	wall coverings Robert Barton Fabrics	120.00	120.00
1/20/04	12000 Merchandise Inventory 20000 Accounts Payable	RB710	flooring Linda Lucks Products	432.00	432.00
1/24/04	12000 Merchandise Inventory 20000 Accounts Payable	VCMRB710	flooring Linda Lucks Products	54.00	54.00
1/27/04	12000 Merchandise Inventory 20000 Accounts Payable	VCM150JR	hardware--restoration Jessica Johnson Hardware	100.00	100.00
				1,506.00	1,506.00

5. To print the Cash Disbursements Journal, highlight Cash Disbursements Journal, then make the selections to print.

Matt's Service Merchandise
Cash Disbursements Journal
For the Period From Jan 1, 2004 to Jan 31, 2004
Filter Criteria includes: Report order is by Date. Report is printed in Detail Format.

Date	Check #	Account ID	Line Description	Debit Amount	Credit Amount
1/23/04	2030	70000	Maintenance Expense	130.00	
		10200	Jack Guth		130.00
1/23/04	2031	73500	Postage Expense	37.00	
		10200	U.S. Post Office		37.00
1/23/04	2032	75500	Supplies Expense	110.82	
		10200	La Jolla Office Supplies		110.82
1/24/04	2033	76000	Telephone Expense	73.60	
		10200	MCA Phone Service		73.60
1/24/04	2034	39007	Matt Lowe, Drawing	500.00	
		10200	Matt Lowe		500.00
1/24/04	2035	39009	Sharon Albert, Drawing	500.00	
		10200	Sharon Albert		500.00
1/24/04	2036	59500	Discounts Taken		7.56
		20000	Invoice: RB710	378.00	
		10200	Linda Lucks Products		370.44
1/28/04	2037	59500	Discounts Taken		8.00
		20000	Invoice: 150JR	400.00	
		10200	Jessica Johnson Hardware		392.00
1/28/04	2038	59500	Discounts Taken		2.40
		20000	Invoice: 201	120.00	
		10200	Robert Barton Fabrics		117.60
	Total			2,249.42	2,249.42

Comment

Observe that the Line Description on the Cash Disbursements Journal shows the account name (e.g. Account No. 70000, Maintenance Expense) for the amount debited. The person to whom the check was written (e.g. Jack Guth) is shown for the amount credited.

VENDOR LEDGERS

Follow these steps to print a Vendor Ledger for Matt's Service
Merchandise:

1. If necessary, from the Reports menu, select Accounts Payable.

2. Highlight Vendor Ledgers then make the selections to print.

Page: 1

Matt's Service Merchandise
Vendor Ledgers
For the Period From Jan 1, 2004 to Jan 31, 2004
Filter Criteria includes: Report order is by ID.

Vendor ID Vendor	Date	Trans No	Typ	Pai	Debit Amt	Credit Amt	Balance
JJH06	1/2/04	64JR	PJ			300.00	300.00
Jessica Johnson Hardwar	1/20/04	150JR	PJ	*		500.00	800.00
	1/27/04	VCM150JR	PJ	*	100.00		700.00
	1/28/04	2037	CDJ		8.00	8.00	700.00
	1/28/04	2037	CDJ		400.00		300.00
LLP07	1/20/04	RB710	PJ	*		432.00	432.00
Linda Lucks Products	1/24/04	VCMRB710	PJ	*	54.00		378.00
	1/24/04	2036	CDJ		7.56	7.56	378.00
	1/24/04	2036	CDJ		378.00		0.00
RBF08	1/20/04	201	PJ	*		120.00	120.00
Robert Barton Fabrics	1/28/04	2038	CDJ		2.40	2.40	120.00
	1/28/04	2038	CDJ		120.00		0.00

PRINTING THE GENERAL LEDGER TRIAL BALANCE

1. In the Report Area, highlight General Ledger. Then, in the Report List,
    highlight General Ledger Trial Balance.

2. Click [Print]. Make the selections to print. Compare your printout
    with the one shown on the next page.

Matt's Service Merchandise
General Ledger Trial Balance
As of Jan 31, 2004

Filter Criteria includes: Report order is by ID. Report is printed in Detail Format.

Account ID	Account Description	Debit Amt	Credit Amt
10200	La Jolla Bank	48,468.54	
10400	Stockmen's Savings & Loa	22,000.00	
12000	Merchandise Inventory	28,938.00	
13000	Supplies	1,750.00	
14000	Prepaid Insurance	2,400.00	
15000	Furniture and Fixtures	5,000.00	
15100	Computers & Equipment	7,500.00	
15500	Building	100,000.00	
20000	Accounts Payable		300.00
27000	Long-Term Notes Payable		20,500.00
27400	Mortgage Payable		75,000.00
39006	Matt Lowe, Capital		60,795.00
39007	Matt Lowe, Drawing	500.00	
39008	Sharon Albert, Capital		60,795.00
39009	Sharon Albert, Drawing	500.00	
59500	Purchase Discounts		17.96
70000	Maintenance Expense	130.00	
73500	Postage Expense	37.00	
75500	Supplies Expense	110.82	
76000	Telephone Expense	73.60	
	Total:	217,407.96	217,407.96

BACKING UP CHAPTER 11 DATA

Follow these steps to back up Chapter 11 data:

1. Put your backup disk in drive A. You may use the same disk that you used to back up data on pages 392-393.

2. From the menu bar, select File, then Back up.

3. Click | Back Up Now |.

4. Click on the down-arrow in the Save in field. If necessary, scroll up the list, then click on 3½ Floppy (A:) to select drive A. *Or*, select the appropriate location to back up to the network drive. Peachtree's default location for backups is your company's hard drive location; for example, c:\Program Files\Peachtree\Company\matserme. If you used a unique company name, your path will differ.

5. Type **Chapter 11** in the File name field.

6. Click [Save].

7. When the screen prompts that This company backup will require approximately 1 diskette, click [OK].

8. When the screen prompts you to insert the first disk, click [OK]. When the Back Up Company scale is 100% completed, you have successfully backed up to the current point in Chapter 11. You are returned to the menu bar.

9. Click on File, Exit to exit Peachtree.

	INTERNET ACTIVITY
1.	From your Internet browser, go to the book's website at http://www.mhhe.com/yacht2004.
2.	In the Student Edition list, link to Internet Activities.
3.	Link to WEB EXERCISES PART 3.
4.	Complete the ACCOUNTING LIST – Chapter 10 exercise. Read steps 1 – 4.
5.	Follow the steps shown on the book's website to complete this Internet activity.
6.	Using a word processing program write a brief summary of what you find. Include all appropriate website addresses.

SUMMARY AND REVIEW

SOFTWARE OBJECTIVES: In Chapter 11, you used the software to:

1. Set up company information for Matt's Service Merchandise.

2. Enter the following general ledger information: chart of accounts and account beginning balances.

3. Enter the following accounts payable information: vendor defaults and vendor records.

4. Enter the following inventory information: inventory defaults, inventory items, inventory beginning balances.

5. Record accounts payable transactions: merchandise purchases, purchase orders, cash purchases, and purchase returns.

6. Make four backups using two blank, formatted disks: two backups for Matt's Service Merchandise data; one backup for Exercise 11-1; one backup for Exercise 11-2.

WEB OBJECTIVES: In Chapter 11, you did these Internet activities:

1. Used your Internet browser to go to the book's website. (Go online to www.mhhe.com/yacht2004.)

2. Went to the Internet Activity link on the book's website. Then, select WEB EXERCISES PART 3. Complete the first web exercise in Part 3—Accounting List.

3. Used a word processing program to write summaries of the websites that you visited.

4. Completed the Going to the Net exercise.

GOING TO THE NET

Access information about Peachtree's Easy Startup, Easy to Learn features at www.peachtree.com/PeachtreeAccountingLine/Complete/features_easy_startup.cfm. Answer the following questions.

1. List four features that make Peachtree easy to learn.

2. How do you take advantage of Online Help?

3. How many sample company chart of accounts can you choose from?

True/Make True: Write the word True in the space provided if the statement is true. If the statement is not true, write the correct answer.

1. Vendor default information needs to be set up to establish the criteria used when computing vendor discounts.

   _____

   _____

2. The purchase discount offered to Matt's Service Merchandise from their vendors is 2% 10, Net 30 Days.

   _____

   _____

3. Matt's Service Merchandise is organized as a partnership.

   _____

   _____

4. Accounts Payable is money you pay to customers.

   _____

   _____

5. The merchandise that Matt's Service Merchandise buys from Robert Barton Fabrics is classified as wall coverings.

    _____

    _____

6. Each time you use the Purchases/Receive Inventory window, you are journalizing in the Cash Disbursements Journal.

    _____

    _____

7. Each time you use the Payments window, you are journalizing in the Purchase Journal.

    _____

    _____

8. The Maintain Vendors window is used to enter information about vendors from whom you purchase merchandise.

    _____

    _____

9. The Purchases/Receive Inventory task posts to the Purchases Journal.

    _____

    _____

10. The purchase discount amount is debited to Account No. 50000, Purchase Discounts.

Exercise 11-1: Follow the instructions below to complete Exercise 11-1.

1. Set up a sales and service company using *your first and last name*; for example, *Your Name Sales & Service*. For the address use 313 North Aspen Street; Eugene, OR 97403; telephone, 541-555-2800; Fax, 541-555-2900. Your sales and service company is a Sole Proprietorship. For the Tax ID information use the following:

   Federal Employer ID: 53-2051188
   State Employer ID: 92-9153911
   State Unemployment ID: 925478-3

   Leave the Web Site and E-mail address fields blank.

2. At the New Company Setup - Chart of Accounts screen, select Copy settings from an existing Peachtree Accounting company.

3. Highlight Matt's Service Merchandise, then click [Next >].

4. Observe that the information on the Copy Company Information screen includes a selection for Accounting Periods. Since your sales and service company is using the same accounting period (January 1 - 31, 2004) as Matt's Service Merchandise, you can leave that box checked. If you wanted to enter a different accounting period, you would click on the Accounting Periods field to uncheck it. For purposes of Exercise 11-1 accept all the defaults on the Copy Company Information screen by clicking on [Next >].

5. Read the information about the Accounting Method. Accept the default for accrual accounting by clicking on [Next >].

---

6. Accept the default for Real Time posting by clicking on [Next >].

7. The New Company Setup - Finish screen appears. Read the information on this screen. Accept the default for Yes, I would like to follow the Setup Checklist, by clicking on [Finish].

8. Disable the Peachtree Today window at start up.

General Ledger

1. Delete the following accounts:

3900A	Owner's Draw
40600	Sales-Floors
51000	Cost of Goods Sold- Floor

   Change the following accounts:

10200	La Jolla Bank	**Eugene Bank**
10400	Stockmen's Savings & Loan	**Citizens Savings & Loan**
39009	Owner's Contribution	**Student Name, Capital**
		(Equity–doesn't close)
40400	Sales-Wall	**Sales-Tools**
50500	Cost of Goods Sold-Wall	**Cost of Goods Sold-Tools**

   Add the following account:

39010	**Student Name, Drawing**	Equity-gets closed

2. Use the Balance Sheet on the next page to record chart of accounts beginning balances. You purchased your sales and service company in December 2003. Remember to select the period From 12/1/03 through 12/31/03.

Student Name Sales & Service Balance Sheet January 1, 2004		
ASSETS		
Current Assets		
Eugene Bank	$37,000.00	
Citizens Savings & Loan	15,500.00	
Merchandise Inventory	14,750.00	
Supplies	1,000.00	
Prepaid Insurance	2,400.00	
Total Current Assets		$70,650.00
Property and Equipment		
Furniture and Fixtures	$3,500.00	
Computers & Equipment	5,500.00	
Building	85,000.00	
Total Property and Equipment		$94,000.00
Total Assets		$164,650.00
LIABILITIES AND CAPITAL		
Long Term Liabilities		
Long-Term Notes Payable	10,000.00	
Mortgage Payable	60,000.00	
Total Long-Term Liabilities		$70,000.00
Capital		
Student Name, Capital		94,650.00
Total Liabilities and Capital		$164,650.00

Accounts Payable

Follow the instructions below to set up vendor information for your sales and service company.

1. Click on Maintain; Default Information, Vendors. Set up the following vendor defaults:

Standard Terms:	Due in number of days
Net due in:	30 days
Discount in:	10 days
Discount %:	2.00
Credit Limit:	5,000.00

    GL Link Accounts:

Purchase Account:	12000 Merchandise Inventory
Discount GL Account:	59500 Purchase Discounts

2. Click on Maintain; Vendors. Set up the following vendors:

    a.
Vendor ID:	**CPT12**
Name:	**Curt Peters Tools**
Contact:	**Sharon Watson**
Address:	**771 Melrose Ave.**
City, ST Zip	**Los Angeles, CA 90036**
Country:	**USA**
Vendor Type:	**tools**
1099 Type:	**Independent Contractor**
Telephone 1:	**323-555-9500**
Fax:	**323-555-9501**
E-mail:	**curt@curtpeters.com**
Web Site:	**www.curtpeters.com**

    Purchase Defaults:

Tax ID #:	**17-9833567**

    b.
Vendor ID:	**SJH14**
Name:	**Sally Jackson Hardware**
Contact:	**Sally Jackson**

Address:	**241 Moreno Drive**
City, ST Zip	**Beverly Hills, CA 90211**
Country:	**USA**
Vendor Type:	**hardware**
1099 Type:	**Independent Contractor**
Telephone 1:	**310-555-2900**
Fax:	**310-555-2999**
E-mail:	**sally@jacksonhardware.net**
Web Site:	**www.jacksonhardware.net**

Purchase Defaults:

Tax ID #:	**17-4338122**

Inventory

Follow these steps to set up inventory defaults:

1. Click on Maintain; Default Information, Inventory Items.

2. Select the GL_Accts/Costing tab. If necessary, set up Average as the inventory costing method (Stock Method, Master Stock Item, Assembly).

3. If necessary, select Account No. 45500, Shipping Charges Reimbursed as the GL Freight Account.

4. Click on Maintain; Inventory Items. Set up the following inventory stock items:

   a.

Item ID:	**002tools**
Description:	**tools**
Description for Sales:	**tools**
Price Level 1:	**85**
Last Unit Cost:	**30**
Cost Method:	Average
GL Sales Acct:	**40400 Sales-Tools**
GL Inventory Acct:	**12000 Merchandise Inventory**
GL Cost of Sales Acct:	**50500 Cost of Goods Sold-Tools**
Item Type:	**tools**
Unit/Measure:	**each**
Minimum Stock:	**10**

Reorder Quantity: **4**
Vendor ID: **CPT12**

b. Item ID: **003hardware**
    Description: **hardware**
    Description for Sales: **hardware--copper**
    Price Level 1:   **150**
    Last Unit Cost: **50**
    Cost Method: Average
    GL Sales Acct: **40200 Sales-Hardware**
    GL Inventory Acct: **12000 Merchandise Inventory**
    Cost of Sales Acct: **50000 Cost of Goods Sold-Hardware**
    Item Type: **hardware**
    Unit/Measure: **each**
    Minimum Stock: **10**
    Reorder Quantity: **4**
    Vendor ID: **SJH14**

5. Click on Inventory Beginning Balances. Record the following beginning balances:

Item ID	Description	Quantity	Unit Cost	Total Cost
002tools	tools	175	30	5,250.00
003hardware	hardware	190	50	9,500.00

6. Click .

7. Print the chart of accounts.

8. Print the balance sheet.

9. Follow these steps to back up Exercise 11-1:

    a. Put a blank, formatted disk in drive A.

    b. From the menu bar, select File, then Back up.

    c. Click on Back Up Now .

d. Click on the down-arrow in the Save in field. If necessary, scroll up the list, then click on 3½ Floppy (A:) to select drive A. *Or,* select the appropriate location to save to the network location. Peachtree's default location for backups is your company's hard drive location; for example, c:\peachw\xxxxxxxx. Substitute the x's for your company's data path.

e. Type **Exercise 11-1** in the File name field.

f. Click [Save].

g. When the screen prompts that This company backup will require approximately 1 diskette, click [OK].

h. When the screen prompts you to insert the first disk, click [OK]. When the Back Up Company scale is 100% completed, you have successfully backed up to the current point in Exercise 11-1. You are returned to the menu bar. Continue with Exercise 11-2 or exit Peachtree.

Exercise 11-2: Follow the instructions below to complete Exercise 11-2. Exercise 11-1 *must* be completed before starting Exercise 11-2.

1. Follow these steps to restore the data that you backed up in Exercise 11-1.[4]

a. Put your Exercise 11-1 backup disk in drive A. From the menu bar, click on File, Restore.

b. From the Select Backup File screen, click [Browse]. The Open Backup File screen pops up.

c. Click on the down-arrow in the Look in field. Then click on 3½

---

[4]You can restore from your back up file even if *no* Peachtree company exists. Close Peachtree's start up screen. Select File; Restore. Select the location of your backup file. On the Restore Wizard's Select Company screen, select A New Company. The *A New Company* selection allows you to restore your backup data, bypassing the process of new company set up. For more information, refer to Troubleshooting on pages 274 and 275.

Floppy (A:) to select drive A (or the appropriate location of your backup file).

d. Click on the Exercise 11-1.ptb file to highlight it. The File name field displays Exercise 11-1. Click [Open].

e. Make sure that the Location field shows A:\Exercise 11-1.ptb (or the appropriate location for your backup file). Click [Next >].

f. From the Select Company screen make sure that the radio button next to An Existing Company is selected. The Company name field shows your company name; the Location field shows C:\ProgramFiles\Peachtree\Company\xxxxxxxx (the x's represent your subdirectory; or restore from the appropriate location on your computer). Click [Next >].

g. The Restore Options screen appears. Make sure that the box next to Company Data is *checked*. Click [Next >].

h. The Confirmation screen appears. Check the From and To fields to make sure they are correct. Click [Finish]. When the Restore Company scale is 100% completed, your data is restored and you are returned to the menu bar.

i. Remove the backup disk.

2. Journalize and post the following transactions and print each check.

01/02/04 Invoice No. 479PF was received from Curt Peters Tools for the purchase of 10 tool kits for a unit cost of $30.

01/05/04 Invoice No. JK45 was received from Sally Jackson Hardware for the purchase of 8 hardware sets at a unit cost of $50.

01/06/04 Returned two tool kits to Curt Peters Tools, Invoice No. 479PF. You paid $30 for each tool kit.

01/09/04 Issued Check No. 1020 to pay Sally Jackson Hardware for Invoice No. JK45. (*Hint: Type the check number, 1020, in the Check Number field.*)

01/09/04 Issued Check No. 1021 to pay Curt Peters Tools for merchandise purchased on January 2, less the January 6 return, Invoice No. 479PF. (*Hint: Remember to calculate, then type the correct discount amount in the Discount column.*)

01/13/04 Issued Check No. 1022 to Terry Kito for $105 for cleaning and maintenance.

01/15/04 Issued Check No. 1023 to the U.S. Post Office for $37 for postage stamps.

01/16/04 Issued Check No. 1024 to Eugene Office Supplies for $149.65 for cell phone. (Debit Account No. 71000, Office Expense.)

01/16/04 Issued Check No. 1025 to Northwest Telephone for $40.27 to pay the telephone bill.

01/26/04 Issued Check No. 1026 to the owner of the business for $400.

3. Print the Purchase Journal.

4. Print the Cash Disbursements Journal.

5. Print the Vendor Ledgers.

6. Print the General Ledger Trial Balance.

7. Follow these steps to back up Exercise 11-2:

    a. Put your backup disk in drive A. You may use the same disk to back up data that you used on pages 424-425.

    b. From the menu bar, select File, then Back up.

    c. Click | Back Up Now |.

    d. Click on the down-arrow in the Save in field. If necessary, scroll up the list, then click on 3½ Floppy(A:) to select drive A. *Or,* back up to the network or hard drive location.

    e. Type **Exercise 11-2** in the File name field.

    f. Click | Save |.

    g. When the screen prompts that This company backup will require approximately 1 diskette, click | OK |.

    h. When the screen prompts you to insert the first disk, click | OK |. When the Back Up Company scale is 100% completed, you have successfully backed up to the current point in Exercise 11-2. Exit PCA.

CHAPTER 11 INDEX

Chapter

12   Accounts Receivable

SOFTWARE OBJECTIVES: In Chapter 12, you will use the software to:

1. Set up customer default information.
2. Set up sales tax information.
3. Set up customer maintenance information.
4. Record credit sales, cash sales, and sales returns.
5. Record customer receipts, partial payments, and edit invoices.
6. Make four backups using two blank, formatted disks: two backups for Matt's Service Merchandise; two backups for the end-of-chapter exercises.

WEB OBJECTIVES: In Chapter 12, you will do these Internet activities:

1. Use your Internet browser to go to the book's website.
2. Go to the Internet Activity link on the book's website. Then, select WEB EXERCISES PART 3. Complete the second web exercise in Part 3–WebCPA: Tools and Resources for the Electronic Accountant.
3. Use a word processing program to write summaries of the websites that you visited.

In Chapter 11, you learned how to use PCA's Purchases/Receive Inventory and Payments tasks. Now that you have purchased merchandise from vendors, you are ready to sell that merchandise. To do that, you need to learn how to use PCA's Sales/Invoicing task.

In Chapter 3, Customer Transactions, when you entered a sales invoice for Bellwether Garden Supply, the unit price, description, account number, and sales taxes were automatically calculated for you. (See pages 101-109.)

Before you can use the Sales/Invoicing task, you need to set up customer defaults, sales tax information, and customer maintenance information. After you set up these defaults, PCA will use this information when you record a sale.

In Chapter 12, you will see how PCA's accounts receivable system works. ***Accounts receivable*** are what customers owe your business. Credit transactions from customers are called ***accounts receivable transactions***.

Customer receipts work similarly to paying vendor invoices. When a customer pays an existing ***invoice*** there are two steps:

1. Enter the customer's ID code so that a list of existing invoices for the customer displays.

2. Select the invoice that applies to the customer's check, then select the Pay box.

The flowchart below shows how PCA's accounts receivable system works.

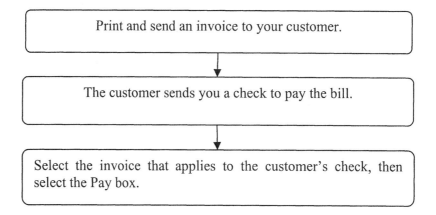

GETTING STARTED

1. Start Windows and Peachtree in the usual way. Open Matt's Service Merchandise, or if you used a unique name, select it. You set up this company in Chapter 11 on pages 373–377.

2.	Follow these steps to restore data from Chapter 11.

a.	Start Windows and Peachtree in the usual way. Open Matt's Service Merchandise. [1]

b.	Put your backup disk in drive A. You backed up Chapter 11 data on pages 414 and 415. From the menu bar, click on File, Restore.

c.	From the Select Backup File screen, click | Browse |. The Open Backup File screen pops up.

d.	Click on the down-arrow in the Look in field. Then click on 3½ Floppy (A:) to select drive A (or the appropriate location of your backup file).

e.	Click on the Chapter 11.ptb file to highlight it. The File name field displays Chapter 11. Click | Open |.

f.	Make sure that the Location field shows A:\Chapter 11.ptb (or the appropriate location for your backup file). Click | Next > |.

g.	From the Select Company screen make sure that the radio button next to An Existing Company is selected. The Company name field shows your company name; the Location field shows C:\ProgramFiles\Peachtree\Company\xxxxxxxx (the x's represent your subdirectory; or restore from the appropriate location on your computer). Click | Next > |.

h.	The Restore Options screen appears. Make sure that the box next to Company Data is *checked*. Click | Next > |.

i.	The Confirmation screen appears. Check the From and To fields to make sure they are correct. Click | Finish |. When the

[1]You can restore from your back up file even if *no* Peachtree company exists. Close Peachtree's start up screen. Select File; Restore. Select the location of your backup file. On the Restore Wizard's Select Company screen, select A New Company. The *A New Company* selection allows you to restore your backup data, bypassing the process of new company set up. For more information, refer to Troubleshooting on pages 274 and 275.

Restore Company scale is 100% completed, your data is restored and you are returned to the menu bar.

j.   Remove the backup disk.

k.   To verify your data, display the General Ledger Trial Balance. Compare it to the one shown on page 414 in Chapter 11.

Setting Up Customer Defaults

In Chapter 11, you entered General Ledger, Accounts Payable, and Inventory Item defaults. The directions that follow show you how to enter customer defaults from the Maintain pull-down menu.

1.   From the menu bar, select Maintain; Default Information, Customers.

2.   Click on the Discount % field. Type **0** (zero) in the Discount % field, then press **<Enter>**. Matt's Service Merchandise does *not* offer a discount to its credit customers.

3.   If necessary, type **2500** in the Credit Limit field, press **<Enter>**.

4.   Accept the default for GL Sales Account 40000, Service Fees by pressing **<Enter>**. (When you set up individual customers, you will select a GL Sales Account for that customer.)

5.   Accept the default for Discount GL Account 49000, Sales Discounts by pressing **<Enter>**.

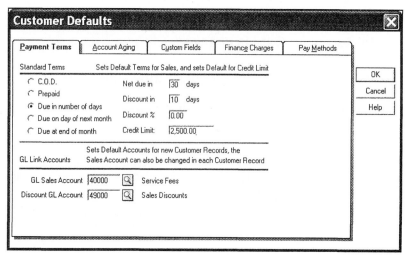

Observe that the default for Standard Terms is Due in number of days.

6. Click [OK].

Setting Up Sales Tax Defaults

You can enter sales tax default information for these areas:

➢ Sales Tax Authorities: codes for governments or other tax authorities and their tax rates. These are used to assemble the sales tax codes.

➢ Sales Tax Codes: the overall rate applied to taxable items on invoices to customers. This is composed of rates entered as Sales Tax Authorities.

Follow these steps to set up sales tax defaults:

1. From the menu bar, select Maintain; then Sales Taxes, Sales Tax Authorities.

2. Your cursor is in the ID field. Type **CA** and press **<Enter>**.

3. In the Description field, type **California sales taxes** and press **<Enter>** two times.

4. In the Sales Tax Payable G/L Account field, select Account No. 23100, Sales Tax Payable. Press **<Enter>**.

5. Type **8** in the Single Tax Rate field.

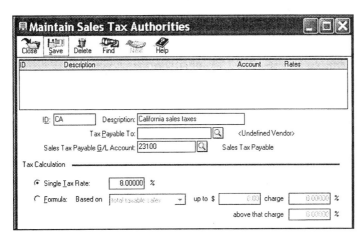

6. Check the accuracy of your work, then click 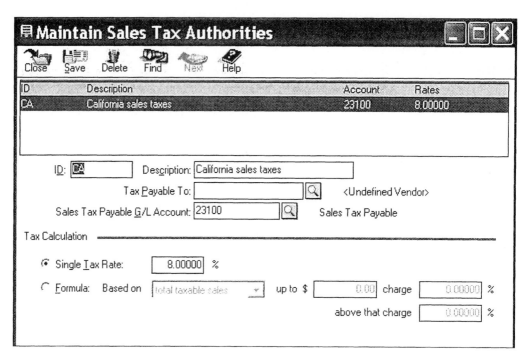.

7. Click ⟨Close⟩ to return to the Menu bar.

Now let's check that the Sales Tax Code for California is correct. Follow these steps to see the Maintain Sales Tax Codes window.

1. From the menu bar, select Maintain; then Sales Taxes, Sales Tax Codes.

2. Type **CA** in the Sales Tax Code field and press **<Enter>** two times. (*Remember Peachtree is case sensitive. Since you used capital letters to abbreviate CA, you must use capital letters again.*)

3. In the Description field, type **California sales taxes** and press **<Enter>**.

4. In the ID column, type **CA** and press **<Enter>**. Observe what gets completed automatically on this screen after you press **<Enter>**.

5. Click .

Maintain Sales Tax Codes

Sales Tax Code	Description	Tax Freight
CA	California sales taxes	

Sales Tax Code: CA   ☐ Tax Freight

Description: California sales taxes

The above tax code is made up of the following taxing authorities:

ID	Description	Rate	G/L Account - Description
CA	California sales taxes	8.00000	23100 - Sales Tax Payable

Total Sales Tax Rate: 8.00000

6. Click Close to return to the menu bar.

Setting Up Customer Maintenance Information

To enter default information about your customers, follow these steps:

1. From the menu bar, select Maintain, then Customers/Prospects.

2. Complete the following fields.

> Customer ID: **ap001** (Use lowercase letters and zeroes)
> Name: **Amy Phelps**
> Address: **160 Clark Street**
> City, ST Zip: **La Jolla, CA 95302**
> Country: **USA**

Sales Ta<u>x</u>:   Select **CA** (for California sales taxes)
Customer Type: **LJ**[2]
Telephone <u>1</u>:   **858-555-9700**
Fa<u>x</u>:   **858-555-7709**
E-mail: **ap@lajolla.com**
Web Site: **www.lajolla.com/amy**

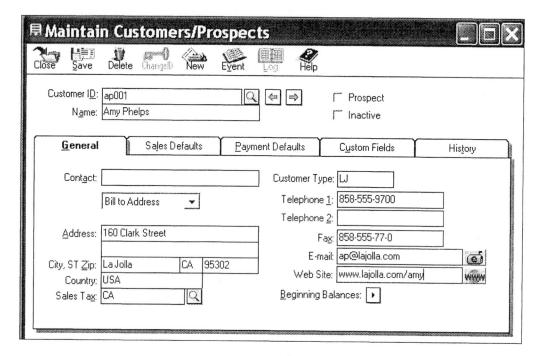

3.   Click on the Sa<u>l</u>es Defaults tab.

4.   In the GL Sales Acct lookup field, click . Select Account No. 40200, Sales-Hardware.

---

[2]It is important to indicate Customer Type. This groups similar customers together. In this case, customers from La Jolla (LJ) are grouped together.

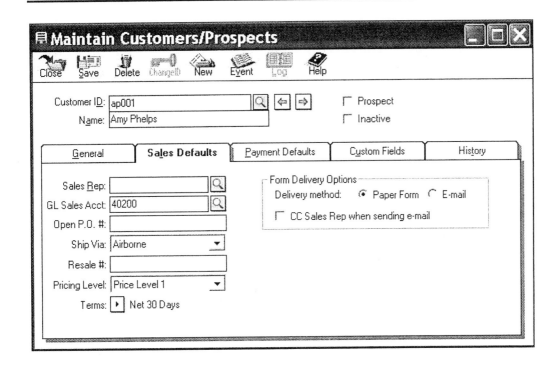

5. Click [Save].

6. Click on the General tab, then click [New]. Add in the following customers:

Customer ID: **bb002**
Name: **Bernard Baker**
Address: **522 North First Avenue**
City, ST Zip: **San Diego, CA 95030**
Country: **USA**
Sales Tax: **CA**
Customer Type: **SD** (for San Diego County)
Telephone 1: **619-555-0632**
Fax: **619-555-9833**
E-mail: **bb513@sandiego.com**
Web Site: **www.sandiego.com/baker**

In the Sales Defaults tab, select the GL Sales Acct 40400, Sales-Wall for Bernard Baker.

Customer ID: **dc003**
Name: **Dana Campbell**
Address: **3203 Howe Road**
City, ST Zip: **Phoenix, AZ 86108**
Country: **USA**
Sales Tax: Skip this field--see footnote. [3]
Customer Type: **Phoenix**
Telephone 1:   **602-555-6331**
Fax: **602-555-6332**
E-mail: **dana@mail.biz**
Web Site: **www.mail.biz/danaC**

In the Sales Defaults tab, select the GL Sales Acct 40600, Sales-Floor for Dana Campbell.

Customer ID: **jp004**
Name: **Jeanne Palmieri**
Address: **7709 W. Spaulding Ave.**
City, ST Zip: **Los Angeles, CA 90046**
Country: **USA**
Sales Tax: **CA**
Customer Type: **LA**
Telephone 1:   **323-555-8733**
Fax: **323-555-8735**
E-mail: **palmieri@lamail.com**
Web Site: **www.lamail.com/jeanne**

In the Sales Defaults tab, select the GL Sales Acct 40200, Sales-Hardware for Jeanne Palmieri.

Customer ID: **pm005**
Name: **Paula Martin**
Address: **1319 N. School St.**
City, ST Zip: **San Diego, CA 95032**
Country: **USA**
Sales Tax: **CA**
Customer Type: **SD**
Telephone 1:   **619-555-2531**

---

[3]Since this customer is out of state, there is no Sales Tax.

Fax: **619-555-2532**
E-mail: **martin@mymail.com**
Web Site: **www.mymail.com/paula**

In the Sales Defaults tab, select the GL Sales Acct 40400, Sales-Wall for Paula Martin. Close the Maintain Customers/Prospects window.

RECORDING SALES

Two types of sales are entered in PCA:

> ➤ Credit sales or invoiced sales--sales where you enter an invoice.

> ➤ Cash sales--sales where you do not enter an invoice.

In PCA, all the information about a sale is recorded on the Sales/Invoicing window. Then, PCA takes the necessary information from the screen and automatically journalizes the transaction in the **sales journal**. Only sales on account are recorded in this special journal. You can also print sales invoices.

Cash sales are entered on the Receipts window (Tasks, Receipts). Then, PCA takes the necessary information from the screen and automatically journalizes the transaction in the **cash receipts journal**.

On the Sales/Invoicing window, you enter invoices for the customers stored in PCA's customer file. You entered five credit customers for Matt's Service Merchandise:

Customer ID	Customer Name
ap001	Amy Phelps
bb002	Bernard Baker
dc003	Dana Campbell
jp004	Jeanne Palmieri
pm005	Paula Martin

All journal entries made to the Sales Journal (Sales/Invoicing window) are posted both to the General Ledger and to the **Customer Ledger** or **Accounts Receivable Ledger**. You can apply transactions to inventory items and jobs.

Entering sales works hand in hand with entering receipts. Once an invoice is posted it is simple to show that a customer has paid. Just display the appropriate invoice and click on the Pay box. PCA takes care of all the correct accounting distributions for you.

Entering Invoices for Credit Sales

In the steps that follow, you will record the following transaction:

Date	Description of Transaction

01/06/04   Amy Phelps purchased two doorknobs on account. (*Hint: Doorknobs are classified as hardware.*)

1. From the Tasks menu, click on Sales/Invoicing.

2. When the Sales/Invoicing window displays, your cursor is in the Customer ID lookup field. Click 🔍 and select **Amy Phelps**. PCA supplies the customer default information: billing address, payment terms, GL account default, A/R Account default, and the sales tax code. (*Hint: If the GL Account column and A/R Account lookup field does* not *display Account Nos. 40200 and 11000, refer to page 56, Changing Global Settings for Accounting Behind the Screens.*)

3. Type **6** in the Date field and press **<Enter>**. Since you want to print an invoice, you will skip the Invoice # field. PCA automatically numbers the invoices for you.

4. Click on the Quantity column, type **2** and press **<Enter>**.

5. In the Item column, click 🔍. Select **001hardware** for hardware.

6. In the Description field, type **Two doorknobs** and press **<Enter>**. Notice that the GL Account,[4] Unit Price, Amount column, A/R Account, and Sales Tax Code are automatically completed.

---

[4]If the G/L Account column and A/R Account fields are *not* displayed on your Sales/Invoicing window, click on Options, Global. Make sure the boxes in the Hide General Ledger Accounts section are unchecked. (For detailed steps, refer to page 56.)

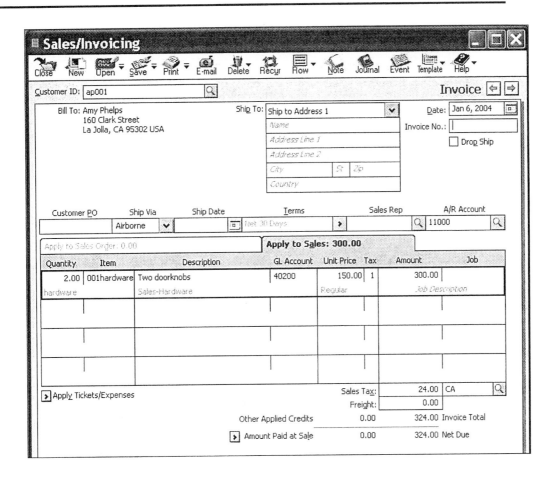

Printing the Sales Invoice

To print this sales invoice, follow these steps:

1. Click Print.

2. The Print Forms: Invoices window pops up. Click Change Form.

3. The Print Forms: Invoices/Pkg. Slips window pops up. Select Invoice Plain Service #2.

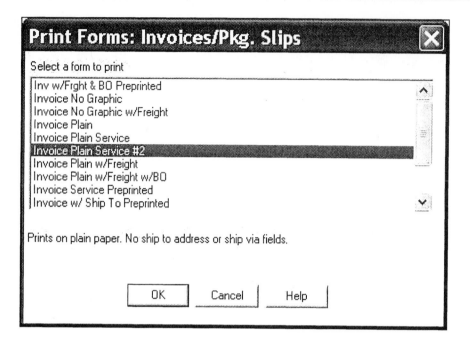

4. Click [OK].

5. The Print Forms: Invoices window appears. The First Invoice Number field displays 101. PCA will number all subsequent invoices consecutively. The Last used form shows Invoice Plain Service #2.

6. Click [Print]. The invoice starts to print. Compare your invoice to the one shown on the next page.

Comment

The form you select is tied to the kind of printer you are using. If your invoice does not print, you should select a different form to print. Refer to instruction 3 on page 443 to change the form for printing invoices.

Invoice

Matt's Service Merchandise
1801 University Drive
La Jolla, CA 95331
USA

Invoice Number:
101

Invoice Date:
Jan 6, 2004

Voice: 858-555-9213
Fax: 858-555-9215

Page:
1

Sold To:
Amy Phelps
160 Clark Street
La Jolla, CA 95302
USA

Customer ID: ap001

Customer PO	Payment Terms	Due Date	Sales Rep ID
	Net 30 Days	2/5/04	

Quantity	Item	Description	Unit Price	Extension
2.00	001hardware	Two doorknobs	150.00	300.00

Subtotal	300.00
Sales Tax	24.00
Total Invoice Amount	324.00
Payment/Credit Applied	
TOTAL	324.00

Check/Credit Memo No:

7. The Sales/Invoicing window is ready for the next sales invoice.

8. Record the following credit sales in the Sales/Invoicing window:

Date   *Description of Transaction*

01/06/04   Dana Campbell purchased three rolls of vinyl flooring on
            account. Print Invoice No. 102. (*Hint: Vinyl flooring is
            classified as floor. Dana Campbell's sales invoice shows
            no tax because this sale is made to an out-of-state
            customer.*)

Matt's Service Merchandise
1801 University Drive
La Jolla, CA 95331
USA

Voice: 858-555-9213
Fax: 858-555-9215

Invoice

Invoice Number:
102

Invoice Date:
Jan 6, 2004

Page:
1

Sold To:
    Dana Campbell
    3203 Howe Road
    Phoenix, AZ 86108
    USA

Customer ID: dc003

Customer PO	Payment Terms	Due Date	Sales Rep ID
	Net 30 Days	2/5/04	

Quantity	Item	Description	Unit Price	Extension
3.00	003floor	Three rolls of vinyl flooring	160.00	480.00

Subtotal	480.00
Sales Tax	
Total Invoice Amount	480.00
Payment/Credit Applied	
TOTAL	480.00

Check/Credit Memo No:

Date	Description of Transaction
01/06/04	Paula Martin purchased three pairs of curtains on account. Print Invoice No. 103. (*Hint: Curtains are classified as wall.*)

Invoice

Matt's Service Merchandise
1801 University Drive
La Jolla, CA 95331
USA

Invoice Number:
103

Invoice Date:
Jan 6, 2004

Voice: 858-555-9213
Fax: 858-555-9215

Page:
1

Sold To:
  Paula Martin
  1319 N. School Street
  San Diego, CA 95032
  USA

Customer ID: pm005

Customer PO	Payment Terms	Due Date	Sales Rep ID
	Net 30 Days	2/5/04	

Quantity	Item	Description	Unit Price	Extension
3.00	002wall	Three pairs of curtains	100.00	300.00

	Subtotal	300.00
	Sales Tax	24.00
	Total Invoice Amount	324.00
Check/Credit Memo No:	Payment/Credit Applied	
	TOTAL	324.00

Date   *Description of Transaction*

01/08/04   Jeanne Palmieri purchased three curtain rods on account.
             Print Invoice No. 104. (*Hint: Curtain rods are classified as
             hardware.*)

Matt's Service Merchandise
1801 University Drive
La Jolla, CA 95331
USA

Voice: 858-555-9213
Fax: 858-555-9215

Invoice

Invoice Number:
104

Invoice Date:
Jan 8, 2004

Page:
1

Sold To:
    Jeanne Palmieri
    7709 W. Spaulding Ave.
    Los Angeles, CA 90046
    USA

Customer ID: jp004

Customer PO	Payment Terms	Due Date	Sales Rep ID
	Net 30 Days	2/7/04	

Quantity	Item	Description	Unit Price	Extension
3.00	001hardware	Three curtain rods	150.00	450.00

Subtotal	450.00
Sales Tax	36.00
Total Invoice Amount	486.00
Payment/Credit Applied	
TOTAL	486.00

Check/Credit Memo No:

---

9. Close the Sales/Invoicing window.

Backing Up Your Data

Follow these steps to back up Chapter 12 data:

1. Put a blank, formatted disk in drive A.

2. From the menu bar, select File, then Back up.

3. Click Back Up Now .

4. Click on the down-arrow in the Save in field. If necessary, scroll up the list, then click on 3½ Floppy (A:) to select drive A. *Or*, back up to the network, hard drive, or other media.

5. Type **Chapter 12 Begin** in the File name field.

6. Click Save .

7. When the screen prompts that This company backup will require approximately 1 diskette, click OK .

8. When the screen prompts you to insert the first disk, click OK . When the Back Up Company scale is 100% completed, you have successfully backed up to the current point in Chapter 12. You are returned to the menu bar.

9. Click on File, Exit to exit Peachtree.

Entering a Service Invoice

Matt's Service Merchandise sells and repairs household items. When repairs are done, a *service invoice* is used. A service invoice is an alternative to the standard invoice. It is used when you want to create an invoice without inventory items.

If you exited PCA, start Windows, then PCA. Open Matt's Service Merchandise or if you used a unique company name, select it. If necessary, restore the Chapter 12 Begin.ptb file.

Follow these steps to enter a service invoice:

1. From the Tasks menu, click on Sales/Invoicing.

2. Click 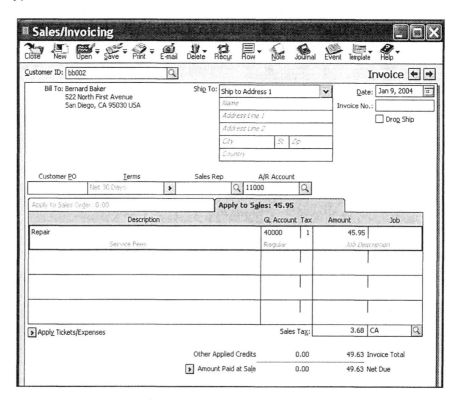Template . Then select <Predefined> Service.

   The Sales/Invoicing window changes to include only the information necessary for a service invoice. This means that you no longer can select inventory items. When you complete the service transaction, you click Template again. Then, you are ready to enter an inventory sale on the Sales/Invoicing window.

3. In the Customer ID field, select Bernard Baker.

4. Type **9** in the Date field, then press **<Enter>**.

5. Click on the Description field. Type **Repair** and press **<Enter>**.

6. In the GL Account column, select Account No. 40000, Service Fees.

7. Type **45.95** in the Amount column.

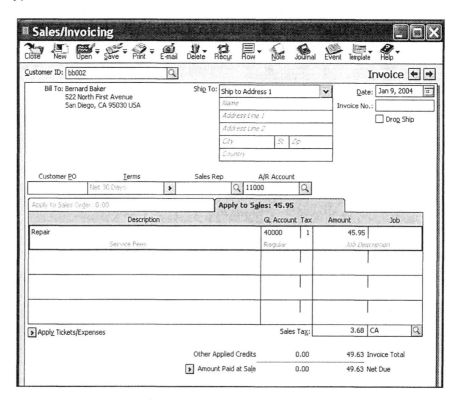

---

8. Print Invoice No. 105 and compare it to the one below.

Invoice

Matt's Service Merchandise
1801 University Drive
La Jolla, CA 95331
USA

Invoice Number:
105

Invoice Date:
Jan 9, 2004

Voice: 858-555-9213
Fax: 858-555-9215

Page:
1

Sold To:
Bernard Baker
522 North First Avenue
San Diego, CA 95030
USA

Customer ID: bb002

Customer PO	Payment Terms	Due Date	Sales Rep ID
	Net 30 Days	2/8/04	

Quantity	Item	Description	Unit Price	Extension
		Repair		45.95

	Subtotal	45.95
	Sales Tax	3.68
	Total Invoice Amount	49.63
Check/Credit Memo No:	Payment/Credit Applied	
	TOTAL	49.63

---

9. Click [Template], then <Predefined> Product. The Sales/Invoicing screen returns to the Sales/Invoice window. Close the screen.

Sales Returns: Tasks; Credit Memos

A sales return, or credit memo, is used when merchandise is returned by a customer. Credit memos for sales returns are entered similarly to vendor credit memos.

Before you can apply a credit, you must post the invoice. Invoice Nos. 101–105 were posted to the sales journal when you printed the sales invoices. When you enter a credit memo, you select the customer's ID code and the appropriate invoice number. Then, the return will be applied to that invoice and the customer's account balance will be adjusted.

In the steps that follow, you will record the following transaction:

Date	Description of Transaction
01/14/04	Paula Martin returned one pair of curtains that she purchased on January 6, Invoice No. 103. She also paid the balance of that invoice.

1. From the Tasks menu, select Credit Memos.

2. In the Customer ID field, select Paula Martin.

3. In the Date field, type **14** and press **<Enter>**.

4. Type **CM103** in the Credit No. field. (CM is an abbreviation of Credit Memo; then you are using the sales invoice number to identify the credit memo.) Press **<Enter>**.

5. The Apply to Invoice No. tab is selected. Click on the down-arrow and select 103.

6. Type **1** in the Returned column. Press **<Enter>**

7. Type **Returned one pair of curtains** in the Description column.

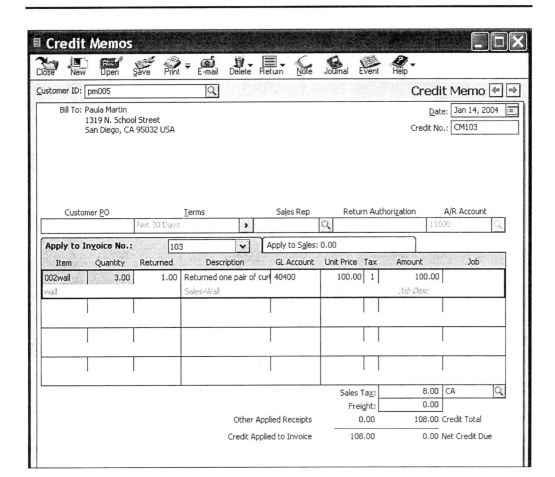

7. Click ![Save] to post, then click ![Close].

Apply a sales return: Follow these steps:

1. From the menu bar, click on Tasks, then Receipts. At the Select a Cash Account window, accept the default for La Jolla Bank by clicking ![OK].

2. Type **01/14/04** in the Deposit ticket ID field. Press **<Enter>**.

3. In the Customer ID field, select Paula Martin.

4. In the Reference field, type **Invoice 103** then press the **<Enter>** key two times.

5. In the <u>D</u>ate field, type **14**, then press the **<Enter>** key two times.

6. The Credit Card Information window appears.

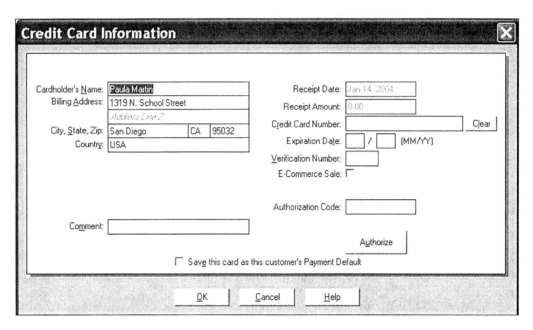

7. Read the information on this screen. Since you are *not* going to record any information, click <u>C</u>ancel . If you were going to charge Ms. Martin's payment to her credit card, you would enter her credit card information on this screen, then select <u>O</u>K .

8. Observe that the Payment Method field displays Check; and that the Cash Account field displays Account No. 10200, La Jolla Bank. In the Apply to <u>I</u>nvoices list, click on the Pay box. Observe that the Receipt Amount shown is 216.00 ($324 - $108). Compare your screen to the one shown on the next page.

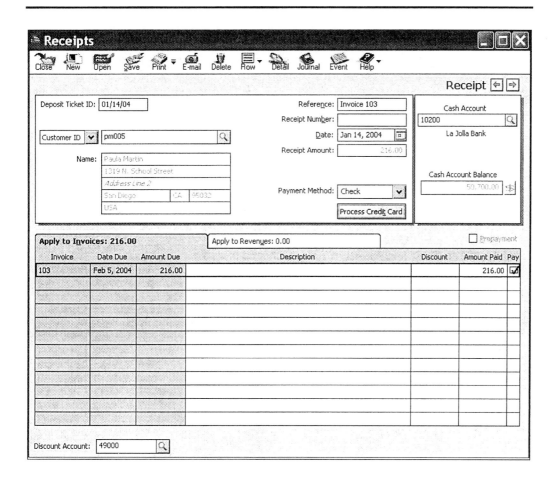

9. Click  to post, then click [Close].

RECORDING RECEIPTS AND CASH SALES

You enter all checks, cash, and credit card slips that you receive and deposit in your checking account using the Receipts window. Then, PCA takes the necessary information from the Receipts window and automatically journalizes the transactions in the Cash Receipts Journal. If the receipt is from a credit customer, then the receipt is posted to the customer's subsidiary ledger as well.

There are two categories for receipts that result from sales:

➢ Receipts for which an invoice was entered in the Sales/Invoicing window.

➢ Direct sales receipts for which no invoice was entered in the Sales/Invoicing window.

Entering A Receipt

Date   Description of Transaction

01/21/04   Matt's Service Merchandise received a check in the amount of $324 from Amy Phelps in payment of Invoice 101.

Follow these steps to enter this receipt:

1.   If necessary, from the menu bar, click on Tasks, then Receipts. The Receipts window appears.

2.   Type **01/21/04** in the Deposit ticket ID field.

3.   In the Customer ID field, select Amy Phelps.

4.   In the Reference field, type **Invoice 101**. (This is the Invoice that is being paid.) Press the **<Enter>** key two times.

5.   Type **21** in the Date field.

6.   Verify that Account No. 10200, La Jolla Bank, is displayed in the Cash Account lookup field. At the bottom of the screen, the Apply to Invoices tab is selected. Click on the Pay box for Invoice 101. Compare your screen to the one shown on the next page.

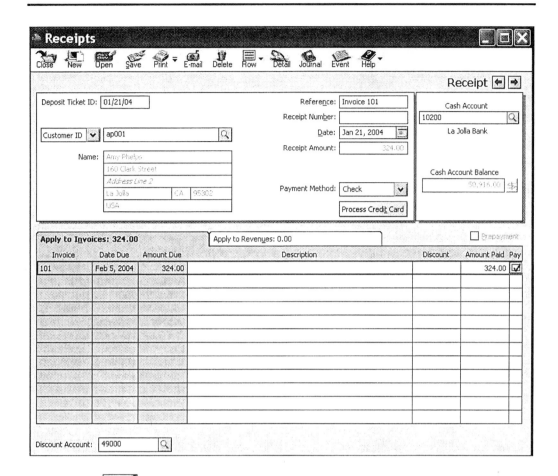

7. Click to post this receipt. The Receipts window is ready for another transaction.

In the preceding steps, each customer paid the invoice in full. What if a customer made a partial payment on an invoice?

Date   *Description of Transaction*

01/22/04   Jeanne Palmieri paid $95 on account, Invoice No. 104.

Follow these steps for partial payment:

1. The Receipts window should be displayed on your screen. Type **01/22/04** in the Deposit ticket ID field.

2. Select Jeanne Palmieri as the Customer.

3. Type **Invoice 104** in the Reference field. Press the **<Enter>** key two times.

4. Type **22** in the Date field.

5. Jeanne Palmieri's Invoice number, Date Due, and Amount Due display in the Apply to Invoices table. Click on the Amount Paid column. Type **95** in the Amount Paid column and press **<Enter>**. A check mark is automatically placed in the Pay box.

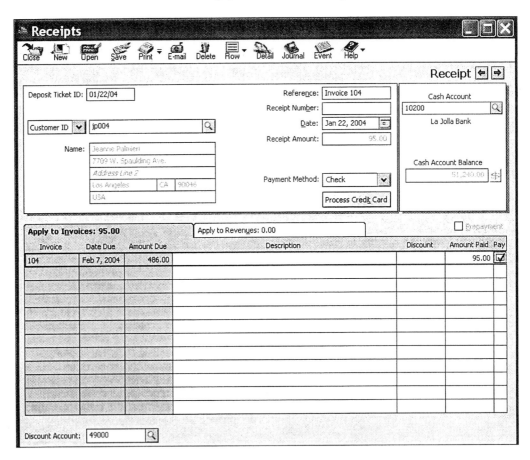

6. Click ![Save] to post.

Enter the following receipts:

Date   *Description of Transaction*

01/28/04   Received a check in the amount of $49.63 from Bernard Baker in full payment of Invoice No. 105.

01/28/04   Received a check in the amount of $480 from Dana Campbell in full payment of Invoice No. 102.

Cash Sales

Follow these steps to record a cash sale.

Date   *Description of Transaction*

01/29/04   Debi Clarke bought two pairs of curtains for cash, $200.

1. If necessary, from the menu bar, click on Tasks, then Receipts. Type **01/29/04** in the Deposit ticket ID field.

2. Click on the Name field, then type **Debi Clarke**. You do not enter address information for a cash sale.

3. Since this is a cash sale, type **Cash** in the Reference field. Press **<Enter>** two times.

4. Type **29** as the date.

5. Verify that account 10200, La Jolla Bank, is displayed in the Cash Account field.

6. Make sure that the Apply to Revenues tab is selected.

   PCA assumes you are going to apply the receipt to revenue unless you select a customer with open invoices.

   You can also apply a portion of the receipt to both invoices and revenue. You do this by selecting each heading, then entering the distribution information for that portion of the receipt. A running subtotal is kept beside the heading to show how much of the receipt has been applied.

7. Type **2** in the Quantity column.

8. Select 002wall as the inventory item.

9. Type **Two pairs of curtains** as the Description and press the **<Enter>** key. (Notice that the GL Account defaults to Account No. 40400, Sales-Wall).

10. Go to the Sales Tax Code lookup field and select California sales taxes. Observe that 16.00 is automatically calculated in the Sales Tax field.

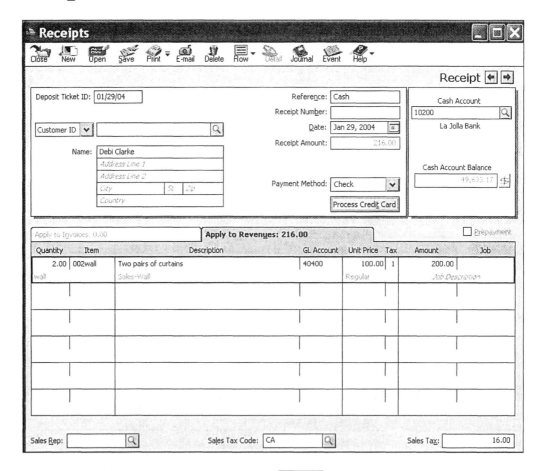

11. Click [Save] to post, and then click [Close].

Finance Charges

PCA includes a feature in the Tasks menu for computing finance or interest charges. This option of the Tasks menu computes and applies finance charges for customers and/or prints a report listing all finance charges.

You use this feature by selecting the Finance Charge option. You may want to try this out on your own. Use the Tasks menu and select Finance Charge to see how this feature works.

PRINTING CUSTOMER FORMS

PCA provides forms for the following types of customer correspondence:

➢ Invoices.

➢ Statements.

➢ Mailing labels.

➢ Collection letters.

You can access these reports by selecting Reports, then Accounts Receivable. You select a predefined form to print your customer information or you can design your own form. In Part 4 of this book you will learn more about Custom Forms.

Printing Invoices

You can print a single invoice from the Sales/Invoicing window by selecting [Print]. This saves and prints the invoice.

You can also print a batch of invoices from the Reports menu by selecting Accounts Receivable and then selecting Invoices/Pkg. Slips. There are several types of predefined invoices available for printing customer information or you can design your own form.

Printing Statements

The information that is printed on customer statements is defined in the Statement/Invoices Defaults which are set up from the Maintain menu. You can set up collection letters and also select from these print options.

➢ Whether to print your company name, address, phone, and fax on the statement.

➢ Whether to print zero and credit balance statements.

➢ The minimum balance necessary to print a statement.

➢ The number of grace days before printing a statement.

➢ Whether to print statements for accounts with no activity.

You can print or display statements. Or, if you want to display customer information before printing, you can display or print the customer ledger.

You print statements from the Reports menu by selecting Accounts Receivable and then Invoices/Pkg. Slips. There are several types of predefined statements available for printing customer account balances. Select the form that best suits your needs. As mentioned before, you can also design your own statement.

When the statements stop printing, a message box displays, asking if the statements printed okay and if you want to update the customer file. Look at your printed statements carefully before you answer Yes to this question. When you answer Yes, PCA records the statement date in the customer record. This is used as the balance brought forward date the next time you print a statement. This way the ending balance on one statement is the same as the beginning balance on the next statement.

You should enter, print, and post all invoices prior to printing statements. In this way the Balance Forward amounts are correct from month to month.

Printing Mailing Labels

From the Reports menu you can print labels. If you want to try this out, select the Reports menu, Accounts Receivable, then Labels - Customers, select one of the types of labels, and print. There are several predefined labels available for printing. You can elect to use these forms or design your own.

When printing labels you can do the following.

➢ Select a range of customers.

➢ Enter all or part of a Zip code to limit the mailing labels to customers in a certain area.

➢ Print labels for customers, prospects, or both.

➢ Enter a Status for customers so that you print labels for all, active, or inactive customers.

➢ Enter a Type Code for customers so that only customers of a specific Type Code will print.

Preparing Collection Letters

What if credit customers are slow to pay their bills? Collection letters can play an important role in generating revenue from customers who are slow to pay off their balances. Sometimes just a friendly reminder is all that is needed.

The table below shows how important it is to get paid on time because the longer a bill remains unpaid, the less chance there is of collecting.

Number of Days Overdue	Percent Uncollectible
1 to 30 days	2%
31 to 60 days	10%
61 to 90 days	20%
91 to 180 days	30%
181 to 365 days	50%
over 365 days	90%

Collection letters are an effective way to remind customers to pay their unpaid balances. Most customers will pay after they receive a friendly reminder of a past-due account. It is worthwhile to send these letters because past-due amounts can be a burden on a company's cash flow.

Depending on how late the payment is, collection letters vary in tone and urgency. For example, a friendly reminder may be all that's needed for someone who is 30 days past due, but a different letter may be needed for someone who is more than 90 days past due. Remember that while it is important to collect past-due amounts, you would also like to keep the customer.

PCA's letters are grouped by lateness of payment and severity of tone. The less than 30 days overdue letter is soft while the 61-90 days overdue letter is much firmer. You may edit all of these letters to suit your needs.

To print a collection letter you use the analysis pull-down menu. Follow these steps to do that:

1. Click on Analysis, then Collection Manager.

2. Type **01/31/04** in the As of Date field. Press **<Enter>**. The Collection Aging bar graph appears.

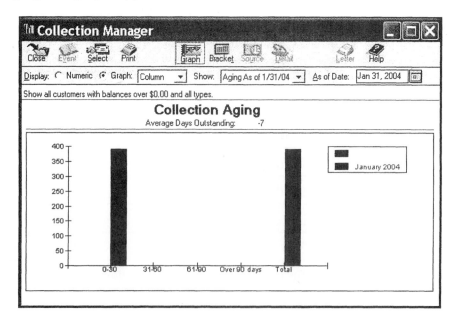

3. Click 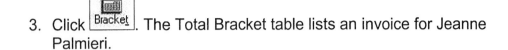. The Total Bracket table lists an invoice for Jeanne Palmieri.

4. Click on the Letter box on the Total Bracket table. Then, click on
   Letter .

5. The Print Forms: Collection Letters window pops up. Click Change Form . You may want to try one of these selections and see what Peachtree's collection letters look like. The sample letters are sorted as follows.

   ➢ Overdue < 30 Soft
   ➢ Overdue >90 Agency
   ➢ Overdue >90 Days
   ➢ Overdue 31-60 Med
   ➢ Overdue 61-90 Firm

6. Select a form to print, then click OK .

7. Click Print . A collection letter prints. Read the letter that you printed.

8. Close the Collection Manager.

PRINTING THE SALES JOURNAL

The Sales/Invoicing window is the Sales Journal in PCA. Like a Sales Journal, credit sales are recorded in the Sales/Invoicing window. Follow these steps to print the Sales Journal:

1. From the Reports menu, select Accounts Receivable.

2. In the Report List, highlight Sales Journal.

3. Click . The Sales Journal Filter window displays. Click
OK.

4. The Print window pops up. Click OK. The Sales Journal starts
to print.

Matt's Service Merchandise
Sales Journal
For the Period From Jan 1, 2004 to Jan 31, 2004
Filter Criteria includes: Report order is by Invoice/CM Date. Report is printed in Detail Format.

Date	Account ID	Invoice/CM #	Line Description	Debit Amnt	Credit Amnt
1/6/04	23100	101	CA: California sales taxes		24.00
	40200		Two doorknobs		300.00
	50000		Cost of sales	100.00	
	12000		Cost of sales		100.00
	11000		Amy Phelps	324.00	
1/6/04	40600	102	Three rolls of vinyl flooring		480.00
	51000		Cost of sales	162.00	
	12000		Cost of sales		162.00
	11000		Dana Campbell	480.00	
1/6/04	23100	103	CA: California sales taxes		24.00
	40400		Three pairs of curtains		300.00
	50500		Cost of sales	90.00	
	12000		Cost of sales		90.00
	11000		Paula Martin	324.00	
1/8/04	23100	104	CA: California sales taxes		36.00
	40200		Three curtain rods		450.00
	50000		Cost of sales	150.00	
	12000		Cost of sales		150.00
	11000		Jeanne Palmieri	486.00	
1/9/04	23100	105	CA: California sales taxes		3.68
	40000		Repair		45.95
	11000		Bernard Baker	49.63	
1/14/04	23100	CM103	CA: California sales taxes	8.00	
	48000		Returned one pair of curtains	100.00	
	50500		Cost of sales		30.00
	12000		Cost of sales	30.00	
	11000		Paula Martin		108.00
		Total		2,303.63	2,303.63

PRINTING THE CASH RECEIPTS JOURNAL

The Receipts window is the Cash Receipts Journal in PCA. Like the
Cash Receipts Journal, payments from customers and cash sales are
recorded in the Receipts window. Follow these steps to print the Cash
Receipts Journal.

1. If the Report List is displayed, highlight Cash Receipts Journal. (Or,
from the menu bar select Reports, then Accounts Receivable, then
highlight Cash Receipts Journal.)

2. Click [Print]. The Cash Receipts Journal Filter window displays. Click [OK].

3. The Print window pops up. Click [OK]. The Cash Receipts Journal starts to print.

Page: 1

Matt's Service Merchandise
Cash Receipts Journal
For the Period From Jan 1, 2004 to Jan 31, 2004
Filter Criteria includes: Report order is by Check Date. Report is printed in Detail Format.

Date	Account ID	Transaction Ref	Line Description	Debit Amnt	Credit Amnt
1/14/04	11000	Invoice 103	Invoice: 103		216.00
	10200		Paula Martin	216.00	
1/21/04	11000	Invoice 101	Invoice: 101		324.00
	10200		Amy Phelps	324.00	
1/22/04	11000	Invoice 104	Invoice: 104		95.00
	10200		Jeanne Palmieri	95.00	
1/28/04	11000	Invoice 105	Invoice: 105		49.63
	10200		Bernard Baker	49.63	
1/28/04	11000	Invoice 102	Invoice: 102		480.00
	10200		Dana Campbell	480.00	
1/29/04	23100	Cash	CA: California sales taxes		16.00
	40400		Two pairs of curtains		200.00
	50500		Cost of sales	60.00	
	12000		Cost of sales		60.00
	10200		Debi Clarke	216.00	
				1,440.63	1,440.63

PRINTING THE CUSTOMER LEDGERS

Follow these steps to print the Customer Ledgers for Matt's Service Merchandise:

1. From the Report List , highlight Customer Ledgers, click [Print]. The Customer Ledgers Filter window displays. Click [OK].

2. The Print window pops up. Click [OK].

Matt's Service Merchandise
Customer Ledgers
For the Period From Jan 1, 2004 to Jan 31, 2004
Filter Criteria includes: Report order is by ID. Report is printed in Detail Format.

Customer ID Customer	Date	Trans No	Type	Debit Amt	Credit Amt	Balance
ap001	1/6/04	101	SJ	324.00		324.00
Amy Phelps	1/21/04	Invoice 101	CRJ		324.00	0.00
bb002	1/9/04	105	SJ	49.63		49.63
Bernard Baker	1/28/04	Invoice 105	CRJ		49.63	0.00
dc003	1/6/04	102	SJ	480.00		480.00
Dana Campbell	1/28/04	Invoice 102	CRJ		480.00	0.00
jp004	1/8/04	104	SJ	486.00		486.00
Jeanne Palmieri	1/22/04	Invoice 104	CRJ		95.00	391.00
pm005	1/6/04	103	SJ	324.00		324.00
Paula Martin	1/14/04	CM103	SJ		108.00	216.00
	1/14/04	Invoice 103	CRJ		216.00	0.00

PRINTING THE GENERAL LEDGER TRIAL BALANCE

1. In the Report Area, highlight General Ledger. Then, in the Report List, highlight General Ledger Trial Balance.

2. Click [Print]. Make the selections to print. Compare your printout with the one shown on the next page.

Matt's Service Merchandise
General Ledger Trial Balance
As of Jan 31, 2004

Filter Criteria includes: Report order is by ID. Report is printed in Detail Format.

Account ID	Account Description	Debit Amt	Credit Amt
10200	La Jolla Bank	49,849.17	
10400	Stockmen's Savings & Loa	22,000.00	
11000	Accounts Receivable	391.00	
12000	Merchandise Inventory	28,406.00	
13000	Supplies	1,750.00	
14000	Prepaid Insurance	2,400.00	
15000	Furniture and Fixtures	5,000.00	
15100	Computers & Equipment	7,500.00	
15500	Building	100,000.00	
20000	Accounts Payable		300.00
23100	Sales Tax Payable		95.68
27000	Long-Term Notes Payable		20,500.00
27400	Mortgage Payable		75,000.00
39006	Matt Lowe, Capital		60,795.00
39007	Matt Lowe, Drawing	500.00	
39008	Sharon Albert, Capital		60,795.00
39009	Sharon Albert, Drawing	500.00	
40000	Service Fees		45.95
40200	Sales-Hardware		750.00
40400	Sales-Wall		400.00
40600	Sales-Floor		480.00
50000	Cost of Goods Sold-Hardw	250.00	
50500	Cost of Goods Sold-Wall	120.00	
51000	Cost of Goods Sold-Floor	162.00	
59500	Purchase Discounts		17.96
70000	Maintenance Expense	130.00	
73500	Postage Expense	37.00	
75500	Supplies Expense	110.82	
76000	Telephone Expense	73.60	
	Total:	219,179.59	219,179.59

EDITING RECEIPTS

Is your Customer Ledger correct? Jeanne Palmieri's account is used to show how to edit the Customer Ledger. Follow these steps to see how the editing feature works:

1. From the menu bar, select Tasks, Receipts, then click

2. The Select Receipt window displays. Highlight Invoice 104, Jeanne Palmieri.

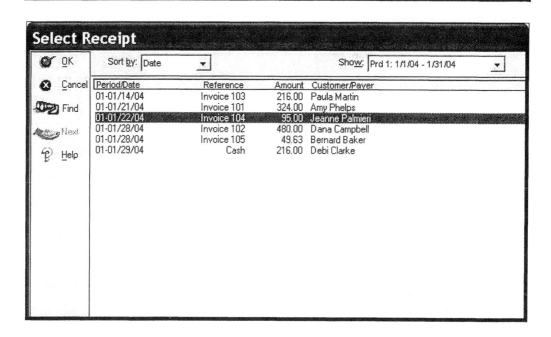

3. Click [✪ OK] and the Receipts window appears with Jeanne Palmieri's partial payment of $95. Check the screen carefully. Make any needed corrections.

4. Close the Receipts window.

BACKING UP CHAPTER 12 DATA

Follow these steps to back up Chapter 12 data:

1. Put your backup disk in drive A. You may use the same disk that you used to back up data on pages 449-450.

2. From the menu bar, select File, then Back up.

3. Click [Back Up Now].

4. Click on the down-arrow in the Save in field. If necessary, scroll up the list, then click on 3½ Floppy (A:) to select drive A. Or, back up to the network or hard drive.

5. Type **Chapter 12** in the File name field.

---

6. Click [Save].

7. When the screen prompts that This company backup will require approximately 1 diskette, click [OK].

8. When the screen prompts you to insert the first disk, click on [OK]. When the Back Up Company scale is 100% completed, you have successfully backed up to the current point in Chapter 12. You are returned to the menu bar.

9. Click on File, Exit to exit Peachtree.

INTERNET ACTIVITY	
1.	From your Internet browser, go to the book's website at http://www.mhhe.com/yacht2004.
2.	In the Student Edition list, link to Internet Activities.
3.	Link to WEB EXERCISES PART 3.
4.	Complete the WebCPA–Tools and Resources for the Electronic Accountant exercise. Read steps 1–3.
5.	Follow the steps shown on the book's website to complete this Internet activity.
6.	Using a word processing program write a brief summary of what you find. Include all appropriate website addresses.

SUMMARY AND REVIEW

SOFTWARE OBJECTIVES: In Chapter 12, you have used the software to:

1. Set up customer default information.

2. Set up sales tax information.

3. Set up customer maintenance information.

4. Record credit sales, cash sales, and sales returns.

5. Record customer receipts, partial payments, and edit invoices.

6. Make four backups using two blank, formatted disks: 2 for Matt's Service Merchandise; 2 for the end-of-chapter exercises.

WEB OBJECTIVES: In Chapter 12, you will do these Internet activities:

1. Use your Internet browser to go to the book's website.

2. Go to the Internet Activity link on the book's website. Then, select WEB EXERCISES PART 3. Complete the second web exercise in Part 3— The Accountant's Web Magazine and Resource Guide: Faulkner & Gray's Electronic Accountant.

3. Use a word processing program to write summaries of the websites that you visited.

GOING TO THE NET

Access the Business Owner's Toolkit website at http://www.toolkit.cch.com/text/P06_1430.asp. Read the accounts receivable page, and then answer the following questions.

1. What is the common abbreviation for accounts receivable?
2. What is the control account for customer sales on account?
3. How is the ending accounts receivable total computed?

Multiple-Choice Questions: In the space provided, write the letter that best answers each question.

_____1. Use the following menu options to record entries in the Sales Journal:

    a. Maintain/Customers Prospects.
    b. Tasks; Receipts.
    c. Tasks; Sales/Invoicing.
    d. Maintain; Default Information, Customers.
    e. None of the above.

_____2. The money that your customers owe to the business is known as:

a. Accounts payable.
b. Revenue.
c. Accounts receivable.
d. Cash in bank.
e. None of the above.

_____3. PCA's accounts receivable system allows you to set up all of the following, EXCEPT:

a. Customers.
b. Inventory items.
c. Finance charges.
d. Vendors.
e. None of the above.

_____4. Use the following menu options to record entries in the Cash Receipts Journal:

a. Tasks/Receipts.
b. Maintain/Company Information.
c. Maintain/Customers Prospects.
d. Tasks/Sales/Invoicing.
e. None of the above.

_____5. Matt's Service Merchandise charges sales tax to all sales made in:

a. Arizona.
b. Oregon.
c. Washington.
d. California.
e. None of the above.

_____6. The owner(s) of Matt's Service Merchandise are:

a. Matt Lowe.
b. Sharon Albert.
c. both a. and b.
d. Jeanne Palmieri.
e. None of the above.

_____7. The sales tax rate is:

a. 6%.
b. 7%.
c. 8%.
d. 9%.
e. None of the above.

_____8. The sales tax payable account is:

a. Account No. 52000.
b. Account No. 53000.
c. Account No. 23100.
d. Account No. 12000.
e. None of the above.

_____9. The Customer ID for Amy Phelps is:

a. AAP001.
b. ap001.
c. ap002.
d. AP002.
e. None of the above.

_____10. The Cash Account number is shown on which of the following windows:

a. Sales/Invoicing.
b. Purchases/Receive Inventory.
c. Receipts.
d. General Journal Entry.
e. None of the above.

_____11. The account used for hardware sales is:

    a. Account No. 40000.
    b. Account No. 40800.
    c. Account No. 40200.
    d. Account No. 40400.
    e. None of the above.

_____12. All journal entries made to the Sales Journal are posted to the General ledger and to the:

    a. Accounts payable ledger.
    b. Customer ledger.
    c. Job cost ledger.
    d. Payroll register.
    e. None of the above.

_____13. A sales return is also called a/an:

    a. Credit memo.
    b. Debit memo.
    c. Invoice.
    d. Receipt.
    e. None of the above.

_____14. The GL Sales Account for wall is:

    a. Account No. 44200.
    b. Account No. 44300.
    c. Account No. 44400.
    d. Account No. 40400.
    e. None of the above.

_____15. To back up all of Chapter 12's data to drive A (or to your network or hard drive), the following file name is typed:

    a. Chapter 12 Begin.
    b. Chapter 12b.
    c. Backup.
    d. Chapter 12.
    e. None of the above.

Exercise 12-1: You must complete Exercises 11-1 and 11-2 before starting Exercise 12-1.

1. Start Windows, then PCA. Open the company that you set up in Exercise 11-1 on pages 419-420.

2. Restore your data from Exercise 11-2. (*Hint: This backup was made on page 428.*) To make sure you are starting in the right place, display Exercise 11-2's general ledger trial balance (step 6, page 427).

3. Enter the following customer defaults:

   a. Standard Terms: Due in number of days

   b. Net due in: 30 days
      Discount in: 10 days
      Discount %:   0.00
      Credit Limit: 2,500.00
      GL Sales Account: 40000 Service Fees
      Discount GL Account: 49000 Sales Discounts

4. Enter the following customer maintenance information:

   a. Customer ID: **ac001**
       Name: **Alene Carter**
       Address: **1556 Mesquite Ave.**
       City, ST Zip: **Eugene, OR 97412**
       Country: **USA**
       Sales Tax: Skip this field. There are no sales taxes in Oregon.
       Customer Type: **EU** (for Eugene, Oregon)
       Telephone 1:   **541-555-3323**
       Fax: **541-555-3324**
       E-mail: **alene@alenecarter.com**
       Web Site: **www.alenecarter.com**

   In the Sales Defaults tab, select the GL Sales Acct 40400, Sales-Tools for Alene Carter.

   b. Customer ID: **bd002**
       Name: **Bruce Davidson**

Address:	**519 Aspen Road**
City, ST Zip:	**Eugene, OR 97413**
Country:	**USA**
Sales Tax:	n/a
Customer Type:	**EU**
Telephone 1:	**541-555-3169**
Fax:	**541-555-3299**
E-mail:	**bruce@brucedavidson.net**
Web Site:	**www.brucedavidson.net**

In the Sales Defaults tab, select the GL Sales Acct 40200, Sales-Hardware for Bruce Davidson.

c.
Customer ID:	**rn003**
Name:	**Robert Norton**
Address:	**5116 Main Street**
City, ST Zip:	**Eugene, OR 97402**
Country:	**USA**
Sales Tax:	n/a
Customer Type:	**EU**
Telephone 1:	**541-555-9901**
Fax:	**541-555-9905**
E-mail:	**robert@robnorton.com**
Web Site:	**www.robnorton.com**

In the Sales Defaults tab, select the GL Sales Acct 40200, Sales-Hardware for Robert Norton.

5. Make a backup of your work. (Use **Exercise 12-1** as the file name.)

Exercise 12-2: Exercise 12-1 must be completed before Exercise 12-2.

1. Start Windows, then PCA. Open your service merchandise company.

2. Restore data from Exercise 12-1.

3. Record the following transactions:

    01/06/04   Sold four tool kits on account to Alene Carter, Customer ac001. Type **101** in the Invoice No. field. Subsequent invoices will be numbered automatically.

    01/06/04   Sold three hardware sets on account to Bruce Davidson, Customer bd002.

    01/06/04   Sold six hardware sets on account to Robert Norton, Customer rn003.

    01/09/04   Alene Carter returned one of the tool kits that she purchased on January 6, Invoice No. 101, CM101. Ms. Carter also paid the balance of Invoice 101. (*Hint: This transaction requires two entries.*)

    01/13/04   Received a check in full payment of Invoice No. 102 from Bruce Davidson.

    01/16/04   Made a cash sale to Katie Fowler for two hardware sets *and* two tool kits.

4. Print the Sales Journal.

5. Print the Cash Receipts Journal.

6. Print the Customer Ledgers.

7. Print the General Ledger Trial Balance.

8. Make a backup. Use **Exercise 12-2** as the file name.

CHAPTER 12 INDEX

Chapter 13   Merchandise Inventory

SOFTWARE OBJECTIVES: In Chapter 13, you will use the software to:

1. Enter inventory maintenance and default information.
2. Enter inventory item information, including Sales account, Merchandise Inventory account, and Cost of Sales account.
3. Enter item codes when recording purchases and sales.
4. Enter inventory adjustments.
5. Make three backups using two blank, formatted disk: two for Matt's Service Merchandise; one for the end-of-chapter exercises.

WEB OBJECTIVES: In Chapter 13, you will do these Internet activities:

1. Use your Internet browser to go to the book's website.
2. Go to the Internet Activity link on the book's website. Then, select WEB EXERCISES PART 3. Complete the third web exercise in Part 3— Accountant's World.
3. Use a word processing program to write summaries of the websites that you visited.

Merchandise inventory includes all goods owned by the business and held for sale. The account used for Matt's Service Merchandise's merchandise inventory is Account No. 12000, Merchandise Inventory.

PCA uses a perpetual inventory system. In a perpetual inventory system a *merchandising business* continuously updates inventory each time an item is purchased or sold.

Inventory calculations include FIFO, LIFO, and average cost methods. The *FIFO* (first in, first out) method assumes that the items in the beginning inventory are sold first. The *LIFO* (last in, first out) method assumes that the goods received last are sold first. The average cost method (also known as weighted average method) is the default that PCA uses for inventory items sold. The formula used is: Average Cost x Quantity Sold = Cost of Goods Sold.

PCA tracks the inventory items you buy and sell. After you post, PCA automatically updates the cost and quantity of each inventory item. Generally, all of your inventory should use the same costing method.

Tracking inventory is a three-step process:

➢ Enter item information, including Sales account, Merchandise Inventory account, and Cost of Sales account.

➢ Use item codes when entering purchases and sales. PCA automatically calculates and tracks average cost, which is the default, using this to calculate and enter the Cost of Goods Sold. You can change the cost method to LIFO (last in, first out) or FIFO (first in, first out). This chapter will explain these inventory cost methods in detail.

➢ If necessary, enter inventory adjustments.

PCA does the rest automatically: adjusts inventory levels each time you post a purchase or sale of an inventory item, tracks the cost of each item, and makes a Cost of Goods Sold journal entry at the end of the accounting period.

COST METHODS

PCA includes three types of cost methods for inventory: average cost, LIFO, and FIFO. Once you select the costing method for an inventory item, you cannot change it if transactions have been posted. Therefore, if you want to change the cost method for an item with posted transactions, you must enter the item again.

Average Cost

When you set up inventory items for Matt's Service Merchandise, you selected the Average cost method. In Chapter 11, Matt's Service Merchandise purchased four pairs of curtains from Robert Barton Fabrics for $30 each (Invoice 201, page 398). What happens when these curtains are sold?

The journal entries would look like this:

Purchased four pairs of curtains from Robert Barton Fabrics at $30 each.

Account ID	Account Description, Purchase Invoice 201	Debit	Credit
12000	Merchandise Inventory	120.00	
20000/RBF08	Accounts Payable/Robert Barton Fabrics		120.00

Sold three pairs of curtains to Paula Martin for $100 each (Invoice 103, page 447).

Account ID	Account Description, Sales Invoice 103	Debit	Credit
50500	Cost of Goods Sold-Walls	90.00	
11000/pm005	Accounts Receivable/Paula Martin	324.00	
12000	Merchandise Inventory		90.00
40400	Sales-Walls		300.00
23100	Sales Tax Payable		24.00

You can see from these journal entries that the Merchandise Inventory account is updated with each purchase and sale. After these transactions, the balance in Merchandise Inventory looks like this:

Merchandise Inventory, Account No. 12000

Purchased inventory	120	Sold Inventory	90
Balance	30		

LIFO (Last In, First Out)

The LIFO (last in, first out) method of inventory pricing assumes that the last goods received are sold first. LIFO assumes that cost is based on replacement and that the last price paid for merchandise is more accurate.

Accountants recommend that you select LIFO when you desire to charge the most recent inventory costs against revenue. LIFO yields the lowest amount of net income in periods of rising costs because the cost of the most recently acquired inventory more closely approximates the replacement cost.

FIFO (First In, First Out)

The FIFO (first in, first out) method of inventory pricing assumes that the items in the beginning inventory are sold first. FIFO costs your sales and values your inventory as if the items you sell are the ones that you have had in stock for the longest time.

Accountants recommend that you select FIFO when you desire to charge costs against revenue in the order in which costs occur. FIFO yields a higher amount of profit during periods of rising costs. This happens because merchandise was acquired prior to the increase in cost.

TYPES OF INVENTORY ITEMS

There are nine types of inventory items in PCA:

➤ Stock item: This is the default in the Item Class list. It is the traditional inventory item where the program tracks descriptions, unit prices, stock quantities, and cost of goods sold. For stock items, you should complete the entire window. Once an item has been designated as a stock item, the type cannot be changed.

➤ Master Stock Item: PCA uses this item class as a special item that does not represent inventory stocked but contains information (item attributes) shared with a number of substock items.

➤ Non-stock item: PCA tracks the description and a unit price for sales. You can also track default accounts. You might use this type for service items such as hours where the unit price is set.

➤ Description only: PCA keeps track of the description of an Inventory Item. This saves time when entering purchases and sales because you don't have to retype the description. You might use this type for service items where the price fluctuates.

➤ Service: This is for services you can apply to your salary and wages account.

➤ Labor: This is for labor you can apply to your salary and wages account. You cannot purchase labor items but you can sell them.

> Assembly: You can specify items as assembly items and create a bill of materials for a unit made up of component stock or subassembly items.

> Activity item: To indicate how time is spent when performing services for a customer, for a job, or for internal administrative work. Activity items are used with the Time & Billing feature.

> Charge item: Expenses recorded by an employee or vendor when company resources are used for a customer or job.

GETTING STARTED

In the preceding chapters, you set up inventory items. The instructions that follow show you how to add inventory items to Matt's Service Merchandise.

1. Start Windows and Peachtree in the usual way. Open Matt's Service Merchandise. If you used a unique name, select it.

2. Follow these steps to restore data from Chapter 12.

   a. Start Windows and Peachtree in the usual way. Open Matt's Service Merchandise.[1]

   b. Put your backup disk in drive A. You backed up Chapter 12 data on pages 470 and 471. From the menu bar, click on File, Restore.

   c. From the Select Backup File screen, click [Browse]. The Open Backup File screen pops up.

   d. Click on the down-arrow in the Look in field. Then click on 3½ Floppy (A:) to select drive A (or the appropriate location of your backup file).

   e. Click on the Chapter 12.ptb file to highlight it. The File name field displays Chapter 12. Click [Open].

---

[1]You can restore from your back up file even if *no* Peachtree company exists. Close Peachtree's start up screen. Select File; Restore. Select the location of your backup file. On the Restore Wizard's Select Company screen, select A New Company. The *A New Company* selection allows you to restore your backup data, bypassing the process of new company set up. For more information, refer to Troubleshooting on page 274.

f. Make sure that the Location field shows A:\Chapter 12.ptb (or the appropriate location for your backup file). Click [Next >].

g. From the Select Company screen make sure that the radio button next to An Existing Company is selected. The Company name field shows your company name; the Location field shows C:\ProgramFiles\Peachtree\Company\xxxxxxxx (the x's represent your subdirectory; or restore from the appropriate location on your computer). Click [Next >].

h. The Restore Options screen appears. Make sure that the box next to Company Data is *checked*. Click [Next >].

i. The Confirmation screen appears. Check the From and To fields to make sure they are correct. Click [Finish]. When the Restore Company scale is 100% completed, your data is restored and you are returned to the menu bar.

j. Remove the backup disk.

k. To verify your data, display the General Ledger Trial Balance. Compare it to the one shown on page 469 in Chapter 12.

3. From the Menu bar, select Maintain; Default Information, Inventory Items. The Inventory Item Defaults window displays. Click on the GL Accts/Costing tab. The default for inventory costing is the Average method. Since this is what Matt's Service Merchandise uses, there is no need to make any changes to this screen.

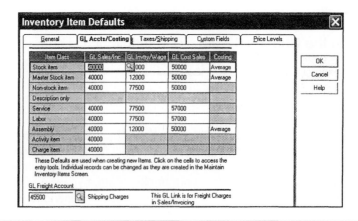

4. Click on the Taxes/Shipping tab.

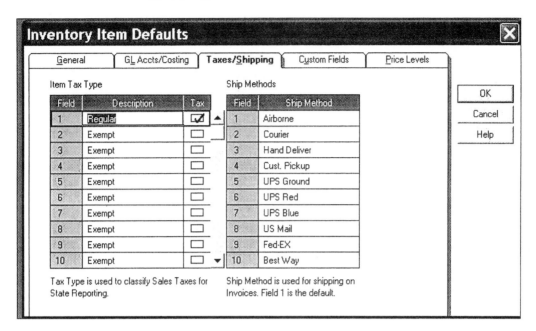

The Regular tax type is selected with a check mark. This is correct because there is an 8% sales tax in California. (Remember: If you click [Cancel], you close the screen without saving any changes. If you would like to learn more about this screen, press the function key <F1>. This opens a topic-specific Help window.)

The Ship Methods that appear on this tab are also shown on the Sales/Invoicing and Purchases/Receive Inventory windows. You can also use these ship methods to set up defaults for customers and vendors.

5. Click [OK] to close this window and return to the menu bar.

ENTERING INVENTORY ITEM MAINTENANCE INFORMATION

Inventory items are set up through the Maintain menu. You can establish general ledger accounts, vendors, tax exemptions, sales prices and reorder quantities. The information on the Maintain Inventory Items window is displayed as five tabs: General, Custom Fields, History, Bill of Materials, and Item Attributes. The fields are visible on one tab at a time, but you can view others by selecting a tab.

Follow these steps to enter inventory maintenance information:

1. From the menu bar, select Maintain, then Inventory Items. The Maintain Inventory Items window displays.

2. Complete the following information:

Item ID:	**004lights**
Description:	**lighting**
Item Class:	**Stock item**
Description(for Sales):	**light fixtures**
Price Level 1:	**175**
Item Tax Type:	1
Last Unit Cost:	**64**
Cost Method:	Average
GL Sales Acct:	Add Account No. **40700 Sales-Lights** (Income)
GL Inventory Acct:	**12000 Merchandise Inventory**
GL Cost of Sales Acct:	Add Account No. **51500 Cost of Goods Sold-Lights** (Cost of Sales)
Item Type:	**PRODUCTS**
Unit/Measure:	**each**
Minimum Stock:	**8**
Reorder Quantity:	**4**

Preferred Vendor ID:

You need to add a new vendor. To add a vendor, click 🔍 in the Preferred Vendor ID field, then click [New]. The Maintain Vendors window displays.

Vendor ID:	**PSS09**
Name:	**Poland Sales & Service**
Contact:	**Mildred Poland**
Address:	**5132 Burbank Blvd.**
City, ST Zip:	**Los Angeles, CA 90231**
Country:	**USA**
Vendor Type:	**lights**
1099 Type:	**Independent Contractor**
Telephone 1:	**818-555-5912**
Fax:	**818-555-5213**

E-Mail: **mildred@ps&s.com**
Web Address: **www.ps&s.com/poland**

Purchase Defaults folder:

Tax ID #: **16-4312898**

Click [Save], then close the Maintain Vendors window. You are returned to the Maintain Inventory Items window. Select Poland

Sales & Service as the vendor. Click [Save].
Click on the Beginning Balances arrow (lower right corner of the Maintain Inventory Items window.) The Inventory Beginning Balances window displays. Select lighting. Complete the following information:

Quantity: 125
Unit Cost: 64.00
Total Cost: 8,000.00 (completed automatically)

3. Click [OK] to close the Inventory Beginning Balances window. You are returned to the Maintain Inventory Items window.

4. Save, then close the Maintain Inventory Items window.

INVENTORY ADJUSTMENTS

Follow these steps to record the following purchase and inventory adjustment.

Date	Description of Transaction
01/14/04	Poland Sales & Service sent Invoice No. 912 for the purchase of eight light fixtures for a unit cost of $64 each, and a total of $512.

1. From the Tasks menu, select Purchases/Receive Inventory. Record the January 14, 2004, transaction.

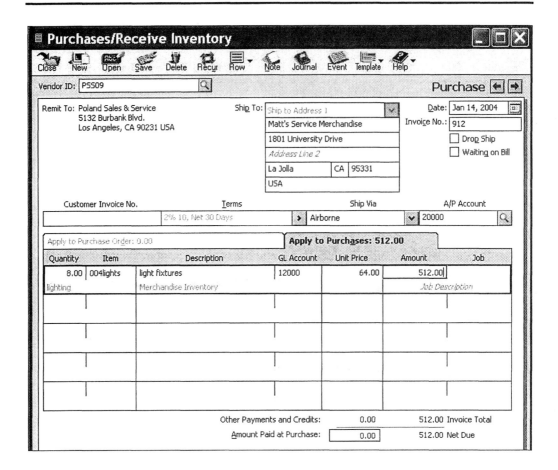

2. Post, then close.

The transaction that follows needs to be recorded.

Date   *Description of Transaction*

01/15/04   Two light fixtures were damaged when they were dropped on the floor by the owner, Matt Lowe.

Follow these steps to make an inventory adjustment.

1. From the Tasks menu, select Inventory Adjustments.

2. In the Item ID lookup field, select lighting.

3. In the Reference field, type **ML** (Matt Lowe's initials).

4. Type **15** in the <u>D</u>ate field.

5. Type **-2** in the <u>A</u>djust Quantity By field. (PCA calculates the New Quantity after you enter the adjustment.)

6. In the Reason to Adjust field, type **Two damaged light fixtures**.

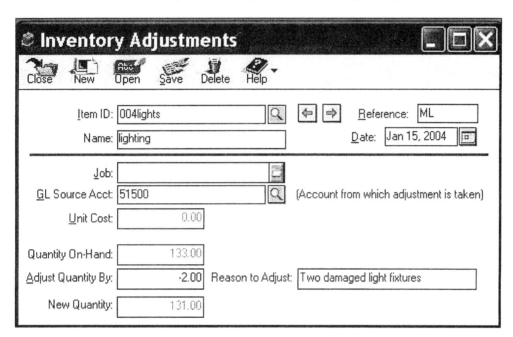

7. Click to post, then close the Inventory Adjustments window. You are returned to the menu bar.

Backing Up Your Data

Follow these steps to back up Chapter 13 data:

1. Put a blank, formatted disk in drive A.

2. From the menu bar, select File, then Back up.

3. Click Back Up Now .

4. Click on the down-arrow in the Save in field. If necessary, scroll up the list, then click on 3½ Floppy (A:) to select drive A. *Or*, back up to the network or hard drive.

5. Type **Chapter 13 Begin** in the File name field.

6. Click [Save].

7. When the screen prompts that This company backup will require approximately 1 diskette, click [OK].

8. When the screen prompts you to insert the first disk, click [OK]. When the Back Up Company scale is 100% completed, you have successfully backed up to the current point in Chapter 13. You are returned to the menu bar.

9. Exit PCA or continue.

ADDITIONAL TRANSACTIONS

Record the following transactions for Matt's Service Merchandise.

Date	*Description of Transaction*
01/19/04	Sold two doorknobs on account to Amy Phelps. Type Invoice **106** in the Invoice No. field. Subsequent invoices will be numbered automatically. (*Hint: Select hardware as the inventory item for doorknobs.*)
01/19/04	Sold two rolls of vinyl flooring on account to Dana Campbell, Invoice No. 107. There is no sales tax because merchandise is being shipped out of state.
01/19/04	Sold two pairs of curtains on account to Paula Martin, Invoice No. 108. (*Hint: Select wall as the inventory item for curtains.*)
01/20/04	Matt's Service Merchandise completed repair work for Bernard Baker at a cost of $70, Invoice No. 109. (*Hint: Remember to credit Account No. 40000, Service Fees.*)

01/23/04	Cash sales in the amount of $1,404 ($1,300 plus $104, CA sales taxes) were deposited at San Diego Bank: 10 pairs of curtains, $1,000; 2 doorknobs, $300. (*Hint: If a screen pops up saying that reference has been used before, click OK.*)
01/24/04	Received a check in the amount of $324 from Amy Phelps in full payment of Invoice 106.
01/26/04	Received a check in the amount of $216 from Paula Martin in full payment of Invoice No. 108.
01/30/04	Issued Check No. 2039 to US Mortgage Co. in the amount of $685.80 for the mortgage payment. (*Hint: On the Write Checks window, **2039** in the Check number field.*)
01/30/04	Issued Check No. 2040 in the amount of $500 to Matt Lowe.
01/30/04	Issued Check No. 2041 in the amount of $500 to Sharon Albert.
01/31/04	Cash sales in the amount of $2,376 ($2,200 plus $176, CA sales taxes) were deposited at San Diego Bank: 8 doorknobs, $1,200; 10 pairs of curtains, $1,000.

PRINTING REPORTS

1. Print the Sales Journal and compare it to the one shown on the next page.

Page: 1

Matt's Service Merchandise
Sales Journal
For the Period From Jan 1, 2004 to Jan 31, 2004
Filter Criteria includes: Report order is by Invoice/CM Date. Report is printed in Detail Format.

Date	Account ID	Invoice/CM #	Line Description	Debit Amnt	Credit Amnt
1/6/04	23100	101	CA: California sales taxes		24.00
	40200		Two doorknobs		300.00
	50000		Cost of sales	100.00	
	12000		Cost of sales		100.00
	11000		Amy Phelps	324.00	
1/6/04	40600	102	Three rolls of vinyl flooring		480.00
	51000		Cost of sales	162.00	
	12000		Cost of sales		162.00
	11000		Dana Campbell	480.00	
1/6/04	23100	103	CA: California sales taxes		24.00
	40400		Three pairs of curtains		300.00
	50500		Cost of sales	90.00	
	12000		Cost of sales		90.00
	11000		Paula Martin	324.00	
1/8/04	23100	104	CA: California sales taxes		36.00
	40200		Three curtain rods		450.00
	50000		Cost of sales	150.00	
	12000		Cost of sales		150.00
	11000		Jeanne Palmieri	486.00	
1/9/04	23100	105	CA: California sales taxes		3.68
	40000		Repair		45.95
	11000		Bernard Baker	49.63	
1/14/04	23100	CM103	CA: California sales taxes	8.00	
	40400		Returned one pair of curtains	100.00	
	50500		Cost of sales		30.00
	12000		Cost of sales	30.00	
	11000		Paula Martin		108.00
1/19/04	23100	106	CA: California sales taxes		24.00
	40200		Two doorknobs		300.00
	50000		Cost of sales	100.00	
	12000		Cost of sales		100.00
	11000		Amy Phelps	324.00	
1/19/04	40600	107	Two rolls of vinyl flooring		320.00
	51000		Cost of sales	108.00	
	12000		Cost of sales		108.00
	11000		Dana Campbell	320.00	
1/19/04	23100	108	CA: California sales taxes		16.00
	40400		Two pairs of curtains		200.00
	50500		Cost of sales	60.00	
	12000		Cost of sales		60.00
	11000		Paula Martin	216.00	
1/20/04	23100	109	CA: California sales taxes		5.60
	40000		Repair		70.00
	11000		Bernard Baker	75.60	
		Total		3,507.23	3,507.23

If any of your transactions do *not* agree with the Sales Journal, you can

drill-down (⊘) to the original entry, make any needed corrections, then save and reprint.

2. Print the Cash Receipts Journal and compare it to the one shown.

Matt's Service Merchandise
Cash Receipts Journal
For the Period From Jan 1, 2004 to Jan 31, 2004
Filter Criteria includes: Report order is by Check Date. Report is printed in Detail Format.

Date	Account ID	Transaction Ref	Line Description	Debit Amnt	Credit Amnt
1/14/04	11000	Invoice 103	Invoice: 103		216.00
	10200		Paula Martin	216.00	
1/21/04	11000	Invoice 101	Invoice: 101		324.00
	10200		Amy Phelps	324.00	
1/22/04	11000	Invoice 104	Invoice: 104		95.00
	10200		Jeanne Palmieri	95.00	
1/23/04	23100	Cash	CA: California sales taxes		104.00
	40400		Ten pairs of curtains		1,000.00
	50500		Cost of sales	300.00	
	12000		Cost of sales		300.00
	40200		Two doorknobs		300.00
	50000		Cost of sales	100.00	
	12000		Cost of sales		100.00
	10200		Cash sales	1,404.00	
1/24/04	11000	Invoice 106	Invoice: 106		324.00
	10200		Amy Phelps	324.00	
1/26/04	11000	Invoice 108	Invoice: 108		216.00
	10200		Paula Martin	216.00	
1/28/04	11000	Invoice 105	Invoice: 105		49.63
	10200		Bernard Baker	49.63	
1/28/04	11000	Invoice 102	Invoice: 102		480.00
	10200		Dana Campbell	480.00	
1/29/04	23100	Cash	CA: California sales taxes		16.00
	40400		Two pairs of curtains		200.00
	50500		Cost of sales	60.00	
	12000		Cost of sales		60.00
	10200		Debi Clarke	216.00	
1/31/04	23100	Cash	CA: California sales taxes		176.00
	40200		Eight doorknobs		1,200.00
	50000		Cost of sales	400.00	
	12000		Cost of sales		400.00
	40400		Ten pairs of curtains		1,000.00
	50500		Cost of sales	300.00	
	12000		Cost of sales		300.00
	10200		Cash sales	2,376.00	
				6,860.63	6,860.63

3. Print the Customer Ledgers.

Matt's Service Merchandise
Customer Ledgers
For the Period From Jan 1, 2004 to Jan 31, 2004
Filter Criteria includes: Report order is by ID. Report is printed in Detail Format.

Customer ID Customer	Date	Trans No	Type	Debit Amt	Credit Amt	Balance
ap001	1/6/04	101	SJ	324.00		324.00
Amy Phelps	1/19/04	106	SJ	324.00		648.00
	1/21/04	Invoice 101	CRJ		324.00	324.00
	1/24/04	Invoice 106	CRJ		324.00	0.00
bb002	1/9/04	105	SJ	49.63		49.63
Bernard Baker	1/20/04	109	SJ	75.60		125.23
	1/28/04	Invoice 105	CRJ		49.63	75.60
dc003	1/6/04	102	SJ	480.00		480.00
Dana Campbell	1/19/04	107	SJ	320.00		800.00
	1/28/04	Invoice 102	CRJ		480.00	320.00
jp004	1/8/04	104	SJ	486.00		486.00
Jeanne Palmieri	1/22/04	Invoice 104	CRJ		95.00	391.00
pm005	1/6/04	103	SJ	324.00		324.00
Paula Martin	1/14/04	CM103	SJ		108.00	216.00
	1/14/04	Invoice 103	CRJ		216.00	0.00
	1/19/04	108	SJ	216.00		216.00
	1/26/04	Invoice 108	CRJ		216.00	0.00

4. Print the Purchase Journal.

Matt's Service Merchandise
Purchase Journal
For the Period From Jan 1, 2004 to Jan 31, 2004
Filter Criteria includes: Report order is by Date. Report is printed in Detail Format.

Date	Account ID Account Description	Invoice/CM #	Line Description	Debit Amoun	Credit Amount
1/2/04	12000 Merchandise Inventory	64JR	hardware--restoration	300.00	
	20000 Accounts Payable		Jessica Johnson Hardware		300.00
1/14/04	12000 Merchandise Inventory	912	light fixtures	512.00	
	20000 Accounts Payable		Poland Sales & Service		512.00
1/20/04	12000 Merchandise Inventory	150JR	hardware--restoration	500.00	
	20000 Accounts Payable		Jessica Johnson Hardware		500.00
1/20/04	12000 Merchandise Inventory	201	wall coverings	120.00	
	20000 Accounts Payable		Robert Barton Fabrics		120.00
1/20/04	12000 Merchandise Inventory	RB710	flooring	432.00	
	20000 Accounts Payable		Linda Lucks Products		432.00
1/24/04	12000 Merchandise Inventory	VCMRB710	flooring		54.00
	20000 Accounts Payable		Linda Lucks Products	54.00	
1/27/04	12000 Merchandise Inventory	VCM150JR	hardware--restoration		100.00
	20000 Accounts Payable		Jessica Johnson Hardware	100.00	
				2,018.00	2,018.00

5. Print the Cash Disbursements Journal.

Matt's Service Merchandise
Cash Disbursements Journal
For the Period From Jan 1, 2004 to Jan 31, 2004
Filter Criteria includes: Report order is by Date. Report is printed in Detail Format.

Date	Check #	Account ID	Line Description	Debit Amount	Credit Amount
1/23/04	2030	70000	Maintenance Expense	130.00	
		10200	Jack Guth		130.00
1/23/04	2031	73500	Postage Expense	37.00	
		10200	U.S. Post Office		37.00
1/23/04	2032	75500	Supplies Expense	110.82	
		10200	La Jolla Office Supplies		110.82
1/24/04	2033	76000	Telephone Expense	73.60	
		10200	MCA Phone Service		73.60
1/24/04	2034	39007	Matt Lowe, Drawing	500.00	
		10200	Matt Lowe		500.00
1/24/04	2035	39009	Sharon Albert, Drawing	500.00	
		10200	Sharon Albert		500.00
1/24/04	2036	59500	Discounts Taken		7.56
		20000	Invoice: RB710	378.00	
		10200	Linda Lucks Products		370.44
1/28/04	2037	59500	Discounts Taken		8.00
		20000	Invoice: 150JR	400.00	
		10200	Jessica Johnson Hardware		392.00
1/28/04	2038	59500	Discounts Taken		2.40
		20000	Invoice: 201	120.00	
		10200	Robert Barton Fabrics		117.60
1/30/04	2039	27400	Mortgage Payable	685.80	
		10200	US Mortgage Co.		685.80
1/30/04	2040	39007	Matt Lowe, Drawing	500.00	
		10200	Matt Lowe		500.00
1/30/04	2041	39009	Sharon Albert, Drawing	500.00	
		10200	Sharon Albert		500.00
	Total			**3,935.22**	**3,935.22**

6. Print the Vendor Ledgers and compare your printout to the one shown on the next page.

Matt's Service Merchandise
Vendor Ledgers
For the Period From Jan 1, 2004 to Jan 31, 2004

Filter Criteria includes: Report order is by ID.

Vendor ID Vendor	Date	Trans No	Typ	Pai	Debit Amt	Credit Amt	Balance
JJH06	1/2/04	64JR	PJ			300.00	300.00
Jessica Johnson Hardwar	1/20/04	150JR	PJ	*		500.00	800.00
	1/27/04	VCM150JR	PJ	*	100.00		700.00
	1/28/04	2037	CDJ		8.00	8.00	700.00
	1/28/04	2037	CDJ		400.00		300.00
LLP07	1/20/04	RB710	PJ	*		432.00	432.00
Linda Lucks Products	1/24/04	VCMRB710	PJ	*	54.00		378.00
	1/24/04	2036	CDJ		7.56	7.56	378.00
	1/24/04	2036	CDJ		378.00		0.00
PSS09	1/14/04	912	PJ			512.00	512.00
Poland Sales & Service							
RBF08	1/20/04	201	PJ	*		120.00	120.00
Robert Barton Fabrics	1/28/04	2038	CDJ		2.40	2.40	120.00
	1/28/04	2038	CDJ		120.00		0.00

7. Follow these steps to print the Cost of Goods Sold Journal and the Inventory Adjustment Journal:

   a. From the Report Area, select Inventory.

   b. Highlight Cost of Goods Sold Journal, then make the selections to print. Compare your printout to the one shown on the next page.

Page: 1

Matt's Service Merchandise
Cost of Goods Sold Journal
For the Period From Jan 1, 2004 to Jan 31, 2004
Filter Criteria includes: Report order is by Date. Report is printed in Detail Format and with Truncated Long Descriptions.

Date	GL Acct ID	Reference	Qty	Line Description	Debit Amount	Credit Amount
1/6/04	12000	101	2.00	Two doorknobs		100.00
	50000		2.00	Two doorknobs	100.00	
1/6/04	12000	102	3.00	Three rolls of vinyl floorin		162.00
	51000		3.00	Three rolls of vinyl floorin	162.00	
1/6/04	12000	103	3.00	Three pairs of curtains		90.00
	50500		3.00	Three pairs of curtains	90.00	
1/8/04	12000	104	3.00	Three curtain rods		150.00
	50000		3.00	Three curtain rods	150.00	
1/14/04	12000	CM103	-1.00	Returned one pair of curt	30.00	
	50500		-1.00	Returned one pair of curt		30.00
1/19/04	12000	106	2.00	Two doorknobs		100.00
	50000		2.00	Two doorknobs	100.00	
1/19/04	12000	107	2.00	Two rolls of vinyl flooring		108.00
	51000		2.00	Two rolls of vinyl flooring	108.00	
1/19/04	12000	108	2.00	Two pairs of curtains		60.00
	50500		2.00	Two pairs of curtains	60.00	
1/23/04	12000	Cash	10.00	Ten pairs of curtains		300.00
	50500		10.00	Ten pairs of curtains	300.00	
	12000		2.00	Two doorknobs		100.00
	50000		2.00	Two doorknobs	100.00	
1/29/04	12000	Cash	2.00	Two pairs of curtains		60.00
	50500		2.00	Two pairs of curtains	60.00	
1/31/04	12000	Cash	8.00	Eight doorknobs		400.00
	50000		8.00	Eight doorknobs	400.00	
	12000		10.00	Ten pairs of curtains		300.00
	50500		10.00	Ten pairs of curtains	300.00	
		Total			1,960.00	1,960.00

c. Highlight the Inventory Adjustment Journal, then make the selections to print.

Page: 1

Matt's Service Merchandise
Inventory Adjustment Journal
For the Period From Jan 1, 2004 to Jan 31, 2004
Filter Criteria includes: Report order is by Date. Report is printed in Detail Format and with Truncated Long Descriptions.

Date	GL Acct ID	Reference	Qty	Line Description	Debit Amount	Credit Amount
1/15/0	12000	ML	-2.00	lighting		128.00
	51500		-2.00	Two damaged light fixture	128.00	
		Total			128.00	128.00

8. Print the General Ledger Trial Balance.

Matt's Service Merchandise
General Ledger Trial Balance
As of Jan 31, 2004

Filter Criteria includes: Report order is by ID. Report is printed in Detail Format.

Account ID	Account Description	Debit Amt	Credit Amt
10200	La Jolla Bank	52,483.37	
10400	Stockmen's Savings & Loan	22,000.00	
11000	Accounts Receivable	786.60	
12000	Merchandise Inventory	27,422.00	
13000	Supplies	1,750.00	
14000	Prepaid Insurance	2,400.00	
15000	Furniture and Fixtures	5,000.00	
15100	Computers & Equipment	7,500.00	
15500	Building	100,000.00	
20000	Accounts Payable		812.00
23100	Sales Tax Payable		421.28
27000	Long-Term Notes Payable		20,500.00
27400	Mortgage Payable		74,314.20
39006	Matt Lowe, Capital		60,795.00
39007	Matt Lowe, Drawing	1,000.00	
39008	Sharon Albert, Capital		60,795.00
39009	Sharon Albert, Drawing	1,000.00	
40000	Service Fees		115.95
40200	Sales-Hardware		2,550.00
40400	Sales-Wall		2,600.00
40600	Sales-Floor		800.00
50000	Cost of Goods Sold-Hardware	850.00	
50500	Cost of Goods Sold-Wall	780.00	
51000	Cost of Goods Sold-Floor	270.00	
51500	Cost of Goods Sold-Lights	128.00	
59500	Purchase Discounts		17.96
70000	Maintenance Expense	130.00	
73500	Postage Expense	37.00	
75500	Supplies Expense	110.82	
76000	Telephone Expense	73.60	
	Total:	223,721.39	223,721.39

Backing Up Chapter 13 Data

If your reports agree with the ones shown, make a backup of Chapter 13 data. If your printouts do not agree with the ones shown, make the necessary corrections.

Follow these steps to back up Chapter 13 data:

1. If necessary, put your backup disk in drive A. You may use the same disk that you used to back up data on pages 491-492.

2. From the menu bar, select File, then Back up.

3. Click [Back Up Now].

4. Click on the down-arrow in the Save in field. If necessary, scroll up the list, then click on 3½ Floppy (A:) to select drive A. *Or*, back up to the network, hard drive, or other media.

5. Type **Chapter 13** in the File name field.

6. Click [Save].

7. When the screen prompts that This company backup will require approximately 1 diskette, click [OK].

8. When the screen prompts you to insert the first disk, click [OK]. When the Back Up Company scale is 100% completed, you have successfully backed up to the current point in Chapter 13. You are returned to the menu bar.

9. Exit PCA or continue.

INTERNET ACTIVITY	
1.	From your Internet browser, go to the book's website at http://www.mhhe.com/yacht2004.
2.	In the Student Center list, link to Internet Activities.
3.	Link to WEB EXERCISES PART 3.
4.	Complete the Accountant's World-Chapter 13 exercise. Read steps 1 and 2.
5.	Follow the steps shown on the book's website to complete this Internet activity.
6.	Using a word processing program write a brief summary of what you find. Include all appropriate website addresses.

SUMMARY AND REVIEW

SOFTWARE OBJECTIVES: In Chapter 13, you have used the software to:

1. Enter inventory maintenance and default information.

2. Enter inventory item information, including Sales account, Merchandise Inventory account, and Cost of Sales account.

3. Enter item codes when recording purchases and sales.

4. Enter inventory adjustments.
5. Make three backups using two blank, formatted disks: two disks for Matt's Service Merchandise; one disk for the end-of-chapter exercises
   .

WEB OBJECTIVES: In Chapter 13, you did these Internet activities:

1. Used your Internet browser to go to the book's website.

2. Went to the Internet Activity link on the book's website. Then, selected WEB EXERCISES PART 3. Complete the third web exercise in Part 3–Accountant's World.

3. Used a word processing program to write summaries of the websites that you visited.

GOING TO THE NET

Access the Small Business Knowledge Base website at http://www.bizmove.com/finance/m3d3.htm. Scroll down the screen to Merchandise Inventories: Perpetual Inventory. Answer these questions about perpetual inventory.

1. What is a perpetual inventory at retail?
2. When is a physical count of inventory necessary?

Short-Answer Questions: Write an answer to each question in the space provided.

1. Identify and explain the three-step process for tracking inventory.

   _____

   _____

2. Explain how PCA uses a perpetual inventory system.

   _____

   _____

3. Define the term merchandise inventory.

   _____

   _____

4. Explain the terms Average Cost, LIFO and FIFO.

   _____

   _____

   _____

   _____

5. What do Invoice Nos. 106, 107, and 108 show? Identify to whom the merchandise was sold, what was purchased, and the amount of the invoice.

_____

_____

_____

6. What are the journal entries for the following transactions when a perpetual inventory system is used: Purchased four pairs of curtains from Robert Barton Fabrics at $30 each? Sold three pairs of curtains to Paula Martin for $300?

_____

_____

_____

_____

7. What kind of invoice is 109? Identify this transaction and the amount.

_____

_____

Exercise 13-1: Follow the instructions below to complete Exercise 13-1. Exercises for Chapters 11 through 13 must be completed before starting Exercise 13-1.

1. Start Windows, then PCA. Open the company that you set up in Exercise 11-1.

2. Restore the data that you backed up in Exercise 12-2. This back up was made on page 478.

3. Make the following inventory purchase.

    01/27/04   Curt Peters Tools sent Invoice No. 73CP for the purchase of 8 tool kits for a unit cost of $30.

4. Make the following inventory adjustment:

    01/28/04   Two tool kits were accidentally damaged.

5. Complete the following additional transactions:

    01/29/04   Received check in the amount of $900 from Robert Norton in payment of Invoice No. 103.

    01/30/04   Cash Sales in the amount of $2,415 were deposited at Eugene National Bank: 9 tool kits, $765; 11 hardware sets, $1,650.

6. Make a backup of Exercise 13-1. (Use **Exercise 13-1** as the file name.)

Exercise 13-2: Follow the instructions below to complete Exercise 13-2.

1. Print the Cash Receipts Journal.

2. Print the Purchase Journal.

3. Print the Cost of Goods Sold Journal.

4. Print the Inventory Adjustment Journal.

5. Print the General Ledger Trial Balance.

CHAPTER 13 INDEX

Chapter 14 Payroll

SOFTWARE OBJECTIVES: In Chapter 14, you will use the software to:

1. Explore the Payroll Setup Wizard.
2. Enter initial payroll fields.
3. Enter employee and employer default information.
4. Journalize and post Payroll Journal entries.
5. Print paychecks.
6. Print the financial statements.
7 Make four backups using two blank, formatted disks: two for Matt's Service Merchandise; two for the end-of-chapter exercises.

WEB OBJECTIVES: In Chapter 14, you will do these Internet activities:

1. Use your Internet browser to go to the book's website.
2. Go to the Internet Activity link on the book's website. Then, select WEB EXERCISES PART 3. Complete the fourth web exercise in Part 3–Salary Calculator.
3. Use a word processing program to write summaries of the websites that you visited.

As you know from your study of accounting, employees and employers are required to pay local, state, and federal payroll taxes. Employers must withhold taxes from each employee's paycheck. The amount withheld for federal taxes is determined from tax tables published by the Internal Revenue Service (IRS). Circular E, Employer's Tax Guide, is available from the IRS. It shows the applicable tax tables and forms that are necessary for filing employee payroll information. PCA has payroll tax tables built into the software. In this chapter you will learn how to access and use the payroll tax tables.

The amount withheld also depends on the employee's earnings and the number of *exemptions* or *withholding allowances* claimed by the employee. The number of withholding allowances usually includes one for the employee, one for the employee's spouse, and one for each dependent. PCA will automatically calculate the amounts withheld from employees' paychecks.

Also deducted from employees' paychecks are **FICA taxes** or social security taxes. This deduction from wages provides qualified workers who retire at age 62 or older with monthly payments from the federal government. The retiree also receives medical benefits called **Medicare** after reaching age 65. In addition to these retirement benefits, social security also provides payments to the surviving family of a qualified deceased worker. PCA will automatically compute FICA and Medicare taxes.

By January 31 of each year employers are required to issue **W-2 Forms** to employees and to the Internal Revenue Service. The W-2 Form is an annual report of the employee's wages subject to FICA and federal income tax and shows the amounts that were withheld.

In PCA, the employee's W-2 Form shows the Federal Income Tax, State Income Tax, Social Security, and Medicare withheld. In 2004, yearly income up to $87,900 is subject to FICA tax. Each year the wage base for Social Security (FICA tax) increases. There is no income limit on amounts subject to the Medicare tax. Congress adjusts the FICA tax annually. The FICA tax percentage for social security in 2004 is 6.2%; the percentage for Medicare, 1.45 %.

Employees may also voluntarily deduct other amounts from wages. These voluntary deductions include: charitable contributions, medical insurance premiums, U.S. savings bonds, or union dues.

It is the purpose of this chapter to show you how to use PCA to enter payroll default information, add employees, make the correct journal entries for payroll, and to print the various payroll reports. Once you set up the default information and employee information, PCA automates the payroll process.

You will establish the following default information for processing payroll:

1. The cash account to credit when disbursing paychecks. Matt's Service Merchandise uses Account No. 10300, Payroll Checking Account.

2. The accounts that comprise the employee's fields.

3. The accounts that comprise the employer's fields.

4. The payroll fields that go on the W-2 form.

5. The employee-paid taxes.

6. The employer-paid taxes.

At the Maintain Employees level, you enter the following types of information:

1. The employee name, address, telephone number, and information from the Employee's Withholding Allowance Certificate, Form W-4.

2. Information about employee pay: hourly, salaried, and amount.

3. The tax filing status of the employee for federal, state, and local purposes, including withholding allowances.

You process payroll through the Tasks menu. All you need to do is select the employee you want to pay, date the paycheck and pay period, and post the paycheck. For a yearly fee, Peachtree's payroll tax service offers the appropriate state's payroll tax amounts. For more information, go online to Peachtree's website at www.peachtree.com, then link to Services, Payroll Tax.

The flowchart on the next page shows you the steps for setting up and using PCA's payroll system.

Default and Setup Information	
Deductions:	*Cash Account:*
FICA, Federal Payroll Tax, State Payroll Tax	10300, Payroll Checking Account

Maintain Employees	
Rate of Pay:	*Frequency:*
$10 per hour, regular rate $15 per hour, overtime rate	Weekly

Payroll Journal

Paycheck, net pay: $428.99

Wages Expense	550.00	
FICA: Soc. Sec.		34.10
FICA: Medicare		7.98
Federal Payroll Tax		60.53
State Payroll Tax		13.45
SDI		4.95
Payroll Checking Account		428.99

GETTING STARTED

Follow these steps to start PCA:

1. Start Windows and Peachtree in the usual way. Open Matt's Service Merchandise. If you used a unique name, select it.

2. Follow these steps to restore data from Chapter 13

   a. Put your backup disk in drive A. You backed up Chapter 13 data on pages 500 and 501. From the menu bar, click on File, Restore.

---

b. From the Select Backup File screen, click [Browse]. The Open Backup File screen pops up.

c. Click on the down-arrow in the Look in field. Then click on 3½ Floppy (A:) to select drive A (or the appropriate location of your backup file).

d. Click on the Chapter 13.ptb file to highlight it. The File name field displays Chapter 13. Click [Open].

e. Make sure that the Location field shows A:\Chapter 13.ptb (or the appropriate location for your backup file). Click [Next >].

f. From the Select Company screen make sure that the radio button next to An Existing Company is selected. The Company name field shows your company name; the Location field shows C:\ProgramFiles\Peachtree\Company\xxxxxxxx (the x's represent your subdirectory; or restore from the appropriate location on your computer). Click [Next >].

g. The Restore Options screen appears. Make sure that the box next to Company Data is *checked*. Click [Next >].

h. The Confirmation screen appears. Check the From and To fields to make sure they are correct. Click [Finish]. When the Restore Company scale is 100% completed, your data is restored and you are returned to the menu bar.

i. Remove the backup disk.

j. To verify your data, display the General Ledger Trial Balance. Compare it to the one shown on page 500 in Chapter 13.

Checking Your Global Tax Table Version

In this chapter, you record payroll transactions for the month of January 2004. Follow these steps to see what payroll tax table is included with the software you are using.

1. From the menu bar, click on Help, then About Peachtree Accounting. The Peachtree Complete® Accounting 2004 window appears. The screen illustration for the educational version is shown below. If you are using the commercial release of Peachtree, your screen may differ.

If your Tax Table Version is 19000101, a generic tax table is installed on your computer. The tax table supplied with the educational version of the software is provided for example purposes only and should not be relied upon for accurate withholding amounts. For purposes of this chapter and subsequent payroll work in the textbook, you will use the tax tables supplied with the PCA 2004, Educational Version.

For an additional fee, Peachtree Software has a payroll tax service. To learn more about the Peachtree Payroll Tax Service, access their website at http://www.peachtree.com/taxtable.

2. After reading the information on the screen, click ☐ OK ☐.

Establishing the Payroll Account

In order to establish the payroll checking account, transfer funds from La Jolla Bank (Account No. 10200) to the Payroll Checking Account (Account No. 10300). Journalize and post the following General Journal transaction:

Date	*Description of Transaction*
01/08/04	Matt's Service Merchandise transferred $6,500 from Account No. 10200, La Jolla Bank, to Account No. 10300, Payroll Checking Account.

After posting this general journal entry, display the general journal. (*Hint: Click on Reports, General Leger, General Journal, Pre*v*iew, OK.*)

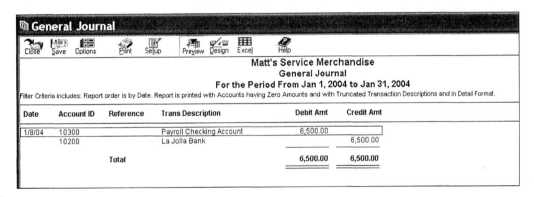

To return to the menu bar, close the General Journal window and the Select a Report window.

INITIAL PAYROLL FIELDS

1. From the menu bar, click on Maintain; Default Information, Payroll Setup Wizard. The Payroll Setup Wizard window displays. Read the information on this screen. Compare your screen to the one shown on the next page.

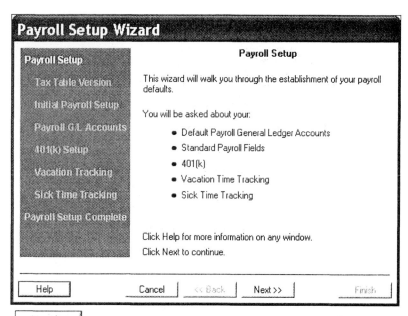

2. Click Next >>. The Payroll Tax Table Information screen appears. Read the information on this screen.

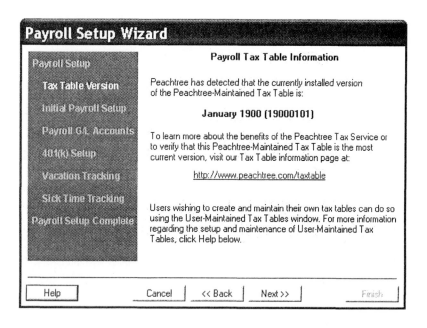

3. Click Next >>.

4. The Initial Payroll Setup window asks you to Please specify the following basic payroll information. Make sure that CA is shown in the In What State Do You Pay Your Employees. If not, select CA for California.

    If PCA has a locality tax table for a town in the state you enter, then this field is accessible. If there is no locality tax table for the state you enter, then the field remains gray, and is not accessible. This is the case with California.

5. Type **3.4** in the Unemployment Percent for Your Company field.[1] Press the **<Enter>** key to accept the default No for Do You Want to Record Employee Meals and Tips?

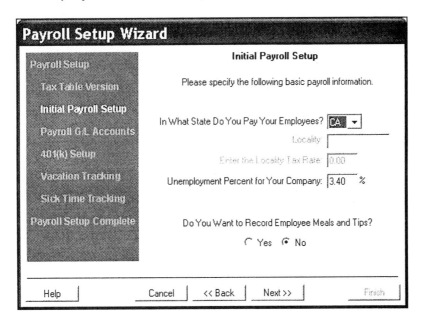

---

[1]All states support their unemployment insurance programs by placing a payroll tax on employers. In most states, the basic rate is 5.4% of the first $7,000 paid each employee. The employer's experience in creating or avoiding unemployment allows the employer to pay more or less than the basic 5.4% rate.

6. Click [Next >>]. The Default Payroll G/L Accounts window shows the defaults for the payroll accounts in the general ledger. Compare your screen to the one shown below.

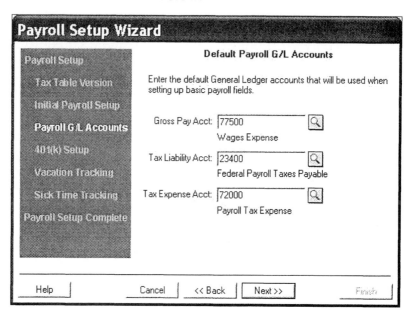

7. You will make changes to these default accounts on pages 522 and 523. For now, accept these default accounts by clicking [Next >>].

8. Read the information on the 401(k) Setup Information screen.

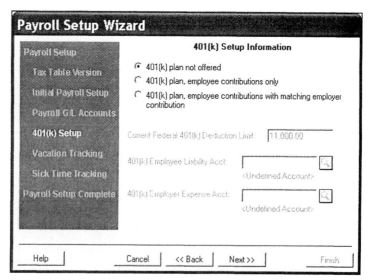

9. Accept the default for 401(k) plan not offered by clicking [Next >>].

10. The Tracking Vacation Time window appears. Accept the default for Vacation time not tracked by clicking [Next >>].

11. The Tracking Sick Time window appears. Accept the default for Sick time not tracked by clicking [Next >>].

12. Read the information on the Payroll Setup Complete window. Click [Finish]. You are returned to the menu bar.

ENTERING EMPLOYEE AND EMPLOYER DEFAULT INFORMATION

Follow these steps to enter employee and employee default information:

1. From the menu bar, click on Maintain; Default Information, Employees. The Employee Defaults window displays. In the Employee Defaults window, you enter constant information that serves as the basis for payroll processing. There are four tabs:

   ➢ General

   ➢ Pay Levels

   ➢ EmployEE Fields

   ➢ EmployER Fields

   There are two other areas on this screen: Assign Payroll Fields for and Custom Fields. These are fields that can be used for specific information, such as employees' birthdays. You are not going to use these fields at this time.

Follow these steps to enter General information in the Employee Defaults window:

1. The General tab should be selected. Notice that CA is already entered in the State field.

2. Under Assign Payroll Fields for: click on the arrow for W-2s.

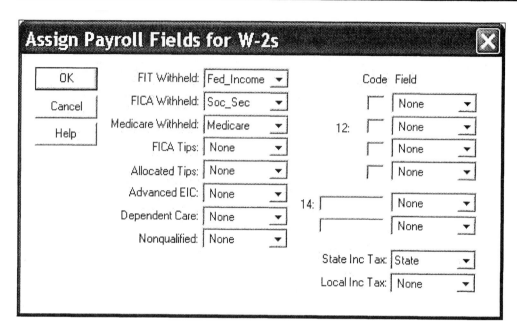

Each line in this window is identified by its field number on the 2004 Form W-2 Wage and Tax Statement.

3. Click [OK].

4. Click on the arrow next to EmployeEE Paid Taxes.

5. Click [OK].

6. Click on the arrow next to EmployER Paid Taxes. Then, click on the down-arrow in the State Disability (SDI) field. Select SDI. Compare your screen to the one below.

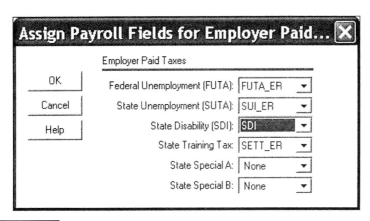

7. Click [OK] to return to the Employee Defaults window.

8. Select the Pay Levels tab.

9. Matt's Service Merchandise employees are paid $10/hour and $15/hour for overtime. Click on the G/L Account column for Overtime. The magnifying-glass icon displays. Type or select Account No. **77600** for Overtime Expense. Press **<Enter>**.

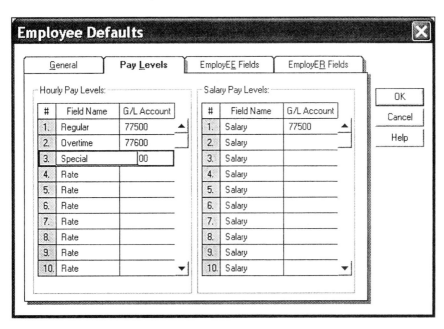

10. Click on the EmployEE Fields tab.

11. The Fed_Income line shows the default G/L Account as 23400 (Federal Payroll Taxes Payable) for FIT. This was also shown as the Tax Liability Acct: on page 516, step 6. Account No. 23400, Federal Payroll Taxes Payable, is the correct account for the Fed Income line. To see this, click on the G/L Account field for Fed Income then click Cancel.

12. Click on the G/L Account field for Soc_Sec and select Account No. 24000, FICA Employee Taxes Payable.

13. Click on the G/L Account field for Medicare and select Account No. 24200, Medicare Employee Taxes Payable.

14. Click on the G/L Account field for State and select Account No. 23600, State Payroll Taxes Payable.

15. Click on the Tax Name field for State and select CASIT.

16. In the G/L Account field on the SDI row, add Account No. 23650, State Disability Insurance (Other Current Liabilities) to the Chart of Accounts. (*Hint: Be sure this account is selected for SDI.*)

17. In the Tax Name field for SDI, select CASDI.

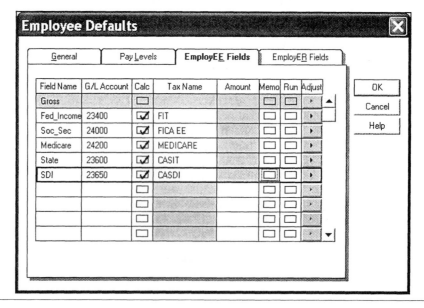

18. Click on the EmployER Fields tab. Change the following account numbers:

	Liability Column	*Expense Column*
Soc_Sec_ER	24100, FICA Employer Taxes Payable	72510, FICA Expense
Medicare_ER	24400, Medicare Employer Taxes Payable	Add Account No. 72520, Medicare Expense (Expenses)
FUTA_ER	23500, FUTA Tax Payable	72530, FUTA Expense
SUI_ER	23700, SUTA Payable	72540, SUTA Expense

There is a third column to change for SUI_ER. Click on the Tax Name column for **SUI ER, then select CASUI ER.

	Liability Column	*Expense Column*
SETT_ER	Add Account No. 23800, State Training Tax (Other Current Liabilities)	Add Account No. 72550, State Training Tax Expense (Expenses)

There is a third column to change for SETT_ER. In the Tax Name column for **SETT ER, select CASETT ER.

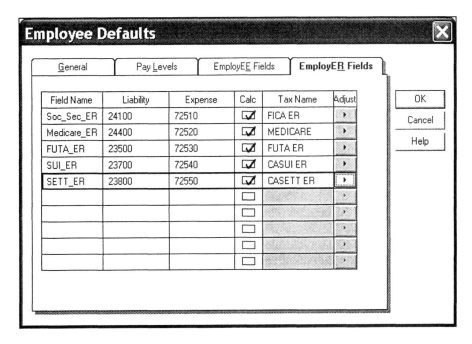

19. Click [OK] to save your changes and return to the menu bar.

ENTERING EMPLOYEE MAINTENANCE INFORMATION

In the Maintain menu there is a selection for Employees/Sales Reps. This includes information about your employees or sales representatives. The information is displayed as six tabbed folders: General, Custom Fields, Pay Info, Withholding Info, EmployEE Fields, and EmployER Fields. The fields are visible for one tab at a time. Follow these steps to set up employee maintenance information.

1. From the menu bar, select Maintain; Employees/Sales Reps. The Maintain Employees/Sales Reps window appears.

2. Complete the following fields.

Employee ID:	**A001**
Name:	**Terry Armstrong**
Accept the default for Employee	
Address:	**71 East 63rd Street**
City, ST Zip:	**La Jolla, CA 95001**
Telephone 1:	**619-555-9901**
E-mail:	**terry@mail.com**
Social Security #:	**688-25-3398**
Type:	**FULL**
Hired:	**1/2/04**

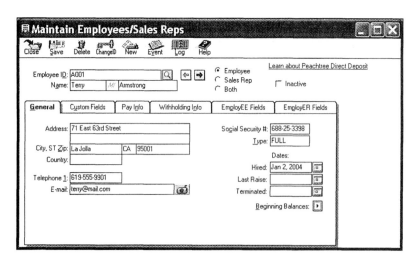

3. Click on the Withholding Info tab. Complete the following fields.

    Filing Status: **Single** for Federal, State, and Local
    Allow: **1** for Federal, State, and Local

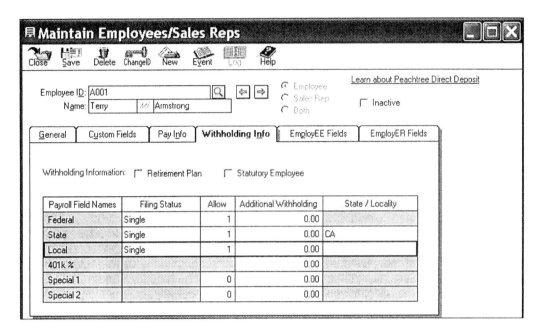

4. Click on the Pay Info tab.

5. Highlight the Regular row in the table. Type **10** in the Hourly Rate column. Press the **<Enter>** key two times.

6. Type **15** in the Hourly Rate column for Overtime. Press the **<Enter>** key. Make sure that the Pay Method field displays Hourly - Hours per Pay Period, and that the Frequency field displays Weekly. Compare your screen to the one shown on the next page.

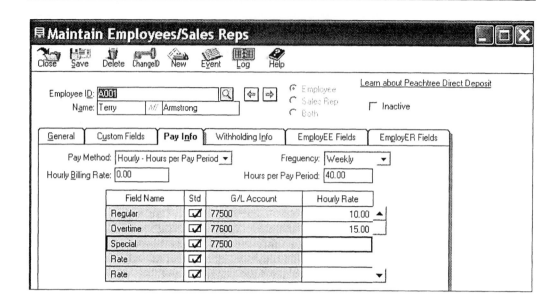

7. Select the EmployEE Fields tab. Notice that the Employee Default information matches the screen illustration on page 520, step 17.

8. Click on the EmployER Fields tab. Notice that the Employer Default information matches the screen illustration on page 521, step 18.

9. Click on [Save], then the General tab.

10. Click [New] to record another employee.

Employee ID:	**G001**
Name:	**Lily Gibson**
Accept the default for Employee.	
Address:	**2051-B Prince Avenue**
City, ST Zip:	**La Jolla, CA 92352**
Telephone 1:	**619-555-3255**
E-mail:	**lily@mail.com**
Social Security #:	**902-11-9872**
Type:	**FULL**
Hired:	**1/2/04**

Withholding Info:

Filing Status: **Married** for Federal, State, and Local
Allow: **2** for Federal, State, and Local

11. Ms. Gibson is paid hourly. Her regular pay is $10 per hour and her overtime pay is $15. Select the Pay Info tab and record this information.

12. Save, then close the Maintain Employee/Sales Reps window.

Backing Up Your Data

Follow these steps to back up Chapter 14 data:

1. If you are backing up to a floppy disk, put a blank formatted disk in drive A.

2. From the menu bar, select File, then Back up.

3. Click | Back Up Now |.

4. Click on the down-arrow in the Save in field. If necessary, scroll up the list, then click on 3½ Floppy (A:) to select drive A. *Or,* back up to the network or hard drive.

5. Type **Chapter 14 Begin** in the File name field.

6. Click | Save |.

7. When the screen prompts that This company backup will require approximately 1 diskette, click | OK |.

8. When the screen prompts you to insert the first disk, click on | OK |. When the Back Up Company scale is 100% completed, you have successfully backed up to the current point in Chapter 14. You are returned to the menu bar.

9. Exit PCA or continue.

PAYROLL ENTRY

Once the defaults for payroll are properly set up, you have very little work to do. In Chapter 4, Employees, the sample company, Bellwether Garden Supply, already had the default information set up for you. Since the payroll tax tables were included for the sample company, all you needed to do for payroll was:

➢ Enter or select the Employee ID.

➢ Specify the pay period (period-ending date).

➢ Verify the information the screen displays (name and address of employee, amount of hours, and employee/employer fields.)

➢ Print or post the paycheck.

In Chapter 14, you will use the payroll tax tables included with the software. The payroll tax tables provided with PCA 2004, Educational Version, are for example purposes only.

In Peachtree, the Payroll Entry window is also the **payroll journal**. All entries made in the Payroll Entry window show up in the payroll journal, and then they are posted to both the General Ledger and to the Employee file.

Payroll entry is a simple process after completing the Payroll Setup Wizard and employee/employer default and maintenance information. When you set up employee and employer defaults, you set up the liability and expense accounts for payroll. When you set up the employee maintenance information, you set up the employee's name; address; social security number; Federal, State, and Local withholding allowances; and pay levels.

All journal entries made to the Payroll Journal are posted both to the General Ledger and to the Employee file. Once an Employee ID is selected, the rest of the employee information is completed automatically. Enough information is entered in the Maintain Employees record, Default Information, and the payroll tax tables included with the software to determine what the paycheck amount should be. If the information is correct, you print or post the paycheck and proceed to the next employee.

The check amount (or net pay) is automatically credited to Account No. 10300, Payroll Checking Account. The withholding amounts are calculated based on the Payroll Fields which were also defined in the Default Information that you previously entered. The rate and frequency of pay were set up in the Employee/Sales Rep record. For Matt's Service Merchandise, employees are paid weekly.

To issue a payroll check, follow these steps:

1. From the menu bar, select Tasks, then Payroll Entry.

2. The Select a Cash Account window displays. Select the Payroll Checking Account.

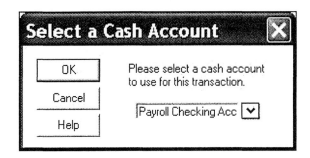

3. Click [OK]. The Payroll Entry window appears.

4. In the Employee ID lookup field, select Terry Armstrong.

5. Leave the Check Number field blank. Type or select **9** as the Date.

6. Make sure that Account No. 10300, Payroll Checking Account, is displayed in the Cash Account lookup field.

7. In the Pay Period End field, type **9** and press **<Enter>**.

8. Accept the default for Weeks in Pay Period which is 1 week.

9. In the Hours Worked table go to the Overtime Hours field. Type **10** and press **<Enter>**. Compare your screen to the one shown on the next page.

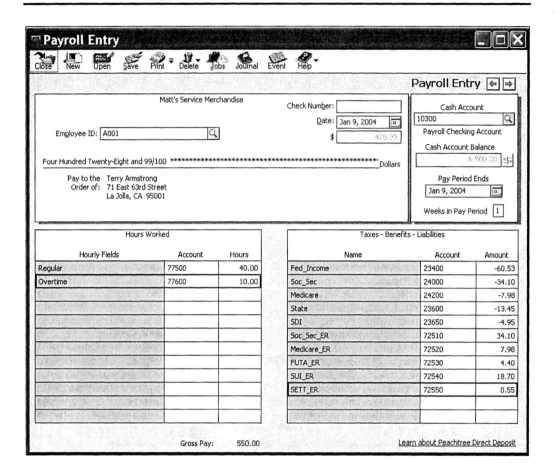

Comment

Observe that the Taxes- Benefits - Liabilities table on the Payroll Entry window includes withholding amounts. These amounts are for example purposes only and do not reflect accurate payroll taxes.

A separate service provided by Peachtree Software at an additional cost includes payroll tax tables. More information about Peachtree's Payroll Tax Service is included on their website at http://www.peachtree.com/taxtable.

10. Click

11. The Print Forms: Payroll Checks window pops up. Click 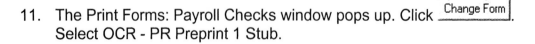. Select OCR - PR Preprint 1 Stub.

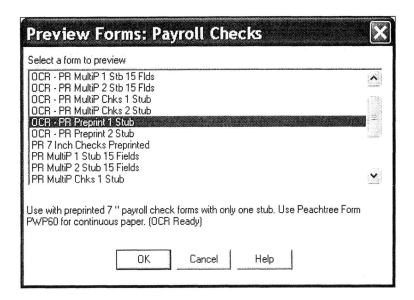

Comment

The form you select is tied to the kind of printer you are using. For example, if you are using an HP DeskJet 680C, the form that you should select is OCR - PR Preprint 2 Stub. You may need to make a different selection depending on your printer.

12. Click [OK].

13. The Print Forms: Payroll Checks window appears. Make sure that the form you chose is shown in the Last used form field.

14. Type **101** as the First check number.

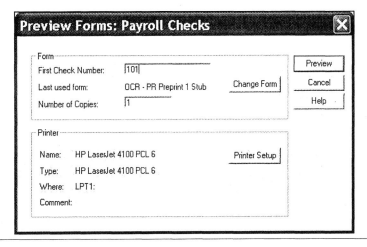

15.   Click [Print]. Your check starts to print.

```
A001      Terry Armstrong              688-25-3398    1/3/04 - 1/9/04    1/9/04


Regular        10.00    40.00       400.00   Gross              550.00          550.00
Overtime       15.00    10.00       150.00   Fed Income         -60.53          -60.53
                                             Soc Sec            -34.10          -34.10
                                             Medicare            -7.98           -7.98
                                             State              -13.45          -13.45
                                             SDI                 -4.95           -4.95




       1        50.00        550.00          550.00            $428.99             101



                           Check Number:   101                    Jan 9, 2004


                                                                  428.99


   Four Hundred Twenty-Eight and 99/100 Dollars

      Terry Armstrong
      71 East 63rd Street
      La Jolla, CA 95001
```

16.   Make the selections to pay Ms. Gibson on January 9, 2004. She worked 40 regular hours for Matt's Service Merchandise.

17.   Print Check No. 102. Compare your check to the one shown on the next page.

```
G001      Lily Gibson                    902-11-9872    1/3/04 - 1/9/04     1/9/04


Regular     10.00    40.00         400.00    Gross            400.00         400.00
                                             Fed Income       -16.06         -16.06
                                             Soc Sec          -24.80         -24.80
                                             Medicare          -5.80          -5.80
                                             State             -0.47          -0.47
                                             SDI               -3.60          -3.60




        1      40.00         400.00          400.00        $349.27            102




                      Check Number:  102                   Jan 9, 2004


                                                             349.27


     Three Hundred Forty-Nine and 27/100 Dollars

     Lily Gibson
     2051-B Prince Avenue
     La Jolla, CA 92352
```

18. Make the following payroll entries for Terry Armstrong and Lily Gibson.

Date	Name	Hours Worked	Overtime	Check No.
1/16/04	T. Armstrong	40	3	103
	L. Gibson	40	2	104
1/23/04	T. Armstrong	40		105
	L. Gibson	40	1	106
1/30/04	T. Armstrong	40		107
	L. Gibson	40		108

After recording the paycheck information, type the check number, then click [Save] to post. You do *not* need to print the paychecks.

19. Close the Payroll Entry window.

PRINTING THE PAYROLL JOURNAL

Follow these steps to print the Payroll Journal:

1. From the menu bar, select Reports, then Payroll.

2. In the Report List, highlight Payroll Journal, then make the selections to print.

Matt's Service Merchandise				
Payroll Journal				
For the Period From Jan 1, 2004 to Jan 31, 2004				
Filter Criteria includes: Report order is by Check Date. Report is printed in Detail Format.				
Date Employee	GL Acct ID	Reference	Debit Amt	Credit Amt
1/9/04	77500	101	400.00	
Terry Armstrong	77600		150.00	
	23400			60.53
	24000			34.10
	24200			7.98
	23600			13.45
	23650			4.95
	24100			34.10
	24400			7.98
	23500			4.40
	23700			18.70
	23800			0.55
	72510		34.10	
	72520		7.98	
	72530		4.40	
	72540		18.70	
	72550		0.55	
	10300			428.99
1/9/04	77500	102	400.00	
Lily Gibson	23400			16.06
	24000			24.80
	24200			5.80
	23600			0.47
	23650			3.60
	24100			24.80
	24400			5.80
	23500			3.20
	23700			13.60
	23800			0.40
	72510		24.80	
	72520		5.80	
	72530		3.20	
	72540		13.60	
	72550		0.40	
	10300			349.27
1/16/04	77500	103	400.00	
Terry Armstrong	77600		45.00	
	23400			44.78
	24000			27.59
	24200			6.45
	23600			7.66
	23650			4.01
	24100			27.59
	24400			6.45
	23500			3.56
	23700			15.13
	23800			0.45
	72510		27.59	
	72520		6.45	
	72530		3.56	
	72540		15.13	
	72550		0.45	
	10300			354.51
1/16/04	77500	104	400.00	
Lily Gibson	77600		30.00	
	23400			19.06
	24000			26.66
	24200			6.24
	23600			1.07
	23650			3.87
	24100			26.66
	24400			6.24

Matt's Service Merchandise
Payroll Journal
For the Period From Jan 1, 2004 to Jan 31, 2004

Filter Criteria includes: Report order is by Check Date. Report is printed in Detail Format.

Date Employee	GL Acct ID	Reference	Debit Amt	Credit Amt
	23500			3.44
	23700			14.62
	23800			0.43
	72510		26.66	
	72520		6.24	
	72530		3.44	
	72540		14.62	
	72550		0.43	
	10300			373.10
1/23/04 Terry Armstrong	77500	105	400.00	
	23400			38.03
	24000			24.80
	24200			5.80
	23600			5.86
	23650			3.60
	24100			24.80
	24400			5.80
	23500			3.20
	23700			13.60
	23800			0.40
	72510		24.80	
	72520		5.80	
	72530		3.20	
	72540		13.60	
	72550		0.40	
	10300			321.91
1/23/04 Lily Gibson	77500	106	400.00	
	77600		15.00	
	23400			17.56
	24000			25.73
	24200			6.02
	23600			0.77
	23650			3.74
	24100			25.73
	24400			6.02
	23500			3.32
	23700			14.11
	23800			0.42
	72510		25.73	
	72520		6.02	
	72530		3.32	
	72540		14.11	
	72550		0.42	
	10300			361.18
1/30/04 Terry Armstrong	77500	107	400.00	
	23400			38.03
	24000			24.80
	24200			5.80
	23600			5.86
	23650			3.60
	24100			24.80
	24400			5.80
	23500			3.20
	23700			13.60
	23800			0.40
	72510		24.80	
	72520		5.80	
	72530		3.20	
	72540		13.60	
	72550		0.40	
	10300			321.91

Matt's Service Merchandise
Payroll Journal
For the Period From Jan 1, 2004 to Jan 31, 2004

Filter Criteria includes: Report order is by Check Date. Report is printed in Detail Format.

Date Employee	GL Acct ID	Reference	Debit Amt	Credit Amt
1/30/04	77500	108	400.00	
Lily Gibson	23400			16.06
	24000			24.80
	24200			5.80
	23600			0.47
	23650			3.60
	24100			24.80
	24400			5.80
	23500			3.20
	23700			13.60
	23800			0.40
	72510		24.80	
	72520		5.80	
	72530		3.20	
	72540		13.60	
	72550		0.40	
	10300			349.27
			3,851.10	3,851.10

PRINTING THE GENERAL LEDGER TRIAL BALANCE

1. In the Report Area, highlight General Ledger. Then, in the Report List, highlight General Ledger Trial Balance.

2. Click [Print]. Make the selections to print. Compare your printout to the one shown on the next page.

Matt's Service Merchandise
General Ledger Trial Balance
As of Jan 31, 2004

Filter Criteria includes: Report order is by ID. Report is printed in Detail Format.

Account ID	Account Description	Debit Amt	Credit Amt
10200	La Jolla Bank	45,983.37	
10300	Payroll Checking Account	3,639.86	
10400	Stockmen's Savings & Loa	22,000.00	
11000	Accounts Receivable	786.60	
12000	Merchandise Inventory	27,422.00	
13000	Supplies	1,750.00	
14000	Prepaid Insurance	2,400.00	
15000	Furniture and Fixtures	5,000.00	
15100	Computers & Equipment	7,500.00	
15500	Building	100,000.00	
20000	Accounts Payable		812.00
23100	Sales Tax Payable		421.28
23400	Federal Payroll Taxes Paya		250.11
23500	FUTA Tax Payable		27.52
23600	State Payroll Taxes Payabl		35.61
23650	State Disability Insurance		30.97
23700	SUTA Payable		116.96
23800	State Training Tax		3.45
24000	FICA Employee Taxes Pay		213.28
24100	FICA Employer Taxes Paya		213.28
24200	Medicare Employee Taxes		49.89
24400	Medicare Employer Taxes		49.89
27000	Long-Term Notes Payable		20,500.00
27400	Mortgage Payable		74,314.20
39006	Matt Lowe, Capital		60,795.00
39007	Matt Lowe, Drawing	1,000.00	
39008	Sharon Albert, Capital		60,795.00
39009	Sharon Albert, Drawing	1,000.00	
40000	Service Fees		115.95
40200	Sales-Hardware		2,550.00
40400	Sales-Wall		2,600.00
40600	Sales-Floor		800.00
50000	Cost of Goods Sold-Hardw	850.00	
50500	Cost of Goods Sold-Wall	780.00	
51000	Cost of Goods Sold-Floor	270.00	
51500	Cost of Goods Sold-Lights	128.00	
59500	Purchase Discounts		17.96
70000	Maintenance Expense	130.00	
72510	FICA Expense	213.28	
72520	Medicare Expense	49.89	
72530	FUTA Expense	27.52	
72540	SUTA Expense	116.96	
72550	State Training Tax Expense	3.45	
73500	Postage Expense	37.00	
75500	Supplies Expense	110.82	
76000	Telephone Expense	73.60	
77500	Wages Expense	3,200.00	
77600	Overtime Expense	240.00	
	Total:	224,712.35	224,712.35

PRINTING THE FINANCIAL STATEMENTS

1. Print the \<Standard\> Balance Sheet.

```
                                              Matt's Service Merchandise
                                                   Balance Sheet
                                                  January 31, 2004

                                                       ASSETS

Current Assets
La Jolla Bank                       $        45,983.37
Payroll Checking Account                      3,639.86
Stockmen's Savings & Loan                    22,000.00
Accounts Receivable                             786.60
Merchandise Inventory                        27,422.00
Supplies                                      1,750.00
Prepaid Insurance                             2,400.00

Total Current Assets                                          103,981.83

Property and Equipment
Furniture and Fixtures                        5,000.00
Computers & Equipment                         7,500.00
Building                                    100,000.00

Total Property and Equipment                                 112,500.00

Other Assets

Total Other Assets                                                 0.00

Total Assets                        $                        216,481.83


                                             LIABILITIES AND CAPITAL

Current Liabilities
Accounts Payable                    $           812.00
Sales Tax Payable                               421.28
Federal Payroll Taxes Payable                   250.11
FUTA Tax Payable                                 27.52
State Payroll Taxes Payable                      35.61
State Disability Insurance                       30.97
SUTA Payable                                    116.96
State Training Tax                                3.45
FICA Employee Taxes Payable                     213.28
FICA Employer Taxes Payable                     213.28
Medicare Employee Taxes Payabl                   49.89
Medicare Employer Taxes Payabl                   49.89

Total Current Liabilities                                      2,224.24

Long-Term Liabilities
Long-Term Notes Payable                      20,500.00
Mortgage Payable                             74,314.20

Total Long-Term Liabilities                                   94,814.20

Total Liabilities                                            97,038.44

Capital
Matt Lowe, Capital                           60,795.00
Matt Lowe, Drawing                          (1,000.00)
Sharon Albert, Capital                       60,795.00
Sharon Albert, Drawing                      (1,000.00)
Net Income                                    (146.61)

Total Capital                                               119,443.39

Total Liabilities & Capital         $                       216,481.83
```

2. Print the \<Standard\> Income Stmnt (Income Statement).

	Current Month			Year to Date	
Matt's Service Merchandise Income Statement For the One Month Ending January 31, 2004					
Revenues					
Service Fees	$ 115.95	1.91	$	115.95	1.91
Sales-Hardware	2,550.00	42.04		2,550.00	42.04
Sales-Wall	2,600.00	42.86		2,600.00	42.86
Sales-Floor	800.00	13.19		800.00	13.19
Total Revenues	6,065.95	100.00		6,065.95	100.00
Cost of Sales					
Cost of Goods Sold-Hardware	850.00	14.01		850.00	14.01
Cost of Goods Sold-Wall	780.00	12.86		780.00	12.86
Cost of Goods Sold-Floor	270.00	4.45		270.00	4.45
Cost of Goods Sold-Lights	128.00	2.11		128.00	2.11
Purchase Discounts	(17.96)	(0.30)		(17.96)	(0.30)
Total Cost of Sales	2,010.04	33.14		2,010.04	33.14
Gross Profit	4,055.91	66.86		4,055.91	66.86
Expenses					
Maintenance Expense	130.00	2.14		130.00	2.14
FICA Expense	213.28	3.52		213.28	3.52
Medicare Expense	49.89	0.82		49.89	0.82
FUTA Expense	27.52	0.45		27.52	0.45
SUTA Expense	116.96	1.93		116.96	1.93
State Training Tax Expense	3.45	0.06		3.45	0.06
Postage Expense	37.00	0.61		37.00	0.61
Supplies Expense	110.82	1.83		110.82	1.83
Telephone Expense	73.60	1.21		73.60	1.21
Wages Expense	3,200.00	52.75		3,200.00	52.75
Overtime Expense	240.00	3.96		240.00	3.96
Total Expenses	4,202.52	69.28		4,202.52	69.28
Net Income	$ (146.61)	(2.42)	$	(146.61)	(2.42)

3.   Print the <Standard> Cash Flow.

	Matt's Service Merchandise Statement of Cash Flow For the one Month Ended January 31, 2004	
	Current Month	Year to Date
Cash Flows from operating activities		
Net Income	$ (146.61) $	(146.61)
Adjustments to reconcile net income to net cash provided by operating activities		
Accounts Receivable	(786.60)	(786.60)
Merchandise Inventory	318.00	318.00
Accounts Payable	812.00	812.00
Sales Tax Payable	421.28	421.28
Federal Payroll Taxes Payable	250.11	250.11
FUTA Tax Payable	27.52	27.52
State Payroll Taxes Payable	35.61	35.61
State Disability Insurance	30.97	30.97
SUTA Payable	116.96	116.96
State Training Tax	3.45	3.45
FICA Employee Taxes Payable	213.28	213.28
FICA Employer Taxes Payable	213.28	213.28
Medicare Employee Taxes Payabl	49.89	49.89
Medicare Employer Taxes Payabl	49.89	49.89
Total Adjustments	1,755.64	1,755.64
Net Cash provided by Operations	1,609.03	1,609.03
Cash Flows from investing activities Used For		
Net cash used in investing	0.00	0.00
Cash Flows from financing activities Proceeds From Used For		
Mortgage Payable	(685.80)	(685.80)
Matt Lowe, Drawing	(1,000.00)	(1,000.00)
Sharon Albert, Drawing	(1,000.00)	(1,000.00)
Net cash used in financing	(2,685.80)	(2,685.80)
Net increase <decrease> in cash	$ (1,076.77) $	(1,076.77)
Summary		
Cash Balance at End of Period	$ 71,623.23 $	71,623.23
Cash Balance at Beg of Period	(72,700.00)	(72,700.00)
Net Increase <Decrease> in Cash	$ (1,076.77) $	(1,076.77)

BACKING UP CHAPTER 14 DATA

Follow these steps to back up Chapter 14 data:

1. If you are using a floppy disk to back up, put a disk in drive A. You may use the same disk that you used to back up on page 525.

2. From the menu bar, select File, then Back up.

3. Click | Back Up Now |.

4. Click on the down-arrow in the Save in field. If necessary, scroll up the list, then click on 3½ Floppy (A:) to select drive A. *Or*, back up to the network or hard drive.

5. Type **Chapter 14** in the File name field.

6. Click | Save |.

7. When the screen prompts that This company backup will require approximately 1 diskette, click | OK |.

8. When the screen prompts you to insert the first disk, click on | OK |. When the Back Up Company scale is 100% completed, you have successfully backed up to the current point in Chapter 14. You are returned to the menu bar.

9. Click on File, Exit to exit Peachtree.

	INTERNET ACTIVITY
1.	From your Internet browser, go to the book's website at http://www.mhhe.com/yacht2004.
2.	In the Student Edition list, link to Internet Activities.
3.	Link to WEB EXERCISES PART 3.
4.	Complete the SALARY CALCULATOR-Chapter 14 exercise. Read steps 1-3.
5.	Follow the steps shown on the book's website to complete this Internet activity.
6.	Using a word processing program write a brief summary of what you find. Include all appropriate website addresses.

SUMMARY AND REVIEW

SOFTWARE OBJECTIVES: In Chapter 14, you used the software to:

1. Explore the Payroll Setup Wizard.

2. Enter initial payroll fields.

3. Enter employee and employer default information.

4. Journalize and post Payroll Journal entries.

5. Print paychecks.

6. Print the financial statements.

7 Make four backups: 2 for Matt's Service Merchandise; 2 for the end-of-chapter exercises.

WEB OBJECTIVES: In Chapter 14, you did these Internet activities:

1. Used your Internet browser to go to the book's website.

2. Went to the Internet Activity link on the book's website. Then, selected WEB EXERCISES PART 3. Completed the fourth web exercise in Part 3— Salary Calculator.

3. Used a word processing program to write summaries of the websites that you visited.

GOING TO THE NET

Access the Employer Reporting and Instructions website at http://www.ssa.gov/employer/. Link to General W-2 Filing Information, then answer these questions.

1. What are dates that employers must send W-2 information to the Social Security Administration? (Include the dates for *both* electronic and paper filing.)
2. When must employers give employees their W-2?
3. What two forms do employers send to the Social Security Administration?

Multiple-Choice Questions: In the space provided, write the letter that best answers each question. (*The questions that follow assume PCA 2004, Educational Version, payroll tax amounts were used.*)

_____1. The cash account to credit when disbursing checks for Matt's Service Merchandise employees is:

    a. Account No. 10200, La Jolla Bank.
    b. Account No. 10300, Payroll Checking Account.
    c. Account No. 23200, Wages Payable.
    d. Account No. 77500, Wages Expense.
    e. None of the above.

_____2. The amount withheld from employees' paychecks depends on:

    a. How many employees a company has.
    b. The amount withheld changes on every paycheck.
    c. There are no withholdings.
    d. The number of withholding allowances.
    e. None of the above.

_____3. Guidelines for employee and employer withholdings are found in the following IRS publication:

    a. Circular E, Employer's Tax Guide.
    b. Circular E, Employee's Tax Guide.
    c. Circular F, Employee/Employer Tax Guide.
    d. Both a. and b.
    e. None of the above.

_____4. At the Maintain Employees level, you enter the following types of information:

    a. Employee name, address, and telephone number.
    b. The way an employee is paid.
    c. Tax filing status and withholding allowances.
    d. All of the above.
    e. None of the above.

_____5. Terry Armstrong received a January 9[h] paycheck in the amount of:

    a. $495.00.
    b. $428.99
    c. $400.00.
    d. $550.00.
    e. None of the above.

_____6. The entry in the General Journal for the transfer of funds on January 3, 2004 is:

    a. Debit, Account No. 10200, La Jolla Bank, $6,500; Credit, Account No. 10300, Payroll Checking Account, $6,500.
    b. Debit, Account No. 10300, Payroll Checking Account, $6,500; Credit, Account No. 10200, La Jolla Bank, $6,500.
    c. Debit, Account No. 10400, Stockmen's & Loan, $6,500; Credit, Account No. 10200, La Jolla Bank, $6,500.
    d. Debit, Account No. 10200, La Jolla Bank, $6,500; Credit, Account No. 10400, Stockmen's & Loan, $6,500.
    e. None of the above.

_____7. All of these payroll tax deductions are subtracted from an employee's gross pay EXCEPT:

    a. Federal income tax (FIT).
    b. Social security tax (FICA).
    c. Medicare tax.
    d. Federal unemployment tax (FUTA).
    e. None of the above.

_____8. The Gross Pay Account is:

    a. Account No. 72000, Payroll Tax Expense.
    b. Account No. 23400, Federal Payroll Taxes Payable.
    c. Account No. 77500, Wages Expense.
    d. Account No. 24000, FICA Employee Tax Payable.
    e. None of the above.

_____9. Lily Gibson received a January 16th paycheck in the amount of:

  a. $373.10
  b. $338.59.
  c. $430.00.
  d. $360.00.
  e. None of the above.

_____10. The unemployment percent used for Matt's Service Merchandise is:

  a. 3.4%.
  b. 5.4%.
  c. 4.5%.
  d. Since no one is collecting unemployment compensation, Matt's Service Merchandise does not have to pay this tax.
  e. None of the above.

Exercise 14-1: Follow the instructions below to complete Exercise 14-1. Exercises for Chapters 11, 12 and 13 must be completed before starting Exercise 14-1.

1. Start Windows, then PCA. Open the company that you set up in Exercise 11-1.

2. Restore your data from Exercise 13-1. You made this back upon page 505.

3. Journalize and post the following General Journal entry:

   01/8/04   Transferred $5,500 from Account No. 10200, Eugene Bank, to Account No. 10300, Payroll Checking Account.

4. Print the January 8, 2004 General Journal.

5. Use the following information for the Payroll Setup Wizard:

   State: OR
   Locality: Tri-Met
   Unemployment Percent for Your Company: 3.4

Do You Want to Record Employee Meals and Tips? No
<u>G</u>ross Pay Acct: 77500 Wages Expense
<u>T</u>ax Liability Acct: 23400 Federal Payroll Taxes Payable
Ta<u>x</u> Expense Acct: 72000 Payroll Tax Expense

Your store does not offer a 401(k) plan, and vacation and sick time are not tracked.

6. Set up the Pay Levels for your employees using Account No. 77500 for Regular wages and Account No. 77600 for Overtime wages.

7. Use the following Employ<u>EE</u> Fields:

For Fed_Income, accept the default for Account No. 23400, Federal Payroll Taxes Payable.

Soc_Sec, Account No. 24000, FICA Employee Taxes Payable

Medicare, Account No. 24200, Medicare Employee Taxes Payable

State, Account No. 23600, State Payroll Taxes Payable

8. Use the following Employ<u>ER</u> Fields:

	Liability column	*Expense column*
Soc_Sec_ER	24100, FICA Employer Taxes Payable	72510, FICA Expense
Medicare_ER	24400 Medicare Employer Taxes Payable	Add Account No. 72520, Medicare Expense (Expenses)
FUTA_ER	23500, FUTA Tax Payable	72530, FUTA Expense
LIT_ER	Add Account No. 25000 Local Payroll Taxes Payable (Other Current Liabilities)	Add Account No. 72535, Local Payroll Taxes Expense (Expenses)
SUI_ER	23700, SUTA Payable	72540, SUTA Expense

9.   Add the following employees.

Employee I<u>D</u>:   C50
N<u>a</u>me: Roger Carberry
Accept the default for Employee
Address: 1211 N. Farrington Road, Apt. 3
City, ST <u>Z</u>ip: Eugene, OR 97214
Telephone <u>1</u>:   503-555-1289
E-mail: carberry@email.com
So<u>c</u>ial Security #: 677-90-0021
<u>T</u>ype: FULL
Hired: 1/2/04

Withholding I<u>n</u>fo:

Filing Status: Single for Federal, State, and Local
Allow: 1 for Federal, State, and Local

Pay I<u>n</u>fo: Hourly, $10/hour; $15/hour, overtime; paid weekly

Employee I<u>D</u>:   M60
N<u>a</u>me: Minnie Matson
Accept the default for Employee
Address: 5134 Branch Drive
City, ST <u>Z</u>ip: Eugene, OR 97204
Telephone <u>1</u>:   503-555-7822
E-mail: Matson@eugene.com
So<u>c</u>ial Security #: 455-88-3821
<u>T</u>ype: FULL
Hired: 1/2/04

Withholding I<u>n</u>fo:

Filing Status: Married for Federal, State, and Local
Allow: 1 for Federal, State, and Local

Pay I<u>n</u>fo: Hourly, $10/hour; $15/hour, overtime; paid weekly

10.   Print an employee list: Reports, Payroll, Employee List.

11.   Make a backup of your work. (Use **Exercise 14-1** as the file name.)

12. Exit PCA or continue.

Exercise 14-2: Follow the instructions below to complete Exercise 14-2.

1. Start Windows, then PCA. Open your company.

2. If necessary, restore your data from Exercise 14-1.

3. On January 9, 2004, issue payroll check 2050 to Roger Carberry. Mr. Carberry worked 40 regular hours. Issue paychecks from the Payroll Checking Account. Type **2050** in the Check Num_ber field.

4. On January 9, 2004, issue payroll check 2051 to Minnie Matson. Ms. Matson worked 40 regular hours.

5. Make the following payroll entries for Roger Carberry and Minnie Matson.

Date	Name	Hours Worked	Overtime	Check No.
1/16/04	R. Carberry	40		2052
	M. Matson	40	2	2053
1/23/04	R. Carberry	40	1	2054
	M. Matson	40		2055
1/30/04	R. Carberry	40		2056
	M. Matson	40	2	2057

After recording the paycheck information, type the check number, then post. You do *not* need to print paychecks 2050–2057.

6. Print the Payroll Journal.

7. Print the General Ledger Trial Balance.

8. Print the following financial statements: Balance Sheet, Income Statement, and Statement of Cash Flow.

9. Make a backup. (Use **Exercise 14-2** as the file name.)

CHAPTER 14 INDEX

In Project 2, you will complete the Computer Accounting Cycle for Copper Bicycles, a merchandising business. Copper Bicycles sells mountain bicycles, road bicycles, and children's bicycles. It is organized as a corporation.

It is the purpose of Project 2 to review what you have learned in Part 3 of the book, Peachtree Complete Accounting for Merchandising Businesses. Accounts payable, accounts receivable, payroll, and inventory transactions are included in this project.

Vendors offer Copper Bicycles a purchase discount of 2% 15, Net 30 days.

A checklist is shown listing the printed reports that you should have at the end of this project. The step-by-step instructions also remind you to print reports at certain intervals.

Follow these steps to complete Project 2, Copper Bicycles:

Step 1: Start Windows and Peachtree in the usual way.

Step 2: At the Peachtree Accounting startup screen, click on Set up a new company.

Step 3: Complete the following company information:

Company Name:	Copper Bicycles (use your last name, then the company name; for example Smith Bicycles)
Address Line 1:	1200 North Peoria Road
City, State, Zip:	Mesa, AZ 83606
Country:	USA
Phone:	480-555-9211
Fax:	480-555-9212

Business Type: Corporation
Federal Employer ID: 35-5249973
State Employer ID: 27-0193201
State Unemployment ID: 274297-2
Web Site: www.copperbicycles.com
E-mail: mail@copperbicycles.com

Step 4:   Select Set up a new company using an extensive chart of accounts from one of many sample companies.

Step 5:   Scroll down the list, then select Retail Company.

Step 6:   Accept the default for Accrual accounting.

Step 7:   Accept the default for Real Time posting.

Step 8:   Accept the default for 12 monthly accounting periods.

Step 9:   On the Monthly Accounting Periods screen, make the following selections:

When do you want your first fiscal year to start?   Month: **January**   Year   **2004**

What is the first month you will be entering data?   Month: **January**   Year   2004

What is the first year you will be entering payroll?   2004

Step 10:   Accept the information on the Defaults screen.

Step 11:   Read the information on the Congratulations! screen. Then click | Finish |.

Step 12:   Disable the Peachtree Today window at startup.

General Ledger

1. Delete the following accounts:

    10000   Petty Cash
    10100   Cash on Hand
    10300   Payroll Checking Account
    11500   Allowance for Doubtful Account

14200   Notes Receivable-Current
15400   Leasehold Improvements
15500   Building
15600   Building Improvements
16900   Land
17400   Accum. Depreciation - Leasehold
17500   Accum. Depreciation - Building
17600   Accum. Depreciation - Bldg Imp
19000   Deposits
19200   Note Receivable-Noncurrent
19900   Other Noncurrent Assets
23000   Accrued Expenses
24200   Current Portion Long-Term Debt
60500   Amortization Expense
63000   Charitable Contributions Exp
63500   Commissions and Fees Exp
65000   Employee Benefit Programs Exp
66000   Gifts Expense
68000   Laundry and Cleaning Exp
89000   Other Expense

Change these account names:

10200   Regular Checking Accounting to Mesa Bank
10400   Savings Account to Arizona Savings & Loan
12000   Product Inventory to Inventory-Mountain Bikes
14000   Prepaid Expenses to Prepaid Insurance
23300   Deductions Payable to Medicare Employee Taxes Payabl
23800   Local Payroll Taxes Payable to Medicare Employer Taxes Payabl
24000   Other Taxes Payable to FICA Employee Taxes Payable
24100   Employee Benefits Payable to FICA Employer Taxes Payable
24800   Other Current Liabilities to Short-Term Notes Payable
27000   Notes Payable-Noncurrent to Long-Term Notes Payable
40000   Sales-Merchandise to Sales-Mountain Bikes
50000   Cost of Goods Sold to Cost of Goods Sold-Mountain Bi
72500   Penalties and Fines Exp to FUTA Expense
73000   Other Taxes to SUTA Expense
74000   Rent or Lease Expense to Rent-Mall Space

Add these accounts:

12020	Inventory-Road Bikes	Inventory
12030	Inventory-Children's Bikes	Inventory
40020	Sales-Road Bikes	Income
40030	Sales-Children's Bikes	Income

50020	Cost of Goods Sold-Road Bikes	Cost of Sales
50030	Cost of Goods Sold-Children's	Cost of Sales
73200	FICA Expense	Expenses
73300	Medicare Expense	Expenses

2. Click on <u>B</u>eginning Balances.

3. You purchased Copper Bicycles in December of 2003. Use the Balance Sheet below to record the chart of account beginning balances.

Copper Bicycles Balance Sheet January 1, 2004		
ASSETS		
Current Assets		
Mesa Bank	$ 40,000.00	
Arizona Savings & Loan	12,500.00	
Inventory-Mountain Bikes	6,000.00	
Inventory-Road Bikes	8,250.00	
Inventory-Children's Bikes	4,050.00	
Prepaid Insurance	2,400.00	
Total Current Assets		$73,200.00
Property and Equipment: Furniture and Fixtures	6,000.00	
Other Assets: Organization Costs	500.00	
Total Property and Equipment and Other Assets		6,500.00
Total Assets		$79,700.00
LIABILITIES AND STOCKHOLDERS' EQUITY		
Short-Term Notes Payable	4,000.00	
Long-Term Notes Payable	6,500.00	
Total Liabilities		$10,500.00
Stockholder's Equity: Common Stock		69,200.00
Total Liabilities and Stockholders' Equity		$79,700.00

Accounts Payable

Follow the instructions below to set up vendor information for Copper Bicycles.

1. Click on Vendor Defaults. Set up the following vendor defaults.

Standard Terms:	Due in number of days
Net due in:	30 days
Discount in:	15 days
Discount %	2.00
Credit Limit:	15,000.00

GL Link Accounts:

Purchase Account:	12000 Inventory-Mountain Bikes
Discount GL Account:	59500 Purchase Discounts

2. Set up the following vendors.

Vendor ID:	BSR111
Name:	BSR Gear
Contact:	Jesse Burke
Address:	709 Orange Avenue
City, ST Zip:	Los Angeles, CA 90036
Vendor Type:	mountain
1099 Type:	Independent Contractor
Telephone 1:	323-555-9525
Fax:	323-555-9416
E-Mail	burke@bsrgear.biz
Web Site:	www.bsrgear.biz

Purchase Defaults:

Purchase Acct:	12000 Inventory-Mountain Bikes
Tax ID #:	27-9117731

Vendor ID:	ERB112
Name:	Ellison's Road Bikes
Contact:	Lisa Ellison
Address:	8230 Rio Grande

City, ST Zip:	El Paso, TX 76315
Vendor Type:	road
1099 Type:	Independent Contractor
Telephone 1:	915-555-2365
Fax:	915-555-2366
E-mail:	ellison@roadbikes.net
Web Site:	www.roadbikes.net

Purchase Defaults:

| Purchase Acct: | 12020 Inventory-Road Bikes |
| Tax ID #: | 84-8276448 |

Vendor ID:	TTW113
Name:	Tiny Tots Wheels
Contact:	Katie Wood
Address:	23913 Route 66
City, ST Zip:	Flagstaff, AZ 86001
Vendor Type:	children
1099 Type:	Independent Contractor
Telephone 1:	928-555-8900
Fax:	928-555-8901
E-mail:	katie@tinytotswheels.com
Web Site:	www.tinytotswheels.com

Purchase Defaults:

| Purchase Acct: | 12030 Inventory-Children's Bikes |
| Tax ID #: | 60-7893213 |

Accounts Receivable

Follow the instructions below to set up customer information for Copper Bicycles.

1. Complete the following customer defaults.

Standard Terms:	Due in number of days
Net due in:	30 days
Discount in:	0 days
Discount %:	0.00
Credit Limit:	5,000.00

GL Sales Account:	40000 Sales-Mountain Bikes
Discount GL Account:	49000 Sales Discounts

2. Complete the following customer maintenance records.

Customer ID:	DB001
Name:	Danny Benoit
Address:	701 North 75th Street
City, ST Zip:	Phoenix, AZ 86002
Sales Tax:	

Follow these steps to add AZ sales taxes:

a. In the Sales Tax field, click [Q].

b. Click [New].

c. Type **AZ** in the Sales Tax Code field.

d. Type **Arizona sales tax** in the Description field.

e. Double-click on the ID column. The Maintain Sales Tax Authorities screen pops up.

f. Type **AZ** in the ID field.

g. Type **Arizona sales tax** in the Description field.

h. In the Sales Tax Payable G/L Account field, type **23100** for Sales Tax Payable. Then, press **<Enter>** two times.

i. Type **7** in the Single Tax rate field.

j. Click [Save], then [Close]. You are returned to the Maintain Sales Tax Codes screen. Type **AZ** in the ID field. Press **<Enter>**. The Description, Rate, and G/L Account - Description columns are completed automatically.

k. Click [Save], then [Close]. You are returned to the Maintain Customer/Prospects screen.

Sales Tax:	Select AZ
Customer Type:	MAR (for Maricopa County)
Telephone 1:	602-555-9211
Fax:	602-555-9212
E-mail	benoit@phoenix.com
Web Site:	www.phoenix.com/benoit

Sales Defaults:

G/L Sales Acct:	40000, Sales-Mountain Bikes

Customer ID:	RL002
Name:	Robert Lanning
Address:	5741 Paradise Avenue
City, ST Zip:	Sedona, AZ 86336
Sales Tax:	AZ
Customer Type:	YAV (for Yavapai County)
Telephone 1:	928-555-3203
Fax:	928-555-3204
E-mail:	robert@sedona.com
Web Site:	www.sedona.com/lanning

Sales Defaults:

G/L Sales Acct:	40020, Sales-Road Bikes

Customer ID:	SW003
Name:	Sandy Westcott
Address:	4114 North Roosevelt
City, ST Zip:	Tempe, AZ 86203
Sales Tax:	AZ
Customer Type:	MAR
Telephone 1:	480-555-8892
Fax:	480-555-9824
E-mail:	westcott@valley.net
Web Site:	www.valley.net/sandy

Sales Defaults:

G/L Sales Acct:	40030, Sales-Children's Bikes

Payroll

1. Use the Payroll Setup Wizard for the following information.

State:	AZ
Unemployment Percent for Your Company:	3.4
Do You Want to Record Employee Meals and Tips:	No

Gross Pay Acct: 77500 Wages Expense
Tax Liability Acct: 23400 Federal Payroll Taxes Payable
Tax Expense Acct: 72000 Payroll Tax Expense

2. Accept the following defaults:

401(k) plan not offered
Vacation time not tracked
Sick time not tracked

3. Click [Finish] to exit the Payroll Setup Wizard.

4. Complete the following employee defaults. Click on the Pay Levels tab. Account No. 77500, Wages Expense, is used for wages.

5. Click on the EmployEE Fields tab. Select the following accounts:

Accept the default for Fed_Income, Account No. 23400, Federal Payroll Taxes Payable

Soc_Sec, 24000, FICA Employee Taxes Payable

Medicare, 23300, Medicare Employee Taxes Payable

State, 23600, State Payroll Taxes Payable

6. Click on the EmployER Fields tab. Select the following accounts:

	Liability column	*Expense column*
Soc_Sec_ER	24100, FICA Employer Taxes Payable	73200, FICA Expense
Medicare_ER	23800, Medicare Employer Taxes Payable	73300, Medicare Expense
FUTA_ER	23500, FUTA Tax Payable	72500, FUTA Expense
SUI_ER	23700, SUTA Payable	73000, SUTA Expense

7. Click [OK].

8. Add the following employee maintenance records.

Employee ID:	1ML
Name:	Michael Larson
Accept the default for Employee	
Address:	203 N. Hill Street
City, ST Zip:	Tempe, AZ 86312
Telephone 1:	480-555-2315
E-mail:	Michael@email.net
Social Security #:	999-22-7623
Type:	FULL
Hired:	1/2/04

Withholding Info:

Filing Status:	Married for Federal, State, and Local
Allow:	2 for Federal, State and Local
State–Additional Withholding:	25.00

Pay Info: Salary, $500 per week.

Employee ID:	2JW
Name:	Jessica Williams
Accept the default for Employee	
Address:	605 North Genesee
City, ST Zip:	Phoenix, AZ 86023
Telephone 1:	602-555-6510
E-mail:	jessica@mail.net
Social Security #:	333-11-7622
Type:	FULL
Hired:	1/2/04

Withholding Info:

Filing Status:	Single for Federal, State, and Local
Allow:	1 for Federal, State and Local
State–Additional Withholding:	25.00

Pay Info: Salary, $500 per week.

9. Click

Inventory

1. Select Maintain; Default Information, Inventory Items. Click on the G<u>L</u> Accts/Costing tab.

2. Set up LIFO as the inventory costing method.

3. Set up the following Inventory Item maintenance information.

Item ID:	mbikes
Description:	mountain bikes
Item Class:	Stock item
Description for Sales:	mountain bikes
Price Level 1:	300.00
Item Tax Type:	1
Last Unit Cost:	150.00
Cost Method:	LIFO
GL Sales Acct:	40000 Sales-Mountain Bikes
GL Inventory Acct:	12000, Merchandise Inventory-Mountain Bikes
GL Cost of Sales Acct:	50000, Cost of Goods Sold- Mountain Bi
Item Type:	mountain
Unit/Measure:	each
Minimum Stock:	10
Reorder Quantity:	5
Preferred Vendor ID:	BSR Gear

Beginning Balances: mountain bikes

Quantity:	40.00
Unit Cost:	150.00
Total Cost:	6,000.00

Item ID:	rbikes
Description:	road bikes
Item Class:	Stock item
Description for Sales:	road bikes
Price Level 1:	150.00
Item Tax Type:	1
Last Unit Cost:	75.00
Cost Method:	LIFO

GL Sales Acct:	40020, Sales-Road Bikes
GL Inventory Acct:	12020, Inventory-Road Bikes
GL Cost of Sales Acct:	50020, Cost of Goods Sold-Road Bikes
Item Type:	road
Unit/Measure:	each
Minimum Stock:	10
Reorder Quantity:	5
Preferred Vendor ID:	Ellison's Road Bikes

Beginning Balances: Road Bikes

Quantity:	110.00
Unit Cost:	75.00
Total Cost:	8,250.00

Item ID:	cbikes
Description:	children's bikes
Item Class:	Stock item
Detailed Description:	children's bikes
Price Level 1:	90.00
Item Tax Type:	1
Last Unit Cost:	45.00
Cost Method:	LIFO
GL Sales Acct:	40030, Sales-Children's Bikes
GL Inventory Acct:	12030, Inventory-Children's Bikes
GL Cost of Sales Acct:	50030, Cost of Goods Sold-Children's Bikes
Item Type:	children
Unit/Measure:	each
Minimum Stock:	10
Reorder Quantity:	5

Vendor ID: Tiny Tots Wheels

Beginning Balances: children's bikes

Quantity:	90.00
Unit Cost:	45.00
Total Cost:	4,050.00

4. Make the selections to disable Peachtree Today at startup.

5. Make a backup. Use **Copper Bicycles Begin** as the file name.

Journalize and post the following transactions:

purchase recieve ✓

Date	Description of Transaction

01/09/04   Invoice No. 55XR was received from BSR Gear for 10 mountain bikes for $150 each.   ✓

01/09/04   Invoice No. 75 was received from Tiny Tots Wheels for 15 children's bikes for $45 each.   ✓

01/09/04   Invoice No. G42 was received from Ellison's Road Bikes for 12 road bikes for $75 each.   ✓

01/9/04   Issued pay checks 1001 and 1002 to Michael Larson and Jessica Williams.   (*Hint: Select Mesa Bank as the cash account for payroll checks. Type the check number, then post the payroll entry.*)   ✓

01/13/04   Deposited cash sales of $2,670, plus sales taxes of $186.90: 4 mountain bikes, $1,200; 5 road bikes, $750; 8 children's bikes, $720. Cash sales are deposited in the Mesa Bank.   ✓

01/15/04   Deposited cash sales of $1,950, plus sales taxes of $136.50: 5 children's bikes, $450; 4 road bikes, $600; and 3 mountain bikes, $900.

01/16/04   Sold one mountain bike to Danny Benoit on account, Sales Invoice 101. (*Hint: Type the invoice number in the Invoice # field.*)   ✓

01/16/04   Issued pay checks 1003 and 1004 for Michael Larson and Jessica Williams. (*Hint: If necessary, complete the Check Num\underline{b}er field.*)   ✓

01/21/04   Deposited cash sales, $1,920, plus sales taxes of $134.40: 3 children's bikes, $270; 2 mountain bikes, $600; 7 road bikes, $1,050.   ✓

01/23/04   Issued Check No. 1005 to BSR Gear in payment of purchase Invoice No. 55XR. Complete the Check Num\underline{b}er field. Issue checks from the Mesa Bank account. (Make sure that the Discount Account field shows 59500 for Purchase Discounts.)

01/23/04 Issued Check No. 1006 to Ellison's Road Bikes in payment of purchase Invoice No. G42.

01/23/04 Issued Check No. 1007 to Tiny Tots Wheels in payment of purchase Invoice No. 75.

01/23/04 Deposited cash sales of $3,810, plus sales taxes of $266.70: 6 mountain bikes, $1,800; 8 road bikes, $1,200; 9 children's bikes, $810.

01/23/04 Issued Check No. 1008 to Greene Rentals for $1,250 in payment of mall space rent for Copper Bicycles. (*Hint: Remember to complete the Check Number field.*)

01/23/04 Issued pay checks 1009 and 1010 for Michael Larson and Jessica Williams.

01/28/04 Sold one children's bike to Sandy Westcott on account, Sales Invoice 102. (*Hint: Type the invoice number in the Invoice # field.*)

01/28/04 Invoice No. 68XR was received from BSR Gear for three mountain bikes for $150 each.

01/28/04 Invoice No. 96 was received from Tiny Tots Wheels for five children's bikes for $45 each.

01/28/04 Invoice No. G82 was received from Ellison's Road Bikes for five road bikes for $75 each.

01/30/04 Deposited cash sales of $3,240 plus sales taxes of $226.80: 6 mountain bikes, $1,800; 6 road bikes, $900; 6 children's bikes, $540.

01/30/04 Issued Check No. 1011 to Sharon Clark for $195 in payment of Short-Term Notes Payable.

01/30/04 Issued Check No. 1012 to Mesa Bank for $135.40 in payment of Long-Term Notes Payable.

01/30/04 Issued Check No. 1013 to Mesa Utilities for $190.57 in payment of utilities.

01/30/04 Issued pay checks 1014 and 1015 for Michael Larson and Jessica Williams.

Print the following reports:

1. Print the General Ledger Trial Balance.

2. Print the financial statements: Balance Sheet, Income Statement, and Statement of Cash Flow.

3. Print the Customer Ledgers and Vendor Ledgers.

4. Make a backup of Project 2, Copper Bicycles. Use **Copper Bicycles January** as the file name.

	CHECKLIST OF PRINTOUTS, Copper Bicycles
	General Ledger Trial Balance
	Balance Sheet
	Income Statement
	Statement of Cash Flow
	Customer Ledgers
	Vendor Ledgers
	OPTIONAL PRINTOUTS
	Chart of Accounts
	General Ledger
	Check Register
	Customer List
	Vendor List
	Purchase Journal
	Cash Disbursements Journal
	Sales Journal
	Cash Receipts Journal
	Payroll Journal
	Cost of Goods Sold Journal

Student Name_____**Date**_____

CHECK YOUR PROGRESS: PROJECT 2, Copper Bicycles

1. What are the total debit and credit balances on your General Ledger Trial Balance?   _____

2. What are the total assets on January 31?   _____

3. What is the balance in the Mesa Bank account on January 31?   _____

4. How much are total revenues as of January 31?   _____

5. How much net income (net loss) is reported on January 31?   _____

6. What is the balance in the Inventory-Mountain Bikes account on January 31?   _____

7. What is the balance in the Inventory-Road Bikes account on January 31?   _____

8. What is the balance in the Inventory-Children's Bikes account on January 31?   _____

9. What is the balance in the Short-Term Notes Payable account on January 31?   _____

10. What is the balance in the Common Stock account on January 31?   _____

11. What are the total expenses reported on January 31?   _____

12. Were any Accounts Payable incurred during the month of January? (Circle your answer.)   YES   NO

The McGraw-Hill Companies, Inc., *Computer Accounting with Peachtree Complete 2004, 8e*

Project

2A

Student-Designed Merchandising Business

In Chapters 11, 12, 13, 14 and Project 2, you learned how to complete the Computer Accounting Cycle for merchandising businesses. Project 2A gives you a chance to design a merchandising business of your own.

You will select the type of merchandising business you want, edit your business's Chart of Accounts, create an opening Balance Sheet and transactions, and complete PCA's computer accounting cycle. Project 2A also gives you an opportunity to review the software features learned so far.

You should think about the kind of business you want to create. In Chapters 11, 12, 13 and 14 you worked with Matt's Service Merchandise, a partnership form of business. In Project 2, you worked with Copper Bicycles, a corporate form of business. You might want to design businesses similar to these. Other merchandising businesses include: jewelry store, automobile dealer, bakery, convenience store, florist, furniture dealer, etc.

Before you begin, you should design your business. You will need the following:

1. Company information that includes business name, address, telephone number, and form of business.
2. One of PCA's sample companies.
3. A Chart of Accounts: 80 accounts minimum, 110 accounts maximum.
4. A Balance Sheet for your business.
5. One month's transactions for your business. These transactions must include accounts receivable, accounts payable, inventory, and payroll. You should have a minimum of 25 transactions; a maximum of 35 transactions. These transactions should result in a net income.
6. Complete another month of transactions that result in a net loss.

After you have created your business, you should follow the steps of PCA's computer accounting cycle to complete Project 2A.

Part 4

Advanced Peachtree Complete 2004 Applications

In Part 4 of the book, you complete four chapters and three projects:

Chapter 15, Customizing Forms, shows how to change the preprinted forms included with the software.

Chapter 16, Import/Export, shows how to use PCA 2004 with a word processing program.

Chapter 17, Using Peachtree Complete 2004 with Microsoft Excel and Word, shows you how to use Peachtree with two Microsoft Office applications. You need Microsoft Office 97 or higher to complete the Excel and Word exercises in Chapter 17.

Chapter 18, Dynamic Data Exchange, shows you how to share data with Microsoft Excel with Windows.

Projects 3 and 4 complete your study of *Computer Accounting with Peachtree Complete 2004, Eighth Edition*. All features of the software are included for review in these projects.

Project 4A gives you an opportunity to add another month's worth of transactions to any of the projects that you have already completed.

The chart below shows that you can two disks to back up all the data in Chapters 16, 17, 18, Project 3 and Project 4. You may also back up to the hard drive, network, or other media. If you are using floppy disks, the author suggests that you reformat disks used in earlier chapters. There is no data to save in Chapter 15. *Remember: do not reformat the Exercise 6-2 backup. Exercise 6-2 will be used in Chapters 15-18 of the textbook.*

Disk Label	Chapter	File Name	Kilobytes	Page No.
Disk 1 of 2	16	customer.csv	28 KB	601-602
		customer.lst	28 kB	603
	17	balance sheet.xls	20 KB	614
		balance sheet & income statement.xls	27 KB	617
		Bellwether Garden Supply.doc	20 KB	618-619
	18	bgsbar2.xls	14 KB	634
		bgsbar1.xls	14 KB	634
		balsht.bgs.xls	18 KB	635
		Exercise 18-1	17 KB	639
		Exercise 18-2	14 KB	639
	Project 3	Valley Computers.Begin.ptb	444 KB	646
		Valley Computers January.ptb	458 KB	648
Disk 2 of 2	Project 4	Woods Mftg Begin.ptb	465 KB	664
		Woods Mftg January.ptb	523 KB	669

The size of your backup files may differ from the amounts shown on the table. This is okay. The differences are usually insignificant.

Chapter

15   Customizing Forms

SOFTWARE OBJECTIVES: In Chapter 15, you will use the software to:

1. Select a form.
2. Select the filter, format, align, and design options.
3. Explore the data, text, command, group, picture, and line objects.
4. Design a Balance Sheet with the Financial Statement Wizard.

WEB OBJECTIVES: In Chapter 15, you will do these Internet activities:

1. Use your Internet browser to go to the book's website.
2. Go to the Internet Activity link on the book's website. Then, select WEB EXERCISES PART 4. Complete the first web exercise in Part 4–Academic Website.
3. Use a word processing program to write summaries of the websites that you visited.

You have used many different kinds of forms: invoices, statements, checks, etc. There may be times when you want to create your own form or customize one of the formats that come with PCA. You can customize forms with PCA's Form Designer.[1]

PRINTING FORMS

There are three types of documents that can be accessed from the Reports menu:

➢ Reports

➢ Financial Statements

➢ Forms

---

[1]You need a mouse to use the Form Designer.

The rules for each type of document are different for printing and designing. This chapter will explain the rules for printing and designing forms.

WHAT IS A FORM?

A form in Peachtree is a document that you exchange with customers, vendors, or employees. The forms that come with PCA include checks, tax forms, invoices, statements, mailing labels, quotes, and collection letters.

Usually, these documents are printed on preprinted forms, but you can also design a form and print to blank paper. When you are ready to print or design a form, you select Reports from the menu bar, and look for the documents contained in file folders. The illustration below shows an open folder for the Accounts Payable report, Disbursements Checks.

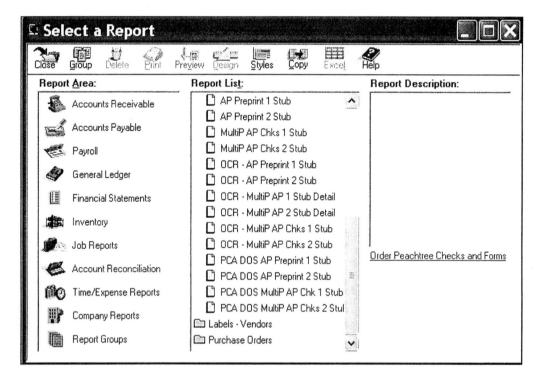

The following table lists the forms that can be printed or edited:

Accounts Receivable	Accounts Payable	Payroll
Invoices	Disbursements checks	Payroll checks
Statements	1099 Forms	W-2's
Customer Mailing Labels	Purchase Orders	940 and 941 Forms
Quotes	Vendor Mailing Labels	State Quarterly Tax Forms
Collection Letters		Employee Mailing Labels

Preprinted paper forms require special attention because the forms must be aligned in the printer correctly and the printer must be configured to accommodate the form. That is why forms cannot be displayed on your screen prior to printing. You can print practice forms to test alignment and printer configuration, or you can view the layout of the form in the Form Designer.

GETTING STARTED

In this chapter, you are going to use Bellwether Garden Supply (the sample company that you used in Chapters 1 through 7).

1. Start Windows and Peachtree in the usual way.

2. Open the sample company, Bellwether Garden Supply.

Comment

You can use beginning Bellwether data or any subsequent Bellwether backup. To install Bellwether's starting data, exit Peachtree and any other open programs. Put the PCA 2004 CD in your CD drive. Select Peachtree Complete Accounting to start the InstallShield Wizard. Select Add Components. Uncheck all the boxes *except* Sample Company Data. (Use the keyboard's down-arrow to select the component; use the space bar to remove the check mark. There *should be a check mark* next to Sample Company Data.) Exit installation and remove the PCA 2004 CD. Restart the sample company. See Appendix A, Installing Starting Data for the Sample Companies, pages 678 and 679 for detailed steps.

Selecting a Report

1. From the Reports menu, select Accounts Receivable. The Select a Report window displays.

2. Scroll down to the Invoices/Pkg. Slips file folder. Double-click on the folder to open it.

3. Select the Invoice Plain Service #2 form. Observe that the Report Description box explains the invoice.

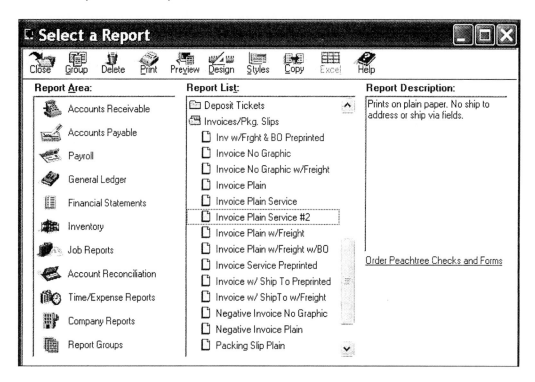

4. Select [Print] or double-click on the form. The Invoice Plain Service #2 window appears and the Filter tab is selected.

5. Select the radio button for Printed Invoices.

6. In the Invoice Number row, click on the From column. Type **10309**. In the To column, type **10311**. Press **<Enter>**.

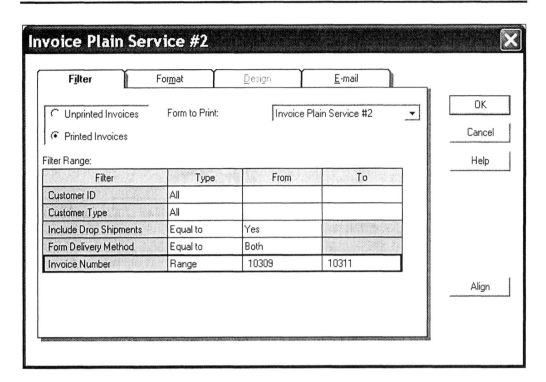

The options that you have are:

If you want to	Then . . . .
Print the form with the default options	Select **<OK>**
Filter the available data	See Filter Options in the next section
Change the Format settings for your printer	See Format Options on page 575
Change the Alignment of your printer	See Align Options on page 577
Test the alignment of forms in your printer	Use the Practice button to print a test invoice

The Filter Options

Filter options vary from form to form. The Filter options you see for customer invoices are different from the options for statements or payroll checks. Entering Filter options works the same for all forms.

1. Make sure the Filter tab is selected. The Filter options are displayed.

2. In the Filter Range for Customer ID and Customer Type, make sure that All is selected as the Type.

   You can set certain options for printing, such as the invoice number, check number, or the last date to include in a batch of checks or invoices.

   You can also set selection criteria. For example, you can specify a range of Customer ID's and Customer Types using the From and To fields. The following table explains the various Filter Types and how to use them.

Filter Type	Use
All	Selects every one of the existing records.
Range	Requires an entry in the From and To fields to set a group of records.
Equal to	Requires a specific response, such as Printed or Unprinted.
Mask	You can filter many records using type codes. For example, if you have set up vendors with either SERVICE or SUPPLY in the Vendor Type field, you could enter SERVICE or SUPPLY to limit the form to only those types of vendors.

If a cell in the Filter Range table has a gray background, no changes can be made to that column entry. If the column entry has a white background, it can be changed.

3. Click [OK]. Then make the selections to print. Three forms print: Retail (Cash) Sales, Invoice 10309 for $508.78; Hensley Park Apartments, Invoice Number 10310 for $845.23; and Tidmore Real Estate, Invoice Number 10311 for $2,005.86.

Comment

The invoices show Duplicate because these invoices have already been printed.

The Format Options

The Format Options let you set certain parameters for printing forms. For example, you can select the printer to use, the margins to set, or the number of copies.

1. If necessary, from the menu bar, click on Reports, Accounts Receivable, Invoices//Pkg. Slips, Invoice Plain Service #2.

2. Click [Print].

3. Click on the Format tab.

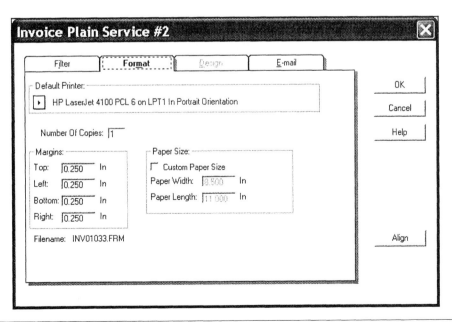

The Default Printer shown on the screen illustration is an HP LaserJet 4100 PCL 6 on LPT1 In Portrait Orientation. ***Portrait orientation*** refers to the direction of the page in which the long edge of the paper runs vertically. It is called portrait orientation because of the similarity to a picture in a frame. Your screen will show the printer that you are using as the Default Printer.

4. Click on the arrow ▸ under Default Printer. The Print Setup window displays.

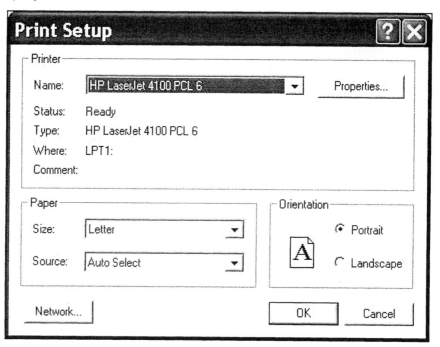

Check this screen before you print to make sure your paper size and orientation are correct. You may be directed to this screen by a message box telling you to adjust paper size.

Printers may have different setup screens. Be sure to set the paper size correctly, especially if the form is not 11 inches high. Some printers default to ***landscape orientation*** when you select 7-inch standard checks. Landscape orientation refers to the direction of the page in which the long edge of the paper runs horizontally. It is called landscape orientation because it resembles the horizon.

5. Select Cancel to return to the Invoice Plain Service #2 Format window.

The Align Options

1. At the Invoice Plain Service #2 window, click 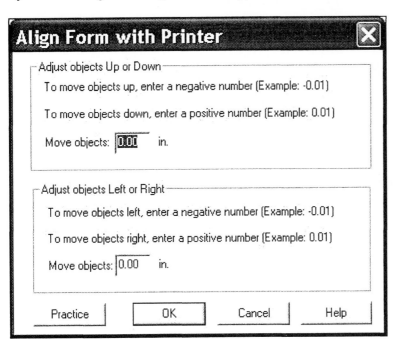 Align . This screen allows you to change the alignment of type on the form.

Align Form with Printer

┌─ Adjust objects Up or Down ──────────────────────
  To move objects up, enter a negative number (Example: -0.01)

  To move objects down, enter a positive number (Example: 0.01)

  Move objects: [0.00] in.

┌─ Adjust objects Left or Right ──────────────────────
  To move objects left, enter a negative number (Example: -0.01)

  To move objects right, enter a positive number (Example: 0.01)

  Move objects: [0.00] in.

| Practice | OK | Cancel | Help |

In the Move objects boxes, you can enter a negative or positive number. Normally you would only move the margins less than an inch. You can enter up to 3 decimal places. If you have a tractor-feed printer, you can align the paper instead.

In the Adjust objects Up or Down section, you enter a negative number to move objects up a fraction of an inch or more. To move objects down, you enter a positive number.

In the Move objects Left or Right area, you enter a negative number to shift the text to the left by the amount you specify. You enter a positive number to shift the text to the right by the amount you specify.

2. Click Cancel two times to return to the Select a Report window.

3. Click Close to return to the menu bar.

DESIGNING FORMS

You build the image of a form on the screen using Form Designer. The image of a form is built using different types of objects: data fields, text objects, bit mapped graphics, commands, lines, or rectangles.

Follow these steps to use the Form Designer:

1. From the Reports menu, click on Payroll.

2. Double-click on the Payroll Checks folder.

3. Select OCR - PR Preprint 1 Stub.

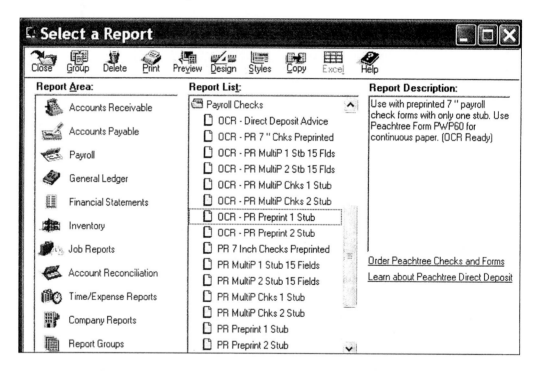

4. Click [Design]. The OCR - PR Preprint 1 Stub window appears.

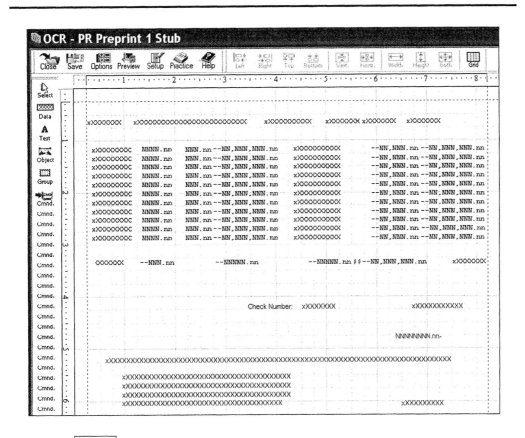

5. Click [Save]. Since you cannot overwrite an existing file name, save the form under a new name. In the Form Name field type **Practice**.

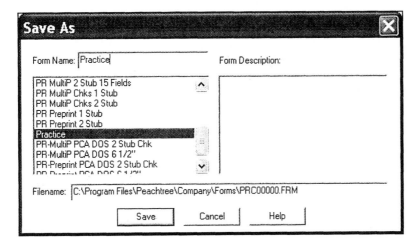

6. Click [Save].

7. To type information into a field, click on the 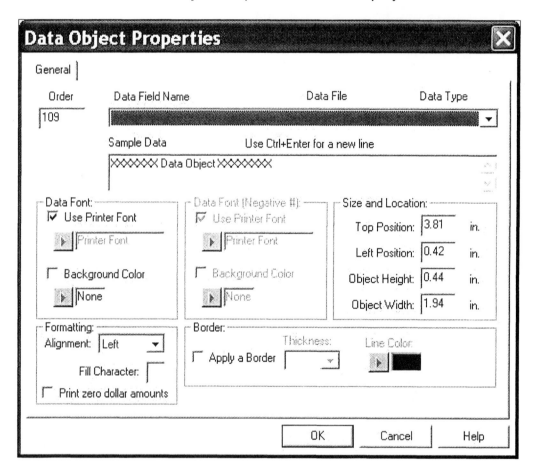 tool from the toolbar on the left side of the window.

8. Move to any blank area on the form. In the blank area, click and hold the left mouse button. Drag the mouse pointer downward and to the left or right to draw a small rectangle. The words Data Object appear in the rectangle that you drew. Release the left mouse button. The Data Object Properties window displays.

9. Click the down arrow button on the right side of the Data Field Name list field.

10. Select Company Name. Then, click OK.

11. With the mouse pointer on the object you just drew, click and hold the left mouse button. Drag the shape to a blank area at the bottom of the screen. (You may need to scroll down the screen to find a blank area.)

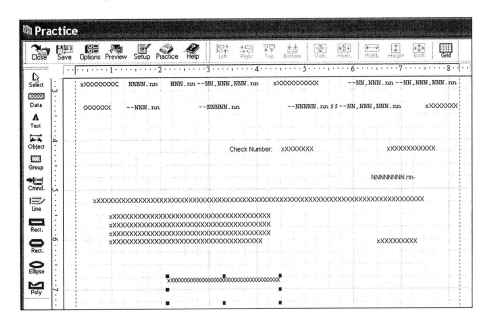

12. Click on this data object. Then, click the right mouse button. A drop-down menu displays. You can change the Font, Auto Size, Order, Properties, etc. You can also Cut, Copy, and Paste.

13. From the drop-down menu, click on the Order option. The Edit Print Order window pops up. The Company Name selection is highlighted.

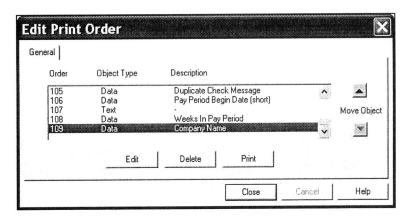

The order determines what prints first. For example, if you draw a rectangle and place a text object inside, you want to give the rectangle a prior order number to the text object. The text inside the rectangle prints first.

When objects are placed on the form, they are given an order number relative to their position on the page. If you move the object, you need to reorder it.

14. Close the Edit Print Order window.

15. Click [Close] , then [No] to the question Save changes to Practice?

16. Close the Select a Report window. You are returned to the menu bar.

EDITING A FORM DESIGN

1. From the menu bar, click on Reports, then Accounts Payable.

2. Double-click on the Disbursements Checks folder.

3. Click on AP Preprint 1 Stub, then [Design].

On the left side of the screen is a toolbar. You can select or create objects that are the building blocks of forms. The toolbar icons allow you to build an image on the screen. Here's how each icon works:

➤ Use the [Select] tool to highlight or select one or more form objects.

➤ Use the [Data] tool to insert a data field on the form (for example, a customer name or item price).

➤ Use the [Text] tool to insert text that will not change from form to form.

➤ Use the [Object] tool to insert an OLE object (object linked and embedded technology). An OLE object is any object from an application that supports Microsoft's OLE standard (for example, a Word file, a *bitmap* file, an Excel chart, etc.). A bitmap refers to the dots (pixels or picture elements) on the display screen.

➤ Use the [Group] tool to create a grid or table of data objects (for example, line items on an invoice).

➤ Use the [Cmnd.] tool to tell PCA to go to the next file or line item.

➤ Use the [Line] tool to draw line graphics that stay the same from form to form.

➤ Use the [Rect.] tool to draw a field that will print on each form.

➤ Use the [Rect.] tool to draw a rectangle with rounded corners.

➤ Use the [Ellipse] tool to draw an ellipse or circular object.

➤ Use the [Poly] tool to draw a polygon, or a figure with three or more sides.

Objects Defined:

Data Objects: A data object is either taken directly from information you have typed or derived from such information. An example of derived data is that you can select a data object called Taxable Invoice Amount when creating invoices. There is no such data field in the Sales/Invoicing Task. This object is the subtotal of all sales-taxable items. Most data objects are taken directly from a field. Derived objects are not.

Text Objects: A text object is for letters or characters you type onto the form. The same text will appear every time this form is printed.

Picture Objects: Picture Objects are any bitmapped graphic image created or captured in a program that supports OLE (object linked and embedded) Native Format. When files are linked, changes you make in the original data using the program in which it was created are reflected wherever the linked data is inserted. When data is embedded, the data becomes part of the file into which it is pasted. For example, the Paintbrush accessory in Windows supports OLE Native Format.

Group Objects: Group objects are combined data objects arranged in columns. They are treated as a single object with a single order number.

Command Objects: Command objects are used by PCA to tell the program what to do next when printing forms. For example, after one invoice prints, command objects tell the program to read the next Invoice File Record which reads in new invoice information and causes the next invoice to print.

Line and Rectangle Objects: You can draw lines or rectangles on your forms. You can draw lines in color and with shading. Lines can even contain other objects.

4. Experimenting with the toolbar, create a form. Close the window and exit PCA or continue with the next section.

FINANCIAL STATEMENT WIZARD

The Financial Statement Wizard walks you through the process of designing financial statements. Follow these steps to use the Financial Statement Wizard.

1. If necessary start Windows, then Peachtree. Open Bellwether Garden Supply.

2. From the menu bar, select Reports, then Financial Statements. Observe that on the right side of the Select a Report window, there is a Financial Statement Wizard icon.

3. Click .

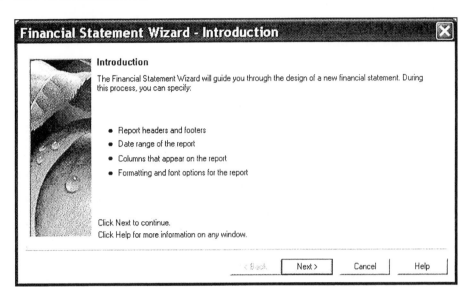

4. After reading the information on the Introduction window, click
Next >.

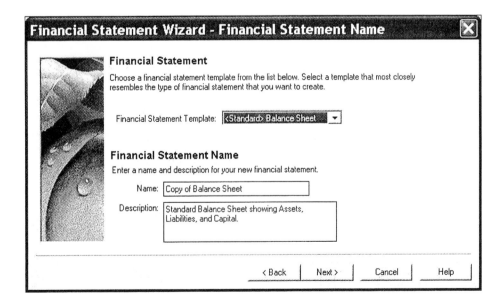

5. After reading the information on the Financial Statement window, click
   | Next > |. The Headers and Footers window appears.

6. The Headers and Footers window allows you to change information at the top and bottom of the balance sheet. For purposes of this exercise, click on the Header 1 line, then type **your name** followed by a comma and a space.

7. In the Header 3 line, click on the beginning of the line, then click
   | Insert ▼ | (down arrow next to Insert). Select Today's Date from the drop-down list. Type a comma after $(Date)$, then put a space between the $(Date)$ and $(enddate)$ comments.

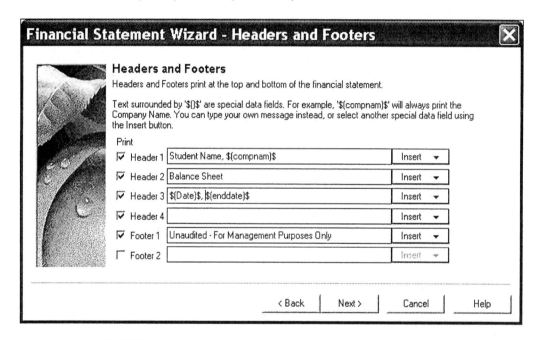

8. Click | Next > |. The Date Range and Account Masking window appears. Read the information in the Dates and General Ledger Account Masking sections. Accept the defaults on this screen, by clicking on | Next > |.

9. Accept the defaults on the Column Properties window by clicking on
   | Next > |.

10. Accept the defaults on the Column Options window by clicking on
     | Next > | .

11. Unless you want to change fonts, accept the defaults on the Fonts
     window by clicking on | Next > | .

12. Accept the defaults on the Formating window by clicking on
     | Next > | .

13. The Congratulations window appears. To display your new financial
     statement, click | Finish | .

     Compare your screen display with the balance sheet shown on the
     next page. The current date on the third line of the header will differ
     on your screen.

     Depending on which chapter of Bellwether data you are using, your
     amounts may differ, too. This balance sheet reflects data from the
     end of Chapter 6. The Exercise 6-2.ptb backup file shows this
     balance sheet.

     Compare your balance sheet to the one shown on the next page.

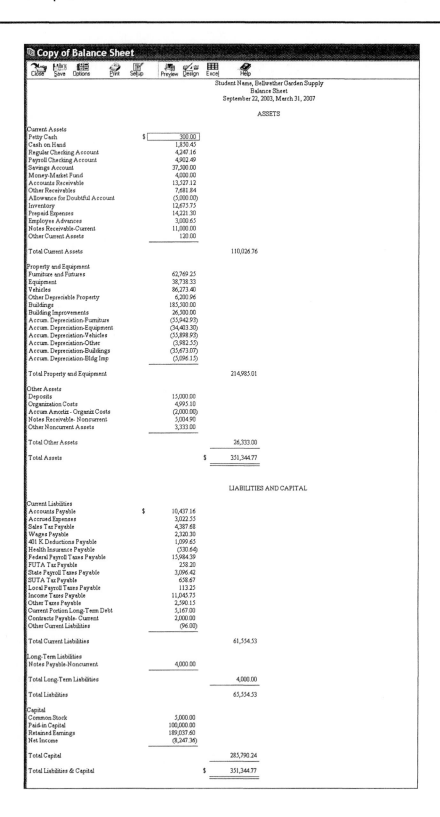

14. Close the balance sheet screen. Then close the Select a Report window. Exit Peachtree.

INTERNET ACTIVITY	
1.	From your Internet browser, go to the book's website at http://www.mhhe.com/business/accounting/yacht2004.
2.	In the Student Center list, link to Internet Activities.
3.	Link to WEB EXERCISES PART 4.
4.	Complete the ACADEMIC WEBSITE exercise. Read steps 1–3.
5.	Follow the steps shown on the book's website to complete this Internet activity.
6.	Using a word processing program write a brief summary of what you find. Include all appropriate website addresses.

SUMMARY AND REVIEW

SOFTWARE OBJECTIVES: In Chapter 15, you have learned to use the software to:

1. Select a form.

2. Select the filter, format, align, and design options.

3. Explore the data, text, command, group, picture, and line objects.

4. Design a Balance Sheet with the Financial Statement Wizard.

WEB OBJECTIVES: In Chapter 15, you did these Internet activities:

1. Used your Internet browser to go to the book's website.

2. Went to the Internet Activity link on the book's website. Then, selected WEB EXERCISES PART 4. Completed the first web exercise in Part 4— Academic Website.

3. Used a word processing program to write summaries of the websites that you visited.

GOING TO THE NET

Access Success Stories about the Peachtree Accounting Product Line at http://www.peachtree.com/pressroom/case_studies.cfm.

1.   Select an article about a company using Peachtree software.

2.   Identify two or three reasons why the use of Peachtree software is helping this company. Include the website address in your answer.

Multiple-choice questions: In the space provided, write the letter that best answers each question.

_____1.   The definition of a form in Peachtree is:

   a. Preprinted paper forms that can be displayed on your screen.
   b. A form in Peachtree is a document that you exchange with customers, vendors, or employees.
   c. Reports that are selected from the menu bar.
   d. Options selected from the menu bar.
   e. None of the above.

_____2.   The three types of documents accessed from the Reports menu are:

   a. Reports, Financial Statements, Forms.
   b. Payroll Checks, Disbursements Checks, Invoices.
   c. Sales Invoices, Purchase Invoices, Cash Receipts.
   d. Filter, Forms Designer, Report List.
   e. None of the above.

_____3. The Accounts Payable forms that can be printed or edited are:

  a. Payroll Checks, W2s, 940's and 941's, State Quarterly Tax Forms, Employee Mailing Labels.
  b. Disbursement Checks, 1099 Forms, Purchase Orders, Vendor Mailing Labels.
  c. Invoices, Statements, Customer Mailing Labels, Quotes, Collection Letters.
  d. All of the above.
  e. None of the above.

_____4. The Accounts Receivable forms that can be printed or edited are:

  a. Payroll checks, 940's and 941's.
  b. Purchase Orders, 1099 Forms, Disbursement Checks, Vendor Mailing Labels.
  c. Invoices, Statements, Customer Mailing Labels, Quotes, Collection Letters.
  d. All of the above.
  e. None of the above.

_____5. Information taken directly from what you have typed is called:

  a. Data Objects.
  b. Text Objects.
  c. Picture Objects.
  d. Group Objects.
  e. None of the above.

_____6. The Payroll forms that can be printed or edited are:

  a. Payroll Checks, 940's and 941's, State Quarterly Tax Forms, Employee Mailing Labels.
  b. Disbursement Checks, 1099 Forms, Purchase Orders, Vendor Mailing Labels.
  c. Invoices, Statements, Customer Mailing Labels, Quotes, Collection Letters.
  d. All of the above.
  e. None of the above.

_____7.   Letters or other characters that you type are called:

    a.   Data Objects.
    b.   Text Objects.
    c.   Picture Objects.
    d.   Group Objects.
    e.   None of the above.

_____8.   If a cell in the Filter Range Table has a gray background, it means:

    a.   Changes can be made to that column entry.
    b.   Gray backgrounds are not used.
    c.   Changes cannot be made to that column entry.
    d.   The Filter Range Table masks all column entries.
    e.   None of the above.

_____9.   The Format Options let you set parameters for printing forms such as:

    a.   Paper width.
    b.   Paper length.
    c.   Top and left margins.
    d.   All of the above.
    e.   None of the above.

_____10.   Objects that tell the program what to do next when printing forms are called:

    a.   Data Objects.
    b.   Text Objects.
    c.   Picture Objects.
    d.   Command Objects.
    e.   None of the above.

Exercise 15-1: Use PCA's Form Designer to experiment with different formats and type fonts.

Exercise 15-2: Print the form that you designed in Exercise 15-1.

CHAPTER 15 INDEX

Chapter

16 Import/Export

SOFTWARE OBJECTIVES: In Chapter 16, you will use the software to:

1. Export information from Peachtree to a word processing program. (In this chapter Microsoft Word 2002 and Windows XP is used.)
2. Select the customer list from Bellwether Garden Supply to export.
3. Save two files.

WEB OBJECTIVES: In Chapter 16 you will do these Internet activities:

1. Use your Internet browser to go to the book's website.
2. Go to the Internet Activity link on the book's website. Then, select WEB EXERCISES PART 4. Complete the second exercise in Part 4—Women's Business Center.
3. Use a word processing program to write summaries of the websites that you visited.

Importing translates data from other programs into a format that Peachtree can use. The flowchart below shows how importing works.

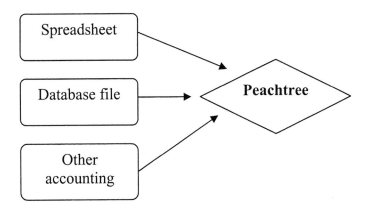

Exporting copies Peachtree data into a format that other programs can read and use. The flowchart below shows how exporting works.

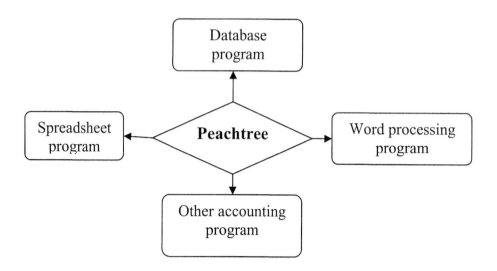

The chart below shows how Peachtree organizes data.

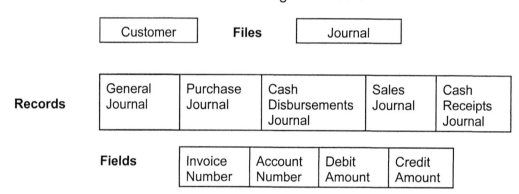

> *Files* are a group of related records; for example, customer files and journal files.

> *Records* are a group of fields that contain information on one subject; for example, the general journal, purchase journal, cash disbursements journal, sales journal, or cash receipts journal.

> *Fields* are an individual piece of data; for example, invoice numbers, account numbers, debit amount, credit amount.

Files

When you import or export files, you use templates to format the data. The templates included in Peachtree are:

➢ Accounts Receivable: Customer List, Sales Journal, and Cash Receipts Journal

➢ Accounts Payable: Vendor List, Purchase Journal, and Cash Disbursements Journal

➢ Payroll: Employee List

➢ General Ledger: Chart of Accounts and General Journal

➢ Inventory: Inventory Item List

➢ Job Reports: Jobs List

Records

When you select a file to export, you can define which information you want. For instance, when you select the Customer List, you can select which customers you want to export.

Fields

When you export in Peachtree, you export individual fields of information. You can see what fields are exported by selecting the Format folder tab. You may uncheck fields to exclude them from being exported or move fields around to change their order.

When you export, the information is exported in a comma-separated format. This means that the fields for each record are written in one line, with commas between them. You will see how this works when you export one of Peachtree's customer lists into Microsoft Word 2002.

The file created during the export process is an *ASCII* file, which contains only text characters. Each record is on a separate line. ASCII is an acronym for American Standard Code for Information Interchange. It is one of the standard formats used for representing characters on a computer. Most word processing, spreadsheet, and database programs can read ASCII files.

GETTING STARTED: EXPORTING

1. Start Windows and Peachtree in the usual way.

2. Open Bellwether Garden Supply. (In this chapter data is used from the Exercise 6-2.ptb backup file.)

3. From the menu bar, select File, then Select Import/Export.

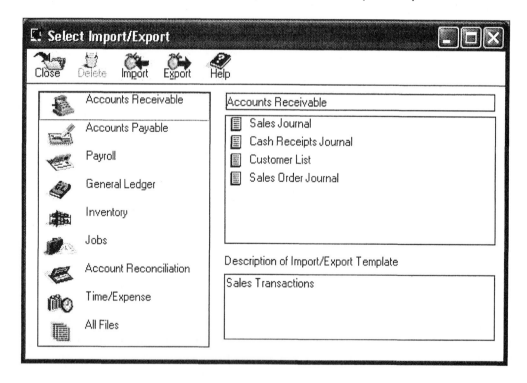

4. In the Accounts Receivable list, highlight Customer List.

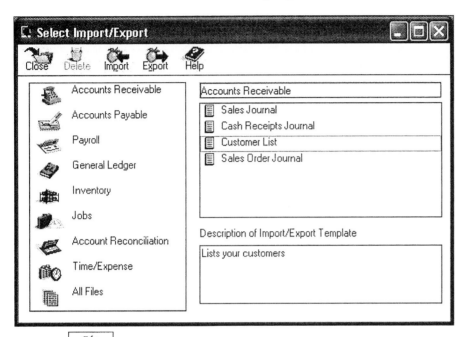

5. Click 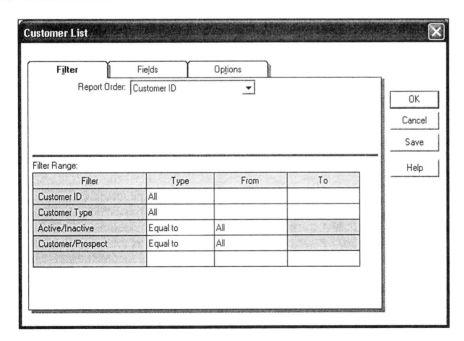.

6. Click on the Fields tab, then click .

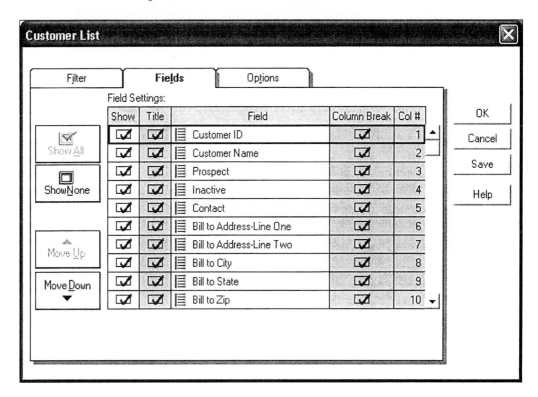

Comment
Show All places a check mark in all the fields.

7. Click on the Options tab.

Comment
The radio button next to Ask, Then Overwrite is the default.

8. Put a disk in drive A. Click on the arrow 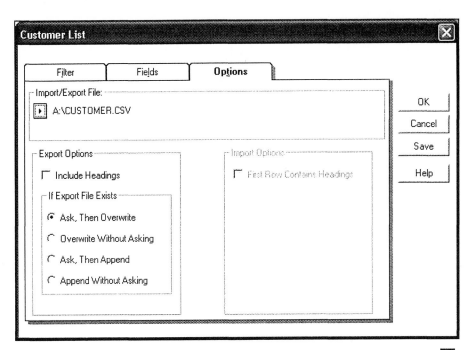 underneath Import/Export File. The File name field shows CUSTOMER; the Files of type field shows Import/Export Files (*.CSV). Type

A:\CUSTOMER in the File Name field. Then click ⌊ Open ⌋.

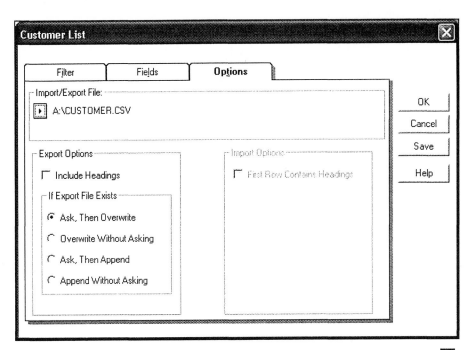

Observe that A:\CUSTOMER.CSV is shown next to the arrow 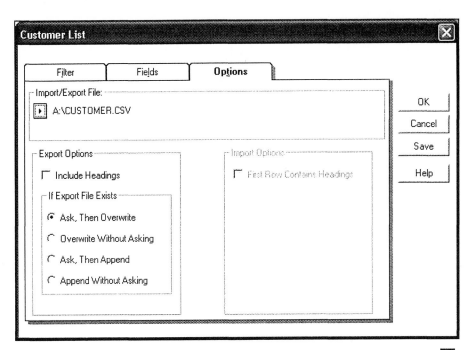 underneath Import/Export File.

9. Click ⌊ Save ⌋. The Save As window pops up. The Customer List is highlighted. Type **Customers** in the Name field.

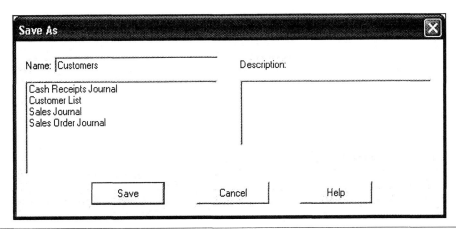

10. Click  .

11. You are returned to the Customer Options window. Make sure that the screen shows A:\CUSTOMER.CSV as the Import/Export File name. Click | OK | .

12. Close the Select Import/Export window. You are returned to the menu bar.

13. Go to the Windows desktop. Start your word processing program. In this chapter, Microsoft Word 2002 and Windows XP are used. (You may use any word processing program that supports ASCII.)

14. Follow these steps to open the Peachtree file from Microsoft Word 2002.

   a. Start Word or other word processing program. Click [icon] (the open file icon).

   b. In the Look in field, select drive A. (If you put the CUSTOMER.CSV file on the hard drive, select that location.)

   c. Highlight the CUSTOMER.CSV file, then click | Open | .

   The data on your screen was exported in a comma-separated format. The fields for each record are written in one line, with commas between them. To use this information, you would need to edit its contents, then save it.

   Compare your screen to the one shown on the next page. If you used a different word processing screen, your screen will look different but the text portion of the data is the same.

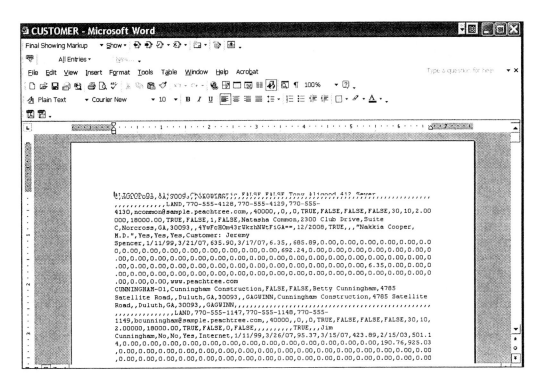

d. To keep the original ASCII file, use Word's Save <u>A</u>s command and rename the file **CUSTOMER.lst**. When you save, the file will convert into a text document file from its original ASCII format.

e. Exit your word processing program.

IMPORTING

Importing data from another accounting, database, or spreadsheet program into Peachtree works similarly to exporting. Any information that is entered in Peachtree during setup and maintenance can be imported.

When you use the Select Import/Export command, you can:

➢ Select specific fields to import from other programs, such as Quicken.

➢ Create templates for importing. When you create a template, you can exclude information from the imported files or change the order of the imported fields.

➢ You can import all the files for a fiscal year.

Importing is an important tool, especially if you are switching from another accounting program to Peachtree. For example, if you have a Chart of Accounts set up in another accounting program, you can import it into Peachtree.

In this chapter you saw the steps for exporting data from Peachtree to Microsoft Word 2002. Since importing works similarly to exporting, you may want to try to import data from another accounting program into Peachtree. Remember to select the Import icon on the Select Import/Export window to start the import process.

	INTERNET ACTIVITY
1.	From your Internet browser, go to the book's website at http://www.mhhe.com/yacht2004.
2.	In the Student Center list, link to Internet Activities.
3.	Link to WEB EXERCISES PART 4.
4.	Complete the WOMEN'S BUSINESS CENTER exercise. Read steps 1 – 4.
5.	Follow the steps shown on the book's website to complete this Internet activity.
6.	Using a word processing program write a brief summary of what you find. Include all appropriate website addresses.

SUMMARY AND REVIEW

SOFTWARE OBJECTIVES: In Chapter 16, you have used the software to:

1. Export information from Peachtree to a word processing program. (In this chapter Microsoft Word 2002 and Windows XP is used.)

2. Select the customer list from Bellwether Garden Supply to export.

3. Save two files.

WEB OBJECTIVES: In Chapter 16, you did these Internet activities:

1. Used your Internet browser to go to the book's website.

2. Went to the Internet Activity link on the book's website. Then, selected WEB EXERCISES PART 4. Completed the second exercise in Part 4—Women's Business Center.

3. Used a word processing program to write summaries of the websites that you visited.

GOING TO THE NET

Access Peachtree's 25th anniversary article at http://www.peachtree.com/pressroom/pr_25th_anniversary.cfm.

Answer the following questions.

1. Why is Peachtree Software celebrating more than 25 years in business?
2. Where was Peachtree Software first sold?
3. What milestone occurred in 1980?
4. What is Peachtree's Internet accounting or Application Service Provider software called?

Multiple-Choice Questions: In the space provided, write the letter that best answers each question.

_____1. A group of related records is called a/an:

    a. File.
    b. Record.
    c. Field.
    d. Balance Sheet.
    e. All of the above.

_____2.   A group of fields that contains information on one subject is
called a/an:

a. File.
b. Record.
c. Field.
d. Income statement.
e. All of the above.

_____3.   An individual piece of data such as an account number or
customer's name is called a/an:

a. File.
b. Record.
c. Field.
d. Income statement.
e. All of the above.

_____4.   Exporting copies Peachtree data into a format that the
following programs can read and use:

a. Spreadsheet programs.
b. Database programs.
c. Accounting programs.
d. Word processing programs.
e. All of the above

_____5.   Importing allows you to translate data from the following types
of programs:

a. Spreadsheet programs.
b. Database programs.
c. Accounting programs.
d. None of the above.
e. All of the above.

_____6. Information that appears on Peachtree's reports can be:

    a. Imported.
    b. Exported.
    c. Formatted into an ANSI file.
    d. A macro.
    e. None of the above

_____7. The name of the company from which you exported data is:

    a. Carol's Jewelry Store.
    b. Woods Manufacturing, Inc.
    c. Copper Bicycles.
    d. Taylor Rinaldi, Graphic Artist.
    e. None of the above.

_____8. When you import or export files, you use one of the following to format the data:

    a. Template.
    b. File.
    c. Field.
    d. Record.
    e. None of the above.

_____9. The type of file that is exported into a word processing program is called a/an:

    a. DOS text file.
    b. ANSI file.
    c. ASCII file.
    d. WordStar file.
    e. None of the above.

_____10. The data on your screen was exported in the following format:

    a. Comma separated.
    b. Line separated.
    c. Field separated.
    d. File separated.
    e. None of the above.

Exercise 16-1: Follow the instructions below to complete Exercise 16-1.

1. Select one of the companies that have a vendor list.

2. Export the vendor list to a word processing program.

3. Open the vendor list.

Exercise 16-2: Follow the instructions below to complete Exercise 16-2.

1. Select one of the companies that have a customer list.

2. Export the customer list to a word processing program.

3. Open the customer list.

CHAPTER 16 INDEX

Chapter 17

Using Peachtree Complete Accounting 2004 with Microsoft Excel and Word

SOFTWARE OBJECTIVES: In Chapter 17, you will use the software to:

1. Copy Peachtree report data to an Excel spreadsheet.
2. Copy Peachtree report data to Word.
3. Save Microsoft Excel and Word files.

WEB OBJECTIVES: In Chapter 17 you will do these Internet activities:

1. Use your Internet browser to go to the book's website.
2. Go to the Internet Activity link on the book's website. Then, select WEB EXERCISES PART 4. Complete the third exercise in Part 4– Web Development.
3. Use a word processing program to write summaries of the websites that you visited.

If you have Microsoft Office 97 or higher, you can use PCA 2004 data in numerous ways. For example, you can add data to an Excel spreadsheet. Or, you can add Peachtree financial statements to a Microsoft Word document that can be used for year-end reports.

This chapter describes several procedures for adding Peachtree data to Microsoft Office applications. In this chapter, you will see how to insert Peachtree report data into a Microsoft Excel spreadsheet or a Word document. Then you can view or format that data using the features of Excel or Word.

GETTING STARTED

If you have Microsoft Excel 97 (or higher) installed on your computer, you can copy a PCA report or financial statement to an Excel spreadsheet.

1. Start Windows.

2. Start PCA, then open the sample company, Bellwether Garden Supply.

COPYING PEACHTREE REPORT DATA TO MICROSOFT EXCEL

Bellwether Garden Supply's menu bar should be displayed on your screen. Follow these steps to copy Bellwether's balance sheet and income statement data to Excel.

1. Restore data from the end of Chapter 6. (On page 203, the backup name used was Exercise 6-2.ptb.)

> **Comment**
>
> If you no longer have your back up disk from Exercise 6-2, use starting data for Bellwether Garden Supply. If you use Bellwether's starting data, your screen illustrations will differ from those shown in this chapter. If necessary, refer to Appendix A, Installing Starting Data for the Sample Company, pages 678 and 679.

2. If necessary, close the Peachtree Today window.

Balance Sheet

1. From the menu bar, select Reports, Financial Statements. Highlight <Standard> Balance Sheet.

2. Click . The <Standard> Balance Sheet window appears, with the Options tab selected. Click OK.

> **Comment**
>
> Microsoft Office 2002 and Windows XP are used for the illustrations in this chapter. If you are using Microsoft Office 97 or other version of MS Office you may notice some differences with the screen displays shown in Chapter 17.

3. The Copy Report to Excel window pops up.

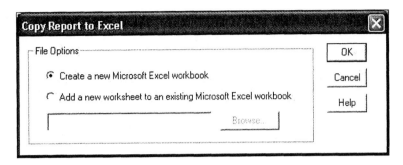

4. Accept the default for Create a new Microsoft Excel workbook by clicking on [OK]. Peachtree will start the Excel program and copy Bellwether's balance sheet into a blank worksheet.[1]

1		
2	ASSETS	
3		
4	Current Assets	
5	Petty Cash	300.00
6	Cash on Hand	1,850.45
7	Regular Checking Account	4,247.16
8	Payroll Checking Account	4,902.49
9	Savings Account	37,500.00
10	Money-Market Fund	4,000.00
11	Accounts Receivable	13,527.12
12	Other Receivables	7,681.84
13	Allowance for Doubtful Account	(5,000.00)
14	Inventory	12,675.75
15	Prepaid Expenses	14,221.30
16	Employee Advances	3,000.65
17	Notes Receivable-Current	11,000.00
18	Other Current Assets	120.00
19		
20	Total Current Assets	110,026.76
21		
22	Property and Equipment	
23	Furniture and Fixtures	62,769.25
24	Equipment	38,738.33
25	Vehicles	86,273.40
26	Other Depreciable Property	6,200.96
27	Buildings	185,500.00
28	Building Improvements	26,500.00
29	Accum. Depreciation-Furniture	(55,942.93)
30	Accum. Depreciation-Equipment	(34,403.30)
31	Accum. Depreciation-Vehicles	(55,898.93)
32	Accum. Depreciation-Other	(3,982.55)
33	Accum. Depreciation-Buildings	(35,673.07)
34	Accum. Depreciation-Bldg Imp	(5,096.15)
35		
36	Total Property and Equipment	214,985.01

[1]If you are using Bellwether's starting data, your account balances will differ.

5. To see the rest of the balance sheet, scroll down the report.

6. To see the header for the report, from Excel's menu bar, click on File, Print Preview. Observe that Bellwether's header information is included. To see page 2 of the balance sheet, click [Next]. Click [Next] to see page 3 of the balance sheet. Close the print preview window.

   Now that Bellwether's balance sheet is in Excel format, you can use Excel's features to make changes to this report.

7. From Excel's menu bar, click on File, Save As.

8. Put your data disk in drive A. You can use the same disk that you used to save Chapter 16 data. In the Save in field, select drive A.

9. The File name field displays Book1. The Save as type field displays Microsoft Excel Workbook. Highlight the file name. Type **balance sheet** in the File name field.

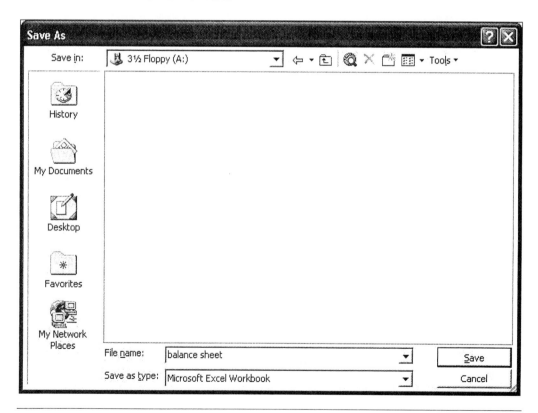

10. Click 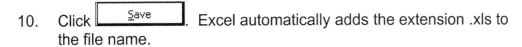 . Excel automatically adds the extension .xls to
     the file name.

11. Minimize the Excel window. Bellwether's Select a Report window
     appears. (*Hint: You can also click on Peachtree from the task bar.*)

Income Statement

1. From the Select a Report window, highlight <Standard> Income
    Stmnt.

2. Click Excel. When the <Standard> Income Stmnt window
    appears, uncheck the Print Page Numbers and Show Zero Amounts
    boxes. Then click OK .

3. At the Copy Report to Excel window, you have *two* choices. Create
    a new Microsoft Excel workbook *or* Add a new worksheet to an
    existing Microsoft Excel workbook. Select Add a new worksheet.

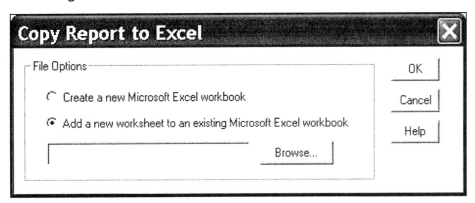

4. Click Browse... and go to drive A (or other location where you saved
    the balance sheet.xls file). Click on the balance sheet file. Make sure
    that the File name field shows balance sheet. Then, click Open .
    The Browse field shows A:\balance sheet.xls (or other location). Click
    OK .

5. If necessary, from the task bar click on ![Microsoft Excel - ...] . The
   Excel spreadsheet for Bellwether's income statement appears.[2]
   Observe that you have two sheet tabs (at the bottom of the Excel
   worksheet). The active sheet, **Income Stmnt,** is shown.

	A	B	C	D	E
1		Current Month		Year to Date	
2	Revenues				
3	Sales	5,175.00	7.73	8,250.95	10.05
4	Sales - Aviary	5,523.13	8.25	6,622.91	8.07
5	Sales - Books	149.75	0.22	3,654.60	4.45
6	Sales - Equipment	2,969.66	4.43	7,731.28	9.42
7	Sales - Food/Fert	367.60	0.55	697.24	0.85
8	Sales - Furniture	30,000.00	44.79	30,000.00	36.55
9	Sales - Hand Tools	199.92	0.30	801.64	0.98
10	Sales - Landscape Services	2,059.53	3.07	2,939.34	3.58
11	Sales - Miscellaneous	18,199.98	27.17	18,199.98	22.17
12	Sales - Nursery	1,182.48	1.77	1,420.34	1.73
13	Sales - Pots	510.58	0.76	580.53	0.71
14	Sales - Seeds	223.17	0.33	766.24	0.93
15	Sales - Soil	351.48	0.52	365.46	0.45
16	Other Income	100.00	0.15	100.00	0.12
17	Sales Discounts	(28.30)	(0.04)	(42.02)	(0.05)
18					
19	Total Revenues	66,983.98	100.00	82,088.49	100.00
20					
21					
22	Cost of Sales				
23	Product Cost	394.50	0.59	394.50	0.48
24	Product Cost - Aviary	1,573.10	2.35	2,012.00	2.45
25	Product Cost - Books	14.27	0.02	1,415.37	1.72
26	Product Cost - Equipment	1,350.45	2.02	3,413.65	4.16
27	Product Cost - Food/Fert	146.00	0.22	278.40	0.34
28	Product Cost - Hand Tools	76.40	0.11	316.45	0.39
29	Product Cost - Pots	209.35	0.31	237.10	0.29
30	Product Cost - Seeds	89.15	0.13	305.30	0.37
31	Product Cost - Soil	148.92	0.22	156.42	0.19
32	Materials Cost	1,547.45	2.31	1,547.45	1.89
33	Materials Cost - Nursery	198.90	0.30	270.30	0.33
34	Subcontractors - Landscaping	335.50	0.50	335.50	0.41
35					
36	Total Cost of Sales	6,083.99	9.08	10,682.44	13.01

6. Scroll down the screen to see the rest of the income statement. Or,
   click on File, Print Preview to see it.

---

[2]If you are using Bellwether's starting data, your account balances will differ.

7. Save the income statement to drive A. Use **balance sheet & income statement** as the file name.

8. Click on File, Exit to exit Excel.

9. Close the Select a Report window, then exit Peachtree.

COPYING PEACHTREE REPORT DATA TO MICROSOFT WORD

A displayed PCA report or financial statement can be copied to the Windows clipboard. Then you can paste that data into other applications, such as Microsoft Word or another word processing program. The steps that follow show you how to copy and paste a report using Microsoft Word 97 or higher.

1. Start Windows.

2. Start PCA, then open the sample company, Bellwether Garden Supply.

3. If necessary restore data from the end of Chapter 6. Use the Exercise 6-2.ptb file. If you do not have that backup, use Bellwether's starting data. Refer to Appendix A, Installing Starting Data for the Sample Companies, pages 678 and 679.

4. If necessary, close the Peachtree Today window.

5. From Bellwether's menu bar, select Reports, Financial Statements, scroll down the list, then select <Standard> Retained Earnings.

6. Click Preview . At the <Standard> Retained Earnings window, uncheck the Print Page Numbers and Show Zero Amounts boxes. Click OK . The Statement of Retained Earnings displays on your screen.

7. From the menu bar, click on Edit, Copy.

8. Start Microsoft Word or other word processing program. From Word's menu bar, click on Edit, Paste. Bellwether's statement of retained earnings appears on your word processor's screen. You will need to format the statement in order for it to look like the one below.[3]

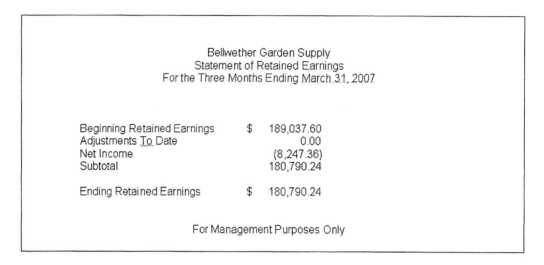

Bellwether Garden Supply
Statement of Retained Earnings
For the Three Months Ending March 31, 2007

Beginning Retained Earnings	$	189,037.60
Adjustments To Date		0.00
Net Income		(8,247.36)
Subtotal		180,790.24
Ending Retained Earnings	$	180,790.24

For Management Purposes Only

9. Click on File, Save As. In the Save in field, select drive A (or other location). Accept the file name Bellwether Garden Supply. Observe that the File as type field shows Word Document.

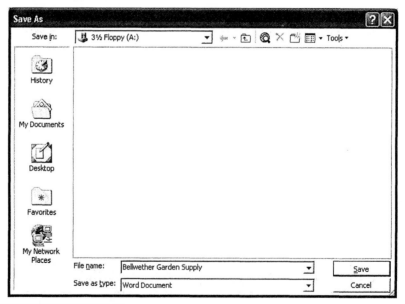

[3]These account balances reflect data from the Exercise 6-2.ptb backup file. If you are using a different back up file, your account balances will differ.

10. Click .

11. Exit Word or other word processing program.

12. Exit PCA.

INTERNET ACTIVITY	
1.	From your Internet browser, go to the book's website at http://www.mhhe.com/yacht2004.
2.	In the Student Center list, link to Internet Activities.
3.	Link to WEB EXERCISES PART 4.
4.	Complete the WEB DEVELOPMENT exercise. Read steps 1 and 2.
5.	Follow the steps shown on the book's website to complete this Internet activity.
6.	Using a word processing program write a brief summary of what you find. Include all appropriate website addresses.

SUMMARY AND REVIEW

SOFTWARE OBJECTIVES: In Chapter 17, you have used the software to:

1. Copy Peachtree report data to an Excel spreadsheet.

2. Copy Peachtree report data to Word.

3. Save Microsoft Excel and Word files.

WEB OBJECTIVES: In Chapter 17, you did these Internet activities:

1. Used your Internet browser to go to the book's website at http://www.mhhe.com/yacht2004.

2. Go to the Internet Activity link on the book's website. Then, select WEB EXERCISES PART 4. Complete the third exercise in Part 4— Web Development.

3. Used a word processing program to write summaries of the websites that you visited.

GOING TO THE NET

Access the Microsoft Office website at http://office.microsoft.com. To answer the questions below, link to the appropriate Microsoft Office program.

1. What is the website address for Word?
2. After linking to the Word website, briefly describe what kind of information can be obtained. If you link to other websites, include the appropriate address(es) in your answer.
3. What is the website address for Excel?
4. After linking to the Excel website, briefly describe what kind of information can be obtained. If you link to other websites, include the appropriate address(es) in your answer.

Short-Answer Questions: Write an answer to each question in the space provided.

1. Explain what Peachtree feature you use to export report data to an Excel spreadsheet.

_____

_____

2. What data do you use if you do not have the recommended back up file?

_____

_____

3. In Chapter 17, do you create a new Microsoft Excel workbook or add a new worksheet to an existing Microsoft Excel workbook?

_____

4. In Chapter 17, it is recommended that you use data from what Bellwether back up file?

_____

_____

5. Why do you use Excel's Print Preview feature?

_____

_____

6. What extension does Word automatically add to saved files?

_____

_____

7. When you save the Peachtree data in Microsoft Word, what file name is automatically given to the report?

_____

_____

8. What extension does Excel automatically add to saved spreadsheets?

_____

_____

_____

9. After copying the Peachtree data to Microsoft Word, do you need to format the document?

_____

_____

_____

10. In Chapter 17, what Peachtree report do you use with Microsoft Word?

_____

_____

_____

Exercise 17-1: Copy Peachtree data to Microsoft Excel. Experiment with different PCA reports.

Exercise 17-2: Copy Peachtree data to Microsoft Word. Experiment with different PCA reports.

CHAPTER 17 INDEX

Chapter

18 Dynamic Data Exchange

DOWNLOADING FILES FROM THE INTERNET TO PEACHTREE

In order to complete Chapter 18, ask your instructor if the following files have been copied to Peachtree's program path.

1. DDE-BalSheet.xls
2. DDE-Graph.xlm
3. DDE-Requests.xls
4. DDE-TrialBal-EmpList.xls

These files are included on Peachtree's website. The steps that follow explain how to download the files from the Internet to Peachtree's program path. (*Remember you do* not *have to download these files if your instructor has already done so.*)

Comment

If you do *not* know where Peachtree is installed on your hard drive, go to your desktop. Right-click on Peachtree's icon, then left-click on Properties. If necessary, select the Shortcut tab. The Target field shows where Peachtree is installed; for example, c:\Program Files\Peachtree\peachw.exe The subdirectory identified as \peachw.exe is the executable file for the program.

---

1. Log on to the Internet.

2. Start Peachtree; open Bellwether Garden Supply.

3. From the menu bar, select, Help; Contents and Index. Make sure the Index tab is selected.

4. Type **DDE** in the Type in keyword to find field. Select | Display |. Peachtree and Dynamic Data Exchange are highlighted. Compare your screen to the one shown on the next page.

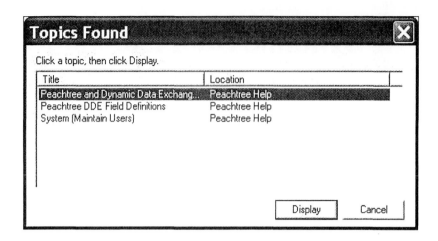

5.   Click [Display]. Read the information on the Peachtree and Dynamic Data Exchange (DDE) help screen.

6.   If necessary, scroll down to the link to www.peachtree.com/support.dde. Click on this link to go to the Internet site.

7.   The Download Peachtree DDE Examples website appears.

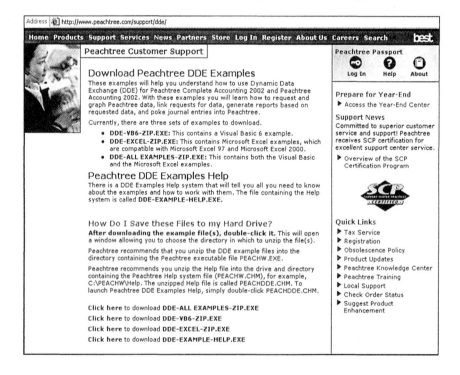

8. Read the information on this screen. You are going to unzip the DDE-EXCEL-ZIP.EXE file. To do that select
    ┃ **Click here** to download **DDE-EXCEL-ZIP.EXE** ┃ .

9. The File Download window appears.

10. Click ┃ Open ┃ .

11. When the WinZip Self-Extractor – DDE-EXCEL window appears, click ┃ Browse... ┃ . Go to C:\Program Files\Peachtree (or the location where Peachtree is installed) to unzip to file. Then, click ┃ OK ┃ .

12. You are returned to the WinZip Self-Extractor – DDE-EXCEL window. Observe that the Unzip to folder field shows Peachtree's program path. Click ┃ Unzip ┃ .

13. A screen displays that says four files were unzipped. Click ┃ OK ┃ .

14. Close the WinZip Self-Extractor window.

15. Close your Internet browser. To make sure these files were unzipped and copied to C:\Program Files\Peachtree go to Windows Explorer and open the C:\Program Files\Peachtree folder. The four DDE files are shown.

DDE-BalSheet	18 KB	Microsoft Excel Worksheet	6/18/2001	12:12 PM
DDE-Graph	116 KB	Microsoft Excel 4.0 Macro	6/18/2001	12:14 PM
DDE-Request	134 KB	Microsoft Excel Worksheet	6/18/2001	12:16 PM
DDE-TrialBal-EmpList	25 KB	Microsoft Excel Worksheet	6/18/2001	12:13 PM

16. Close Windows Explorer.

SOFTWARE OBJECTIVES: In Chapter 18, you will use the software to:

1. Work with two Windows programs at the same time: Peachtree Complete Accounting for Windows and Microsoft Excel for Windows.
2. Use macros to create spreadsheets from Bellwether Garden Supply data.
3. Display and save bar graphs.
4. Save Excel files.

WEB OBJECTIVES: In Chapter 18, you will do these Internet activities:

1. Use your Internet browser to go to Peachtree's website.
2. Unzip the DDE-EXCEL-ZIP.EXE files to Peachtree's program path.[1]
3. Go to the Internet Activity link on the book's website. Then, select WEB EXERCISES PART 4. Continue to explore the third exercise in Part 4–Web Development.
4. Use a word processing program to write summaries of the websites that you visited.

What is **Dynamic Data Exchange**? DDE is a method that allows Windows programs to share data. DDE is like an automatic export/import.

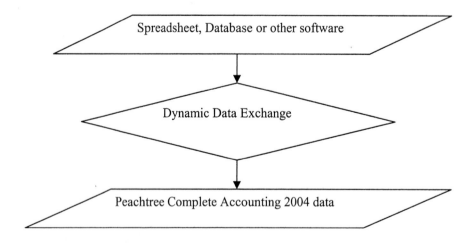

---

[1]If your instructor has already copied these files, you do not need to copy them again.

When using DDE, one application provides some form of data (either text or graphics) to another application. The application that is the source of the data is called the *server*; the application that is receiving the data is called the *client*. Peachtree uses DDE as a client.

Using DDE, you could enter a formula into an Excel spreadsheet cell that would refer to a field of data in PCA . Whenever you used that spreadsheet in the future, that cell would be updated with the current data from PCA. Built into Peachtree software is the ability to respond to requests for information.

In order to learn about DDE you are going to use income statement data from Bellwether Garden Supply

GETTING STARTED

You are going to use an Excel *macro* named DDE-Graph.xlm. The extension .xlm identifies an Excel macro file. A macro is a series of commands and keystrokes that automate frequently performed tasks. For example, the DDE-Graph.xlm macro lets you select a Peachtree company, open the company, then read activity and budget information for the current year. The DDE-Graph.xlm macro can only read information from General Ledger accounts that are identified as Income, Cost of Sales, and Expense account types, i.e., the Income Statement accounts.

Whenever you use DDE, you must start PCA first, open the appropriate company, then the other software. Follow these steps to see how DDE works with PCA.

1. The menu bar for Bellwether Garden Supply should be displayed on your screen. If necessary, click on the Peachtree icon

   on your taskbar to maximize Peachtree.

2. Restore the Exercise 6-2 file. This back up was made on page 203.

> **Comment**
>
> If you no longer have your back up disk from Exercise 6-2, use starting data for Bellwether Garden Supply. If you use Bellwether's starting data, your screen illustrations will differ from those shown in this chapter. If necessary, refer to Appendix A, Installing Starting Data for the Sample Companies, pages 678 and 679.

3. Minimize Peachtree to return to the desktop.

4. Start Microsoft Excel. Microsoft Excel's spreadsheet window displays.

> **Comment**
>
> The version of Excel used in this chapter is Microsoft Excel 2002 with Windows XP. If you do not have Excel 2002, you may use Excel 97 or higher. You may need to modify the directions slightly to accommodate the version of Excel that you are using.

5. From Excel's menu bar, click on File, then Open.

6. In the Look in field, select drive C. (This might be on a different drive if you are using a network or have more than one hard drive.)

7. Double-click on Peachtree's folder (program path) to open it; for example the C:\Program Files\Peachtree folder. (If PCA 2004 is installed in a different folder, open that one.)

8. Highlight the DDE-Graph file.

9. Click Open .

Comment

In some versions of Excel, a Microsoft Excel window pops up that says that you are opening a workbook that contains macros. Click Enable Macros.

If an Excel window pops up that says you have to set the security settings, follow these steps:
   a. Click OK.
   b. From the menu bar, click on Tools, then Macro. Then, select Security.
   c. In the Security dialog box, click Medium. Click OK.
   d. Open the DDE-Graph file from the C:\peachw folder. If necessary, click on Enable Macros.

---

10. A window displays with two buttons: Open Company and Graphs.

11. Read the information on this screen. Click on Open Company. If Peachtree opens, minimize it.

12. When the Select Company window displays, Bellwether Garden Supply should be highlighted.

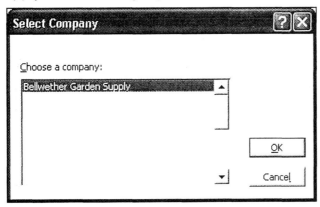

13. Click OK.

The macro is reading activity and budget data for Bellwether's income and expense accounts. When the macro is finished reading and writing records and formatting the data sheet, you are returned to the screen that shows Open Company and Graphs. (Remember, your instructor must provide you with the macro files to complete the activities in Chapter 18.)

---

14. To view the spreadsheet that was just created, follow these steps:

    a. From the menu bar, select <u>W</u>indow.

    b. Click on DATASHT.

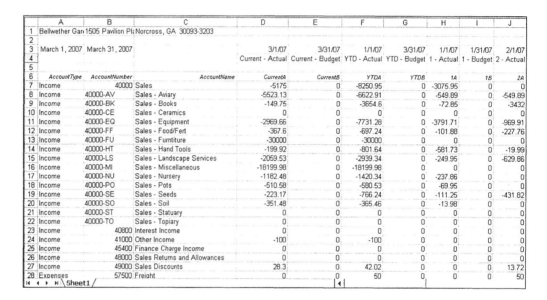

	A	B	C	D	E	F	G	H	I	J
1	Bellwether Gar	1505 Pavilion Pl	Norcross, GA 30093-3203							
2										
3	March 1, 2007	March 31, 2007		3/1/07	3/31/07	1/1/07	3/31/07	1/1/07	1/31/07	2/1/07
4				Current - Actual	Current - Budget	YTD - Actual	YTD - Budget	1 - Actual	1 - Budget	2 - Actual
5										
6	*AccountType*	*AccountNumber*	*AccountName*	*CurrentA*	*CurrentB*	*YTDA*	*YTDB*	*1A*	*1B*	*2A*
7	Income	40000	Sales	-5175	0	-8250.95	0	-3075.95	0	0
8	Income	40000-AV	Sales - Aviary	-5523.13	0	-6622.91	0	-549.89	0	-549.89
9	Income	40000-BK	Sales - Books	-149.75	0	-3654.6	0	-72.85	0	-3432
10	Income	40000-CE	Sales - Ceramics	0	0	0	0	0	0	0
11	Income	40000-EQ	Sales - Equipment	-2969.66	0	-7731.28	0	-3791.71	0	-969.91
12	Income	40000-FF	Sales - Food/Fert	-367.6	0	-697.24	0	-101.88	0	-227.76
13	Income	40000-FU	Sales - Furntiture	-30000	0	-30000	0	0	0	0
14	Income	40000-HT	Sales - Hand Tools	-199.92	0	-801.64	0	-581.73	0	-19.99
15	Income	40000-LS	Sales - Landscape Services	-2059.53	0	-2939.34	0	-249.95	0	-629.86
16	Income	40000-MI	Sales - Miscellaneous	-18199.98	0	-18199.98	0	0	0	0
17	Income	40000-NU	Sales - Nursery	-1182.48	0	-1420.34	0	-237.86	0	0
18	Income	40000-PO	Sales - Pots	-510.58	0	-580.53	0	-69.95	0	0
19	Income	40000-SE	Sales - Seeds	-223.17	0	-766.24	0	-111.25	0	-431.82
20	Income	40000-SO	Sales - Soil	-351.48	0	-365.46	0	-13.98	0	0
21	Income	40000-ST	Sales - Statuary	0	0	0	0	0	0	0
22	Income	40000-TO	Sales - Topiary	0	0	0	0	0	0	0
23	Income	40800	Interest Income	0	0	0	0	0	0	0
24	Income	41000	Other Income	-100	0	-100	0	0	0	0
25	Income	45400	Finance Charge Income	0	0	0	0	0	0	0
26	Income	48000	Sales Returns and Allowances	0	0	0	0	0	0	0
27	Income	49000	Sales Discounts	28.3	0	42.02	0	0	0	13.72
28	Expenses	57500	Freight	0	0	50	0	0	0	50

I ◄ ► H \ Sheet1 /

Comment

This screen represents Bellwether's data from Exercise 6-2. If you are using different data from the sample company, your screen illustration will differ. Continue with step 15.

---

15. To create a graph based on the DATASHT spreadsheet, follow these steps:

    a. From Excel's menu bar, click on <u>W</u>indow, then DDE-Graph.

    b. Click on the Graphs button. The Peachtree Accounting for Windows – Graphs window appears. The Select <u>G</u>raph list includes five types of graphs.

    c. Accept the defaults for the graph, Income vs. Expenses (Bar Chart) and the <u>Y</u>ear to Date range.

    d. Click on [Run].

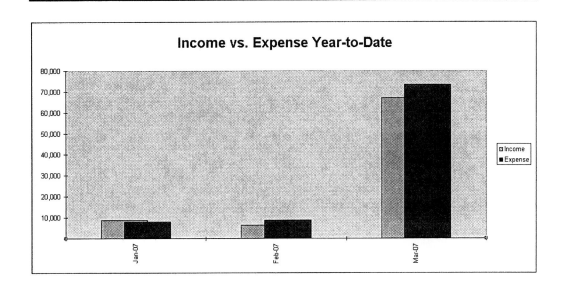

16. To display another type of Bar Chart, follow these steps:

    a. Click on <u>W</u>indow, then DDE-Graph.

    b. Click on the Graphs button.

    c. In the Select <u>G</u>raph list, highlight Income by Account (Pie Chart).

    d. Accept the <u>Y</u>ear to Date default.

    e. Click ⟦ Run ⟧. Compare your screen to the one shown on the next page.

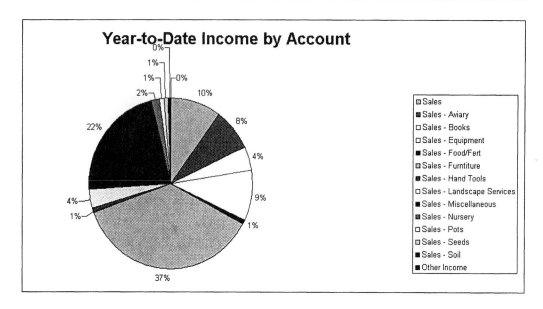

On your screen the income accounts are shown in color.

17. To save these bar charts, put a disk in drive A; then click on File, then Save As.

18. In the Save in field, select drive A.

19. In the File name field, type **bgspie2** and click [Save].

20. On the menu bar, click on Window, select Chart1, then File, Save As. Make sure that drive A is selected in the Save in field. Type **bgsbar1** as the filename. Click [Save].

Follow these steps to do another DDE with Peachtree and Excel.

1. Click on File, then Open.

2. In the Look in field, select drive C or the appropriate drive.

3. Double-click on the folder (program path) for Peachtree: C:\Program Files\Peachtree. (You may have installed Peachtree in a different folder. Make sure you open Peachtree's program path or folder.)

4.   Highlight the DDE-BalSheet. Click [Open ▾].

5.   A window pops up that says This workbook contains links to other data sources. Click [Update].

6.   Scroll down this screen to see the Payroll Summary Information.

Payroll Summary Information	
Total Gross	49,643.54
Total FICA	-3,077.93
Total FWT	-4,915.56
Total State WT	-2,111.09
Total Net	39,538.96

To see how DDE works when using remote links, follow these steps:

1. Click on View. A check mark should be placed next to Formula Bar.

2. Click on cell D10 to see the formula for Total Assets. The Formula for D10 is shown below Excel's menu bar. The formula, =SUM(D6:D9) was used to compute the amount of Total Assets: $351,344.77.[2] You can go to any cell where the data is computed and display the formula.

3. To save this spreadsheet, select File, then Save As. Select drive A. Type the file name **balsht.bgs** and click [Save].

4. To exit Excel, click on File, Exit.

5. Return to PCA, then exit.

---

[2]If you restored Exercise 6-2, the amount for Total Assets is $351,344.77. If you are using beginning data for Bellwether, the amount of Total Assets is $354,718.91.

INTERNET ACTIVITY	
1.	From your Internet browser, go to the book's website at http://www.mhhe.com/yacht2004.
2.	In the Student Center list, link to Internet Activities.
3.	Link to WEB EXERCISES PART 4.
4.	Since this exercise was started in Chapter 17, continue to explore the WEB DEVELOPMENT links.
5.	Using a word processing program write a brief summary of what you find. Include all appropriate website addresses

SUMMARY AND REVIEW

SOFTWARE OBJECTIVES: In Chapter 18, you have used the software to:

1. Work with two Windows programs at the same time: Peachtree Complete Accounting for Windows and Microsoft Excel for Windows.

2. Use macros to create spreadsheets from Bellwether Garden Supply data.

3. Display and save bar graphs.

4. Save Excel files.

WEB OBJECTIVES: In Chapter 18, you did these Internet activities:

1. Use your Internet browser to go to Peachtree's website.

2. Unzip the DDE-EXCEL-ZIP.EXE files to Peachtree's program path.[3]

3. Go to the Internet Activity link on the book's website. Then, select WEB EXERCISES PART 4. Continue to explore the third exercise in Part 4—Web Development.

---

[3]If your instructor has already copied these files, you do not need to copy them again.

4. Use a word processing program to write summaries of the websites that you visited.

GOING TO THE NET

Access the MSDN Online Library website at http://msdn.microsoft.com/library/. Answer the following questions.

1. What is the MSDN library?
2. Type **What is DDE?** in the Search for field. Then, select GO. Define term Dynamic Data Exchange.

True/Make True questions: Write the word True in the space provided if the statement is true. If the statement is not true, write the correct answer.

1. Using Dynamic Data Exchange, you can enter a formula into an Excel spreadsheet cell that would refer to a field of data in PCA.

_____

_____

2. Macros are unnecessary for automating frequently performed tasks.

_____

_____

3. Dynamic Data Exchange is a method that allows Windows programs to share data.

_____

_____

4. The only type of data that the graph95.xlm or graph97.xlm macro reads is Balance Sheet data in the form of assets, liabilities, and capital.

_____

_____

5. According to the Actual vs. Budget (Income) Year-to-Date bar chart, budgeted expenditures exceeded actual expenditures for the month of March 2004.

_____

_____

6. The PCA company used in this chapter is Copper Bicycles.

_____

_____

7. According to the Income vs. Expense Year-to-Date bar chart, income was higher than expenses for the month of February 2004.

_____

_____

Exercise 18-1: Follow the instructions below to complete Exercise 18-1.

1. Use Bellwether Garden Supply's Income Statement to print a year-to-date Expenses by Account (Bar Chart).

2. To print an Excel bar chart, select File, Print, **<OK>**. Use portrait orientation when printing.

3. Save your spreadsheet. (A suggested file name is **Exercise 18-1**.)

Exercise 18-2: Follow the instructions below to complete Exercise 18-2.

1. Use Bellwether Garden Supply's Balance Sheet to display the March 31, 2007 Balance Sheet in Excel.

2. Print the Balance Sheet with the Payroll Summary Information. (*Hint:* Print cells A1 through D20.)

3. Save your spreadsheet. (A suggested file name is **Exercise 18-2**.)

CHAPTER 18 INDEX

Project

3 Valley Computers

In Project 3, you will complete the computer accounting cycle for Valley Computers which is located in Reseda, California. Valley Computers is a computer club that is a nonprofit business organized as a corporation.

Because Valley Computers is a nonprofit business, you will notice some differences in its Chart of Accounts and some of its transactions. For example, revenues are derived from membership fees and seminars. Club members can also contribute computers to local schools. You will see how these transactions are handled when you work with this project.

The club sponsors a trip to Comdex, a computer trade-show in Las Vegas. The trip involves expenses for bus rental, motel rooms, meals, and entrance fees to the trade show. Since so many club members attend Comdex, a special rate is offered to them.

In this project you will complete the accounting cycle for the month of January 2004. Valley Computers' Balance Sheet, checkbook register, and bank statement are provided as source documents.

At the end of this project you will find a Checklist that lists the printed reports you should have. The step-by-step instructions also remind you when to print. Your instructor may ask you to turn in these printouts for grading purposes. Remember to make backups at periodic intervals.

Follow these steps to complete Project 3, Valley Computers:

Step 1: Start Windows and Peachtree in the usual way.

Step 2: Make the selections to set up a new company.

Step   3:   The company information for Valley Computers is:

Company Name:	Valley Computers
Address Line 1:	2100 White Oak Blvd.
City, State, Zip:	Reseda, CA 91732
Country:	USA
Phone:	818-555-9772
Fax:	818-555-8712
Business Type:	Corporation
Federal Employer ID:	55-7877365
State Employer ID:	40-1292240
State Unemployment ID:	405958-2
Web Site:	www.valleycomputers.com
E-mail:	valley@computers.com

Step   4:   At the New Company Setup - Chart of Accounts window, select Set up a new company using an extensive chart of accounts from one of the many sample companies.

Step   5:   Select Non-Profit Company.

Step   6:   Accept the default for Accrual accounting.

Step   7:   Accept the default for Real Time posting.

Step   8:   At the Accounting Periods screen, accept the default for 12 monthly accounting periods.

Step   9:   On the Monthly Accounting Periods screen, make the following selections:

	Month	Year
When do you want your first fiscal year to start?	January	2004
What is the first month you will be entering data?	January	2004

Step   10:   Accept the defaults for payment terms and credit limits.

Step   11:   At the Congratulations screen, click [Finish]. The menu bar for your company appears.

Step 12: When the Peachtree Today window appears, make the selections to disable Peachtree Today each time the company is opened.

Step 13: Delete, add, and change the following General Ledger accounts in the Chart of Accounts:

Delete these accounts:

Acct. #   Account Name

Acct. #	Account Name
10000	Petty Cash
10100	Cash on Hand
10300	Payroll Checking Account
10500	Special Account
10600	Cash-Restricted Fund
10700	Investments
11400	Other Receivables
11500	Allowance for Doubtful Account
12100	Inventory-Kitchen
12150	Inventory-Golf & Tennis
12200	Inventory-Snack Stand
14100	Employee Advances
14700	Other Current Assets
15200	Automobiles
15300	Other Depreciable Property
15400	Leasehold Improvements
15500	Building
15600	Building Improvements
16900	Land
17200	Accum. Depreciation-Automobi
17300	Accum. Depreciation-Other
17400	Accum. Depreciation-Leasehold
17500	Accum. Depreciation-Building
17600	Accum. Depreciation-Bldg Imp
19000	Deposits
19150	Accum Amortiz - Org. Costs
19200	Note Receivable-Noncurrent
19900	Other Noncurrent Assets
23000	Accrued Expenses
23100	Sales Tax Payable

23300	Deductions Payable
23400	Federal Payroll Taxes Payable
23500	FUTA Tax Payable
23600	State Payroll Taxes Payable
23700	SUTA Payable
23800	Local Payroll Taxes Payable
24000	Other Taxes Payable
24100	Employee Benefits Payable
24200	Current Portion Long-Term Debt
24800	Other Current Liabilities
24900	Suspense-Clearing Account
27000	Notes Payable-Noncurrent
27100	Deferred Revenue
27400	Other Long-Term Liabilities
40200	Sales-Kitchen/Dining Room
40400	Sales-Golf & Tennis
40600	Sales-Snack Stand
40800	Sales-Other
41000	Contributions-Unrestricted
41200	Grants
41400	Program Service Revenue
41800	Investment Income
42000	Realized gain in Investment
42200	Miscellaneous Income
42400	Contributions-Restricted
42600	Investment Income-Restricted
43000	Other Income
48000	Fee Refunds
58000	Cost of Sales-Other
59000	Purchase Returns and Allowance
60000	Default Purchase Expense
60100	Grant and Allocation Exp.
61500	Bad Debt Expense
65000	Employee Benefit Programs Exp
65500	Other Employee Benefits
72000	Payroll Tax Expense
76500	Compensation of Officers
77000	Salaries Expense
89000	Other Expense

Change these accounts:

Acct. #	Account Name	New Account Name
10200	Regular Checking Account	Reseda Bank
12000	Inventory-Bar	Inventory-Computers/Schools
14000	Prepaid Expenses	Prepaid Rent
15100	Equipment	Computer Equipment
17000	Accum. Depreciation-Furnitur	Accum. Depreciation-Furn & Fix
17100	Accum. Depreciation-Eq.	Accum. Depreciation-Comp Equip
20000	Accounts Payable	Credit Card Payable
40000	Sales-Bar	Fees-Seminars/Classes
66000	Supplies Expense	Office Supplies Expense
67500	Occupancy Expense	Rent Expense
70000	Travel Expense	Bus Rental-Comdex
72500	Depreciation Expense	Depr. Exp.-Furniture & Fixture

Add these accounts:

Acct. #	Account Name	Account Type
39002	Membership Contributions	Equity-doesn't close
60000	Advertising Expense	Expenses
60400	Bank Service Charge	Expenses
70010	Meals-Comdex	Expenses
70020	Motel-Comdex	Expenses
70030	Fees-Comdex	Expenses
72520	Depr. Exp.-Comp Equip	Expenses

Continue with step 14 on the next page.

Step 14: Use Valley Computers Balance Sheet to record the chart of accounts beginning balances.

Valley Computers Balance Sheet January 1, 2004		
ASSETS		
Current Assets		
Reseda Bank	$7,100.00	
Inventory-Computers/Schools	500.00	
Inventory-Office	1,500.00	
Total Current Assets		$9,100.00
Property and Equipment		
Furniture and Fixtures	1,200.00	
Computer Equipment	3,000.00	
Total Property and Equipment		4,200.00
Other Assets: Organization Costs		300.00
Total Assets		$13,600.00
LIABILITIES		
Credit Card Payable	250.00	
Total Liabilities		250.00
CAPITAL		
Retained Earnings		13,350.00
Total Liabilities and Capital		$13,600.00

Step 15: Back up your data. The suggested file name is Valley Computers Begin.ptb.

Step 16: The checkbook register that follows provides you with the information necessary for Valley Computers' Cash Receipts Journal and Cash Disbursements Journal entries for January.

Check Number	Date	Description of Transaction	Payment/Dr. (-)	Deposit/Cr. (+)	Balance
					7,100.00
	1/2/04	Deposit (membership dues)[1]		2,700.00	9,800.00
9001	1/8/04	Payment - Credit Card	250.00		9,550.00
9002	1/8/04	Melody Advertising	170.00		9,380.00
9003	1/9/04	Boulevard Office Supplies	192.78		9,187.22
9004	1/17/04	Meals, Comdex	750.00		8,437.22
9005	1/17/04	Bus Rental, Comdex	500.00		7,937.22
9006	1/17/04	Comdex Entrance Fees	725.00		7,212.22
9007	1/17/04	Motel Rooms, Comdex	820.65		6,391.57
9008	1/26/04	Western Telephone Co.	47.40		6,344.17
9009	1/26/04	U.S. Post Office	37.00		6,307.17
	1/29/04	Deposit (seminar fees)		605.00	6,912.17

Step 17: *Additional journal entry*: On January 31, a club member donated a computer system and printer to the club. The value of the computer and printer is $300. (Debit, Inventory - Computers/Schools; Credit, Membership Contributions. Use the General Journal for this entry)

---

[1] For each deposit shown on the check register, type the date of the transaction in the Deposit ticket ID field. For each check, use the Write Checks task.

Step 18: Valley Computers bank statement is shown below. Journalize and post the entry for the bank service charge. Then complete the Account Reconciliation for the checking account.

Statement of Account Reseda Bank Jan. 1 to Jan. 31, 2004 Account #80355-1205			Valley Computers 2100 White Oak Blvd. Reseda, CA 91732	
REGULAR CHECKING				
Previous Balance	12/31/04	$ 7,100.00		
3 Deposits(+)		3,305.00		
7 Checks (-)		2,730.83		
Service Charges (-)		12.00		
Ending Balance	1/31/04	**$ 7,662.17**		
DEPOSITS				
	1/3/04	2,700.00	1/31/04	605.00
CHECKS (Asterisk * indicates break in check number sequence)				
	1/10/04	9001	250.00	
	1/11/04	9002	170.00	
	1/17/04	9003	192.78	
	1/26/04	9004	750.00	
	1/28/04	9005	500.00	
	1/29/04	9007*	820.65	
	1/31/04	9008	47.40	

Step 19: Make a backup. The suggested file name is Valley Computers January.ptb.

Your instructor may want to collect this project. A Checklist of Printouts is shown on the next page.

Checklist of Printouts, Project 3: Valley Computers
Chart of Accounts
Account Reconciliation
Cash Account Register
Cash Disbursements Journal
Cash Receipts Journal
General Journal
General Ledger Trial Balance
General Ledger
Balance Sheet
Income Statement
Statement of Cash Flow
Statement of Changes in Financial Position
Statement of Retained Earnings

Student Name_____**Date**_____

CHECK YOUR PROGRESS: PROJECT 3
VALLEY COMPUTERS

1. What are the total debit and credit balances on your
    general ledger trial balance?   _____

2. What is the total amount of checks outstanding?   _____

3. How much are the total expenses on January 31?   _____

4. How much are the total revenues on January 31?   _____

5. How much is the net income (net loss) on January 31?   _____

6. What is the account balance in the Membership
    Contributions account on January 31?   _____

7. What are the total assets on January 31?   _____

8. What is the ending retained earnings on
    January 31, 2004?   _____

9. What is the balance in the Credit Card Payable
    account on January 31?   _____

10. What is the balance in the Office Supplies Expense
    account on January 31?   _____

11. Is there an Increase or Decrease in cash for the
    month of January?   _____

12. Was any Credit Card Payable incurred during the
    month of January? (Circle your answer)   YES   NO

In Project 4, you will complete the computer accounting cycle for Woods Manufacturing, Inc. This company manufactures backpacks, sleeping bags, and tents.

Woods Manufacturing, Inc. offers its customers a sales discount of 2% 15, Net 30 days. Vendors offer Woods Manufacturing a purchase discount of 1% 15, Net 30 days.

Follow these steps to complete Project 4, Woods Manufacturing, Inc.

Step 1:   Start Windows and Peachtree in the usual way.

Step 2:   Make the selections to set up a new company.

Step 3:   Type the following company information for Woods Manufacturing:

Company Name:	Woods Manufacturing, Inc. (*use your name, then Manufacturing, Inc.*)
Address Line 1:	414 Farrington Road
City, State, Zip:	Philadelphia, PA 19141
Country:	USA
Phone:	215-555-5522
Fax:	215-555-5524
Business Type:	Corporation
Federal Employer ID:	79-3243135
State Employer ID:	20-5544321
State Unemployment ID:	201206-9
Web Site:	www.phila.net/Woodsmftg
E-mail:	Woodsmftg@phila.net

Step 4: Select Set up new company using an extensive chart of accounts from one of the many sample companies.

Step 5: Scroll down the Available Charts of Accounts list, then select Manufacturing Company.

Step 6: Accept the default for Accrual accounting.

Step 7: Accept the default for Real Time posting.

Step 8: Accept the default for 12 monthly accounting periods.

Step 9: On the Monthly Accounting Periods screen, make the following selections:

	Month	*Year*
When do you want your first fiscal year to start?	January	2004
What is the first month you will be entering data?	January	2004
What is the first year you will be entering payroll?	2004	

Step 10: Accept the information on the Defaults screen.

Step 11: At the Congratulations screen, click [Finish]. The menu bar for your company appears.

Step 12: Disable Peachtree Today.

General Ledger

1. At the Setup Checklist, select Chart of Accounts.

   Delete the following accounts:

10100	Cash on Hand
10400	Savings Account
10500	Special Account
10600	Investments-Money Market
15400	Leasehold Improvements
16900	Land

17300   Accum. Depreciation-Other
17400   Accum. Depreciation-Leasehold
24800   Other Current Liabilities

Change these account names:

10200   Regular Checking Accounting to Bank of Philadelphia
10300   Payroll Checking Account to Penn Savings
14000   Prepaid Expenses to Prepaid Insurance
15100   Equipment to Computers & Equipment
15200   Automobiles to Trucks/Autos
17100   Accum. Depreciation-Equipment to Accum. Depreciation-
        Comp & Equ
17200   Accum. Depreciation-Automobil to Accum. Depreciation-
        Trucks/Aut
23300   Deductions Payable to Medicare Employee Taxes Payabl
24000   Other Taxes Payable to FICA Employee Taxes Payable
24100   Employee Benefits Payable to FICA Employer Taxes
        Payable
27000   Notes Payable-Noncurrent to Mortgage Payable
40000   Sales #1 to Sales-Backpacks
40200   Sales #2 to Sales-Sleeping Bags
40400   Sales #3 to Sales-Tents
72500   Penalties and Fines Exp to Employer FUTA Expense
73000   Other Taxes to Employer SUTA Expense

Add these accounts:

Acct. ID	Acct. Description	Account Type
12010	Inventory-Backpacks	Inventory
12020	Inventory-Sleeping Bags	Inventory
12030	Inventory-Tents	Inventory
22000	Credit Card Payable	Other Current Liabilities
23350	Medicare Employer Taxes Payabl	Other Current Liabilities
73200	Employer FICA Taxes Expense	Expenses
73300	Employer Medicare Expense	Expenses

2. You purchased Woods Manufacturing in December 2003. Use the
    Balance Sheet below to record the chart of account beginning
    balances.

Woods Manufacturing, Inc. Balance Sheet January 1, 2004		
ASSETS		
Current Assets		
Bank of Philadelphia	$40,000.00	
Penn Savings	30,500.00	
Investments-Cert. of Deposit	13,000.00	
Inventory-Backpacks	1,612.50	
Inventory-Sleeping Bags	1,760.00	
Inventory-Tents	2,679.60	
Prepaid Insurance	3,600.00	
Total Current Assets		$93,152.10
Property and Equipment		
Furniture and Fixtures	2,500.00	
Computers & Equipment	6,000.00	
Trucks/Autos	25,000.00	
Building	105,000.00	
Total Property and Equipment		138,500.00
Organization Costs	1,000.00	
Total Assets		$232,652.10
LIABILITIES AND STOCKHOLDER'S EQUITY		
Credit Card Payable	15,900.00	
Mortgage Payable	97,500.00	
Total Liabilities		$113,400.00
Stockholder's Equity: Common Stock		119,252.10
Total Liabilities and Stockholder's Equity		$232,652.10

Accounts Payable

1. Set up the following vendor defaults.

Standard Terms:	Due in number of days
Net due in:	30 days
Discount in:	15 days
Discount %	1.00
Credit Limit:	20,000.00

   GL Link Accounts:

Purchase Account:	12010 Inventory-Backpacks
Discount GL Account:	59500 Purchase Discounts

2. Set up the following vendors:

Vendor ID:	dd22
Name:	D&D Fabrics
Contact:	Helen Marchon
Address:	173 North 75th Street
City, ST Zip:	Hartford, CT 06108
Vendor Type:	slpg bgs
1099 Type:	Independent Contractor
Telephone 1:	860-555-5462
Fax:	860-555-5463
E-mail:	helen@hartford.com
Web Site:	www.hartford.com/helenM

   Purchase Defaults tab:

Purchase Acct:	12020 Inventory-Sleeping Bags
Tax ID #:	23-9838306

Vendor ID:	ep33
Name:	Eastern Products
Contact:	Dudley Birney
Address:	7300 Cleveland Heights Blvd.
City, ST Zip:	Cleveland, OH 44192
Vendor Type:	tents
1099 Type:	Independent Contractor

Telephone 1:	216-555-0909
Fax:	216-555-0911
E-mail:	dudley@easternprod.com
Web Site:	www.easternprod.com

Purchase Defaults tab:

Purchase Acct:	12030 Inventory-Tents
Tax ID #:	41-7733932

Vendor ID:	rk44
Name:	RK Materials
Contact:	Richard Kantor
Address:	21223 Oak Street
City, ST Zip:	Trenton, NJ 07092
Vendor Type:	backpack
1099 Type:	Independent Contractor
Telephone 1:	609-555-8855
Fax:	609-555-9966
E-mail:	rich@rkmaterials.net
Web Site:	www.rkmaterials.net

Purchase Defaults tab:

Purchase Acct:	12010 Inventory-Backpacks
Tax ID #:	23-7891245

Accounts Receivable

1. Set up the following customer default settings:

Standard Terms:	Due in number of days
Net due in:	30 days
Discount in:	15 days
Discount %:	2.00
Credit Limit:	15,000.00
GL Sales Account:	40000 Sales-Backpacks
Discount GL Account:	49000 Sales Discounts

2. Enter the following customer records:

Customer ID:	001BOS
Name:	Barson's Outdoor Supplies
Contact:	Benjamin Barson
Address:	131 East Pima Ave.
City, ST Zip:	Tucson, AZ 85711
Customer Type:	PIMA (for Pima County)
Telephone 1:	520-555-1132
Fax:	520-555-9832
E-mail:	ben@barson.biz
Web Site:	www.barson.biz

Sales Defaults tab:

G/L Sales Acct:	40000, Sales-Backpacks
Resale #:	7836215-7

Customer ID:	002SCS
Name:	Susan's Camping Store
Contact:	Susan Mills
Address:	901 Cornell Street
City, ST Zip:	Portland, OR 97218
Customer Type:	PORT (for Portland County)
Telephone 1:	971-555-8831
Fax:	971-555-9912
E-mail:	susan@campingstore.com
Web Site	www.campingstore.com

Sales defaults tab:

G/L Sales Acct:	40200, Sales-Sleeping Bags
Resale #:	2857825-6

Customer ID:	003WST
Name:	West's Store
Contact:	Danny West
Address:	2100 Lincoln Street
City, ST Zip:	Cincinnati, OH 45227
Customer Type:	HAM (for Hamilton County)
Telephone 1:	513-555-4092
Fax:	513-555-5498

E-mail: dan@weststore.com
Web Site: www.weststore.com

Sales defaults tab:

G/L Sales Acct: 40400, Sales-Tents
Resale #:   8732335-8

Payroll

1. Enter the following employee defaults:

    State: PA
    Locality: Phila
    Enter the Locality Tax Rate: 1.00
    Unemployment Percent for Your Company: 3.4
    Do You Want to Record Employee Meals and Tips?: No
    Gross Pay Acct: 51000 Direct Labor Costs
    Tax Liability Acct: 23400 Federal Payroll Taxes Payable
    Tax Expense Acct: 72000 Payroll Tax Expense

2. Accept the following defaults: 401(k) plan not offered, Vacation time not tracked, Sick time not tracked.

3. Click [Finish] to exit the Payroll Setup Wizard.

4. The Help screen pops up. Review any necessary information. Then, close the Help screen.

5. Go to the Employee Defaults screen. Observe that the State / Locality shows PA (for Pennsylvania) as the State, and Phila (for Philadelphia) as the locality

6. Select the Pay Levels tab. In the Salary Pay Levels table, select G/L Account 77000, Salaries Expense, for the salaried employee, Rosalyn Klein.

7. Select the following EmployE<u>E</u> Fields:

The Fed_Income line displays Account No. 23400, Federal Payroll Taxes Payable, for FIT.

Soc_Sec, 24000, FICA Employee Taxes Payable

Medicare, 23300, Medicare Employee Taxes Payable

State, 23600, State Payroll Taxes Payable

Local, 23800, Local Payroll Taxes Payable

8. Select the following EmployE<u>R</u> Fields:

	Liability column	*Expense column*
Soc_Sec_ER	24100, FICA Employer Taxes Payable	73200, Employer FICA Taxes Expense
Medicare_ER	23350, Medicare Employer Taxes Payabl	73300, Employer Medicare Expense
FUTA_ER	23500, FUTA Tax Payable	72500, Employer FUTA Expense
SUI_ER	23700, SUTA Payable	73000, Employer SUTA Expense

9. Enter the following employee records:

Employee ID:	RK40
Name:	Rosalyn Klein
Accept the default for Employee	
Address:	183 Montgomery Road
City, ST Zip:	Upper Darby, PA 19112
Telephone 1:	215-555-4411
E-mail:	roz@mail.net
Social Security #:	207-22-3339
Type:	FULL
Hired:	1/2/04

Pay Info: Salary, $1,000. Ms. Klein is paid monthly.

Withholding Info:

Filing Status:	Single for US Federal, State, and Local
Allow:	1 for US Federal, State and Local

Employee ID: JS50
Name: Judy Smythe
Accept the default for Employee
Address: 971 Brockton Avenue
City, ST Zip: Philadelphia, PA 19191
Telephone 1:   215-555-3582
E-mail: judy@mail.net
Social Security #:   982-11-9900
Type: FULL
Hired: 1/2/04

Pay Info: Hourly, $9.75 per hour; Overtime, $14.63. Ms. Smythe is paid weekly.

Withholding Info:

Filing Status:	Married for Federal, State, and Local
Allow:	3 for Federal, State, and Local

Employee ID: LS60
Name: Larry Simms
Accept the default for Employee
Address: 9302 N. 83rd Street
City, ST Zip: Philadelphia, PA 19122
Telephone 1:   215-555-0632
E-mail: larry@mail.net
Social Security #:   209-99-0033
Type: FULL
Hired: 1/2/04

Pay Info: Hourly, $9.75 per hour; Overtime, $14.63. Mr. Simms is paid weekly.

Withholding Info:

Filing Status:	Single for Federal, State, and Local
Allow:	1 for Federal, State, and Local

Employee ID: OW70

Name: Oscar Williams

Accept the default for Employee

Address:	302 Lancaster Road
City, ST Zip:	Philadelphia, PA 19135
Telephone 1:	215-555-9542
E-mail:	oscar@mail.net
Social Security #:	209-33-7228
Type:	FULL
Hired:	1/2/04

Pay Info: Hourly, $9.75 per hour; Overtime, $14.63. Mr. Williams is paid weekly.

Withholding Info:

Filing Status:	Married for Federal, State, and Local
Allow:	2 for Federal, State, and Local

Inventory

1. Enter the following inventory default settings.

2. Make sure that FIFO is the inventory costing method.

3. Set up the following inventory items and assembly records:

Item ID:	backpacks
Description:	backpacks
Item Class:	Stock item
Description for Sales:	backpacks
Price Level 1:	150.00
Item Tax Type:	2 Exempt
Last Unit Cost:	37.50
Cost Method:	FIFO
GL Sales Acct:	40000 Sales-Backpacks

GL Inventory Acct:	12010, Inventory-Backpacks
GL Cost of Sales Acct:	50500, Raw Material Purchases
Item Type:	backpack
Unit/Measure:	each
Minimum Stock:	10
Reorder Quantity:	5
Preferred Vendor ID:	rk44, RK Materials

Beginning Balances: backpacks

Quantity:	43.00
Unit Cost:	37.50
Total Cost:	1,612.50

Item ID:	sleeping bags
Description:	sleeping bags
Item Class:	Stock item
Description for Sales:	sleeping bags
Price Level 1:	105.00
Item Tax Type:	2 Exempt
Last Unit Cost:	27.50
Cost Method:	FIFO
GL Sales Acct:	40200, Sales-Sleeping Bags
GL Inventory Acct:	12020, Inventory-Sleeping Bags
GL Cost of Sales Acct:	50500, Raw Material Purchases
Item Type:	slpg bgs
Unit/Measure:	each
Minimum Stock:	10
Reorder Quantity:	5
Preferred Vendor ID:	dd22, D&D Fabrics

Beginning Balances: sleeping bags

Quantity:	64.00
Last Unit Cost	27.50
Total Cost:	1,760.00

Item ID:	tents
Description:	tents
Item Class:	Stock item
Description for Sales:	tents

Price Level 1:	175.00
Item Tax Type:	2 Exempt
Last Unit Cost:	47.85
Cost Method:	FIFO
GL Sales Acct:	40400, Sales-Tents
GL Inventory Acct:	12030, Inventory-Tents
GL Cost of Sales Acct:	50500, Raw Material Purchases
Item Type:	tents
Unit/Measure:	each
Minimum Stock:	10
Reorder Quantity:	5
Preferred Vendor ID:	ep33, Eastern Products

Beginning Balances: tents

Quantity:	56.00
Unit Cost:	47.85
Total Cost:	2,679.60

Jobs

1. Set up the following job records:

Job ID: 13-221
Description: backpacks
For Customer: 001BOS
Start Date: 1/5/04
End Date: 12/31/04
Job Type: backpack

Job ID: 14-331
Description: sleeping bags
For Customer: 002SCS
Start Date: 1/5/04
End Date: 12/31/04
Job Type: slpg bgs

Job ID: 15-441
Description: tents
For Customer: 003WST
Start Date: 1/5/04

End Date: 12/31/04
Job Type: tents

2. Backup your data. Use **Woods Mftg Begin.ptb** as the filename.

3. Exit or continue with Project 4.

Journalize and post the following transactions:

Date   *Description of Transaction*

01/07/04 Invoice No. 315 was received from D&D Fabrics for 15
          sleeping bags @ $27.50 each for a total of $412.50. Post
          invoice 315.

01/07/04 Invoice No. 45 was received from RK Materials for 20
          backpacks @ $37.50 each for a total of $750.00. Post invoice
          45.

01/07/04 Invoice No. 800 was received from Eastern Products for 16
          tents @ $47.85 each for a total of $765.60. Post invoice 800.

01/09/04 Pay the factory employees for 40 hours of direct labor. Select
          Account No. 10300, Penn Savings, as the Cash Account. In
          the Check Number field, type **101** for Ms. Smythe's paycheck.
          The check numbers for Mr. Simms and Mr. Williams will be
          automatically completed. (You will *not* print the payroll

          checks.) Remember to click on , then and

          . Complete the following:

Check No.	Employee	Job	Hours
101	Judy Smythe	15-441	40
102	Larry Simms	14-331	40
103	Oscar Williams	13-221	40

Remember to click [Save] *after each payroll entry.*

01/15/04 Sold 20 backpacks on account to Barson's Outdoor Supplies for a total of $3,000.00, Job 13-221. In the Invoice # field, type **101**.[1] Post sales invoice 101.

01/15/04 Sold 12 sleeping bags on account to Susan's Camping Store for a total of $1,260.00, Job 14-331. Post sales invoice 102.

01/15/04 Sold 20 tents on account to West's Store for a total of $3,500.00, Job 15-441. Post sales invoice 103.

01/16/04 Pay the factory employees for 40 hours of direct labor. *Remember to post each payroll entry.*

Check No.	Employee	Job	Hours
104	Judy Smythe	15-441	40
105	Larry Simms	14-331	40
106	Oscar Williams	13-221	40

01/16/04 Issued Check No. 1001 to RK Materials in payment of purchase Invoice No. 45. Select Account No. 10200, Bank of Philadelphia as the cash account. In the Check Number field, type **1001**. You will *not* print vendor checks. In the Discount Account field, make sure that Account No. 59500, Purchase Discounts is shown. Post Check No. 1001 in the amount of $742.50.

01/16/04 Issued Check No. 1002 to D&D Fabrics in payment of purchase Invoice No. 315. Post Check No. 1002 in the amount of $408.37.

01/16/04 Issued Check No. 1003 to Eastern Products in payment of purchase Invoice No. 800. Post Check No. 1003 in the amount of $757.94.

---

[1]Since you are not printing sales invoices, it is necessary to complete this field.

01/23/04   Invoice No. 328 was received from D&D Fabrics for 15 sleeping bags @ $27.50 each for a total of $412.50. Post invoice 328.

01/23/04   Invoice No. 900 was received from Eastern Products for 20 tents @ $47.85 each for a total of $957.00. Post invoice 900.

01/23/04   Pay the factory employees for 40 hours of direct labor. *Remember to click on Save after each payroll check is recorded.*

Check No.	Employee	Job	Hours
107	Judy Smythe	15-441	40
108	Larry Simms	14-331	40
109	Oscar Williams	13-221	40

01/27/04   Received payment from Barson's Outdoor Supplies for sales invoice 101. Select Account No. 10200, Bank of Philadelphia, as the cash account. Use the date of the transaction in the Deposit ticket ID field. In the Reference field, type **Inv. 101**. Post this receipt in the amount of $2,940.

01/27/04   Received payment from Susan's Camping Store for sales invoice 102. In the Reference field, type **Inv. 102**. Post this receipt in the amount of $1,234.80.

01/27/04   Received payment from West's Store for sales invoice 103. In the Reference field, type **Inv. 103**. Post this receipt in the amount of $3,430.

01/27/04   Sold 25 sleeping bags on account to Susan's Camping Store for a total of $2,625.00, Job 14-331. In the Invoice # field, type **104**. Post sales invoice 104.

01/29/04   Sold 21 tents on account to West's Store for a total of $3,675.00, Job 15-441. Post sales invoice 105.

01/30/04   Issued Check No. 1004 to Bank of Philadelphia for $709.23 in payment of Mortgage Payable. In the Check Number field, type **1004**. (Use the Write Checks task; and make sure that account 10200, Bank of Philadelphia, is selected as the Cash Account.) Post Check No. 1004.

01/30/04   Issued Check No. 1005 to Penn Savings for $795 in payment of Credit Card Payable. Post Check No. 1005.

01/30/04   Issued Check No. 1006 to Phila. Electric for $200.92 in payment of utilities. (Debit Utilities Expense, Account No. 78000.) Post Check No. 1006.

01/30/04   Issued Check No. 1007 to Area Phone Co. for $175.15 in payment of telephone bill. Post Check No. 1007.

01/30/04   Received payment from West's Store for sales invoice 105. In the Reference field, type **Inv. 105**. Post this receipt in the amount of $3,601.50.

01/30/04   Pay the factory employees for 40 hours of direct labor. *Remember to click on Save after each payroll check is recorded.*

Check No.	Employee	Job	Hours
110	Judy Smythe	15-441	40
111	Larry Simms	14-331	40
112	Oscar Williams	13-221	40

01/30/04   Pay the salaried employee, Rosalyn Klein. In the Salary Amounts table, make sure that account 77000, Salaries Expense, is shown in the Account column. If not, select that account. *Post Check No. 113.*

Continue with Account Reconciliation on pages 668 and 669.

Account Reconciliation

Complete the bank reconciliation for Bank of Philadelphia and Penn Savings. The January 31, 2004, bank statements are shown on this page and page 669.

Statement of Account Bank of Philadelphia January 1 to January 31, 2004		Account #863-993344	Woods Manufacturing, Inc. 414 Farrington Road Philadelphia, PA 19141	
REGULAR CHECKING				
Previous Balance	12/31/01	$40,000.00		
2 Deposits(+)		11,206.30		
3 Checks (-)		1,908.81		
Service Charges (-)	1/31/04	22.00		
Ending Balance	1/31/04	**$49,275.49**		
DEPOSITS				
	1/28/04	7,604.80		
	1/30/04	3,601.50		
CHECKS (Asterisk * indicates break in check number sequence)				
	1/30/04	1001	742.50	
	1/30/04	1002	408.37	
	1/31/04	1003	757.94	

Statement of Account Penn Savings January 1 to January 31, 2004		Account #991-345-881	Woods Manufacturing, Inc. 414 Farrington Road Philadelphia, PA 19141	
PAYROLL CHECKING				
Previous Balance	12/31/01	30,500.00		
Deposits(+)				
9 Checks (-)		2,925.42		
Service Charges (-)	1/31/04	20.00		
Ending Balance	1/31/04	**27,554.58**		
DEPOSITS				
CHECKS (Asterisk * indicates break in check number sequence)				
	1/12/04	101	336.05	
	1/12/04	102	308.81	
	1/12/04	103	330.28	
	1/19/04	104	336.05	
	1/19/04	105	308.81	
	1/19/04	106	330.28	
	1/27/04	107	336.05	
	1/27/04	108	308.81	
	1/27/04	109	330.28	

Back up your data. Use **Woods Mftg January.ptb** as the file name.

Your instructor may want to collect this project. A Checklist of Printouts is shown below.

CHECKLIST OF PRINTOUTS, WOODS MANUFACTURING, INC.	
	Account Reconciliation Report: Bank of Philadelphia
	Account Reconciliation Report: Penn Savings
	Cash Account Register: Bank of Philadelphia
	Cash Account Register: Penn Savings
	General Ledger Trial Balance
	General Ledger
	Balance Sheet
	Income Statement
	Statement of Cash Flow
	Statement of Changes in Financial Position
	Statement of Retained Earnings
	Customer Ledgers
	Vendor Ledgers
	Job Ledger
	Job Profitability Report
	Inventory Profitability Report
	Payroll Register
Optional printouts, Woods Manufacturing, Inc.	
	Chart of Accounts
	Customer List
	Vendor List
	Payroll Journal
	Purchase Journal
	Cash Disbursements Journal
	Sales Journal
	Cash Receipts Journal
	Cost of Goods Sold Journal
	General Journal

Student Name_____**Date**_____

CHECK YOUR PROGRESS: PROJECT 4
WOODS MANUFACTURING, INC.

1. What are the total debit and credit balances on your
    General Ledger Trial Balance?   _____

2. What are the total assets on January 31?   _____

3. What is the balance in the Bank of Philadelphia
    account on January 31?   _____

4. What is the balance in the Penn Savings
    account on January 31?   _____

5. What is the balance in the Susan's Camping Store
    account on January 31?   _____

6. What are the direct labor costs on January 31?   _____

7. How many backpacks were sold during the month
    of January?   _____

8. How many sleeping bags were sold during the
    month of January?   _____

9. How many tents were sold during the month of
    January?   _____

10. What is the ending retained earnings amount on
    on January 31?   _____

11. What are the total expenses reported on January 31?   _____

12. Was any Accounts Payable incurred during the
    month of January? (Circle your answer)   YES   NO

Project

4A Student-Designed Project

You have completed four projects: Lena Becker, Consultant; Copper Bicycles; Valley Computers; and Woods Manufacturing, Inc. In each project you completed the Computer Accounting Cycle for one month.

It is the purpose of Project 4A, to have you write the next month's transactions for one of the four projects. You pick the project and complete the accounting cycle: Project 1, Lena Becker, Consultant, a service business; Project 2, Copper Bicycles, a merchandising business; Project 3, Valley Computers, a nonprofit business; or Project 4, Woods Manufacturing, Inc., a manufacturing business. At the end of your month's transactions, you are required to complete the appropriate depreciation entries and adjusting entries.

Good luck! It is your turn to create the transactions for another month and complete the Computer Accounting Cycle. Remember to back up periodically.

Appendix A

Installing the Software

INSTALLING ON A SINGLE MACHINE

This section gives you instructions for installing Peachtree Complete Accounting 2004 (PCA) software on an IBM-PC or compatible computer. *You may need to check with your instructor to see if Peachtree has already been installed in the classroom or computer lab.* On the CD included with the textbook, a site license for individual use or computer lab network installation is included in the Doc folder; PAWGS.pdf file; Registration/Copyright bookmark. PCA may be used with Windows XP/2000/Me/98/95, or Windows NT 4.0 with Service Pack 6.

Follow these steps to install PCA 2004 on an individual computer (non-networked).

Step 1:   Turn on your computer and start Windows. Exit all programs and disable virus-protection and screen saver programs on your computer. This frees up memory and avoids interference with the Peachtree Complete Accounting setup process. Insert the Peachtree Complete Accounting 2004 CD that came with this book.

Step 2:   After a few moments, the Peachtree Accounting Educational Version 2004 screen appears. Click on Peachtree Complete Accounting, and continue with the next step. If the Welcome screen does not appear automatically, click on Start, then Run. Type x:\setup and select OK. (Substitute the appropriate CD drive letter for x.)

Step 3:   At the Peachtree Complete Accounting Educational Version 2004 Welcome screen, click [Next >]. Read the Licensing Agreement, then click on the radio button next to I accept the terms of the License Agreement. Click [Next >].

Step 4:   The Setup Options screen appears. Click on the Standard Setup radio button to select it. (If you do *not* have Standard Setup as an option, then you have a previous version of Peachtree installed. The author suggests that you delete the earlier version. See page 680, Deleting Peachtree.) Click [Next >]. Peachtree starts to install.

The McGraw-Hill Companies, Inc., *Computer Accounting with Peachtree Complete 2004, 8e*

675

Step 5: When the Finish screen appears, accept the default for Yes, I would like to start Peachtree Complete Accounting Educational Version by clicking on [Finish]. After a few moments, the startup menu appears.

Step 6: To exit the program, select Close this window. Then, click on File, Exit. If you need to install Adobe Acrobat Reader, go page 678 and follow the Installing Adobe Acrobat Reader instructions. If you do not need to install Adobe Acrobat Reader, click on Exit.

Step 7: Remove the CD from your drive.

Comment: When I start Peachtree, I receive a Btrieve error

For this message: Btrieve version 5.10 is being used by another application . . . follow these steps to copy the necessary file.
1. Click on OK. Then exit the Installation program.
2. Exit Windows and go to the DOS prompt.
3. At the c:\win directory, type **cd. .** then press the <Enter> key.
4. Type **cd peachw** then press <Enter>.
5. At the peachw directory, type **copy wbt*.* c:\windows\system** then press <Enter>.
6. Select **(a) all files to be copied**. Five files should be overwritten.
7. Type **win** to return to Windows.
8. Exit Windows. Power off for at least 10 seconds.
9. Restart your system in the normal way. Start installation again.

NETWORK INSTALLATION

In order to obtain network installation guides, you need to access the Peachtree Knowledge Center. Before accessing Peachtree's Knowledge Center, you need to become a Peachtree Passport member. After setting up your Peachtree Passport account, you can access information from Peachtree's support database.

Peachtree's Knowledge Center

Use the Peachtree Knowledge Center to search for useful information about the software. To use the Knowledge Center, you need to create a Peachtree Passport account first.

Access the Peachtree Knowledge Center to find useful hints for using the software. To use the Knowledge Center, you need to create a Peachtree Passport account.

---

1. Go to this website http://www.peachtree.com/login/newusersignup.cfm to create a Peachtree Passport account. Complete the e-mail address, password, and confirm fields. Complete the contact information. You will be sent a confirmation email. To activate your account, link to your email message.

2. Once your account is activated, click on Support, then from the drop-down list, click on Knowledge Center. The Welcome to the Peachtree Knowledge Center screen appears. Select, Click here to Sign in Now! Complete the E-mail Address and Password fields. Then, click on the Log In button.

3. The Proceed to the Peachtree Knowledge Center screen appears. Select, Click here to Continue Now! Click on Find Answers to search Peachtree's Knowledge Center.

Once you have a Peachtree Passport account, the website for logging in to the Peachtree Knowledge Center is http://www.peachtree.com/support/rightnow/welcome.cfm

---

Comment

Peachtree Complete Accounting 2004, Release 11, Educational Version, was used to write the textbook. All the screen illustrations and Peachtree printouts were done using Windows XP. You may install the CD that is packaged with the textbook on individual computers or on a network. **If you have an earlier release of Peachtree installed (Peachtree Complete Accounting Release 8.0 or PCA 2002, Release 9.0); or Peachtree Accounting for Windows 3.0, 3.5, 5.0, or 7.0, see the Deleting Peachtree steps on page 680.**

INSTALLING MICROSOFT INTERNET EXPLORER

Microsoft Internet Explorer 6.0 is included on the Peachtree Complete Accounting 2004 CD. An Internet connection is *not required* to run Peachtree. Peachtree *does not* require that Microsoft Internet Explorer be your default browser. Peachtree *requires* that Microsoft Internet Explorer 5.x (or higher) be installed on your computer. Peachtree uses components of the Microsoft Internet Explorer Web browser in its application (for example, Peachtree Today).

INSTALLING ADOBE ACROBAT READER

Electronic versions of the Peachtree manuals are automatically installed during the standard Peachtree setup process. To display or use these manuals, you must have Adobe Acrobat 4 (or higher) installed on your computer. Adobe Acrobat Reader can be installed from the Peachtree Complete Accounting 2004 CD or downloaded for free at www.adobe.com. Follow these steps to install Adobe Acrobat Reader from the Peachtree Complete Accounting 2004 CD packaged with the book.

1.   Insert the Peachtree Complete Accounting 2004 CD in your CD-ROM drive. The Peachtree Welcome screen automatically appears.
2.   Click the Adobe Acrobat Reader option. If the Peachtree Welcome menu does not automatically appear, do the following: From Windows Explorer, browse to the Acrobat folder on the Peachtree CD. Then double-click the Acrobat Reader setup file.
3.   Follow the prompts to install Adobe Acrobat Reader.

DISPLAYING THE PEACHTREE ONLINE MANUALS

Adobe Acrobat reader must be installed in order to use Peachtree's online manuals.

1.   From the Windows Start menu, select All Programs.
2.   Point to the Peachtree folder (or the name of the program folder you chose during Peachtree installation).
3.   A drop-down list appears. Select Peachtree Resources & Help. Select one of the following Adobe Acrobat files:

   a.   Getting Started Guide
   b.   User's Guide

Another way to open Peachtree's online manuals is to follow these steps.

1.   Start Windows Explorer. Open the folder where Peachtree is stored; for example, C:\Program Files\Peachtree\Doc.
2.   Double-click on PAWGS.pdf to open the Getting Started Guide.
3.   Double-click on PAWUG.pdf to open the User's Guide.

INSTALLING STARTING DATA FOR THE SAMPLE COMPANIES: BELLWETHER GARDEN SUPPLY AND PAVILION DESIGN GROUP

There are two ways to obtain beginning data for the sample companies. The first way is to restore the first back up made in Chapters 1 and 8. In Chapter 1 you were instructed to back up beginning data for Bellwether Garden Supply. Restore the bgs.ptb file to start Bellwether with beginning data. In Chapter 8 you backed up Pavilion Design Group. Restore the Chapter 8.ptb file to start Pavilion with beginning data.

The second way to obtain beginning data for the sample companies is to install it from the CD that accompanies this textbook. Follow these steps to install starting data for the sample companies.

1. If necessary start Windows. All other programs should be closed. Insert the Peachtree Complete Accounting 2004 CD in your CD drive.
2. At the Welcome to Peachtree Accounting Educational Version screen, select Peachtree Complete Accounting.
3. The InstallShield Wizard screen appears. Select

4. Click Next > . The Add / Components screen appears. With your keyboard's down-arrow, select Standard Forms; then press the space bar to remove the check mark. With your down-arrow select Tutorial And Manual Files; press the space bar to remove the check mark. *Observe that* Sample Company Data *has a check mark next to it*.

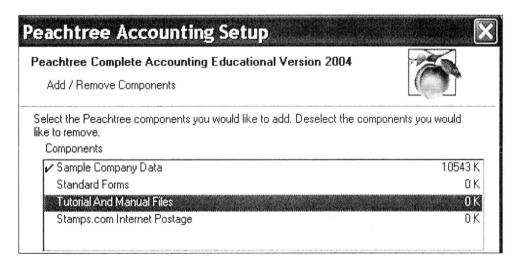

5. Click Next > . Follow the prompts to install the sample company data.
6. Remove the PCA 2004 CD from your CD drive.

DELETING PEACHTREE

To check your software version, start Peachtree, open any company, and then click on Help, About Peachtree Accounting. To delete Peachtree Complete Accounting Release 8 and higher, do the following:

Step 1:   Make a backup of any data files that you have created.

Step 2:   Close Peachtree Complete Accounting.

Step 3:   From the Start menu, select Control Panel, then Add or Remove Programs.

Step 4:   Select Peachtree Complete Accounting from the list; then click Add/Remove Programs.

Step 5:   Select remove to confirm that you want to remove Peachtree Complete accounting program files. (If necessary, click Yes to All to delete shared files.)

Step 6:   Once the program has been removed, click [Finish].

Step 7:   If necessary, delete the c:\windows\pcwXXX.ini file. (Substitute the appropriate numbers for XXX.)

To delete an earlier version of Peachtree (3.0, 3.5, 5.0 or 7.0), follow these steps:

Step 1:   Delete the PAWxx.ini file. The xx stands for a number; for example, PAW35.ini; PAW36.ini, PAW50.ini, PAW70.ini. The PAWxx.ini file is a subdirectory of Windows; for example, c:\windows\PAW70.ini.

Step 2:   Delete the program path; for example, c:\paw7edu. If you do not know where the Peachtree is installed, follow these steps.

a. Right-click on Peachtree's desktop icon. Then, left-click on Properties.
b. If necessary, select the Shortcut folder tab. The Target box shows where Peachtree is installed; for example, C:\paw7edu. The subdirectory identified as \peachw.exe is the executable file for the program.

Step 3:   Empty the Recycle bin.

Step 4:   Restart your computer.

Once you have deleted the one or more .ini file(s), install Peachtree Complete Accounting 2004, Release 11, Educational Version. If you do not get the Standard install option, you did not delete the two files shown in steps 1 and 2.

Appendix B
Review of Accounting Principles

Computer Accounting with Peachtree Complete 2004, Release 11, Eighth *Edition*, is for students who are studying accounting or have used accounting in business. Many of you have completed one or two semesters of accounting using *Fundamental Accounting Principles*, *17e*, Larson et al., McGraw-Hill/Irwin, 2005, or another accounting textbook. Appendix B is a review of basic accounting principles and procedures.

Accounting is concerned with how transactions and other economic events should be described and reported. The Computer Accounting Cycle is shown below. This series of steps is repeated each month for a business's transactions.

Peachtree Complete Accounting Computer Accounting Cycle	
1	New Company Set up and the chart of accounts.
2	Analyze transactions.
3	Journalize entries.
4	Post to the ledger.
5	Print general ledger trial balance (unadjusted).
6	Account reconciliation.
7	Journalize and post adjusting entries.
8	Print the general ledger trial balance (adjusted).
9	Print the financial statements.
10	Change accounting periods.
11	Interpret accounting information.

In the service businesses featured in this book, you used the Cash Payments Journal and Cash Receipts Journal for business transactions. Then you post these transactions to the General Ledger. In a merchandising business you use

Peachtree's Accounts Payable system and Accounts Receivable system. Special journals are used in conjunction with the Accounts Payable and Accounts Receivable ledgers. The special journals include: Cash Receipts Journal, Sales Journal, Cash Disbursements Journal, and Purchases Journal. The General Ledger, Accounts Payable Ledger and Accounts Receivable Ledger systems are taught in Parts 1, 2 and 3 of *Computer Accounting with Peachtree Complete 2004, Release 11.*

Standard accounting procedures are based on the double-entry system. This means that for each business transaction, one or more debits and one or more credits must be made in a journal and posted to the ledger. The debits must equal the credits.

The double-entry accounting system is based on the following premise: each account has two sides–a debit (left) side and credit (right) side. This is stated in the **accounting equation** as:

Assets = Liabilities + Owner's Equity

Assets are the economic resources and other properties that a business owns. Asset accounts include: Cash, Accounts Receivable, Office Supplies, Equipment, Land, Buildings, etc.

Liabilities are the business's debts. Liability accounts include: Accounts Payable, Loans Payable, Unearned Rent, etc.

Equity is the difference between the assets and liabilities or what the business has left after the debts are paid. Equity accounts include: Capital and Withdrawals, Revenue accounts, Cost of Goods Sold accounts, and Expense accounts.

Since assets are on the left side of the accounting equation, the left side of the account increases. This is the usual balance, too; assets increase on the left side and have a debit balance. Liabilities and Equity accounts are on the right side of the equation. Therefore, they increase on the right side and normally carry credit balances.

Another way to show the accounting equation and double-entry is illustrated on the next page.

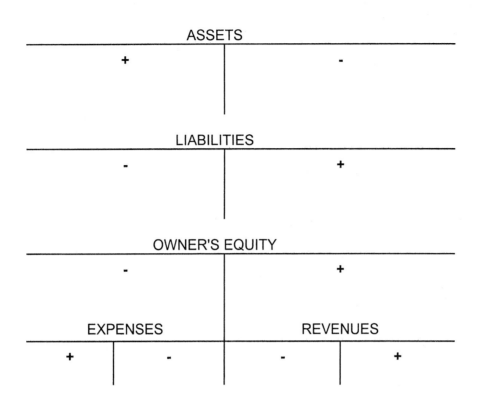

Each element of the accounting equation, Assets, Liabilities, and Equity, behaves similarly to their placement in the equation. Assets have debit balances; Liabilities have credit balances; Equities have credit balances; Expenses have debit balances because they decrease equity; and Revenues have credit balances because they increase equity.

In computerized accounting it is important to number each account according to a system. This is called the Chart of Accounts. The Chart of Accounts is a listing of all the general ledger accounts. The Chart identifies accounts with a number (five digits in Peachtree's extensive chart; four digits in Peachtree's simplified chart), a description of each account, and a Type code. Type codes classify accounts as cash accounts, inventory accounts, accounts receivable accounts, equipment accounts, depreciation accounts, liability accounts, etc.

Peachtree includes over 75 sample companies from which you can copy default information, including the Chart of Accounts. If you want to see which sample companies are included in Peachtree, select Help from the menu bar, then select Contents and Index. If necessary, select the Contents tab; then double-click Help about Your Specific Type of Business. Double -click on the A-Z List of Business Types. An alphabetic list of company types displays. Move your mouse to a company that you want to see and single click. To see the chart of accounts, click on <u>Display a sample chart of accounts for this type of business</u>.

If you want a printout, click | 🖶 Print |. Click | ⇦ Back | to select another

business type; or click ⊠ on the title bar to close the Peachtree Help screen.

Reporting information in the form of financial statements is important to accounting. The Balance Sheet reports the financial position of the business. It shows that assets are equal to liabilities plus owner's equity--the accounting equation. The Income Statement shows the difference between revenue and expenses for a specified period of time (month, quarter, year). The Statement of Cash Flow reports the operating, financial, and investing activities for the period. The Statement of Changes In Financial Position describes changes in a company's financial position that may not be obvious from the other financial statements.

Peachtree tracks income and expense data for an entire year. At the end of the year, all revenue and expense accounts are closed to equity. All you need to do is select Tasks, System, then Year-End Wizard. This step closes all revenue and expense accounts to equity. The income and expense accounts have zero balances and you are ready to start the next year.

Appendix C   Glossary

Appendix C lists a glossary of terms used in *Computer Accounting with Peachtree Complete 2004, Release 11, Eighth Edition*. The number in parentheses refers to the textbook page. Appendix C is also included on the textbook website (www.mhhe.com/yacht2004) <u>Student Edition</u> link.

accounting equation	The accounting equation is stated as assets = liabilities + owner's equity. (p. 682)
accounts payable	The money a company owes to a supplier or vendor. (p. 372)
accounts payable ledger	Shows the account activity for each vendor. (p. 394)
accounts payable transactions	Purchases of merchandise for resale, assets, or expenses incurred on credit from vendors. (p. 372)
accounts receivable	Money that is owed by customers to the business. (p. 432)
accounts receivable ledger	Shows the account activity for each customer. (p. 441)
accounts receivable transactions	Credit transactions from customers. (p. 432)
activity items	An item class for time and billing. (p. 232)

ASCII	An acronym for American Standard Code for Information Interchange. A standard format for representing characters on a computer. Most word processing, spreadsheet, and database programs can read ASCII files. (p. 598)
assets	The economic resources and other properties that a business owns. (p. 682)
audit trail	The path from the source document to the accounts. (p. 408)
average cost	A method of computing inventory. (See weighted-average method). (p. 398)
backing up	Saving your data to a floppy disk. (p. 16)
balance sheet	Lists the types and amounts of assets, liabilities, and equity as of a specific date. (p. 200; 263)
bank reconciliation	The process of bringing the balance of the bank statement and the balance of the cash account into agreement. (p. 288)
batch posting	Journal entries are held in temporary storage on your disk and not made part of the permanent records of the company until you decide you are satisfied with them and select Post from the icon bar. After you post, the General Ledger and all other accounting reports are updated. (p. 110)
bitmap	Refers to the dots (pixels or picture elements) on the display screen. (p. 583)
case sensitive	Refers to the use of lowercase and uppercase letters. When coding a customer or vendor, you must use either a capital or lowercase letter. For example, a vendor code that is A002 will not be recognized if a002 is typed. (p. 65)

cash disbursements journal	All payments of cash are recorded in the cash disbursements journal. In Peachtree, the Payments task is the cash disbursements journal. (p. 399)
cash receipts journal	In Peachtree the receipts task posts to the cash receipts journal. (p. 441)
charge items	An item class for time and billing. (p. 232)
chart of accounts	A list of all the accounts used by a company, showing the identifying number assigned to each account. PCA has over 70 sample charts of accounts. (p. 160)
coding system	A combination of letters and numbers that are used to identify customers and vendors. The coding system is case sensitive, for example, A002 is not the same as a002. (See case sensitive.) (p. 64)
command objects	Command objects are used by PCA to tell the program what to do next when printing forms. (p. 584)
credit memos	Refunds for merchandise that is returned by a customer. Also known as a credit invoice. (p. 121)
customer ledger	Shows account activity for each customer (p. 441)
data objects	A data object is either taken directly from information you have typed or derived from such information. (p. 583)
default	Information that displays in windows or information that is automatically used by the system. You can change the default by choosing another command. (p. 33)
desktop	Depending on how your computer is set up, various icons appear on your desktop when you start Windows. (p. 8)

dialog box	A window that appears when the system requires further information. You type information into dialog boxes to communicate with the program. Some dialog boxes display warnings and messages. (p. 32)
drill down	The act of following a path to its origin for further analysis. In certain Peachtree reports, you can click transactions to drill down to the task window. For example, from financial statements, you can drill down to the general ledger report; then you can drill down to the task window. (p. 289)
drop-down list	The down arrow means that this field contains a list of information from which you can make a selection. Many of PCA's screens will have drop down lists. When you click on the arrow next to a field, the list appears. You can press **<Enter>** or click your mouse on an item to select it from the list. (p. 12)
dynamic data exchange (DDE)	A method by which Windows programs share data with each other. For instance, you could enter a formula into an Excel spreadsheet cell that would refer to a field of data in PCA such as the Total Gross Paid to all employees quarter-to-date. Whenever you used that spreadsheet in the future, that cell would be updated with the current data from PCA. (p. 628)
ellipsis (...)	A punctuation mark consisting of three successive periods (...). Choosing a menu item with an ellipsis opens a dialog box. See glossary item, dialog box. (p. 32)
equity	The difference between the assets and liabilities or what the business has left after the debts are paid. (p. 682)

exemptions	These are withholding allowances claimed by the employee. The number of exemptions or withholding allowances usually includes one for the employee, one for the employee's spouse, and one for each dependent. (p. 507)
expense tickets	Used to track and aid in the recovery of customer-related expenses. (p. 230)
exporting	Copies Peachtree data into a format that other programs can read and use. (p. 596)
FICA taxes	This deduction from wages is also called the social security tax and provides qualified workers who retire at age 62 or older with monthly payments from the federal government. A portion of this tax is for Medicare. (See Medicare.) (p. 508)
fields	An individual piece of data, for example, the account number for sales or a customer's name. (p. 596)
FIFO	First in, first out method of inventory assumes that the items in the beginning inventory are sold first. (p. 481)
files	A group of related records; for example, customer files and journal files. (p. 596)
filter	Filtering allows you to select specific types of activities and events. (p. 10)
global options	Settings that affect the entire program. When you set global options for one company, you set them for all companies. You can access these settings from the Options menu. (p. 35)
graphical user interface (GUI)	Consists of procedures which enable you to interact with PCA. The key is the Windows environment: the menus, dialog boxes, and list boxes. A mouse simplifies use of the GUI, but it is not required. (p. 1)

group objects	Group objects are combined data objects arranged in columns. (p. 584)
HTML	HTML is an abbreviation for Hypertext Markup Language. Peachtree's Help topics are displayed in HTML. (p. 160)
icons	Small graphic symbols that represent an application or command. Icons appear on the screen when Windows programs are used: file folder, eraser, clock, hour-glass, etc. (p. 1)
icon bar	The icon bar shows pictures of commands or additional information that pertain to the window. Some icons are common to all windows while other icons are specific to a particular window. (p. 10)
importing	Translates data from other programs into a format that Peachtree can use. (p. 595)
Internet	The worldwide electronic communication network that allows for the sharing of information. To read about the differences between the Internet and the World Wide Web, go to www.webopedia.com/DidYouKnow/Internet/2002/Web_vs_Internet.asp. (p. 44)
invoice	A bill that shows an itemized list of goods shipped or services rendered, stating quantities, prices, fees, and shipping charges. (p. 432)
landscape orientation	The direction of the page in which the long edge of the paper runs horizontally. (p. 576)
liabilities	The business' debts. (p. 682)
LIFO	Last in, first out method of inventory assumes that the last goods received are sold first. (p. 481)

line items	These rows appear on many of Peachtree's windows. On color monitors, a magenta line is placed around the row you select. (p. 11)
line objects	You can draw lines or rectangles on your forms. (p. 584)
lookup field	Lookup fields are indicated by an icon with a magnifying glass. When you are in the text field portion of the lookup field, the cursor changes to an I-bar with a plus sign and question mark, < I +? >. In a lookup field, you can either select from a list of records, such as vendors, customers, accounts, etc. or you can type a new record. (p. 11)
macro	A series of commands and keystrokes that automate frequently performed tasks. (p. 629)
Medicare	A portion of FICA taxes (also called social security taxes) deducted from wages of qualified workers. Retirees receive medical benefits called Medicare after reaching age 65. (p. 508)
merchandise inventory	Includes all goods owned by the business and held for resale. (p. 481)
merchandising business	Retail stores that resell goods and/or perform services. (p. 481)
mouse	A pointing device that is used to interact with images on the screen. The left mouse button is used in PCA. (p. 1)
net income	A net income results when revenues exceed expenses. (p. 207)
net loss	A net loss results when expenses exceed revenues. (p. 207)

option buttons	Circles in dialog boxes which toggle options on and off. Options signal an either or choice. For example, there are two option buttons on the Maintain Employees dialog box: Salary or Hourly pay. You select one or the other; you cannot select both. (p. 40)
payroll journal	In Peachtree, the Payroll Entry window is also the payroll journal. The Payroll Entry window posts to the General Ledger and to the Employee file. (p. 526)
PCA	Abbreviation for Peachtree Complete Accounting. (p. 1)
perpetual inventory	In a perpetual inventory system, an up-to-date record of inventory is maintained and the inventory account is revised each time a purchase or sale is made. (p. 159)
picture objects	Picture objects are any bitmapped graphic image created or captured in a program that supports OLE (object linked and embedded) native format. (p. 584)
portrait orientation	The direction of the page in which the long edge of the paper runs vertically. (p. 576)
posting	The process of transferring information from the journal to the ledger. (p. 245)
purchase discount	Cash discounts from vendors in return for early payment of an invoice, for example, 2% 10 days, net 30. (p. 53)

purchase journal	In the Purchase Journal, or Purchases/Receive Inventory window, you can enter invoices received from vendors or enter and print purchase orders. In manual accounting, a Purchase Journal is a multi-columnar journal in which all purchases on account are recorded. (p. 393)
purchase orders	The business form used by the purchasing department to place an order with a vendor. Purchase Orders, abbreviated P.O., authorize the vendor to ship the ordered merchandise at the stated price and terms. (p. 55)
queue	A list of files waiting to be printed. (p. 36)
radio buttons	Commands that can be turned on from a list of choices in a dialog box or window. (p. 40)
real-time posting	Journal transactions are posted to the General Ledger at the time they are entered and saved. Peachtree Software recommends real-time posting for networked computers. (p. 110).
records	A group of fields that contain information on one subject, for example, the general journal, purchase journal, cash disbursements journal, sales journal, or cash receipts journal. (p. 596)
rectangle objects	You can draw lines or rectangles on your forms. Also called line objects. (p. 584)
restore	Previously backed up data can be restored or retrieved with the File, Restore selection. (p. 16)

sales discount	A cash discount that is offered to customers for early payment of their sales invoices. For example, Bellwether Garden Supply offers Tidmore Real Estate a 5% discount for payments received within 15 days of the invoice date. In PCA the discount period (number of days) and discount percentage can be changed. (p. 99)
sales journal	The Sales/Invoicing task in Peachtree is the sales journal. (p. 441)
service invoice	An alternative to the standard invoice. Use it when you want to create an invoice without inventory items. (p. 449)
shortcut keys	Enable you to perform some operations by pressing two or more keys at the same time. For example **<Alt> + <F4>** closes an application window. (p. 4)
source documents	Written evidence of a business transaction. Examples of source documents are sales invoices, purchase invoices, and a check register. (p. 248)
statement of financial position	Another name for a balance sheet. (See glossary item balance sheet.) (p. 263).
tabs	There are various tabs shown on Peachtree's windows. For example, in the Maintain Customers/Prospects window there are tabs for General, Sales Defaults, Payment Defaults, Custom Fields, and History. You can select one of these tabs to open a window so that more information will display about a customer. (p. 12)

taskbar	In Windows 98, the Start button and taskbar are located at the bottom of your screen. (p. 8)
text objects	Letters or characters you type on to a form. (p. 583)
time tickets	Used to record time-based activities such as research or consultations. A record of activities of either a vendor or an employee. (p. 230)
title bar	The top line of every window is a bar which contains the name of the application or menu in that window. (p. 7)
trackball	A device that works like a built-in mouse. (p. 1)
troubleshooting	Identifying and finding the source of a problem. (p. 13)
unearned revenue	A liability account used to report advance collections from customers. (p. 333)
vendor credit memos	Returns to vendors. (p. 77)
vendor ledger	Shows the account activity for each vendor. (p. 394)
vendors	In PCA, this term refers to businesses that offer credit for merchandise or assets purchased or expenses incurred. (p. 372)
W-2 forms	An annual report of an employee's wages subject to FICA and federal income tax that shows the amounts of these taxes that were withheld. (p. 508)
weighted-average method	This method of inventory pricing divides the cost of the inventory purchased by the quantity of merchandise purchased. This unit cost is multiplied by the ending inventory. (p. 398)

WIMP	The acronym, WIMP, stands for Windows, Icons, Menus, and Pull-downs. This acronym is used to describe the way personal computer software looks and works. (p. 1)
windows	A visual (instead of typographic) format for computer operations. (p. 1)
withholding allowances	Exemptions claimed by the employee. The number of exemptions or withholding allowances often includes one for the employee, one for the employee's spouse, and one for each dependent. (p. 507)
World Wide Web (WWW)	A way of accessing information over the Internet. To read about the differences between the Internet and the World Wide Web, go online to www.webopedia.com/DidYouKnow/Internet/2002/Web_vs_Internet.asp (p. 414)

Index

The McGraw-Hill Companies, Inc., *Computer Accounting with Peachtree Complete 2004, 8e*